Planning Sustainable Cities and Regions

As global warming advances, regions around the world are engaging in revolutionary sustainability planning—but with social equity as an afterthought. California is at the cutting edge of this movement, not only because its regulations actively reduce greenhouse gas emissions, but also because its pioneering environmental regulation, market innovation, and Left Coast politics show how to blend the "three Es" of sustainability—environment, economy, and equity. *Planning Sustainable Cities and Regions* is the first book to explain what this grand experiment tells us about the most just path moving forward for cities and regions across the globe.

The book offers chapters about neighborhoods, the economy, and poverty, using stories from practice to help solve puzzles posed by academic research. Based on the most recent demographic and economic trends, it overturns conventional ideas about how to build more livable places and vibrant economies that offer opportunity to all. This thought-provoking book provides a framework to deal with the new inequities created by the movement for more livable—and expensive—cities, so that our best plans for sustainability are promoting more equitable development as well.

This book will appeal to students of urban studies, urban planning, and sustainability, as well as policymakers, planning practitioners, and sustainability advocates around the world.

Karen Chapple is Professor of City and Regional Planning at the University of California, Berkeley, USA, and serves as Interim Director of the Institute for Urban and Regional Development.

Routledge Equity, Justice and the Sustainable City Series
Series editors: Julian Agyeman, Zarina Patel,
AbdouMaliq Simone, and Stephen Zavestoski

This series positions equity and justice as central elements of the transition toward sustainable cities. The series introduces critical perspectives and new approaches to the practice and theory of urban planning and policy that ask how the world's cities can become "greener" while becoming more fair, equitable, and just.

The Routledge Equity Justice and the Sustainable City series addresses sustainable city trends in the Global North and South and investigates them for their potential to ensure a transition to urban sustainability that is equitable and just for all. These trends include municipal climate action plans, resource scarcity as tipping points into a vortex of urban dysfunction, inclusive urbanization, "complete streets" as a tool for realizing more "livable cities," and the use of information and analytics toward the creation of "smart cities."

The series welcomes submissions for high-level, cutting-edge research books that push thinking about sustainability, cities, justice, and equity in new directions by challenging current conceptualizations and developing new ones. The series offers theoretical, methodological, and empirical advances that can be used by professionals and as supplementary reading in courses in urban geography, urban sociology, urban policy, environment and sustainability, development studies, planning, and a wide range of academic disciplines.

Incomplete Streets
Processes, Practices and Possibilities
Edited by Stephen Zavestoski and Julian Agyeman

Planning Sustainable Cities and Regions
Towards More Equitable Development
Karen Chapple

"Finally, a book about sustainability that fully accepts that the future will not be like the past. Boldly proclaiming that cities are inevitably moving toward livability, Chapple notes how traditional planning techniques cannot fully grapple with our changing demographics, the rise of the networked economy, and the shifting preferences of the next America. Utilizing the experience of the Bay Area—while making the appropriate caveats about the transportability of that experience—she charts a different approach, one that addresses our distributional and environmental crises even as it neatly fits into an emerging economy that is both more regional and more entrepreneurial. Deftly shifting between high-level theory, case study empirics, and practical policy—and insisting along the way that equity be a guiding principle for the future—this volume should be required reading for both students and practitioners of sustainability planning for the 21st Century."

Manuel Pastor, University of Southern California, USA

"In this exceptional book Karen Chapple develops an argument regarding how planning can be used to achieve justice and sustainability within cities and regions. With great originality Chapple shows how sensitivity to local context is key within a larger goal of enlarging people's capabilities, not simply broadening their range of choice."

Susan S. Fainstein, Harvard University, USA

"Linking economic development, environmental protection and improvement, and equity have long been articulated, but rarely achieved, goals of city sustainability programs. This book takes a critical look at how cities in California have sought to achieve these goals, and offers a new way of thinking about their pursuit. It is a must read for anyone seriously interested in understanding the promise and impediments to making cities and their regions more sustainable."

Kent Portney, Tufts University, USA

Planning Sustainable Cities and Regions
Towards More Equitable Development

Karen Chapple

LONDON AND NEW YORK

First published 2015
by Routledge

Published 2014 by Routledge

2 Park Square, Milton Park, Abingdon, Oxfordshire, OX14 4RN

and by Routledge
711 Third Avenue, New York, NY 10017

Routledge is an imprint of the Taylor and Francis Group, an informa business

First issued in paperback 2015

British Library Cataloguing-in-Publication Data
A catalogue record for this book is available from the British Library

Library of Congress Cataloging-in-Publication Data
 Chapple, Karen.
 Planning sustainable cities and regions : towards more equitable
development/Karen Chapple.
 pages cm.—(Routledge equity, justice and the sustainable city series)
 1. Sustainable urban development. 2. City planning—Environmental
aspects. 3. Regional planning—Environmental aspects. 4. Urban
policy—Environmental aspects. 5. Urban economics—Environmental
aspects. I. Title.
 HT241.C423 2015
 307.1'216—dc23
 2014012841

ISBN 978-1-138-78966-1 (hbk)
ISBN 978-1-138-95664-3 (pbk)
ISBN 978-1-315-76470-2 (ebk)

Typeset in Goudy
by Florence Production Ltd, Stoodleigh, Devon, UK

To my teacher and co-conspirator in life, Persis Alexandra

Contents

Figures

Acknowledgments

This book would not have been possible without the help of a veritable army of students and colleagues, and I am grateful beyond measure to all. Coauthors Mason Austin, Ed Goetz, Malo Hutson, Cynthia Kroll, Bill Lester, Carrie Makarewicz, Lizzy Mattiuzzi, Sergio Montero, Tessa Munekiyo, Alison Nemirow, Erica Spaid, and Jake Wegmann will recognize our collaborations in many of the vignettes that follow. Simply indispensable were the research, mapping, and editing efforts of Somaya Abdelgany, Rucker Alex, Chris Andrews, Sean Campion, Victoria Duong, Jenny Gant, Roxanne Glick, Jordan Klein, Jessica Lynch, Anne Martin, Nina Meigs, Ezra Pincus-Roth, Anita Roth, Chris Schildt, Arijit Sen, Jessica Sheldon, Alexis Smith, Laura Wiles, Jessica Zdeb, and Miriam Zuk.

I am indebted to an amazing team of readers who provided many criticisms and ideas along the way. This book would be a much lesser work were it not for Mike Teitz, Dena Belzer, Rolf Pendall, Alison Nemirow, Mason Austin, Bill Lester, Karen Trapenberg Frick, Steve Wertheim, and Mike Condon. Peter Wissoker was my skillful and sensitive editor.

This book is the product of many fascinating conversations with mentors, colleagues, and students. Perhaps the long talks with Jane Jacobs were imaginary, but Mike Teitz, Ron Shiffman, and Herbert Gans have been major influences on my education in three different academic institutions. Two other intellectual heroes influenced this book heavily: Susan Fainstein and Ben Harrison. At the University of Minnesota and the University of California, Berkeley, I have been incredibly lucky to work closely with superb colleagues such as Ed Goetz, Ann Markusen, Anno Saxenian, Betty Deakin, and Robert Cervero, whose insights appear throughout this volume. Many of the ideas also grow out of the wonderful exchanges I have had on long walks with Dena Belzer and Bob Giloth. Working with the students and faculty at the Department of City & Regional Planning, University of California, Berkeley, has taught me a tremendous amount and inspired me in countless ways. Of the many lifelong friends that I gained in the Ph.D. room at Berkeley, Miriam Chion and Rachel Weinberger, in particular, have pushed me hard to clarify my thinking about regional sustainability planning. Outside of the academy, Elena Garella and Alex Chapple have sharpened my contrarian skills.

The most valuable tool for a writer is time. I am grateful to Dean Jennifer Wolch and Professor and Chair Paul Waddell for carving writing time out of my workload—and then pushing me to write the book. The Urban Institute, which housed me for my sabbatical, proved to be a very stimulating environment to start a book. On the home front, I am indebted to the village that has raised my child during many long writing nights and weekends, especially Esther Puga, Ameya Futnani, Ducky, Beth, and Grandma.

Portions of the book have appeared in earlier published work. I thank Taylor & Francis, publishers of *Community Development, Housing Policy Debate, Journal of the American Planning Association*, and *Urban Geography*, for permission to reuse material that appeared in "Spatial justice through regionalism? The inside game, the outside game, and the quest for the spatial fix in the US," coauthored with Edward Goetz, *Community Development: Journal of the Community Development Society*, 42(4) (2011): 458–475; "'You gotta move': advancing the debate on the record of dispersal," coauthored with Edward Goetz, *Housing Policy Debate*, 20(2) (2010): 1–28; "Overcoming mismatch: beyond dispersal, mobility, and development strategies," *Journal of the American Planning Association*, 72(3) (2006): 322–336; and "Out of touch, out of bounds: how social networks shape the labor market radii of women on welfare in San Francisco," *Urban Geography*, 22(7) (2001): 617–640. Other material first appeared (in significantly different form) in "Time to work: job search strategies and commute time for women on welfare in San Francisco," *Journal of Urban Affairs*, 23(2) (2001): 155–173; "Hidden density in single-family neighborhoods: backyard cottages as an equitable smart growth strategy," coauthored with Jake Wegmann, *Journal of Urbanism: International Research on Placemaking and Urban Sustainability*, ahead-of-print (2014): 1–22; "The highest and best use? Urban industrial land and job creation," *Economic Development Quarterly* (2014 in press); "Innovation in the green economy: an extension of the regional innovation system model?" coauthored with Cynthia Kroll, Bill Lester, and Sergio Montero, *Economic Development Quarterly*, 25(1) (2011): 5–25; and "Restricting new infrastructure: bad for business in California?" coauthored by Carrie Makarewicz, *Access*, 34 (2010): 14–21.

1 Introduction

The Challenge of Equitable Regional Planning for Neighborhoods, Housing, and Jobs

Wanted: Lively, Safe, Sustainable, and Healthy Cities

Here at the start of the twenty-first century, we can glimpse the contours of several new global challenges that underscore the importance of far more targeted concern for the human dimension. Achieving the vision of lively, safe, sustainable, and healthy cities has become a general and urgent desire. All four key objectives—lively cities, safety, sustainability, and health —can be strengthened immeasurably by increasing the concern for pedestrians, cyclists, and city life in general. A unified citywide political intervention to ensure that the residents of the city are invited to walk and bike as much as possible in connection with their daily activities is a strong reinforcement of the objectives.

Jan Gehl (2010: 6)

When we examine the writing, professional culture, and popular beliefs about urban planning, it seems that there exists a counterpart to this reaction against rationality and broad social design. For what we are attempting to plan is, indeed, community itself.

Michael B. Teitz (1985)

Around the world, cities are becoming more livable. By reconfiguring cities to make it easier to conduct a variety of activities, we help city residents, workers, and visitors live richer, and presumably happier, lives. As values shift toward livability, the new city paradigm that Jan Gehl refers to above is arising worldwide, not just in the famous examples such as Copenhagen and New York, but also in the more improbable, such as Melbourne and Moscow.

The push to re-engineer our cities and regions also comes from the gradual societal acceptance of the need for more sustainable living patterns— communities that meet the needs of today without compromising the futures of our children and grandchildren. As global warming advances, regions around the world are engaging in sustainability planning. Arguably, California is the cutting edge of regional sustainability planning, not only because state legislation requires land use and transportation planning to target reductions in greenhouse gas emissions, but also because its combination of pioneering environmental regulation, business technological innovation, and Left Coast politics generate a unique conversation about how to blend the "three Es" of sustainability—environment, economy, and equity.

But planning and building sustainable and equitable regions is proving to be a serious challenge. The livable city is an expensive city; our urban playgrounds attract people and businesses, causing land and housing prices to rise. This creates the potential for social exclusion, if protections are not in place.

Yet, over the decades, we have accumulated many layers of urban policies that do not work well for the families and businesses of the twenty-first century. Many transportation agencies still resist linking transportation investment to jobs and housing. Anti-poverty policy seems to be trapped in the 1960s. It does not help that opponents, from business groups, to Tea Partiers, to progressive housing advocates, are lining up for the fight against the rational planning of community, as in Teitz's quote above about the Counter-Enlightenment. And many regions around the world are repeating U.S. mistakes on top of their own.

In this book, I argue that to plan for sustainability that truly incorporates equity, we need to revisit traditional liberal approaches in light of societal changes. Our prescriptions have been, for the most part, backward-looking. Despite the extraordinary demographic and economic changes of the last 50 years, we continue to rely on urban planning and policy dogmas from the 1960s and 1970s. Over time, these legacies have become reified into a planning playbook that does not always reflect today's lived experience—and may not result in the most equitable outcomes. The vestiges of urban renewal and public housing, economic restructuring and redevelopment, concentrated poverty and riots stamp our best-intentioned, most progressive strategies with a misguided impulse to engineer diversity, the economy, and opportunity.

For example, the idea of mixing income levels in housing is core to our notions of fair housing. But given rising income inequality and segregation of the affluent, in practice it has proven ineffective at improving access to opportunity. Though we have adapted our economic development strategies to focus on knowledge and creativity, we ignore the mixed quality of jobs produced. Opportunity is not just about access and proximity to jobs and schools, but stable social networks, institutions, and families in a world of rising racial/ethnic diversity and informal work. The rising land values in livable cities and regions may disrupt this support system.

To plan for equitable and sustainable regions, we need to start from an understanding of how regional economies, economic opportunity, and family lives work today in each region around the world, and then link that to growth management planning. Yet, the standard prescriptions are hard to uproot, all the more so because they stem from a way of thinking about problems that grew out of the French Enlightenment; in liberal policymaking, we appeal to facts and logic to rectify societal problems, applying the power of reason and the scientific method. We believe that society is knowable, and solutions for a new and better world can be designed. However, this flies in the face of another kind of order, the need of individuals for a sense of belonging and mutual support. Thus, communities that planners try to plan react against this rationality (Berlin 1980).

Planning for the Future—Amid the Ghosts of the Past

This book upsets—and reconstructs—three premises that have guided urban planning and policymaking for much of the last century: namely, how to engineer neighborhood density and diversity, how to develop economies for specific places, and how to locate the poor near social and economic opportunities. In a sense, we need to re-conceptualize a series of relationships: between people and plans, economy and place, and the poor and their life chances.

Embracing Diversity

The first premise to address is the idea of engineering diversity, embraced so fervently by planners. Ever since Jane Jacobs showed us the virtues of social and economic diversity in the neighborhood and the region, especially in comparison to the modernist spaces of urban renewal, planners have promoted physical diversity in the interest of social diversity and economic productivity (Fainstein 2010). They have sought to create it through a variety of policies, from mixed-income neighborhoods, to jobs–housing balance, to mixed-use development, to new density.

At face value, these strategies meet sustainability and equity goals. Urban planners and policymakers often try to create more equitable and just cities through redistribution and encounter (Fincher and Iveson 2008).[1] Redistributive policies reduce disparities between groups by remedying locational disadvantage (e.g., neighborhoods with poor-quality schools) and inaccessibility (e.g., distance to job opportunities). The principle of encounter means planning spaces for more interaction between different groups. Both principles entail increasing diversity in places—though, as Agyeman (2013) points out, the concept of diversity may be narrowly defined in race and gender terms, rather than the full array of cultural differences.

But, in practice, fostering diversity at a local or micro scale may actually result in more segregation, or simply outcomes that are unintended. What if, by making it easier for businesses to locate in the core, professional businesses push light manufacturing to the suburbs, resulting in a much larger carbon footprint? What if, in locating near transit lines, low-income households end up much closer to highways, with poor air quality raising asthma levels for children? What if families can live and work in the same neighborhood, but the kids' school is now a 30-minute drive away? What if having neighbors of different incomes triggers resentment and self-esteem problems, particularly among lower-income residents? Planners' efforts to create diversity at specific sites or places can fail miserably, as illustrated by the vacant retail-zoned ground floors of residential development, or the inability to generate high job densities to support transit lines, or the struggles of low-income families to find jobs in the suburbs.

With an increasingly diverse population and rapidly changing preferences for living and working, the approaches learned in previous decades about how to create more heterogeneous environments need to be recreated. Mixing uses within a building, or incomes within a development, or densities in a block is a useful tool in specific contexts, but does not work as a system-wide rule. Instead, we need to consider how to support diversity goals at multiple scales simultaneously. It may be effective to foster diversity at a larger scale, for instance, like that of the community, while allowing more homogeneity at a hyper-local scale, such as a site or block. This, then, could meet equity and sustainability goals of redistribution, encounter, and greenhouse gas reduction, without the restrictiveness that can lead to unintended results. For redistribution, it makes most sense to foster diversity at the scale at which resources are distributed, such as school districts.

Spurring the Economy

The second premise is the artificial separation of the economy and place. Technology and globalization have transformed the economy into a more informal place, while eviscerating the middle class—yet, we continue to plan for a world of corporate offices and well-paying conventional jobs, chasing the manufacturing plant that never responds, or the high-tech firms with their creative workers. Acknowledging a world dominated by workers patching income together from multiple jobs, home-based businesses, the sharing economy, and entrepreneurship—as well as minimum-wage workers—leads to a re-conceptualization of strategies.

The most successful regional economies—Silicon Valley, Boston, Austin, Research Triangle—develop organically around innovation clusters, and even less high-tech regions, such as Houston and Minneapolis, are driven by dynamic sectors, from manufacturing, to the arts (Castells and Hall 1994; Hall 2000). Businesses decide where to locate more through a combination of historical accident and inertia than a conscious decision to optimize production, and when they do select a location intentionally, it is most likely to be driven by labor force needs, either the need for high-skilled labor or low-cost housing (Gottlieb 1995). This suggests a focus on endogenous development—development from within—rather than business attraction.

Yet, rather than supporting businesses to grow in place, urban policymakers and planners either see the economy as exogenous to place or equate economic development with real estate development. The needs of the existing economy are rarely acknowledged. So we plan places such as waterfront parks without regard for the adjacent cement plant that needs to be on the water—and might be subsequently displaced by rising land costs. Or, a city trumpets a new entertainment megaplex as economic development, seemingly without realizing that the profits are only benefiting outsiders and the jobs are simply replacing others in the region. These silos—the distinct practices of land use and economic development—have led us to plan more livable places and regions that simply transfer economic activity from one place to another, and not necessarily to its most efficient location. Since our politically driven economic development policies and incentives support these transfers, their very structure acts counter to sustainability goals, which require planning over a longer-term framework.

How might we reconfigure urban planning and policy to support a more flexible, entrepreneurial economy? Entrepreneurs need low start-up costs and minimal overhead, whether that means operating out of a suburban garage or a mobile van. To expand, businesses need flexible space, where cubicles can be rearranged, functions can be shared, parking can be converted into work-space, and operations can switch easily between development, production, and sales. If workers are traveling among multiple sites instead of at one job center, accessibility becomes key. These changes add up to a new focus on identifying entrepreneurs, building local markets, and assisting businesses to reuse existing spaces effectively, rather than building new urban spaces.

Offering Opportunity

The third premise is how we conceptualize the geography of opportunity, or the distribution of life chances across space. In reaction to the problems of concentrated-poverty neighborhoods, twentieth-century anti-poverty policy tried to identify neighborhoods with concentrations of opportunity, in the form of good schools, low crime, and jobs. Yet, the office building next door may not hire from the neighborhood, the nature of low-skilled work has changed, and quality of life is deteriorating in the suburbs. Beyond trying to locate the poor adjacent to opportunity, we need to think about how to empower people regardless of context.

An abstract principle of equality centered on opportunity and choice undergirds many current progressive policy solutions for poverty (O'Connor 2001). The idea of equality of opportunity, as expounded upon in John Rawls' 1971 book A *Theory of Justice*, is that all should have the opportunity to acquire the skills necessary in order to achieve in a meritocracy. Rawls calls for preventing "excessive concentrations of property and wealth" through policies that support fairer distributions of benefits. The stream of policies in support of equal opportunity since the 1960s have reflected this concern—not just education programs such as school integration and Pell grants for low-income students, but also fair housing enforcement, the Community Reinvestment Act, HOPE VI mixed-income housing, and, most recently, healthcare reform. Many of these policies are implicitly urban, since space (i.e., the uneven distribution of groups across neighborhoods) mirrors societal inequalities. Yet, as Susan Fainstein points out in The Just City (2010: 44), policies remedying unequal opportunity may take an individualistic view that is essentially unjust:

Liberal democratic theory, by treating individuals atomistically, ignores the rootedness of people in class, gender, cultural, and familial relationships. In doing so and by placing liberty at the top of its pantheon of values, it fails to recognize the ties of obligation that necessarily bind people to one another and also the culturally based antagonisms that separate them.

Another key concept for equity, though not always explicitly acknowledged, is choice. Rather than distribute opportunity evenly through policy, for instance by direct subsidies for housing or education, our policies typically work to provide choices—loans for those who choose to attend college, vouchers for those who prefer to live in different neighborhoods, ability to choose between multiple healthcare providers, and so on. Yet, too much choice—especially in the absence of good information about possibilities—may feel overwhelming and detract from happiness and a sense of control. A fascinating literature in psychology debunks the capitalist emphasis on choice, finding that the lower the income of the individual, the greater the association of choice with fear and freedom with instability (Schwartz, Markus, and Snibbe 2006). One example in urban policy is mortgage finance, where deregulation resulted in a large—and intimidating—number of choices for borrowers, making them vulnerable to steering and exploitation by brokers or lenders (Immergluck 2009).

We have based much of our urban policy on three anchors: community development (helping the inner-city poor in their own neighborhoods), dispersal (helping the poor move to the suburbs), and mobility (helping the poor access opportunity in suburbs). One alternative framework is Amartya Sen's (1999) capabilities approach, which suggests that instead of thinking about distribution in terms of the resources people are able to access, we should examine what their environmental context allows them to do or be. The question, then, is how to think about context, since capability may come from scales from the immediate context, such as the family, to the entire region. What might an urban policy, as well as regional sustainability planning, look like that focused on giving disadvantaged communities in both city and suburb the security that will make people capable of achieving their dreams?

The following chapters examine these questions in more detail. But first, what will the future look like? We turn next to a brief overview of the societal changes that compel a new approach.

Planning for the Twenty-First Century

Recent years have seen several demographic trends that are expected to continue until at least mid-century, which is as far as most demographers will project. Many economists also forecast technological and sectoral shifts that will impact future development patterns.

The New Demography

What will the U.S. population look like by 2040? Our population will grow to 391 million (from 314 million today) (Pitkin and Myers 2011). Population change is slow, but two big changes are in store that will make the United States look very different: the minority majority, led by growth in the Latino and, to a lesser extent, Asian population, and the rise of the millennials. Similar factors, albeit with different roles, are reshaping populations around the world.

Immigrants

Almost 120 million (30.5 percent of the population, compared to 22.5 percent today) will be foreign-born residents and their children, a share of immigrant population not seen since 1930 (ibid.). Over half will be long-term residents, with an ever-higher stake in local communities. Many advanced industrial countries, particularly in Western Europe (as well as Australia), will also experience significant increases in immigrant populations. Although proportionately much smaller, immigration is also on the rise in many Latin American and Asian countries.

Millennials

As of this writing, there are already more millennials—those aged 18–32 in 2013—than baby boomers (65 million versus 61 million) (Pendall 2013). Although millennials are most notable—or notorious—for their sense of entitlement, for our purposes, what is most demographically remarkable about this generation is its deferral of marriage and childrearing, its educational attainment, and its poor track record in the labor force. The lack of children is part of a secular trend: in the 1960s, half of all households had children, while today it is less than one-third, and decreasing (Nelson 2011). The number of bachelor's degrees is currently growing twice as fast as the workforce, which puts pressure on a labor market that is already tight because of the reluctance of baby boomers to retire. This generation is thus experiencing higher unemployment rates, while accumulating less work experience and more education debt (Andreason 2013; Pendall 2013). Similar generational patterns are occurring in Europe. Although many developing countries host an even younger population, they, too, are seeing declining birth rates.

The New Economy

The U.S. economy will also grow by over 40 million jobs, to 183 million jobs, by 2040 (Levy 2012). Sectoral changes are likely to mean even higher levels of income inequality than we have today, exacerbated by growing wealth inequality. At the same time, the nature of work will likely continue its shift toward informality, with more entrepreneurship and contingent work.

Income Inequality

The sectors that will grow the fastest, accounting for almost half of the overall economy (up from 37 percent before the recession), will be professional and business services, educational and health services, leisure and hospitality, and other services (ibid.). In absolute or relative decline will be manufacturing (impacted by globalization), retail and financial services (both impacted by information technology), and information technology (reflecting the ongoing loss of jobs in telecommunications).

Even though the labor force is increasingly educated, the majority of the new jobs (at least 65 percent) will not require a college degree, and will be relatively low-paid (Symonds, Schwartz, and Ferguson 2011; Thiess 2012). Moreover, the involuntary part-time workforce is at historic highs (7.6 million workers), and this may not revert to its pre-recession levels (4.4 million in 2007). Thus, in the absence of policies to raise wages, inequality will likely continue its rise (Mishel, Schmitt, and Shierholz 2013). This inequality will be particularly pronounced in the strong markets (i.e., regions where the economic growth rate and land prices are above the national average) in the United States where it exists already: New York, San Francisco, Boston, Washington, DC, Chicago, and other large cities. Worsening the inequality will be income volatility, which has doubled since the 1960s, largely because of lack of male labor market attachment (Hacker 2006). Length of job tenure has declined sharply for men (but not women) in the private sector (25 percent from 1973 to 2006); to the extent that this trend reflects the growth of international competitive pressure, it is likely to continue (Farber 2008). Moreover, with wealth inequality also increasing, and millennials far less likely to buy homes, home equity is less likely to provide the safety net that it has in recent decades (Nelson 2011).

Nature of Work

At the same time, recent changes in the nature of work itself are likely to continue, with a shift away from the traditional notion of a job. Small businesses and start-ups have long been one engine of job creation, and the rise of the Internet will only increase their role (Birch 1979, 1987; Haltiwanger, Jamin, and Miranda 2011; Neumark, Wall, and Zhang 2010). For instance, crowdsourcing makes it easier to raise seed funding, and intermediaries such as eBay help entrepreneurs reach markets. Self-employment is projected to grow by 3 million workers by 2040, to 14 million workers or 7.6 percent of the labor force (Levy 2012). Most advanced industrial countries actually have a much higher share of self-employment (for instance, 14 percent in the United Kingdom), and there is evidence that the new ease of obtaining healthcare will incentivize as many as 1.5 million new entrepreneurs to leave their formal work (Blumberg, Corlette, and Lucia 2013; Schmitt and Lane 2009). And even when employed by others, 30 percent of workers now have flexible schedules (McMenanim 2007).

Development Patterns

These changes in the population and economy will transform demand for space in our cities and suburbs. Again, change will be gradual—for instance, 70–80 percent of Americans prefer single-family detached homes and about 60 percent choose large lots and privacy over ability to walk to stores, and that is unlikely to decrease significantly in the near future (Belden Russonello & Stewart 2011). Just one-fifth of new housing construction at present is infill development (building on vacant or underutilized land in the urban core), and though that share is increasing in many older metropolitan areas, most are still growing outward (EPA 2012). But the millennials and the immigrants, the aging boomers and the childless households, the service businesses, the mobile workers, and the entrepreneurs will constitute the majority, placing new pressure on the market to serve their interests.

Housing Preferences

At first glance, the immigrants, who tend to have children, and the millennials and retired boomers, who do not, would seem to have different residential space needs. Though demographic groups occupy different niches, some trends in housing preferences cut across groups and others overlap (i.e., over one-fifth of immigrants are millennials). While still refusing to trade in their large lots and privacy for smart growth—defined as a compact, walkable development pattern—the majority of households now also express a preference for walkable neighborhoods near multiple transportation options, located close to an urban center (Belden Russonello & Stewart 2011; Nelson 2013; Smart Growth America 2013; Urban Land Institute 2013).[2] Households increasingly value the availability of diverse housing types (i.e., life-cycle housing) in the neighborhood; immigrants, millennials, and baby boomer retirees all benefit from flexible housing arrangements that accommodate changes in lifestyle or the addition of a family member, increasingly without the burden of a mortgage (Belsky 2013).[3] This means neighborhoods with smaller housing units in apartment buildings, townhouses, duplexes, retirement complexes, and accessory dwelling units, as well as multigenerational households in single-family homes (Nelson 2011).

Back-to-the-City Movement

This growing diversity in transportation and housing preferences, along with new appreciation of urban amenities, is driving households back to the city. Almost every large U.S. city (the exceptions are cities such as Detroit and Cleveland) is experiencing a back-to-the-city movement, adding up to millions of new urban households (Pendall 2013). This shift in residential demand complements changes in demand for office and retail space. Living in amenity-rich neighborhoods facilitates home-based work, which increased from

4.8 percent of workers in 1997 to 6.6 percent in 2010—and will likely increase rapidly again with the increase in self-employment and entrepreneurship (Mateyka, Rapino, and Landivar 2012). Over half of the home-based workers are actually not self-employed, but working for others, an indication of the new acceptance of working from home in corporate culture.

Non-Residential Space

When workers need to be around their coworkers, they increasingly work in shared spaces, either mobile offices or cowork spaces (SPUR 2012). This has decreased the need for office space, particularly enclosed offices; for instance, when Facebook moved to the former Sun Microsystems campus in Menlo Park, it fit its 6,600 employees in a campus previously housing 3,400 (ibid.). At the same time, the need for retail space is declining with the rapid rise of Internet retail. E-commerce accounted for just 4 percent of retail sales in 2009, but 5.5 percent in 2013, with growth rates of about 15 percent per year anticipated in this decade (U.S. Census 2012).[4] These transformations create the need not so much for a new type of space, but a reconfiguration of the existing: an analysis of national trends suggests that over two-thirds of nonresidential space will be recycled, rather than built new, in coming decades (Nelson 2013).

The implications of these changes for our cities and regions are powerful. Even with a continued strong preference for single-family residential homes, there will be increasing interest in core neighborhoods with diverse housing and transportation options. At present, 60 percent of households prefer single-family homes on large lots. What if, among the 61 million aging boomers and 65 million millennials, 60 percent prefer smaller lots (i.e., more urban locations)? Even if the 70 million immigrants (not including millennials) maintain today's preferences, there will be a shift from 40 percent preferring urban densities to 53 percent. This means 14 million more city residents just among these groups.

Likewise, what share of work will be unconventional in the future? With 22 percent of the workforce already working flexible hours, including telecommuting (not including part-time workers), and 15 percent of workers who work alternate shifts, overall 37 percent of workers do not belong to the world of 9–5 work. Add to this the share of self-employed workers growing to 10 percent, home-based work (non-self-employed) at 3.5 percent, part-time work and multiple job holding steady at 5.3 percent and 5.2 percent, respectively, and 61 percent of the workforce is nontraditional—not even including the informal workforce, which, though not nearly as large as in Latin America, Africa, or Asia, may comprise as much as 40 percent of employment in the United States (Nightingale and Wandner 2011). Work is dispersed over 24 hours and across places, reducing the need for job centers and transportation networks designed for peak-hour loads.

Again, these trends are not universal, although they are similar in most advanced industrialized countries. For instance, the share of self-employment in Europe has traditionally been much higher than in the United States, and thus is not likely to increase much. Many newly industrialized countries, such as China and Mexico, are experiencing a new infatuation with the automobile that is leading to urban sprawl. But at the same time, these same countries see strong demand for central city neighborhoods and changing use of office space, as evidenced by high land prices in the core, particularly in Asia-Pacific and Latin-American countries (International Housing Coalition 2008; UN-HABITAT 2001).[5] In other words, under the conditions of rapid growth, the disparate development patterns that took almost a century to emerge in the United States are occurring simultaneously, compressed into a much shorter time period. With these shifts in mind, we return to the three premises and the legacies of planning past.

On Planning Sustainable Regions

Our planning legacies have embedded themselves in the new push for sustainable development. Regional sustainability planning has emerged from the confluence of several different movements: the concern of environmentalists that present-day consumption patterns jeopardize the earth's future, the support of urban planners for smarter growth patterns that integrate land use and transportation investments, the growing role of business groups concerned with regional competitiveness, the emergence of a movement for regional equity, and the growing preoccupation with climate change adaptation. The definition of sustainable development in Julian Agyeman, Robert D. Bullard, and Bob Evans' *Just Sustainabilities: Development in an Unequal World* (2003: 2) provides a starting point: "the need to ensure a better quality of life for all, now and into the future, in a just and equitable manner, while living within the limits of supporting ecosystems."

Many planners embrace the idea of sustainable development as a holistic, umbrella concept, in part because it allows for problem-solving across "silos" and the balancing of economic, environmental, and social goals (Gunder 2006; Wheeler 2000). Defining sustainability loosely, as a big tent, gives planners a concept to advance that is arguably in everybody's interest, regardless of values and political views (Gunder 2006; Krueger and Gibbs 2007). This, then, can smooth over value conflicts, such as opposing goals among the three Es.[6]

The complications arise in operationalizing the concept. In practice, sustainable development concepts have been slow to enter plans: sustainability plans look a lot like most city plans today, which embrace the idea of livability—but without much mention of ecological or equity principles (Berke and Conroy 2000).

The U.S. Department of Housing and Urban Development (HUD) (2011: 12) defines livability as a community "with multiple modes of transportation, different types of housing, and destinations located close to home," evoking both diversity and accessibility. But the popularity of livability as a concept is due, in part, to the increasingly global phenomenon of entrepreneurial cities trying to attract capital and its talent (Batchelor and Patterson 2007; Florida 2002; Gibbs and Krueger 2007; Raco 2005). Due to economic restructuring, which has removed heavy industry from most urban cores, and the gradual weakening of political opposition to environmentalism generally, businesses increasingly support environmentally friendly policies and programs (Portney 2007). A new market for environmentalism has emerged, a niche that appreciates quality of life and livability (e.g., reduced commute times, more urban parks), but without major changes in consumption habits (Haughton and Counsell 2004; Krueger and Gibbs 2008; Krueger and Savage 2007; Pares and Sauri 2007). Equity, however, is often an afterthought in the practice of sustainability.

The realization that we cannot solve sustainability issues (or quality of life issues more generally) at the scale of the community has led to a focus on the *regional* scale. The region is both an organic and analytic construct (Teitz 2012). In the organic view, the world consists of a patchwork of distinct regional entities created by the interaction of human life and ecological forces. The region as an analytic construct identifies these areas as functionally distinct areas that provide a lens for studying phenomena or intervening to solve problems, in the Enlightenment sense. Thus, one might study the commute shed—the area within which workers will commute to work, on average—to design transportation interventions. Or one might start from the administrative unit (e.g., examine a designated transportation district to identify the most effective transit investments). But both of these might be different from the organic region within which people move to conduct their daily lives, or businesses cluster.

The problem is that in most countries, the primary administrative units are cities and states, not regions. In the United States, as well as many European and Latin-American countries, after decades of mostly failed attempts to manage growth at the city level, as well as the widespread inability to enact effective growth management regulations at the state level, policymakers began looking to the regional level as the most effective scale to coordinate planning. Not only would the regional lens help to alleviate the challenges of coordinating across many disparate places (i.e., jurisdictional fragmentation), but also it would allow for management across multiple policy areas—such as land use, transportation, housing, energy, water and air quality, and open space and habitat. Two factors have facilitated the shift to the regional scale in the United States: federal and state reforms that allowed regional agencies to use new carrots and sticks to guide transportation investment and regulate the environment, and the emergence of regional blueprint planning exercises across the country (Barbour and Teitz 2006; Calthorpe and Fulton 2001).

The Federal Aid Highway Act of 1962 gave regional agencies (metropolitan planning organizations, or MPOs) a role in deciding where to build transportation infrastructure projects. Subsequent federal transportation legislation that incentivized MPOs to coordinate transportation and air quality planning pushed some to realize the cost efficiencies and environmental benefits of linking transportation investment to land use patterns, specifically jobs and housing. However, federal mandates stop short of regional sustainability planning, and many regions still plan for cars more than human activity patterns.

Blueprint plans, described further in Chapter 2, are regional plans for growth over a long-term framework, typically 30 years—plans that emerge from participatory processes involving both local government actors and communities convened in regional visioning exercises. Often initiated by nonprofit environmental and equity groups, they typically complement the regional transportation plans that MPOs make to guide transportation investment; in some cases, blueprints have even supplanted the role of traditional transportation models as a basis for plans. Thus, instead of regional planners devising a rational form for communities, local sentiment is shaping the region.

The success of blueprint planning exercises at building public support for regional planning is, in part, what led to the Sustainable Communities Regional Planning Grant Program. HUD launched the program in 2010 and provided a total of $165 million to two cohorts of regions throughout the country to develop or implement Regional Plans for Sustainable Development over three-year periods. In its calls for proposals for participation, HUD tries to address the "siloing" of both regional stakeholders (including municipalities, nonprofit and business groups, and regional agencies) and growth management issues. Thus, HUD (2011: 3) defines sustainable development as:

> integrated housing, land use, economic and workforce development, transportation, and infrastructure investments in a manner that empowers jurisdictions to consider the interdependent challenges of: (1) economic competitiveness and revitalization; (2) social equity, inclusion, and access to opportunity; (3) energy use and climate change; and (4) public health and environmental impact.

Nationally, interest in the program has been nothing short of extraordinary, with 360 regional applicants over two years.

What is most interesting about the HUD effort is the explicit integration of economic competitiveness and social equity concerns into the blueprint regional planning framework. Regional development planning, from the Tennessee Valley Authority in the United States, to the work of development organizations in developing countries, had focused on economic development and poverty (Teitz 2012). But that focus has, until now, been largely absent from the blueprint planning processes. Urban models typically take economic change as exogenous; projections of job growth and sectoral change come from state and national models. The blueprint visions have come largely from residents concerned with neighborhood quality of life, not businesses interested in regional growth or communities fighting for social equity. As a result, the key assumptions driving sustainability planning processes across the country do not take economic processes into account. For instance, we plan for a closed region, with the number of new housing units matching the number of new jobs, without taking into account that at the peak of the business cycle, employers may need to look outside of the region for workers. Rather than address the lack of economic opportunity directly, we plan for the proximity of jobs and housing to remedy inequities.

The premise of this book is that if we re-examined our planning dogmas in light of the changes that are occurring in our population, preferences, technology, and economy, we could develop jobs and housing strategies that would enable us to reach environmental, economic, and equity goals more effectively. Attempts to shift the location of jobs and housing need to reflect changes in the structure of home and work. Efforts to grow the regional economy need to acknowledge local context. And rather than ensuring an even spatial distribution of opportunity across metropolitan areas, urban policy and planning should focus on giving disadvantaged communities the security that will allow them to realize their full potential.

One day, a call for help came to my office from a regional council of governments in California. How can we make sure that places have a reasonable balance between their jobs and housing? The agency proposed to plan for "balance"—1.5 jobs for every housing unit—within four miles of every job center in the region.[7] Balance would be achieved by adding housing to places with concentrations of jobs. To allow workers who earn low wages to live nearby to their jobs, two-thirds of the new housing units would need to be affordable.[8] Implementing this vision would be a Herculean challenge.

Though appropriate in the abstract, the proposal would fail to achieve its goals if implemented via a traditional urban modeling paradigm. Since the 1950s, supported by the federal government, metropolitan planning has been dominated by transportation engineers drawn to systems thinking (Brown, Morris, and Taylor 2009; Hansen 1959). As a general principle, the idea of inserting housing into job centers in order to reduce vehicle miles traveled (VMT) is reasonable. But in practice, it will not advance equitable development goals in every context. It might raise land costs and crowd out businesses, some of which hire lower-skilled workers. By adding housing, it might lower job densities, making rail transit systems less viable. It may not be possible to add much affordable housing into job centers, since land is more expensive. This is not to say that diversifying job centers is a bad idea; in some contexts, it will make more livable communities. Jobs–housing balance at the scale of the commute shed is an important goal to reduce VMT. But as a systems rule guiding site planning everywhere, it fails. If, instead, sustainability planning focused on what would make business thrive (and pay workers enough to afford housing), and what would reduce travel (and travel costs) for all members of a household, model results would look quite different—and more viable from the perspective of those battling today's sustainability movement.

Much of the urban and regional analysis that guides policymaking is based on these kinds of simplistic assumptions. Or, worse, analysts, particularly economists, make policy recommendations based on their predictions of the average case—yet there is no average metropolitan area! Nate Silver (2011) captured the dilemma aptly in a column on a Brookings Institution report, *Missed Opportunity: Transit and Jobs in Metropolitan America* (Tomer et al. 2011). Brookings ranked the top U.S. metropolitan areas on the basis of physical access to transit and employment, rather than local transit usage. Thus, the report scored places such as Salt Lake City and Fresno, with a very low share of transit riders, higher than New York City and Chicago, where commuters embrace transit. Silver points out that the researchers did not consider the choices commuters make in particular contexts: they will choose driving over transit if that option is better, as it is in Salt Lake and Fresno. Good transit access to employment means different things in different regions, not just the choices available, but also local culture, job types, household types, and so forth. Planners and policymakers should embrace our regional exceptionalism, rather than masking it with one-size-fits-all analysis.

The Plan of the Book

This book relies on the example of the San Francisco Bay Area to make its case. In many ways, the Bay Area, with its economic resilience amid natural beauty, epitomizes the challenge of reconciling sustainability goals with economic growth and social equity. It has earned its sustainability credentials the hard way: a century-long fight by environmentalists to preserve "the country in the city," a regional planning movement that dates from the late 1930s, the pioneering rise of regional equity groups in the 1990s, and, most importantly, a vibrant, high-tech regional economy that is the envy of the world (Pastor, Benner, and Matsuoka 2009; Walker 2007). With powerful interest groups representing each of the three Es, the Bay Area is a place where the conflicts are intensified. As an early adopter of sustainability planning, the region has been forced to come up with innovative solutions that provide insights for other regions around the world, most of whom have not even begun to take jobs, housing, and poverty into consideration in planning for transportation systems.

Although it is easier to generalize these experiences to similar strong market regions and advanced industrialized countries, the Bay Area story also offers lessons for weaker markets in the developing world, as well as the hundreds of U.S. regions seeking to engage in sustainability planning. Even if these regions are not experiencing gentrification (and displacement) and have not succeeded in creating high-tech economies, they likely experience similar challenges with creating and maintaining diverse neighborhoods in terms of income and use. They suffer from the same toolkit of unsustainable business attraction policies and failure to support local markets. Changes in the economy and population have transformed the nature of economic opportunity in their cities and suburbs as well.

In many ways, the United States is an extreme case study for the study of regional sustainability planning. While nearly leading the world in greenhouse gas emissions (second only to China), the United States lags in policymaking for climate change reduction and social inclusion (UNEP 2012). Because of the lack of federal action on climate change, cities and states have innovated their own strategies. Enabling this local innovation is the country's federalist structure, which gives states and cities autonomy while still providing resources and opportunities through federal programs. Thus, the Bay Area case might be considered an example of a local response within a federal system, not so dissimilar from an E.U. member state.[9] With over 8 million residents in the greater Bay Area, the region is more populous than the majority of countries in the world.[10]

The current push for regional sustainability planning around the world grows out of a combination of local fiscal crisis, the global financial crisis, rapid urbanization, and awareness of climate change, all of which lead to a concern with the sustainability of development patterns. Chapter 2 shows that sustainability planning efforts draw from a long tradition of planning for regional development (mostly in the non-U.S. development context), the rise of regional transportation and blueprint planning, and the broad experience with city-level climate planning. In essence, regional planning processes augment transportation planning processes with planning for neighborhoods, housing, and jobs. In the process, however, it must deal with the multiple legacies of planning. An analysis of 150 proposals for regional sustainability plans submitted to HUD suggests that planners, elected officials, community-based organizations, and engaged citizens are thinking about how to plan for tomorrow's neighborhoods, jobs, and people.

Accommodating future growth in jobs and housing means changing the form and function of neighborhoods, and even thinking beyond the neighborhood to scales that may matter more for sustainability and equity. Part I shows how planners try to reshape neighborhoods for sustainable growth through changes in design, density, and diversity. This section, as well as the next two, use examples (or "vignettes") to highlight the societal changes that create the imperative for new approaches, as well as the common misconceptions that have unwittingly worked their way into sustainability planning. These vignettes also outline some alternatives, although there are many more than this book can possibly cover. In Part I, four chapters, on infill development, job location, mixed-income neighborhoods, and gentrification, answer two key questions:

1.   How do we make places denser (and yet still equitable)?
2.   How do we make places more diverse, without pricing people out?

The chapters describe how planners try to shape neighborhood change along three dimensions: businesses, development, and households. Each dimension has changed: the large lot single-family home no longer experiences the same demand, the conventional job no longer dominates, and household structure and preferences have shifted. And each dimension has its own dynamic: new development is subject to the politics in existing neighborhoods, job growth occurs according to the business cycle, and neighborhood household mix depends on a variety of demographic and economic factors—and is generally very slow to change. In reaction to the unpopularity of the monolithic approach of urban renewal, most interventions proposed now in the United States are sensitive to the existing neighborhood fabric. But most are too narrow to accommodate the growing diversity of the U.S. population and economy.

The regional economy is rarely explicitly considered in sustainability planning: in the urban models, job growth depends on the national economy, rather than local factors, and planners and policymakers, just as they did 40 years ago, tend to assume that job growth will happen simply by building new office buildings, industrial parks, and transit lines. Part II shows how place shapes the regional economy's ability to generate new ideas and jobs, even more than in bygone eras where regions simply competed on costs. In the bifurcated economy dominated by high-tech businesses and low-end services, businesses rely heavily on local talent; since they rarely move, especially between regions, firm start-ups and expansions are key to regional growth. This embeddedness also presents an opportunity to leverage higher-wage jobs for locals. Growing firms also have unique needs for space—from the suburban garage, to core industrial land—that are rarely anticipated in sustainability planning. Though studies frame job sprawl in negative terms, that pattern may actually reflect a combination of home-based entrepreneurship and localized job centering. Given these business location patterns amid growing inequality, our economic development policy toolkit, which focuses on business attraction incentives, is woefully inadequate. Three chapters take on the puzzles of business attraction, local markets, and mixed-use industrial land in turn, answering three key questions:

1. How can we get jobs to locate in specific places (i.e., near transit or in poor neighborhoods)?
2. What type of economy is sustainable?
3. What is the most sustainable metropolitan structure?

Since ineffective and unsustainable economic development practices are common in regions across the globe, the lessons of these vignettes apply broadly.

Decades of anti-poverty policy have been built on the premise that concentrations of poverty in inner cities hinder life chances and the suburbs offer opportunity for the poor. Yet, changes in metropolitan structure have overturned the city-suburb dichotomy, as poverty has grown in the suburbs and the affluent have flocked back to cities. Part III examines the nature of poverty, as well as the meaning and location of opportunity in today's regions. Three chapters look, in turn, at what changing metropolitan structure means for the three anchors of urban policy: community development (helping the inner city poor in their own neighborhoods), dispersal (helping the poor move to the suburbs), and mobility (helping the poor access opportunity in suburbs). Thus, this section looks at two questions:

1.   What is opportunity for the poor?
2.   How do we intervene to create opportunity—for people, or place, or both?

Growing income and wealth inequality at the national level hinders the ability of regions to address poverty, and creates a need to expand anti-poverty policies to address the issue of insecurity for the working poor as well. If regions are to be sustainable for all, planning will need to rethink its one-size-fits-all approach to opportunity.

The concluding chapter begins with an examination of how to plan more just, sustainable, and equitable cities and regions. How might our regions give disadvantaged communities the security that will ensure the development of capabilities, while also preserving the environment? Despite stalemate in global action to reduce emissions, there is still much that local action can achieve.

2040—from the Vantage Point of Berkeley, California

If regional sustainability planning takes hold, the future of America's metropolitan regions will look very different indeed. Without any kind of sustainability planning at all, the "business as usual" scenario will result in more congested highways, more sprawl, longer commutes, more economic disparities, and less competitive regions. Even though more sustainable settlement patterns are not going to reverse climate change, they help reduce our vulnerability and raise awareness.

Why should we care about improving our approach to regional sustainability planning? If we can make our regions work well for business and people, we will win the support that will make sustainability planning meet the goals of the three Es—and win political viability as well. So, consider two alternative futures, using the example of the San Francisco Bay Area.

In the first, most new housing and jobs locate on just 5 percent of the total regional land area, concentrated in the central cities of Oakland, San Francisco, and San Jose—the vision of the Sustainable Communities Strategy put out by the San Francisco Bay Area in 2013. As a result of this focused growth, as well as local political opposition, outer counties retain their open space and agriculture land, and receive very little new housing. This is achieved through infrastructure investment in core areas. At the same time, there are no changes in the existing tax or incentive structure, so there is little new affordable housing, particularly near transit, and jobs continue to decentralize, attracted by entrepreneurial cities both within and outside the region. Because of constraints to infill development, housing and job growth is slower than anticipated. Still, rapidly increasing demand for land in the core—the influx of new households and rise of prices—creates pressures on both existing households and businesses. Displaced households, working in the new low-wage jobs, move to suburban areas, occupying older houses on large lots and traveling long distances to work. Businesses vacate offices in core areas, or, with few low-cost alternatives to expand to within the region, contract. Entrepreneurs struggle to find start-up space. Lost industrial land in the core exacerbates the bifurcation of the economy, as well as VMT. Meanwhile, the poor are isolated from support networks in both city and suburb. These growth patterns mean that there is little or no net reduction in greenhouse gas emissions after all. Other regions point to the failure of the San Francisco experiment as a reason not to pursue sustainability planning.

In the second future, the region has adopted an approach that is at once more pragmatic, more forward-looking, and more closely aligned with federal, state, and local policy incentives, which have been restructured. Policies to make cities more livable also mitigate their rising costs—and potential exclusion. Cities adopt a variety of approaches to infill development that acknowledge rising land prices and accommodate diverse households, combating the increasing income inequality at the national level. They use value recapture and other financing tools to share some of the benefits of transit investment with existing residents. They make transportation investments that support a variety of work patterns and aspects of life. Policies and programs to support income mixing are reconfigured to the scales at which integration is most effective. Economic development policies work together to leverage local markets, foster entrepreneurship in the core, and grow businesses at job centers. Having achieved more sustainable development patterns, planners rethink the old policy toolkit of community development, dispersal, and mobility to planning in order to support families and opportunity throughout the region. This local innovation in sustainability planning is adopted statewide, emulated by regions across the country, and, eventually, adopted by the federal government.

After a brief portrayal of how we found ourselves heading toward the first future, the following chapters outline an approach that will lead us toward the second.

Notes

1. Fincher and Iveson also suggest a third approach, recognition, through which efforts are made to define the attributes of groups of people so that their needs can be met.
2. Smart growth is typically defined as a compact, walkable development pattern, implying the mixing of uses in development that is dense enough that retail and services are readily accessible and transportation choices are viable. According to Smart Growth America (2013), "Smart growth means building urban, suburban and rural communities with housing and transportation choices near jobs, shops and schools. This approach supports local economies and protects the environment."
3. Home ownership rates are currently declining; however, it is unclear whether this trend will continue, since the desire (if not the ability) to own a home remains strong among Americans.
4. E-commerce sales are supposed to double between 2012 and 2017, according to the Internet Retailer (2013).
5. UN-HABITAT (2001) finds that the ratio of land price to income is typically at least 10 times higher on highly developed land than on raw land, and a survey of metropolitan areas in developing countries by the International Housing Coalition (2008) found that two-thirds experienced their highest land prices in the core (with the remaining one-third split between secondary job centers and formal suburbs).

6. Scott Campbell (1996) describes the opposing goals among the three Es. However, Gunder (2006) suggests that the triple bottom line is impossible to achieve, and suggests separating ecological and equity goals so that they are not subsumed to the economic growth imperative.
7. On average, each household has 1.5 members who are employed—thus, 1.5 is considered balanced.
8. An affordable housing unit costs (for rent or ownership) 30 percent or less of the income of a household making 120 percent of the area (county) median income or less.
9. I am indebted to Rolf Pendall for this observation.
10. If it were a country, it would rank about 100th in population of 244 countries in the world.

References

Agyeman, Julian. *Introducing Just Sustainabilities: Policy, Planning, and Practice*. London: Zed Books, 2013.

Agyeman, Julian, Robert D. Bullard, and Bob Evans. *Just Sustainabilities: Development in an Unequal World*. Cambridge, MA: MIT Press, 2003.

Andreason, Stuart. "We Got More Educated, We Are Better Off . . . Right?" Paper presented at the Federal Reserve Community Development Conference, April 12, 2013.

Barbour, Elisa and Michael B. Teitz. *Blueprint Planning in California: Forging Consensus on Metropolitan Growth and Development*. San Francisco, CA: Public Policy Institute of California, 2006.

Batchelor, Anna and Alan Patterson. "Political Modernization and the Weakening of Sustainable Development in Britain," in *The Sustainable Development Paradox*, edited by David D. Gibbs and Rob Kreuger, 192–213. New York: Guilford Press, 2007.

Belden Russonello & Stewart. "The 2011 Community Preference Survey: What Americans are Looking for When Deciding Where to Live." Washington, DC: Belden Russonello & Stewart, 2011. Accessed June 1, 2013. www.stablecommunities. org/sites/all/files/library/1608/smartgrowthcommsurveyresults2011.pdf.

Belsky, Eric S. "The Dream Lives On: The Future of Homeownership in America." *Harvard Joint Center for Housing Studies W13-1*. Cambridge, MA: Harvard University, 2013.

Berke, Philip R. and Maria Manta Conroy. "Are We Planning for Sustainable Development? An Evaluation of 30 Comprehensive Plans." *Journal of the American Planning Association* 66, no. 1 (2000): 21–33.

Berlin, Isaiah. "The Counter-Enlightenment." In *Against the Current: Essays in the History of Ideas*, 1–24. New York: Viking Press, 1980.

Birch, David. *The Job Generation Process*. Cambridge, MA: MIT Program on Neighborhood and Regional Change, 1979.

Birch, David. *Job Creation in America*. New York: Free Press, 1987.

Blumberg, Linda J., Sabrina Corlette, and Kevin Lucia. "The Affordable Care Act: Improving Incentives for Entrepreneurship and Self-Employment." Washington, DC: Urban Institute Press and Robert Wood Johnson Foundation, 2013. Accessed May 30, 2013. www.rwjf.org/content/dam/farm/reports/issue_briefs/2013/rwjf406367.

Brown, Jeffrey R., Eric A. Morris, and Brian D. Taylor. "Planning for Cars in Cities: Planners, Engineers, and Freeways in the 20th Century." *Journal of the American Planning Association* 75, no. 2 (2009): 161–177.

Calthorpe, Peter and William Fulton. *The Regional City*. Washington, DC: Island Press, 2001.

· Campbell, Scott. "Green Cities, Growing Cities, Just Cities? Urban Planning and the Contradictions of Sustainable Development." *Journal of the American Planning Association* 62, no. 3 (1996): 296–312.

Castells, Manuel and Peter Hall. *Technopoles of the World: The Making of the 21st Century Industrial Complexes*. New York: Routledge, 1994.

EPA Office of Sustainable Communities. *Residential Construction Trends in America's Metropolitan Regions*. Washington, DC: EPA, 2012.

Fainstein, Susan S. *The Just City*. Ithaca, NY: Cornell University Press, 2010.

Farber, Henry. "Employment Insecurity: The Decline in Worker-Firm Attachment in the United States." *Princeton University Industrial Relations Section, Working Paper #530* (2008): 23.

Fincher, Ruth and Kurt Iveson. *Planning and Diversity in the City: Redistribution, Recognition and Encounter*. Houndmills, Basingstoke, Hampshire, 2008.

Florida, Richard. *The Rise of the Creative Class and How It's Transforming Work, Leisure and Everyday Life*. New York: Basic Books, 2002.

Gehl, Jan. *Cities for People*. Washington, DC: Island Press, 2010.

Gibbs, David D. and Rob Kreuger, editors. *The Sustainable Development Paradox*. New York: Guilford Press, 2007.

Gottlieb, Paul D. "Amenities, Firm Locations, and Economic Development." *Urban Studies* 32, no. 9 (1995): 1413–1436.

Gunder, Michael. "Sustainability: Planning's Saving Grace or Road to Perdition?" *Journal of Planning Education and Research* 26, no. 2 (2006): 208–221.

Hacker, Jacob. *The Great Risk Shift: The Assault on American Jobs, Families, Health Care, and Retirement—and How You Can Fight Back*. New York: Oxford University Press, 2006.

Hall, Peter. "Creative Cities and Economic Development." *Urban Studies* 37, no. 4 (2000): 639–649.

Haltiwanger, John, Ron S. Jamin, and Javier Miranda. "Who Creates Jobs? Small vs. Large vs. Young." *NBER Working Paper No. 16300*. Cambridge, MA: National Bureau of Economic Research, 2011.

Hansen, Walter G. "How Accessibility Shapes Land Use." *Journal of the American Institute of Planners* 25 (1959): 73–76.

Haughton, Graham and Dave Counsell. "Regions and Sustainable Development: Regional Planning Matters." *The Geographical Journal* 170, no. 2 (2004): 135–145.

Immergluck, Daniel. *Foreclosed: High-Risk Lending, Deregulation, and the Undermining of America's Mortgage Market*. Ithaca, NY: Cornell University Press, 2009.

International Housing Coalition. *Report on Survey of Urban Land Prices in the Developing World*. Washington, DC: World Bank, 2008. Accessed January 20, 2014. www-wds. worldbank.org/external/default/WDSContentServer/WDSP/IB/2012/07/04/000333037 _20120704015038/Rendered/PDF/705730WP0P11030000Report0on0Housing.pdf.

Internet Retailer. "U.S. E-Commerce Sales 2012–17." Accessed June 3, 2013. www.internetretailer.com/trends/sales/

Krueger, Rob and David C. Gibbs, editors. *The Sustainable Development Paradox*. New York: Guilford Press, 2007.

Krueger, Rob and David Gibbs. "'Third Wave' Sustainability? Smart Growth and Regional Development in the USA." *Regional Studies* 42, no. 9 (2008): 1263–1274.

Krueger, Rob and Lydia Savage. "City Regions and Social Reproduction: A 'Place' for Sustainable Development?" *International Journal of Urban and Regional Research* 31, no. 1 (2007): 215–223.

Levy, Stephen. *Bay Area Job Growth to 2040: Projections and Analysis*. Palo Alto, CA: Center for the Continuing Study of the California Economy, 2012.

McMenamin, Terence M. "A Time to Work: Recent Trends in Shift Work and Flexible Schedules." Washington, DC: Bureau of Labor Statistics, 2007. Accessed May 30, 2013. www.bls.gov/opub/mlr/2007/12/art1full.pdf.

Mateyka, Peter J., Melanie R. Rapino, and Liana C. Landivar. *Home-Based Workers in the United States: 2010*. Washington, DC: U.S. Census Bureau, 2012.

Mishel, Lawrence, John Schmitt, and Heidi Shierholz. "Assessing the job polarization explanation of growing wage inequality." Working Paper, Economic Policy Institute, January 11, 2013. Accessed May 1, 2013. www.epi.org/publication/wp295-assessing-job-polarization-explanation-wage-inequality.

Nelson, Arthur C. *The New California Dream: How Demographic and Economic Trends May Shape the Housing Market: A Land Use Scenario for 2020 and 2035*. Washington, DC: Urban Land Institute, 2011.

Nelson, Arthur C. *Reshaping Metropolitan America: Development Trends and Opportunities to 2030*. Washington, DC: Island Press, 2013.

Neumark, David, Brandon Wall, and Junfu Zhang, "Do Small Businesses Create More Jobs? New Evidence for the United States from the National Establishment Time Series." *Review of Economics and Statistics* 93, no. 1 (2010): 16–29.

Nightingale, Demetra and Stephen Wandner. *Informal and Nonstandard Employment in the United States: Implications for Low-Income Working Families*. Washington, DC: Urban Institute Press, 2011.

O'Connor, Alice. *Poverty Knowledge: Social Science, Social Policy, and the Poor in Twentieth-Century U.S. History*. Princeton: Princeton University Press, 2001.

Pares, Marc and David Sauri. "Integrating Sustainabilities in a Context of Economic, Social and Urban Change: The Case of Public Spaces in the Metropolitan Region of Barcelona." In *The Sustainable Development Paradox*, edited by Rob Krueger and David Gibbs, 160–191. Guilford Publications, 2007.

Pastor Jr., Manuel, Chris Benner, and Martha Matsuoka. *This Could be the Start of Something Big: How Social Movements for Regional Equity are Reshaping Metropolitan America*. Ithaca, NY: Cornell University Press, 2009.

Pendall, Rolf. "Big City, Big Ideas: The Millennials in Cities." Presentation at Munk School of Global Affairs, University of Toronto, April 22, 2013. Accessed May 1, 2013. http://munkschool.utoronto.ca/imfg/the-millennials-in-cities-the-coming-change-in-urban-demographics-and-civic-values.

Pitkin, John and Dowell Myers. *Projections of the U.S. Population, 2010–40, by Immigration Generation and Foreign-Born Duration in the U.S.* Los Angeles, CA: USC PopDynamics Research Group, 2011.

Portney, Kent E. "Local Business and Environmental Policies in Cities." In *Business and Environmental Policy: Corporate Interests in the American Political System*, edited by Sheldon Kamieniecki and Michael E. Kraft, 299–326. Cambridge, MA: MIT Press, 2007.

Raco, Mike. "Sustainable Development, Rolled-Out Neoliberalism and Sustainable Communities." *Antipode* 37, no. 2 (2005): 324–347.

Rawls, John. *A Theory of Justice*. Cambridge, MA: Belknap Press, 1971.

San Francisco Planning & Urban Research. *The Urban Future of Work*. San Francisco, CA: SPUR, 2012.

Schmitt, John and Nathan Lane. *An International Comparison of Small Business Employment*. Washington, DC: Center for Economic and Policy Research, 2009. Accessed May 30, 2013. www.cepr.net/documents/publications/small-business-2009-08.pdf.

Schwartz, Barry, Hazel Rose Markus, and Alana Conner Snibbe. "Is Freedom Just Another Word for Many Things to Buy?" *New York Times*, 2006.

Sen, Amartya. *Development as Freedom*. New York: Anchor, 1999.

Silver, Nate. "On the Economics of Mass Transit and the Value of Common Sense." *New York Times*, May 20, 2011. Accessed June 5, 2013. http://fivethirtyeight.blogs.nytimes.com/2011/05/20/thinktanks-gone-wild-on-the-economics-of-mass-transit-and-the-value-of-common-sense.

Smart Growth America. "What is 'Smart Growth'?" Accessed June 1, 2013. www.smart growthamerica.org/what-is-smart-growth.

Symonds, William C., Robert B. Schwartz, and Ronald Ferguson. "Pathways to Prosperity: Meeting the Challenge of Preparing Young Americans for the 21st Century." Report, Pathways to Prosperity Project, Harvard School of Education, 2011.

Teitz, Michael B. "Rationality in Planning and the Search for Community." In *Rationality in Planning*, edited by Michael Breheny and Andrew Hooper, 137–144. London: Pion, 1985.

Teitz, Michael B. "Regional Development Planning." In *Planning Ideas That Matter: Livability, Territoriality, Governance, and Reflective Practice*, edited by Bishwapriya Sanyal, Lawrence J. Vale, and Christina D. Rosan, 127. Cambridge, MA: MIT Press, 2012.

Thiess, Rebecca. *The Future of Work Trends and Challenges for Low-Wage Workers*. Washington, DC: Economic Policy Institute, 2012.

Tomer, Adie, Elizabeth Kneebone, Robert Puentes, and Alan Berube. *Missed Opportunity: Transit and Jobs in Metropolitan America*. Washington, DC: Brookings Institution Press, 2011. Accessed June 5, 2013. www.brookings.edu/research/reports/2011/05/12-jobs-and-transit.

UNEP. *The Emission Gas Report 2012*. Nairobi: United Nations Environment Programme, 2012.

UN-HABITAT. "Urban Shelter: Land." In *The State of the World's Cities Report 2001*, 36–37. New York: United Nations Centre for Human Settlements, 2001.

Urban Land Institute. *America in 2013: A ULI Survey of Views on Housing, Transportation, and Community*. Urban Land Institute, 2013.

U.S. Census. "Wholesale & Retail Trade: Online Retail Sales." Washington, DC: Dept. of Commerce, 2012. Accessed June 3, 2013. www.census.gov/compendia/statab/cats/wholesale_retail_trade/online_retail_sales.html.

U.S. Department of Housing and Urban Development (HUD). "Notice of Funding Availability (NOFA) for HUD's FY 2011 Sustainable Communities Regional Planning Grant Program." FR-5395-N-03, 2011.

Walker, Richard. *The Country in the City: The Greening of the San Francisco Bay Area*. Seattle, WA: University of Washington Press, 2007.

Wheeler, Stephen M. "Planning for Metropolitan Sustainability." *Journal of Planning Education and Research* 20, no. 2 (2000): 133–145.

2   The Landscape of Regional Sustainability Planning, Past and Present

City planning has benefited from rich experience in building cities, starting with Mesopotamia in 3000 BC. In contrast, metropolitan and regional planning dates just to the nineteenth century, and there are no treatises on how to lay out regions: "Regional planning has become a necessity in most countries. But nobody seems to know quite what it is, and no nation seems to know how to do it" (Ross and Cohen, quoted in Gore 1984: 236). In fact, nearly from the onset, there was significant disagreement about strategy. The "metropolitanists" focused on supporting central cities and their economic agglomerations with efficient infrastructure and development patterns, while the "regionalists" advocated for decentralization and the utopian garden city (Fishman 2000).

The idea of sustainable development at the regional scale might be traced back to Ian McHarg's work on green regionalism: a green region embraces its ecological systems, such as water, climate, and topography, and integrates them into planning (McHarg 1969; Steiner 2011). To add the notion of equity to sustainability, it took the advent of the environmental justice movement, as well as the concept of intergenerational equity advanced by the World Commission on Environment and Development's Brundtland Commission. Environmental justice meant recasting healthy food, clean air, and clean water for people as part of "the environment," not something separate from it (Agyeman, Bullard, and Evans 2003). The Brundtland Commission Report framed sustainable development as "development that meets the needs of the present generation without compromising the ability of future generations to meet their own needs" (World Commission on Environment and Development 1987). Sustainability, thus, was to reconcile the "three Es" of development—economy, equity, and environment.

This chapter begins by defining regions and then briefly examines the distinct histories of regional and metropolitan planning and their convergence into the new regionalism and blueprint planning. This then became the basis for regional sustainability planning. The chapter next examines how regions across the world have addressed equitable development and sustainability in their regional planning efforts. The chapter concludes with a description of California's experiment in regional sustainability planning, which, arguably, is leading the world.

The Regional Scale

What is a region? Returning to the distinction between organic and analytic regions from Chapter 1, we can see regions as either an expression of human life or an optimal area for designing and implementing policy solutions—or both. Regions can come in many different shapes, sizes, and forms. Michael Teitz (2012) traces the region back to the fifth century BC and Herodotus, who wrote of regions as people in a place (i.e., not just geographic entities differentiated by physical boundaries such as plains or rivers, but homelands of people differentiated by their interaction with place). This organic region, then, is a subcontinental, subnational, or substate space with homogeneity of natural resources and/or culture; for instance, the California coast or the Andes mountains (Markusen 1987). This homogeneity can mean that common problems arise, making it an appropriate scale for intervention as well.

The region also can be an appropriate scale for understanding sustainability. Viewed from an environmental perspective, sustainability should reflect the underlying ecosystem. Technically, an ecosystem is a complex that supports a community of organisms.[1] The growth of population and economic activity impacts natural systems in specific places, through the destruction of habitat and the degradation of air and water quality. However, the impacts extend beyond localized areas: diminished air quality in one region's atmospheric system can spread to others. Thus, sustainability also requires a global lens.

When we define regions for the purpose of making sustainability plans, we rarely can rely on the boundaries of the organic region. Typically, a sustainability plan defines the spatial entity that is most appropriate to meet its objectives (e.g., transportation and land use linkages, infrastructure provision, or economic development). Thus, the region as an analytic construct for sustainability tends to take either functional or administrative form (i.e., defined either by a function, such as the area within which commutes take place, or the governing entity, such as city, county, multiple counties, or state, that administers the policies and plans to meet the objective).

In practice, then, most regional planning exercises today are based upon the metropolitan nodal region (i.e., urbanization organized around a center or centers), which is the spatial entity that encompasses most functions and administration. Economists and planners have long commented on the formation of urban centers, with density and rents peaking at the core and declining toward the periphery (Alonso 1964; Mills 1972; Muth 1969). Because most of the development needed to accommodate growth occurs within this urban system, this may be the most logical foundation for development policy. Over time, this city-based region may expand to incorporate multiple nodes or sub-centers, but it remains a metropolitan region. In contrast to the ecological region, metropolises tend to be internally heterogeneous—complicating regional planning both technically and politically.

In adopting the analytic construct of the region, rather than a more holistic view, regional planning becomes a rational exercise based on the Enlightenment ideas (i.e., that reason may be applied to challenges and we can remake society for the better). Often, this means losing sight of the desires of and for community (i.e., the Counter-Enlightenment view of the importance of group identity and the rootedness of local populations) (Teitz 1985). It is no wonder, then, that communities often organize in opposition to regional planning, to preserve the home rule authority of local government (though their motive may be preserving property values just as much as place attachment).

Perhaps as a result, in practice the movement for sustainability has largely emerged from cities, rather than regions, and research has followed suit. City governments have taken action against climate change, enacting energy efficiency and recycling programs that encourage individuals to take action, and creating voluntary sustainability plans that set targets for the reduction of greenhouse gas emissions. But reducing automobile dependence is challenging, if not impossible, within city boundaries, since mode choice depends on destinations that are outside the city, and is thus shaped by regional labor and housing markets. Metropolitan fragmentation creates significant challenges for coordinating across cities. And with little discretionary funding of their own, cities struggle to effect changes in behavior.

Meanwhile, most global climate change policymaking occurs at the national and international level. At their best, international agreements and national legislation provide standards that reshape local policymaking and behavior. For example, the Kyoto Protocol sets emission reduction targets, asking developed countries to assume primary responsibility. The United Nations has taken the lead in advocating sustainable development globally, with a 2012 summit (building on the 1992 Earth Summit) that negotiated sustainable development goals. But in the end, such standards will not be effective if there is no funding to incentivize changes in behavior, and if they are enacted at an institutional level—state or city—that does not correspond to the scale of the problem being addressed. If the issue is transportation, or water quality, or housing, or economic development, or labor, that scale is regional.

The Rise of Regional and Metropolitan Planning

The earliest efforts at regional planning emerged in response to the Industrial Revolution, with the specific aim of exploiting natural resources and developing more productive industrial cities (Weaver 1984). This meant the coordination of infrastructure and housing development by the state, to create effective urban agglomerations of labor and capital. It also spurred an anarchistic reaction, with Proudhon, Kropotkin, and others advocating collectivist societies organized in decentralized producers' associations for local markets (Teitz 2012). The first vision meant centralization and a metropolitan structure of strong core-weak periphery. The second was of regional self-sufficiency, in some ways the earliest attempt at sustainability.

As railroad and streetcar suburbs grew into cities in their own right, questions of coordination across cities arose. At the industrial city's peak, most of the

U.S. population was concentrated in the major central cities, but, facilitated by transportation, decentralization was rapid—a pattern now repeated through both developing and industrialized countries. Progressive reforms in most states established home rule authority, protecting local government autonomy from state interference. Since cities could raise their own taxes, issue bonds, and build large-scale infrastructure, this then had the effect of reinforcing piecemeal development patterns.[2] Cities also worked to expand their territories through annexation and consolidation, though progressive reforms made this challenging.

It was Patrick Geddes who, in 1915, popularized the idea of the river basin as an organizing principle for planning, thus maintaining the focus on the organic, homogeneous region. Because of the primacy of the ecological imperative, human activity, even when manifesting itself as a "conurbation" or "regional city," would be balanced with nature (Teitz 2012). In a utopian vision, mutual cooperation would emerge across the region defined by the basin.

These ideas quickly came into practice in the United States with the formation of the Regional Plan Association of America (RPAA) by Clarence Stein in 1922. The RPAA promoted regional planning in the 1920s through the regional city, with the ecological region to be preserved around a system of cities (Parsons 1994). Their first project, conceived of by Benton MacKaye, was the Appalachian Trail, and their ongoing voice was Lewis Mumford, who advocated a form of regional development at a human scale in contraposition to the modern, technology-driven world (Mumford 1961). This then reinforced the focus on the region, rather than the metropolis.

Shaping the emergence of regional planning in its present form were the development of an institutional framework, the rise of neoliberalism, and the growing concern with regional inequity. In the United States, the institutional framework was in place long before issues of competitiveness and equity came to the fore. But countries that began developing later, such as China or Colombia, are dealing with all three at once.

The Emergent Institutional Framework

In the United States, the New Deal had kicked off the period of Keynesian stimulus with a set of programs that invested in and stabilized infrastructure and housing. Most of this investment was not explicitly regional, but it often reinforced the tendency for growth on the periphery of central cities. Development of water, sewer, road systems, and even universities occurred through what Barbour (2002) calls "vertical regionalism." This service framework for urban expansion occurred via funding from federal and state governments, management by single-purpose state agencies, and implementation by regional special districts. Where formal regionalism did not exist, jurisdictions developed their own mechanisms for coordination, in a de facto regionalism. The result was rapid suburban development, with some redevelopment of the core for housing, universities, and other institutional uses.

In the 1960s, another set of regional institutions arose to reshape transportation and land use and the growing uneven development across cities and suburbs. In support of federal requirements mandating planning in transportation, services, and other areas, federal policy enabled the establishment of councils of government (COGs) in the 1960s. COGs are a voluntary organization of local governments that originally channeled federal housing grants. Yet, with a one-city, one-vote structure of governance, and no real power to regulate and incentivize, this horizontal institutional form struggled to shape development. Land use regulation remained local, subject to home rule, and was rarely coordinated across levels or jurisdictions.

More promising was the creation of metropolitan planning organizations (MPOs), required by the Federal-Aid Highway Act of 1962 for any urbanized area with a population greater than 50,000. In order to receive federal funds, MPOs were required to undergo a planning process. MPOs received a major boost in 1991 when Congress enacted the Intermodal Surface Transportation Efficiency Act (ISTEA), increasing their authority to program federal transportation dollars (Goldman and Deakin 2000). While allocating one-fifth of federal transportation funding to MPOs, ISTEA mandates the development of long-range (20 years or more) regional transportation plans that conform to regional air quality plans while realistically taking into account fiscal constraints and other objectives. This then set the stage for regional sustainability planning. But first, the neoliberal era added new fuel to the regionalism movement.

The Rise of Neoliberalism

Beginning in the 1980s, the rise of neoliberal ideology meant government retrenchment and increased privatization of the government role in many countries around the world. In the United States, neoliberalism suggested the rejection of egalitarian liberalism, or the idea of a state that mitigates market failures through regulation and redistribution (Hackworth 2007). Though this market fundamentalism came to be known as the Washington Consensus, a broad movement opening up domestic economies to trade, in practice there were many different paths toward liberalization. For example, in Asia, many governments retained their centralized control over the economy, with an active industrial policy and aggressive protectionism. Other countries, particularly in Latin America, assumed state ownership of key industries.

However welcoming to the market, most countries (including the United States) also began a process of decentralization at this time, what might be called second-generation reforms, or institution building to support sustainable growth (Camdessus 1999). The motive for decentralization, or the transfer of responsibilities, resources, and/or authority from the national to the local and regional level, varies across nation-states. Some seek to improve global competitiveness and attract foreign investment to regions; others are trying to reduce the size of central government out of market ideology; and a few are driven by local political considerations (Falleti 2005). In some cases, political, administrative, and fiscal decentralization processes are leading to increased democratic participation, what Tim Campbell (2003), writing about Latin America, called the "quiet revolution," transforming local governance toward more transparency and accountability.

The retrenchment of central government has also led to the rise of new forms of governance, in which NGOs, the private sector, and other non-state actors are given a more significant and active role in public decisions, policymaking, and planning. Governance is the "self-organized steering of multiple agencies, institutions, and systems which are operationally autonomous from one another yet structurally coupled due to their mutual interdependence" (Jessop 1998: 29). Thus, it occurs via cross-sectoral networks that change in membership depending on the issue. Given the challenges in establishing regional governments, the rise of more flexible forms of governance may better support regional planning for sustainability. At the same time, the rescaling of the state has often occurred without resources, leading places to seek the most effective way to facilitate an influx of capital (Deas and Ward 2000). Neil Brenner (2002) argues that these shifts have themselves led to intensified inter-city competition for capital, greater administrative fragmentation, and uneven development.

The 1950s had brought new awareness of uneven development patterns, with increasingly competitive "growth poles" draining capital and people from other places in a "backwash" effect that created new equity problems (Myrdal 1957; Perroux 1955). Although there was some debate, the expectation remained that benefits would trickle down from growth poles to the poor (Hirschman 1958).[3]

At the regional level, the idea of core and periphery resonated, particularly as inequality among regions increased. Innovation clusters in core regions were clearly starting to drive regional development, lifting the nimble Sunbelt over the less adaptive Rustbelt regions (with the help of supportive federal policies such as military spending) (Markusen et al. 1991). Global city-regions had become the engines of the global economy through innovation, efficiency, and productivity (Scott 2001). But such urban agglomerations only exacerbate differences between core and periphery. Major questions remained about whether to concentrate development efforts on a few key centers or many, as well as whether to concentrate on export sectors or import substitution and endogenous growth (Friedmann and Weaver 1979; Teitz 2012).[4]

New Concern with Intra-Regional Equity

Several development factors also created new awareness of intra-regional inequalities, beginning in the United States and the United Kingdom in the 1970s and continuing in many countries today. In the United States, the rapid decentralization of jobs and housing increased awareness of urban sprawl and its costs, leading to the rise of the smart growth movement. At the same time, cities began feeling the pinch of increasing fiscal constraints, due to simultaneous federal budget cuts and local taxpayer revolts. Particularly in strong markets, budget-conscious cities began increasing impact fees to support rising infrastructure costs, creating higher housing prices. In search of greater efficiencies, transportation planners sought better coordination with land use planning.

Recognizing the growing inequality between, and interdependence of, cities and suburbs, some suggested addressing regional fragmentation through planning and governance. A set of studies first established the relationship between city and suburban well-being, making the case that letting inner cities continue their struggle with poverty was hurting the entire region (Ledebur and Barnes 1993; Rusk 1993; Savitch et al. 1993; Voith 1998). Then, Manuel Pastor and his colleagues (2000) produced *Regions that Work*, demonstrating that regions that were growing faster had less poverty (rather than the reverse). His more recent work with Chris Benner has shown that where income inequality, political fragmentation, and racial segregation are high, regions experience shorter periods of sustained growth (Benner and Pastor 2012).[5]

Experiments around the United States emerged to address regional inequities and fragmentation. Among the most frequently cited were Minneapolis–St. Paul's experiment in tax-base sharing and the regional and state growth management in Portland, Oregon (Swanstrom 1996). Experimentation with regional governance focused on policy areas of transportation, land use, and environmental protection, with new integration across functional areas and emphasis on collaborative decision-making among existing institutions (Barbour 2002). In California, for example, diverse agencies began a new collaboration to manage the water in the Sacramento-San Joaquin Delta (Innes et al. 2006). Where these collaborations worked best, they negotiated and adopted outcome-oriented standards (such as water quality or greenhouse gas reduction), incentivizing participation with funding and allowing stakeholders to devise their own implementation methods (Barbour 2002; Mazmanian and Kraft 2009).

Thus, a concerted focus has emerged on developing the optimal scale and form of governance to guide regional growth and prosperity. But as regions continue to struggle with managing local needs for transportation, infrastructure, and housing, the realization has grown that in order to preserve the current environment and resources, they need to consider future consumption patterns more carefully. This has led to the blossoming of regional planning for the long-term (20–50 years).

The Rise of Regional Sustainability Planning

More specifically, the current generation of regional sustainability planning emerges from the convergence of blueprint planning and the sustainable development movement. Blueprint planning—"collaborative planning processes that engage residents of a region in articulating a vision for the long-term future of their region"—emerged in the 1990s as a civil society response to the costs of sprawl, the market and demographic pressures for smarter growth, and the frustration with the lack of planning and coordination across the policy arenas of transportation, the environment, the economy, and housing (Barbour and Teitz 2006; California Department of Transportation 2012). Enabled by the federal reforms that funded MPOs to take the lead in developing long-range regional transportation plans, planning processes appeared around the country; among the best documented are Portland, Sacramento, Salt Lake City, San Francisco, San Diego, Denver, Chicago, and Washington, DC (Calthorpe and Fulton 2001; Knaap and Lewis 2011). These are not based on the traditional transportation modeling that had guided planning since the 1950s, but instead are more participatory and comprehensive. In a consensus-building process, often taking the form of visioning workshops, local governments and community members settle upon a preferred growth scenario, coordinating across transportation, air quality, and housing goals, with an explicit objective of more compact development. Communities make challenging trade-offs among policy goals (such as land conservation and affordable housing) and also between local and regional costs and benefits of development (Barbour and Teitz 2006).

After adopting the preferred scenario, the MPOs then modify their land use projections. With growth forecasted to concentrate more than it would in the business-as-usual scenario, the allocation of transportation spending must shift. This then spurs the transformation in development patterns by initiating a virtuous cycle, as even more transportation funding must be directed to the growth areas. However, success depends on the local will to change policies: local governments must voluntarily implement policies in support of the increased growth. Winning this support has proved challenging for MPOs, though they can use carrots such as competitive grants for planning in these areas (called priority development areas (PDAs) in the San Francisco Bay Area), or conditioning proposed new transit lines on land use policies that mandate higher density (Barbour and Teitz 2006).

Even if the blueprint plans were implemented fully, the projected benefits are typically not very significant. They typically envision the preservation of much open space along with a small shift in mode choice from auto to alternative modes, with a resultant reduction in vehicle miles traveled (VMT) of about 10 percent per 20-year period (Barbour and Teitz 2006). Moreover, the preferred scenario typically costs more than business as usual because of infrastructure needs.

Blueprint planning had yet to be linked to sustainability. Planning for sustainable development per se first emerged in the form of climate change (or climate action) plans, typically at the city or state scale. What Stephen Wheeler (2008) calls the first generation of climate change plans had occurred in 29 U.S. states by 2008. These plans typically featured targets for reducing greenhouse gas emissions based on the Kyoto goal (7 percent below 1990 emissions by 2008–2012), although there is great variation in target level adopted across states (ibid.). For most states, this means including a variety of strategies in plans, typically including: (1) renewable energy portfolio standards for utilities, generally meaning a shift from coal-based electricity generation to solar and wind; (2) higher vehicle emission standards, as pioneered by the State of California; (3) stricter building codes, including increasing energy efficiency requirements and Leadership in Energy and Environmental Design (LEED) certification for buildings; (4) government vehicle fleets running on alternative fuels; and (5) alternative fuel standards for vehicle use (such as the Iowa plan for 25 percent biologically based fuels by 2020) (ibid.). Though implementation has been slow, there has already been an impact, albeit very small: approximately one half metric ton per person per year, or 2–3 percent of average annual greenhouse gas emissions (Drummond 2010). The most effective policies seem to be residential and commercial building energy efficiency, LEED commercial certification, and vehicle efficiency standards (ibid.).

At the local level, the International Council for Local Environmental Initiatives (ICLEI-Local Governments for Sustainability, formed in 1991) and the U.S. Mayor Climate Protection Agreement (MCPA, formed in 2005) have created a global sustainability network. ICLEI focuses on local sustainability planning via climate action plans, offering technical support to help cities inventory their greenhouse gas emissions and develop strategies to reduce them. Over 1,000 cities in 86 countries are members (ICLEI 2013). About 5 percent of all U.S. cities, nearly 30 percent of the population, have joined one or both of these programs committing to reduction in emissions (Krause 2011).[6] Larger, more affluent cities with more educated, liberal-leaning residents are most likely to participate in these efforts (ibid.). Cities are more likely to participate if their neighbor cities are involved; however, this may stem more from free-riding by suburbs on core city efforts than true regional cooperation (Dierwechter 2010; Krause 2011).

Despite this activity, there is no groundswell of public support for sustainability. There are no surveys on public attitudes toward sustainable development per se; however, evidence suggests that although there is widespread support for environmental goals, individual preferences for material consumption are even stronger (Leiserowitz, Kates, and Parris 2006). Yet, pro-sustainability cities do tend to have higher levels of civic participation (Portney and Berry 2010).

The broadness of the sustainability concept may deter support, and it also conceals its contradictions—conflicts between economic growth and redistribution for social equity, between consuming natural resources to generate growth and preserving the environment, between improving the lives of the poor through growth and protecting the environment from development (Campbell 1996). These conflicts over who benefits—sustainable for whom?—have not been addressed effectively by blueprint and sustainability plans to date.

The Challenges of Incorporating Equity into Regional Sustainability Planning

Regional planning and sustainable development might be intended to improve people's lives, but they have not brought fairness, or social equity, as such. At the most basic level, social equity encompasses two dimensions: equity in outcomes (i.e., the equal distribution of life chances, services meeting basic needs, and the ability to realize one's full potential), and equity in process, or democratic representation (and voice) in planning processes (Fainstein 2010).

Four different forms of outcome-based and procedural equity might be evident in regional sustainability plans and processes. *Accessibility* approaches focus on spatial access to needs and opportunities that, in turn, shape life chances and the ability to realize one's potential: access to services, to amenities, to infrastructure, to fair housing, to education, to jobs, to capital, and to resources generally. *Household budget* approaches focus on basic needs (i.e., the individual household's ability to make ends meet: reducing the cost of living, particularly housing, transportation, and energy costs). *Place* approaches address disparities in a particular neighborhood context, either via infill development, typically mixed-use with both jobs and housing, or by improving neighborhood quality, typically through housing and service improvements in existing communities. The theory of equity underlying place approaches is relatively indirect, albeit still outcome-focused: by increasing densities and improving places, the disadvantaged should be more readily able to meet their basic needs. Finally, *capacity-building* approaches address procedural equity either by training disadvantaged individuals to participate in planning processes or supporting community-based organizations that advocate for disadvantaged places or groups.

Despite the growing interest in sustainable development, "just sustainability" is not yet part of policy and practice (Agyeman 2013). Of course, many equitable strategies have emerged in cities in the areas of land use planning, solid waste, toxic chemical use, residential energy use, transportation, urban agriculture, public utilities, and green businesses. In general, these enable more local control over the economy (such as local businesses or food access), support greater democratic participation (such as the involvement of the public sector in energy generation), have redistributive benefits for low-income households (such as green jobs), or improve the health of low-income groups and thus their capacity to be productive (Hess and Winner 2007). And the benefits of livability strategies, such as improved walkability, do accrue to all.

But in practice, equity is an afterthought. Many sustainability plans neglect environmental and social justice issues, and even if they are incorporated, they may be overlooked in implementation in favor of more prominent concerns such as climate change (Pearsall and Peirce 2010; Saha and Paterson 2008). Surprisingly, even community engagement is uneven across urban sustainability programs, with some cities favoring consulting the public via survey research, while others engage in visioning processes (Portney 2005).

Incorporating equity into regionalism is a challenge, in part, because of the sheer complexity of legislating and governing sustainable development. Given the challenge of enacting holistic policies in a complex system, in practice most policies are incremental and ad hoc (Drummond and Marsden 1995). The governance of sustainability typically occurs via networks and multilevel coalitions of state and non-state actors (Bulkeley and Betsill 2005; Cochrane 2010). With many different interests at stake, local sustainability goals may readily be subsumed by more mainstream development goals (e.g., regional, state, and national planning for highways). And the governance of sustainability via networks, even with nonprofits well represented, does not guarantee the implementation of equitable policies, since the lack of a real government structure means the loss of the accountability so characteristic of the city scale. As Bill Lester and Sarah Reckhow (2012) caution, the networks themselves have power relations embedded within them, so their governance may just replicate existing inequalities. Network participants, particularly municipal political leaders, continue to act based on narrow self-interest, rather than form alternative regional or statewide coalitions (Weir, Wolman, and Swanstrom 2005).

Thus, as Scott Bollens (2003) argues, equity may only find its way into regional policies "through the back door," as regions incorporate equity mostly by responding to federal and state programs and funding opportunities that explicitly or indirectly serve to increase social equity in areas addressing air quality, civil rights, fair housing, and poverty reduction, among others. The back door takes different forms around the world, depending on the institutional context for regional sustainability planning.

The International Landscape of Regional Sustainability Planning

The United Nations has long led the call for sustainable development, from the 1992 Earth Summit in Rio, to the 2012 Conference on Sustainable Development, or Rio+20. At the initial summit, countries adopted Agenda 21, which many still use as the guiding principle for their regional planning and development programs. Agenda 21 is a voluntary blueprint that provides guidance on achieving sustainable growth while combatting poverty and conserving natural resources. Rio+20 developed a set of measures (the "outcome document") for implementing sustainable development (United Nations General Assembly 2012).

The outcome document makes an explicit call for engaging the subnational (i.e., regional) level in planning and implementing sustainable development.[7] It recognizes the need to build new regional capacity and institutions to implement sustainable development policies, and to strengthen their ability to coordinate on the three dimensions of sustainable development.

What does regional sustainability planning look like around the world? In general, regional planning is a cross-jurisdictional, cross-sectoral effort to manage regional transportation, infrastructure, and housing for regional prosperity. A concern with sustainability adds consideration of inter- (and intra-) generational equity, as well as sensitivity to ecosystem limits.

Regional sustainability planning has emerged in many different forms, with just a few model efforts. The best examples are in countries that offer a strong national framework for metropolitan or regional planning, most prominently the European Union and Australia. Both regional and climate policies guide planning for subnational regions in the European Union. The E.U. regional policy (€351 billion from 2014 to 2020) invests in the competitiveness and sustainable development of E.U. regions, with the aim of reducing inter-regional disparities. The 2030 E.U. framework for climate and energy policies sets and allocates targets for greenhouse gas reduction (currently, reduction by 40 percent below the 1990 level by 2030); it also supports investments in renewable energy and energy efficiency. In Australia, states have constitutional authority to conduct spatial and infrastructure planning at the metropolitan level, and thus most major metropolises have strategic plans that direct infrastructure investment (Searle and Bunker 2010). Increasingly, these metropolitan plans incorporate issues of inclusion and sustainability (ibid.). China has been experimenting with new forms of regional governance in the form of provincial organizations, although the central government maintains a powerful role (Wong, Qian, and Zhou 2008). Its 31 provinces have prepared climate change plans, and, with expansion of zoning powers to the regional level, are able to coordinate resource management across cities (European Commission 2013).

At the other end of the spectrum are countries that have retained a more centralized governance framework, as is the case in Africa, the successor states to the Soviet Union, and some Southeast Asian countries. Most common in these regions are metropolitan plans, often prepared for the dominant capital metropolis (e.g., Jakarta or Nairobi). Where the planning process is more regional in scope, it is usually addressing issues of land or resource management (as in, for example, Tajikistan, with its Strategy and Action Plan for Sustainable Land Management in the High Pamir and Pamir-Alai Mountains). Rarely, though, do these regions have any powers for implementation, lacking the enforcement powers of municipalities and relying heavily on budget transfers from the central government.

In between these two poles is a set of countries with emergent regional planning frameworks. These include certain Latin-American countries, the United States and Canada, India, and several other countries. In these cases, policy experiments have taken place, and institutions may be at work, but powers to incentivize and enforce regional planning remain limited.

A scan we conducted of regional sustainability plans around the world reveals a broad diversity of metropolitan and regional plans.[8] Looking at the 29 megacities (metropolises with more than 10 million residents), almost all have metropolitan plans.[9] Most focus on global competitiveness and urban quality of life, and seem to emerge from strong political leadership in the central city. Not surprisingly, they often center on the construction of megaprojects, typically infrastructure, such as rail, highways, or telecommunications (Belsky et al. 2013). Studies of model metropolitan plans in Singapore, London, New York, and Stockholm suggest that their success is due to several best practices, including: (1) a clear division of roles between cities and region; (2) a long-term vision linked to a spatial investment plan; (3) the integration of land use and transportation planning; (4) specific strategies for project design and finance;

and (5) planning staff resources and capacity (Belsky et al. 2013; Sankhe et al. 2010).

In comparison, regional development plans tend to focus on a variety of topics, predominantly transportation and infrastructure development, environmental management, and land use. Many of these regional plans are intended to help peripheral regions that are losing out to the more competitive metropolitan nodes. Thus, they are much less likely to address global competitiveness, instead focusing on the well-being of residents.

Less than half of the metropolitan and regional plans we located mentioned sustainability, or even just the integration of economic, environmental, and equity goals; the more recent the plan, the more likely to incorporate sustainability concerns. Even rarer was the discussion of social equity and inclusion. Regional plans typically addressed inclusion in terms of capacity building for local residents, including both local economic development (LED) and participation in plan making. In the metropolitan plans that do address equity, it was in terms of physical accessibility to opportunity, or generally improving regional competitiveness so that benefits would trickle down to the poor.

Yet, our scan surfaced numerous metropolitan and regional plans that address sustainability in interesting ways. We look next at a selected set, chosen as some of the best examples of regional sustainability planning across a variety of continents and political economies: Melbourne, Australia; La Araucanía, Chile; Shanghai, China; Copenhagen, Denmark; South Transdanubia, Hungary; and Istanbul, Turkey.

Melbourne

Melbourne, a metropolis of over 4 million people and 31 local governments, has experienced the rapid spread of low-density development on the fringe since World War II, led by land speculation and infrastructure development (Sandercock 1979). With jobs and housing highly decentralized, and high rates of car dependency, communities resist attempts to densify and alter the character of suburban life (Dovey et al. 2013). Despite this, the recent growth of some higher-density housing suggests the emergence of a new market for infill and density (Randolph and Tice 2013).

Melbourne has prepared regional plans regularly since 1929, with the state generally taking the lead due, in part, to metropolitan fragmentation. In the 2000s, the state's Department of Infrastructure prepared *Melbourne 2030: Planning for Sustainable Growth*, based on a lengthy participatory process. Following this was the Department of Transport, Planning & Local Infrastructure's *Plan Melbourne: Metropolitan Planning Strategy 2050*, which is more of an outcomes-based, integrated approach to planning and development. In addition, many of the city governments have created climate change strategies (Jones 2013).

Plan Melbourne is a strategy to accommodate the next 2.5 million residents and 1.2 million jobs in a sustainable urban structure (i.e., with healthier natural systems and greater jobs and housing density near public transportation to reduce greenhouse gas emissions) (State Government of Victoria 2013). A new Metropolitan Planning Authority will coordinate planning, with five new subregions empowered to deal with the region's weak local governments, decentralization, and emerging polycentricity. There is almost no mention of social equity in the plan.

La Araucanía

La Araucanía, with almost 870,000 inhabitants, is one of Chile's 15 administrative divisions and comprises two provinces and 38 municipalities. With the lowest GDP per capita in the country, the region seeks to narrow inequality, promote sustainable fishing and tourism industries for economic development, and promote trust and development for the indigenous Mapuche group (Central Bank of Chile 2012; Government of Chile 2010).

Although Chile as a whole has generally experienced dynamic economic growth and poverty reduction, the majority of its regions and municipalities have not benefited (RIMISP 2012). Decentralization reforms beginning in the 1990s strengthened regional development initiatives by empowering local governments and at the same time forcing them, for lack of resources, to involve actors from the private sector and nongovernmental organizations (Helmsing 2001). Still, subnational institutions in Chile are still relatively weak due to the devolution of governing capacity before political authority, which remains centralized (Eaton 2004).

The national and La Araucanía regional government have developed complementary regional plans for 2010–2022, linking spatial investment planning to regional development and social equity goals. The Chilean government's Plan Araucanía is essentially a plan for public investment, proposing $4.4 billion in expenditures in the first four years to help the region catch up to other Chilean regions. It focuses on the indigenous people, educational and health reforms, productive development, and investment in infrastructure and regional connectivity. The regional government's regional development strategy focuses more on sustainable economic development, through social cohesion, economic growth, the sustainable development of cities and territories, regional identity, and regional public institutions. The goal is to reduce inequality through integration, by strengthening urban centers and connectivity and trade networks between them.

Shanghai

The Shanghai metropolitan region (population 24 million) occupies most of the southern region of the Yangtze River Delta, which houses 6 percent of the country's population but more than 21 percent of its gross domestic product (GDP) (Ye 2009). Driving Shanghai's rapid urban expansion are the ongoing rural-urban migration, the spatial dispersion of both the local population and industry, and global investment. Building Shanghai, the largest megacity in the world, into an international financial trading center by opening up the cities along the Yangtze River is not just part of the Chinese economic leap forward, but also a way for regional government to reassert its position in local economic governance for a global city-region (Xu 2008). The challenge is to plan for urban sustainability at the same time as the metropolis is transforming itself. As Solecki and Leichenko (2006: 20) point out:

> The physical layout and expanse of the city for the twenty-first century is being built now, and while some aspects of government policy is [sic] focused on urban sustainability, other policies focus on promoting individual consumerism, and capitalist markets provide a countervailing force of increasingly extensive resource demand and use.

Prior to the 1978 reforms in China, regional policies focused on resource exploitation and industrial production, with a focus on management, rather than planning for economic and social development (Wong, Qian, and Zhou 2008; Ye 2009). The current experiment in regional planning conducts strategic spatial planning with a focus on sustainable development, but still under the eye of the central government.

Both the Yangtze Delta Regional Plan 2005–2010 (2007) and the Shanghai Master Plan (1999–2020) guide development. The Yangtze Delta plan, which was initiated by the central government, but shaped and supported by local authorities, strategizes for the international competitiveness of the region (Wong, Qian, and Zhou 2008). Although it offers detailed policies, it lacks mechanisms for implementation (ibid.).

The Master Plan also focuses on competitiveness for Shanghai, the "Dragon's Head" of the Yangtze River Basin, but through the lens of sustainable development (Shanghai Municipal Government 1998). With 2 million new residents anticipated by 2020, suburban development will need to accelerate, particularly in new job centers. At the same time, the plan seeks to improve the environmental quality and livability of Central Shanghai, the headquarters for finance, insurance, and information technology. Although the plan describes a focus on people as a prominent feature, it seems to interpret that as creating a more livable, rather than equitable, environment.

Copenhagen

With 30 percent of the Danish population (almost 2 million people), but 40 percent of the economy, the Capital Region of Denmark (Copenhagen and 28 other municipalities) is the growth engine of the country. The region, considered a model of regional sustainability, benefits from its 1947 Finger Plan, a metropolitan growth strategy that instituted key transit-supportive principles, including high-density development around train stations on five commuter lines, and open space preservation in wedges between these "fingers" (Vejre,

Skov-Petersen, and Lizia Henschel n.d.). In recent years, though growth has been relatively slow, the incidence of auto commuting has been increasing (Næss et al. 2009).

The national government has recently established a framework for regional development strategies, including: (1) reducing the number of local and regional authorities; (2) giving regions new statutory responsibility for economic development, as well as increasing coordination with the national Globalisation Strategy; and (3) integrating development activities across levels, from the local to the European Union (Halkier 2009). The five new regions, governed by elected councils and subsidized by the central government and municipalities, maintain responsibility for health and social services, as well as formulating the regional spatial development plan; however, land use planning and regulation authority is still shared between municipalities and central government. Undergirding the new focus on regional development is concern about the integration of the peripheral and rural areas left behind (Kragh 2005).

Two regional plans guide development in the Capital Region and Greater Copenhagen: the *Finger Plan* (2007) and the *Regional Development Plan* (2008). The new Finger Plan, which was formulated by the central government, is primarily a physical plan guided by sustainable development principles; it enacts the "Close to Station" principle, whereby large office buildings and commercial facilities are required to locate within a 600-meter radius from train stations (Danish Ministry of the Environment 2007). The *Regional Development Plan* (for 2020) couples a focus on international competitiveness (including business development and education) with quality of life (environmentally friendly infrastructure, open space, environmental quality, and climate change strategies). Given its new focus on business development strategies, critics suggest that a growth-oriented agenda is overriding issues of equity (Halkier 2009). Further, locals seem to conceptualize sustainability as the reduction of the environmental impact from economic development, rather than a reconciliation of conflicting goals (Xue et al. 2011).

South Transdanubia

The South Transdanubia region, one of seven in Hungary, is located in the southwestern part of Hungary and houses almost a million people at the lowest population density in the country. A landscape dominated by small villages and towns, it is experiencing serious economic challenges and outmigration due to the decline of heavy industry and mining, the poor transportation infrastructure, and the struggle to attract foreign direct investment (Pálné Kovács, Paraskevopoulos, and Horváth 2004). With one of the lowest per capita GDPs in the country (44 percent of the E.U. average), regional development planning focuses on the three Es and inequality (European Commission 2013; Government of the Republic of Hungary 2007).

Because of the European Union support (and funding) for regional planning, regional development agencies in Hungary have considerable capacity. Yet, as has occurred in much of Eastern Europe, the European Commission imposed regional definitions on Hungary that did not correspond to traditional regions (in Hungary's case, counties), complicating local politics (Hughes, Sasse, and Gordon 2004). Still, the country is gradually creating new institutions that decentralize state functions and strengthen local governments, as well as private-sector participation (Pálné Kovács, Paraskevopoulos, and Horváth 2004). Though the regional development councils are weakened by the continued power of central state officials and counties to allocate funds, they are increasingly central to the governance structure and have become the main fora for the dialogue about development in the country (Pálné Kovács, Paraskevopoulos, and Horváth 2004).

The *South Transdanubia Operational Programme 2007–2013* prioritizes competitiveness via endogenous development, especially support of small and medium enterprises and local infrastructure development, the strengthening of the tourism sector, the improvement of human services, the sustainable renewal of places occupied by the Roma people to facilitate social cohesion, and improved environmental quality and accessibility. It thus integrates the three Es, with an explicit focus on mitigating disparities both within the region and between South Transdanubia and the rest of Hungary (Government of the Republic of Hungary 2007). Though it is considered one of Hungary's strongest regional plans in terms of promoting sustainable development, critics point to its centralized planning process and resultant exclusion of local voices (Pálné Kovács and Varjú 2009).

Istanbul

Located at the Strait of Istanbul (Bosphorus), which separates Asia and Europe, Istanbul houses about 14 million people in a metropolis with a dominant core and multiple urban nuclei (Yuzer and Kucuk 1998). Rapid growth has led to suburbanization and urban sprawl along its coasts, and real estate speculation is rampant (ibid.). The spread of the *gecekondu*, or illegal squatter settlements, threatens the environment, particularly forestlands and water supplies, and the tendency of planning is to facilitate the development, rather than manage growth strategically (OECD 2008). With its concentration of economic output (38 percent of the country's industrial output and more than 50 percent of services), policymakers have long shared a vision for Istanbul as an international gateway, both symbolic and financial, between Europe, Asia, and the Middle East (OECD 2008; Yuzer and Kucuk 1998). At the same time, the in-migration of low-skilled workers, concentrated in the informal sector, along with the rise of advanced services, has contributed to a sharp rise in income inequality (OECD 2008).

Turkey's political and institutional culture comprises both anti-democratic and democratic elements: it is at once a centralized state run by a corrupt and controlling political system, with a powerful religious network in the background, and a participatory democracy with a high degree of association and representation (Lovering and Evren 2011). The primary regional government is the Istanbul Metropolitan Municipality, created in 1984, although a provincial administration with significantly fewer powers covers the same territory (Daoudov 2011). The Istanbul Metropolitan Municipality comprises 39 district municipalities; all are governed by elected councils and mayors.

The *Istanbul Metropolitan Area Master Plan for 2023* focuses on global competitiveness, social justice and urban integration, and local quality of life and culture (Istanbul Metropolitan Municipality 2007). Its approach to sustainability is through spatial development that protects forest, water, and agricultural areas, and reduces migration to Istanbul, via both horizontal (i.e., among the districts) and vertical (i.e., national) coordination.

In sum, this selection of regions demonstrates the variety of regional sustainability plans, as we will see when we revisit the cases in coming chapters. In general, the plans suggest the importance of spatial investment plans (i.e., plans that are coordinated with real estate development and infrastructure investment, and incentivized via financing mechanisms) (Belsky et al. 2013). Most of the metropolitan plans have such effective structures in place for implementation, often because of the link to infrastructure development. The metropolitan plans (Shanghai, Copenhagen, Istanbul, Melbourne) target the role of the market and global competition, generally ignoring issues of social equity (in part, because the national government maintains control of social services and development). In contrast, the regional plans (La Araucanía and South Transdanubia) deal more explicitly with social equity, avoiding the need for a "back door." Is regional sustainability planning in the United States any more equitable?

Regional Sustainability Planning in the United States in the Twenty-First Century

The United States has established an institutional framework for regional planning in the form of the MPOs, and numerous blueprint plans have experimented with public participation and visioning. But the Housing and Urban Development's (HUD) Sustainable Communities Initiative Regional Planning Grant (SCI-RPG) program provides the first evidence of a nationwide resurgence of interest in regional planning in the twenty-first century.

Funded by Congress in 2010 and 2011, the SCI-RPG provided grants on a competitive basis for collaborative regional planning efforts supporting more sustainable development patterns. With $165 million awarded to 74 grantees from across the country, the program marks the largest federal government investment ever in regional planning in the United States. But even just the process of applying for the grants, with applications from 289 different regions, has spurred conversations about regional sustainability across the country (Figure 2.1). These applications constitute a kind of natural experiment, since they reveal a variety of different approaches to planning sustainable regions.

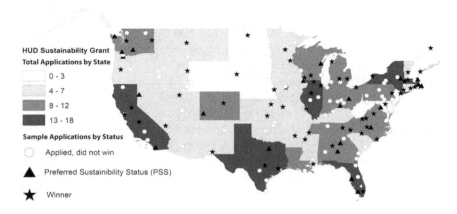

Figure 2.1 SCI-RPG applicants and sample
Source: Chapple and Mattiuzzi (2013)

A content analysis we did of the applications (Chapple and Mattiuzzi 2013) reveals just how diverse these approaches can be.[10]

Overall, applications tended to follow the distribution of population, but there has been a surprising amount of interest in states with non-liberal political leanings, such as Oklahoma and Georgia, as well as weak market states where economic development is clearly a greater concern than environmental preservation. The landscape of regions working on regional sustainability looks slightly different from the United States as a whole: this group is almost twice as likely to include large metropolitan regions and half as likely to include small metros, and also has a slightly higher share of minority groups.

The HUD program asked for consortia of public and nonprofit actors, including either an MPO or regional planning agency, to produce a regional plan, implement such a plan, or develop processes that would ultimately lead to a plan (e.g., building coordination among agencies or collecting new data). Overall, almost 80 percent of the consortia involved an MPO, COG, or joint MPO-COG, with joint involvement much more typical. This suggests that this particular institutional structure may be best prepared to take on the challenges of regional sustainability planning, and not just because they have the carrot of transportation funding. They effectively—but not democratically—combine regional and local governance by incorporating both subregional agencies (e.g., transit districts) and city governments into their governing boards. At their best, they make decisions about regional planning for transportation and air quality (per state and federal mandates) in light of local land use constraints. On the other hand, this balanced structure means that they tend to avoid challenging decisions, such as funding certain cities at the expense of others, instead spreading the benefits equally across jurisdictions (Barbour and Teitz 2006). And ultimately, their authority over land use is only advisory. Change is slow.

To support more sustainable development, the activities would need to integrate housing, land use, economic and workforce development, transportation, and infrastructure investments and advance livability. In support of social equity—through the back door—HUD specified that grantee activities should further Title VI of the Civil Rights Act, Section 504 of the Rehabilitation Act of 1973, and the Fair Housing Act by incorporating inclusionary zoning, environmental justice, and the coordination of housing development and public transportation into their plans. HUD also called for meaningful stakeholder engagement in planning processes, from the development of vision, to its implementation, with particular attention to marginalized communities.

How Regions Define Sustainability

What does sustainability mean to actors in U.S. regions? Most of the applications offered no specific definition of sustainability, though they mentioned the term or provided examples such as recycling and buying local. But most applications implied a definition of sustainability that fell into one of four areas:

1. The three Es or comprehensiveness (31 percent of applicants); for instance, describing sustainability via the Brundtland definition, or as "long-term balance of social, economic, and environmental components of a community," or as coordination and a systems approach.
2. Livability (18 percent of applicants); e.g., by proposing projects that "improve walkability, support existing communities, and increase the access to jobs for these neighborhoods" make places more sustainable.
3. Location efficiency (19 percent of applicants): as one applicant wrote, "The results will be a reduced urban footprint, significant infrastructure savings, more walking and biking, improved public health, inclusionary affordable housing and increased quality of life. This is a sustainable growth scenario that reduces combined transportation/housing costs and travel time and makes the super region more globally competitive." Most of these applicants referred to the cost of sprawl, the inefficient use of existing infrastructure, or the burden on the family budget of high housing plus transportation costs.
4. Environment/climate change (17 percent of applicants), as in the ecological perspective of an applicant that would "advance sustainable development through its consideration of the unique perspectives of its constituents: plant, animal, and human" or the applicants who focus on climate change adaptation, land preservation, or environmental quality.

Approaches to Inclusion and Economic Development

The applications also provide a lens into U.S. regional tools for—and attitudes toward—equity and economic development. Overall, the U.S. regions are much less focused on global competitiveness than are their counterparts around the world, and instead are more likely to target income inequality. As in many metropolitan plans, however, they tend to focus on accessibility and place making as key to more livable and equitable regions.

Social Inclusion and Procedural Equity

Applicants adopted one of four different public participation strategies, roughly based on Sherry Arnstein's 1969 ladder of citizen participation: from simply educating the public (often through websites, reports, or presentations), to interacting with a select group (e.g., via working groups, agency taskforces, or citizen advisory committees), to interacting with the public (typically in community meetings, workshops, or charrettes), to actually building local capacity (typically through intermediaries, leadership development, or training programs). Over 60 percent of the applicants scored high on the participation ladder, proposing two-way strategies rather than a top-down approach; however, most of these propose interactive workshops, rather than local empowerment approaches. In general, the stronger the local market context, the higher the score on the participation ladder. Regions with weaker markets (and more conservative politics) tended to rely on public education strategies or work through committees.

Economic Development and Outcomes-Based Equity

Not only did the SCI emphasize social equity, but, in 2011, it added the creation of an economic development plan as a potential program outcome. Applications proposed some 44 different approaches, from specific strategies (such as promoting green jobs through energy efficiency programs, or revitalizing a neighborhood commercial corridor), to general concepts (targeting equity as a growth strategy, or building on existing business). Overall, 20 percent of the applicants focused on business for their economic development approach, 32 percent targeted people, and 46 percent targeted place (2 percent did not mention economic development) (Figure 2.2). The focus on developing livable places in order to attract skilled labor and thus economic development of course occurs in metropolitan plans around the world, such as Shanghai and Melbourne. But in comparison to other countries around the world, the U.S. regions are much less sophisticated about business development and much more concerned about developing people-based strategies at the local scale for addressing inequities.

The majority of business-focused strategies suggested targeting regional sectors or clusters, mostly in food, clean energy, and tourism; some also suggested

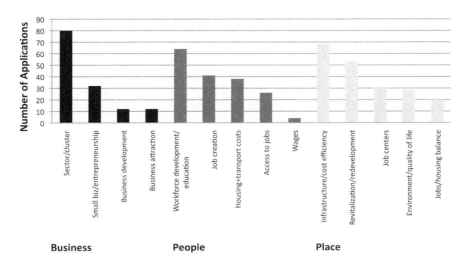

Figure 2.2 Economic development approaches proposed in SCI applications: business, people, or place-based

Source: Author's elaboration

focusing on high-tech, export industries, or research and development (R&D). Less common were approaches to develop small business (typically through entrepreneurship programs or incubators), assist or attract businesses generally, or revitalize commercial corridors. Many blended strategies (e.g., combining business attraction with a sectoral approach) such as the region that would "allow small towns to attract appropriate businesses to their communities while preserving the productive agricultural lands and existing agricultural oriented industry."

People-focused strategies, which address inequities most directly, typically address either access to education or jobs, or household budgets to reduce combined housing and transport costs. Workforce development and, to a lesser extent, higher education dominated the people-focused strategies.[11] Many applicants mentioned job creation or reducing combined housing and transportation costs as a concern, but failed to offer any specific policies. For instance, one applicant wanted to "Increase job education opportunities for those unemployed due to the collapse of tobacco, textiles, and furniture industries and those in need of fundamental skills; pursue economic development clusters that yield more jobs with higher wages." Only a couple of applicants mentioned living wage or other strategies to boost earnings.

Place-based economic development approaches operate under the premise that improving a place will create economic growth: for instance, investing in infrastructure will attract businesses seeking lower costs, fostering job centers will help create agglomeration economies, and improving the quality of life in communities will also attract investment. For these applicants, economic development will occur via efficient infrastructure: as one suggested, the plan will "enhance regional centers' competitiveness through denser, mixed-use development and increase access to centers through transportation improvements, which will create financial incentives and economies of scale that encourage developers to invest in the areas." Others suggested either redevelopment or beautification plans that will attract new residents and shoppers.

A region's economy and politics shape what type of economic development strategy it adopts. Weak market regions, as well as red states, were more likely to focus on place and business, while strong market regions relied on people-focused strategies. The most important factors affecting the decision to emphasize equity, or people-focused economic development, in the application have to do with regional context: Midwestern culture, the presence of a substantial non-white population, and a strong market economy. Also important are several variables representing application and collaboration type: the total grant amount, percent match, and a number of different organization types. In general, the more diverse the collaborative, the more the matching funds offered, and the higher the overall grant funding requested, the more likely the application is to focus on equity. Overall, this analysis suggests that in more affluent regions, there is greater empowerment of non-white populations, as well as capacity and resources to support an equity focus.

It is too early to assess the full impact of HUD's SCI-RPG program, but this overview of the applications suggests that launching the program has planted many seeds and started many conversations across the country. Seventy-four regions have either launched new sustainability planning processes or begun implementing completed plans, many of which will be more equitable than they would have been without HUD's "back door." Even for the regions that did not win a grant, the process of applying mostly likely built new capacity to work on regional planning issues.

The Case of California and the San Francisco Bay Area

California's efforts in regional sustainability planning stand out from the rest of the country and even the world. The state has long pioneered environmental legislation that then becomes a model either adopted by the federal government or individual states. Its 2002 tailpipe standards (regulating automobile greenhouse gas emissions) were adopted by 16 states and ultimately by the federal government. Currently, the implementation of the Global Warming Solutions Act of 2006 (Assembly Bill 32) has established the benchmark goal of reducing the state's carbon emissions to below 1990 levels by 2020. By 2050, the reduction target will be 80 percent below 1990 levels.[12] In implementing this standard, the California Air Resources Board has emphasized the primacy of vehicle fuel economy and low-carbon fuel standards, with sustainable land use and transportation planning as a smaller, third element (Barbour and Deakin

2012). It has created the country's first cap-and-trade system, watched closely by policy analysts across the country. Its system of carrots and sticks to reduce greenhouse gas emissions is motivating residents, businesses, and planners to change business as usual.

California became a leading exemplar of regional sustainability as well following passage of the Sustainable Communities and Climate Protection Act, Senate Bill 375 of 2008, which charges regions with developing a long-range (2020 and 2035) plan to guide transportation funding investment, land use, and affordable housing as means to reduce greenhouse gas emissions from automobiles and light trucks. This plan, or the Sustainable Communities Strategy of the Regional Transportation Plan, not only must meet emissions reduction targets, but also must plan for sufficient (and affordable) housing to accommodate growth, in compliance with the state's fair share housing (Regional Housing Needs Assessment, or RHNA) process.[13] SB 375 offers two incentives for smarter growth: future transportation investment and protection for infill projects from lawsuits during the environmental review process.

As is typical in regional governance, SB 375 uses outcome-oriented standards to guide planning. Yet, it relies on the MPO, which has no real power (other than the limited transportation funds) to make local governments change their land use patterns. Although targets are relatively low, just 6 percent of AB 32 goals, the contribution of land use and transportation planning to overall greenhouse gas reduction is expected to grow substantially over time as new development patterns take hold (Barbour and Deakin 2012; California Air Resources Board 2011). Implementation is also expected to accelerate as revenues from cap-and-trade begin supporting sustainable development patterns. In California, cap-and-trade, or emissions trading, allows firms to discharge excessive emissions in exchange for buying permits or carbon credits from firms that have successfully reduced emissions. Under AB 32, cap-and-trade limits greenhouse gases and creates a carbon market to spur users to invest in clean technologies.

Where California may be truly exceptional is in its preparedness for regional sustainability planning processes. Support for the integration of environmental, transportation, and land use policies comes from both environmental activists interested in preserving diversity in the bioregion and business leaders wanting to protect quality of life within regional commute sheds. For instance, a coalition of environmentalists and developers supported SB 375's trade-offs between environmental quality (reducing greenhouse gas emissions) and development (streamlining environmental reviews for infill development) (Barbour and Deakin 2012). The institutional structure is in place (albeit still weak), not only because MPOs in California have the power to program some long-range state and federal capital investment funds, but also because its RHNA process asks that municipalities provide their fair share of housing needed in the region. This, in turn, means for the first time augmenting transportation planning processes with planning for neighborhoods, housing, and jobs, traditionally the domain of urban policy. This shifts it into the realm of equity regionalism and challenges the technocratic approaches at the heart of transportation planning.

Most California regions have already completed their initial Sustainable Communities Strategy, with modest success in reducing greenhouse gas emissions projected for the region by planning for more compact development near transportation infrastructure. These regional plans begin to address social equity by accommodating future housing needs via higher-density development throughout the region. But they fall short of equitable development in several ways, most importantly failing to identify the funding necessary for new housing to ensure that it is affordable, and neglecting the needs of the regional economy almost entirely.

In 2013, the San Francisco Bay Area approved its Sustainable Communities Strategy, called Plan Bay Area, which will use about $10 billion in transit revenues (about one-third from California's cap-and-trade revenues) to support more sustainable development patterns that reduce greenhouse gas emissions (Cabanatuan 2013). It should be noted, however, that this is just a drop in the bucket of transportation funds, which total almost $300 billion over the next 30 years.

Although Plan Bay Area incorporates equitable development more explicitly than do other California regions, it is far from a model in planning for housing and jobs, as discussed in subsequent chapters. And it is not very popular, either: thus far, it has spawned four lawsuits (two from property rights groups, one from environmental groups, and one from developers) and narrowly avoided a fifth, from fair housing advocates. However, a deep expertise and capacity for regional planning in both professional and civil society sectors in the Bay Area have emerged from its long history of regional planning, including the Bay Vision 2020 in 1991 and the Smart Growth Strategy—Regional Livability Footprint project in 2002.

California is often seen as an exceptional case because of its early adoption of regulations protecting the environment and the unique challenges associated with its rapid population growth. Yet, both its problems and their symptoms are cropping up in both strong and weak markets around the world. Everywhere, fragmentation of growth management responsibilities between different governments, along with contentious planning processes, make it challenging to build infill development, reduce traffic congestion, and slow outward expansion, aka sprawl. Federal and state budget cuts coupled with taxpayer revolts (such as California's Proposition 13) limit the ability of local governments to fund basic services and raise housing costs.

Few (if any) cities and regions will be able to adopt the California model wholesale. But it does offer valuable lessons in reconciling the three Es and building the legislative infrastructure to sustain sustainability. For other regions, it will be important to start from their own strengths, identifying where there is a regional conversation already that crosscuts deep value conflicts and has an institutional basis. This will be easiest to achieve in areas where ecological, functional, and administrative regions coincide—which Patrick Geddes hinted at 100 years ago.

The Future of Regional Sustainability Planning

Regional planning has gone in and out of fashion over the past 100 years, and it is hard to predict its future. Most past efforts at institutionalizing regionalism have long since disappeared: the Tennessee Valley Authority stands as one lonely monument. Other moments, such as the rise of blueprint planning in the United States in the 1990s, seem, in retrospect, to have been fads, yet also having had significant impact on how MPOs envision the future and engage the public.

The sheer variety of regional plans around the world, as well as the number of international organizations involved, suggests the possibility that this movement will gain more traction. What these efforts have in common is that they attempt to construct policy on an appropriate spatial basis. Certainly, awareness of climate change is driving new interest in planning at a regional scale in many different places. Across the world's different continents, the interest stems from different factors. In Latin America and some Asian countries, the rapid decentralization of the government, along with the influence of the United Nations, plays a pivotal role. Interest in both regional integration and climate change drives regional planning in Europe. But what will be most interesting to watch, as the current generation of regional plans emerges, is how they plan and design for a just sustainability.

Notes

1. A. J. Willis (1997: 270) defines ecosystem as "a unit comprising a community (or communities) of organisms and their physical and chemical environment, at any scale, desirably specified, in which there are continuous fluxes of matter and energy in an interactive open system."
2. Yet, Elisa Barbour (2002) argues that this was an early form of metropolitan planning, even though it was within city boundaries, because so much of the population lived within those central cities.
3. Of course, as dependency theorists posited, drawing from Marxist ideas, the dynamic could be working in reverse: resources were flowing from a periphery of poor states to a core of wealthy states, enriching the latter and impeding the former's · development potential (Cardoso and Faletto 1979).
4. The Douglas North-Charles Tiebout debate famously took on the question of whether the success of the export base determines the regional rate of growth, or endogenous, supply-side variables.
5. In a complementary volume with Martha Matsuoka (Pastor, Benner, and Matsuoka 2009), they also document the rise of what they call "social movement regionalism," new alliances for regional equity.
6. As of July 2009.
7. The term "regional" typically refers to a cohesive collection of countries.
8. There is no comprehensive database of regional sustainability plans. For this scan, we conducted a Google search of every country in the world, along with the terms "sustainability" and "regional plan." We also searched separately for the 29 global megacities, with the terms "sustainability" and "metropolitan plan." One limitation of this method is that we were restricted to English-language queries and could thus not identify plans written in a country's native tongue.

9. We could not find any reference (in English) to metropolitan plans for Lagos and Karachi.
10. For this study, we collected data for this project by contacting all of the individual lead applicants and requesting their application materials. In total, we received 144 applications, or 50 percent of the non-duplicated applications that was our universe. The sample slightly overrepresents several regions, including the South Atlantic, Mid Atlantic, East North Central, West North Central, Mountain, and Pacific divisions, and slightly underrepresents East South Central and New England division. Only in the West South Central is there a potential sampling problem, with just 11 of 34 non-duplicate applications (34 percent); response was particularly low in Arkansas and Louisiana.
11. This was perhaps because of the involvement of counties (and their Workforce Investment Boards) in the SCI-RPG consortium.
12. Per Executive Order (S-3-05), signed by then-governor Arnold Schwarzenegger in 2005.
13. RHNA requires cities to ensure through their general plans (specifically the Housing Element) that they can accommodate existing and future housing needs (based on projected job and population growth) through existing housing stock and future development. In order to show that they are accommodating the need for affordable housing, cities must show that they have zoned at high densities (30 units or higher for cities of population 25,000 or more). The State of California must certify that the housing elements accommodate their fair share; without this certification, cities may experience challenges in obtaining state bond and housing funding.

References

Agyeman, Julian. *Introducing Just Sustainabilities: Policy, Planning, and Practice*. London: Zed Books, 2013.

Agyeman, Julian, Robert D. Bullard, and Bob Evans. *Just Sustainabilities: Development in an Unequal World*. Cambridge, MA: MIT Press, 2003.

Alonso, William. *Location and Land Use: Toward a General Theory of Land Rent*. Cambridge, MA: Harvard University Press, 1964.

Arnstein, Sherry R. "A Ladder of Citizen Participation." *Journal of the American Institute of Planners* 35, no. 4 (1969): 216–224.

Barbour, Elisa. *Metropolitan Growth Planning in California, 1900–2000*. San Francisco, CA: Public Policy Institute of CA, 2002.

Barbour, Elisa and Elizabeth Deakin. "Smart Growth Planning for Climate Protection." *Journal of the American Planning Association* 78, no. 1 (2012): 70–86.

Barbour, Elisa and Michael B. Teitz. *Blueprint Planning in California: Forging Consensus on Metropolitan Growth and Development*. San Francisco, CA: Public Policy Institute of California, 2006.

Belsky, Eric S., Nicholas DuBroff, Daniel McCue, Christina Harris, Shelagh McCartney, and Jennifer Molinsky. *Advancing Inclusive and Sustainable Urban Development: Correcting Planning Failures and Connecting Communities to Capital*. Cambridge, MA: Harvard University Joint Center for Housing Studies, 2013.

Benner, Chris and Manuel Pastor. *Just Growth: Inclusion and Prosperity in America's Metropolitan Region*, New York: Routledge, 2012.

Bollens, Scott A. "In Through the Back Door: Social Equity and Regional Governance." *Housing Policy Debate* 13, no. 4 (2003): 631–657.

Brenner, Neil. "Decoding the Newest 'Metropolitan Regionalism' in the USA: A Critical Overview." *Cities* 19, no. 1 (2002): 3–21.

Bulkeley, Harriet and Michele Betsill. "Rethinking Sustainable Cities: Multilevel Governance and the 'Urban' Politics of Climate Change." *Environmental Politics* 14, no. 1 (2005): 42–63.

Cabanatuan, Michael. "Bay Area Sets Transits Spending Target." *SF Gate*, December 18, 2013. Accessed December 18, 2013. www.sfgate.com/default/article/Bay-Area-sets-transit-spending-targets-5077424.php.

California Air Resources Board. *Status of Scoping Plan Recommended Measures.* California Government Code Sections 65080-65086.5, and 65580-65589.8. Sacramento, CA: California Air Resource Board, 2011.

California Department of Transportation. "California Regional Blueprint Planning Program." Last modified 2012. Accessed September 20, 2013. http://calblueprint.dot.ca.gov.

Calthorpe, Peter and William Fulton. *The Regional City.* Washington, DC: Island Press, 2001.

Camdessus, Michel. "Second Generation Reforms: Reflections and New Challenges." Presentation at the IMF Conference on Second Generation Reforms, Washington, DC, November 8, 1999.

Campbell, Scott. "Green Cities, Growing Cities, Just Cities? Urban Planning and the Contradictions of Sustainable Development." *Journal of the American Planning Association* 62, no. 3 (1996): 296–312.

Campbell, Tim. *The Quiet Revolution: Decentralization and the Rise of Political Participation in Latin American Cities.* Pittsburgh, PA: University of Pittsburgh Press, 2003.

Capital Region of Denmark. *Regional Development Plan: The Capital Region of Denmark— an International Metropolitan Region with High Quality of Life and Growth.* The Capital Region of Denmark, 2008. Accessed January 20, 2014. www.regionh.dk/NR/rdonlyres/D07BBC02-EE45-4FDC-AEF7-0BFCA1ECA99C/0/080904_RUP_UK_net.pdf.

Cardoso, Fernando and Enzo Faletto. *Dependency and Development in Latin America.* Berkeley, CA: University of California Press, 1979.

Central Bank of Chile. *National Accounts: Evolution of Economic Activity in 2011.* 2012. Accessed January 14, 2014. www.bcentral.cl/estadisticas-economicas/publicaciones-estadisticas/trimestrales/pdf/CuentasNacionales_cuarto_trimestre2011.pdf.

Chapple, Karen and Elizabeth Mattiuzzi. *Planting the Seeds for a Sustainable Future: HUD's Sustainable Communities Initiative Regional Planning Grant Program.* Berkeley, CA: Center for Community Innovation, 2013.

Cochrane, Allan. "Exploring the Regional Politics of 'Sustainability': Making up Sustainable Communities in the South-East of England." *Environmental Policy and Governance* 20, no. 6 (2010): 370–381.

Danish Ministry of the Environment. *Spatial Planning in Denmark.* Ministry of the Environment, Denmark, 2007. Accessed January 20, 2014. http://commin.org/upload/Denmark/Spatial_Planning_in_Denmark_2007.pdf.

Daoudov, Murat. "Istanbul: Regional Issues, Metropolitan Responses." Presentation at the Session "Regions and Metropolitan Areas—Competition or Partnership?" 5th Local Economic Development Forum of Tbilisi, Tbilisi, Georgia. May 4, 2011.

Deas, Iain and Kevin G. Ward. "From the 'New Localism' to the 'New Regionalism'? The Implications of Regional Development Agencies for City-Regional Relations." *Political Geography* 19, no. 3 (2000): 273–292.

Dierwechter, Yonn. "Metropolitan Geographies of US Climate Action: Cities, Suburbs, and the Local Divide in Global Responsibilities." *Journal of Environmental Policy & Planning* 12, no. 1 (2010): 59–82.

Dovey, Kim, Ian Woodcock, Shane Murray, and Lee-Ann Khor. "Re-Assembling the Car-Dependent City: Transit-Oriented Intensification in Melbourne." Paper presented at State of Australian Cities Conference, November 2013. Accessed December 20, 2013. www.soacconference.com.au/wp-content/uploads/2013/12/Dovey-Structure.pdf.

Drummond, Ian and Terry K. Marsden. "Regulating Sustainable Development." *Global Environmental Change* 5, no. 1 (1995): 51–63.

Drummond, William J. "Statehouse Versus Greenhouse." *Journal of the American Planning Association* 76, no. 4 (2010), 413–433.

Eaton, Kent. "Designing Subnational Institutions Regional and Municipal Reforms in Postauthoritarian Chile." *Comparative Political Studies* 37, no. 2 (2004): 218–244.

European Commission. *Eurostat Regional Yearbook 2013*, 2013. Accessed January 20, 2014. http://epp.eurostat.ec.europa.eu/portal/page/portal/statistics/theme.

European Union. National Development and Reform Commission. *Regional Policy in China and the EU: A Comparative Perspective*. KN-32-11-891-A5-C. Belgium: European Union, 2011.

Fainstein, Susan S. *The Just City*. Ithaca, NY: Cornell University Press, 2010.

Falleti, Tulia G. "A Sequential Theory of Decentralization: Latin American Cases in Comparative Perspective," *American Political Science Review* 99, no. 3 (2005): 327–346.

Fishman, Robert. "The Death and Life of American Regional Planning." In *Reflections on Regionalism*, edited by Bruce Katz, 107–123. Washington, DC: Brookings Institution Press, 2000.

Friedmann, John and Clyde Weaver. *Territory and Function: The Evolution of Regional Planning*. Berkeley, CA: University of California Press, 1979.

Geddes, Patrick. *Cities in Evolution: An Introduction to the Town Planning Movement and to the Study of Civics*. London: Williams & Norgate, 1915.

Goldman, Todd and Elizabeth Deakin. "Regionalism Through Partnerships? Metropolitan Planning Since ISTEA." *Berkeley Planning Journal* 14, no. 1 (2000): 46–75. http://escholarship.org/uc/item/4j0001c4.

Gore, Charles. *Regions in Question: Space, Development Theory and Regional Policy*. London and New York: Methuen, 1984.

Government of Chile. *Araucanía Plan: Investing in People and Opportunities*. 2010. Accessed January 14, 2014. www.minsegpres.gob.cl/wp-content/uploads/files/Plan_Araucania.pdf.

Government of the Republic of Hungary. *South Transdanubia Operational Programme 2007–2013*. 2007.

Hackworth, Jason. *The Neoliberal City: Governance, Ideology, and Development in American Urbanism*. Ithaca, NY: Cornell University Press, 2007.

Halkier, Henrik. "Policy Developments in Denmark: Regional Policy, Economic Crisis and Demographic Change." *EoPRA Paper* 9, no. 2. European Policies Research Centre, 2009.

Helmsing, A. H. J. (Bert). *Partnerships, Meso-Institutions and Learning: New Local and Regional Economic Development Initiatives in Latin America*. The Netherlands: Institute of Social Studies, The Hague, 2001.

Hess, David and Langdon Winner. "Enhancing Justice and Sustainability at the Local Level: Affordable Policies for Urban Governments." *Local Environment* 12, no. 4 (2007): 379–395.

Hirschman, Albert O. *The Strategy of Economic Development*. Yale University Press, 1958.

Hughes, James, Gwendolyn Sasse, and Claire Gordon. "Conditionality and Compliance in the EU's Eastward Enlargement: Regional Policy and the Reform of Sub-National Government." *JCMS: Journal of Common Market Studies* 42, no. 3 (2004): 523–551.

ICLEI. "ICLEI Local Governments for Sustainability." Accessed November 24, 2013. www.iclei.org.

Innes, Judith E., Sarah Connick, Laura Kaplan, and David E. Booher. *Collaborative Governance in the CALFED Program: Adaptive Policy Making for California Water*. UC Berkeley: Institute of Urban and Regional Development, 2006.

Istanbul Metropolitan Municipality. *The Istanbul Master Plan Summary*. 2007. Accessed January 25, 2014. http://tarlabasi.files.wordpress.com/2009/10/master-plan.pdf.

Jessop, Bob. "The Rise of Governance and the Risks of Failure: The Case of Economic Development." *International Social Science Journal* 50, no. 155 (1998): 29–46.

Jones, Stephen. "Climate Change Policies of City Governments in Federal Systems: An Analysis of Vancouver, Melbourne and New York City." *Regional Studies* 47, no. 6 (2013): 974–992.

Knaap, Gerrit J. and Rebecca Lewis. "Regional Planning for Sustainability and Hegemony of Metropolitan Regionalism." In *Regional Planning in America: Practice and Prospect*, edited by Ethan Seltzer and Armando Carbonell, 176–221. Cambridge, MA: Lincoln Institute of Land Policy, 2011.

Kragh, Mette Fosgaard. *New Danish Regional Development Plans*. 2005. Accessed January 20, 2014. www.fig.net/pub/monthly_articles/september_2005/september_2005_kragh.pdf.

Krause, Rachel M. "Policy Innovation, Intergovernmental Relations, and the Adoption of Climate Protection Initiatives by US Cities." *Journal of Urban Affairs* 33, no. 1 (2011): 45–60.

Ledebur, Larry C. and William R. Barnes. *All in it Together: Cities, Suburbs and Local Economic Regions*. National League of Cities, 1993.

Leiserowitz, Anthony A., Robert W. Kates, and Thomas M. Parris. "Sustainability Values, Attitudes, and Behaviors: A Review of Multinational and Global Trends." *Annual Review of Environment and Resources* 31 (2006): 413–444.

Lester, T. William and Sarah Reckhow. "Network Governance and Regional Equity: Shared Agendas or Problematic Partners?" *Planning Theory* (2012): 1–24.

Lovering, John and Yigit Evren. "Urban Development and Planning in Istanbul." *International Planning Studies* 16, no. 1 (2011): 1–4.

McHarg, Ian. *Design with Nature*. New York: Natural History Press, 1969.

Markusen, Ann. *Regions: The Economics and Politics of Territory*. Totowa, NJ: Rowan & Littlefield, 1987.

Markusen, Ann R., Peter Hall, Scott Campbell, and Sabrina Deitrick. *The Rise of the Gunbelt: The Military Remapping of Industrial America*. New York: Oxford University Press, 1991.

Mazmanian, Daniel A. and Michael E. Kraft, editors. *Towards Sustainable Communities: Transition and Transformations in Environmental Policy*. Cambridge, MA: MIT Press, 2009.

Mills, Edwin S. *Studies in the Structure of the Urban Economy*. Baltimore, MD: Johns Hopkins University Press, 1972.

Mumford, Lewis. *The City in History: Its Origins, Its Transformations, and Its Prospects*. Houghton Mifflin Harcourt, 1961.

Muth, Richard F. *Cities and Housing*. Chicago, IL: University of Chicago Press, 1969.

Myrdal, Gunnar. *Economic Theory and Under-Developed Regions*. London: Gerald Duckworth, 1957.

Næss, Petter, Teresa Næss, Morton Skou Nicolaisen, and Esben Clemens. *The Challenge of Sustainable Mobility in Urban Planning and Development in Copenhagen Metropolitan*

Area. 2nd Edition. Aalborg University, 2009. Accessed January 20, 2014. http://vbn. aau.dk/files/19642767/download.pdfPT.pdf.

Organisation for Economic Co-Operation and Development. *OECD Territorial Reviews: Istanbul, Turkey*. Paris: OECD, 2008.

Pálné Kovács, Ilona, C. J. Paraskevopoulos, and Gy Horváth. "Institutional 'Legacies' and the Shaping of Regional Governance in Hungary." *Regional & Federal Studies* 14, no. 3 (2004): 430–460.

Pálné Kovács, Ilona and Viktor Varjú, editors. "Governance for Sustainability—Two Case Studies from Hungary." Discussion Paper 73. Pécs, Hungary: Hungarian Academy of Science Center for Economic and Regional Studies, 2009.

Parsons, Kermit C. "Collaborative Genius: The Regional Planning Association of America." *Journal of the American Planning Association* 60, no. 4 (1994): 462.

Pastor Jr., Manuel, Chris Benner, and Martha Matsuoka. *This Could be the Start of Something Big: How Social Movements for Regional Equity are Reshaping Metropolitan America*. Ithaca, NY: Cornell University Press, 2009.

Pastor, Manuel, editor. *Regions that Work: How Cities and Suburbs Can Grow Together*. Minneapolis, MN: University of Minnesota Press, 2000.

Pearsall, Hamil and Joseph Pierce. "Urban Sustainability and Environmental Justice: Evaluating the Linkages in Public Planning/Policy Discourse." *Local Environment* 15, no. 6 (2010): 569–580.

Perroux, François. "Note sur la notion de pôle de croissance." *Economie Appliquée* 8, no. 1–2 (1955): 307–320.

Portney, Kent. "Civic Engagement and Sustainable Cities in the United States." *Public Administration Review* 65, no. 5 (2005): 579–591.

Portney, Kent E. and Jeffrey M. Berry. "Participation and the Pursuit of Sustainability in US Cities." *Urban Affairs Review* 46, no. 1 (2010): 119–139.

Randolph, Bill and Andrew Tice. "Who Lives in Higher Density Housing? A Study of Spatially Discontinuous Housing Sub-Markets in Sydney and Melbourne." *Urban Studies* 50, no. 13 (2013): 2661–2681.

Regional Government of La Araucanía. *Final Report: Regional Development Strategy 2010–2022*. 2010. Accessed January 14, 2014. www.sernam.cl/sistema_gt/sitio/ integracion/sistema/archivos/file/pdf/a%C3%B1o%202010/erd%20IXregion.pdf.

RIMISP. *Rural Territories in Motion: Rural Territorial Dynamics Program—Final Report 2007–2012*. RIMISP—Centro Latinoamericano para el Desarrollo Rural, 2012. Accessed January 14, 2014. www.rimisp.org/wp-content/files_mf/1362665462Final ReportRTDprogram20072012_2_RIMISP_CARDUMEN.pdf.

Rusk, David. *Cities Without Suburbs*. Washington, DC: Woodrow Wilson Center Press, 1993.

Saha, Devashree and Robert G. Paterson. "Local Government Efforts to Promote the 'Three Es' of Sustainable Development Survey in Medium to Large Cities in the United States." *Journal of Planning Education and Research* 28, no. 1 (2008): 21–37.

Sandercock, Leonie. *The Land Racket: The Real Costs of Property Speculation*. Hale & Iremonger for the Australian Association of Socialist Studies, 1979.

Sankhe, Shirish, Ireena Vittal, Richard Dobbs, Ajit Mohan, and Ankur Gulati. "India's Urban Awakening: Building Inclusive Cities Sustaining Economic Growth." McKinsey Global Institute, 2010.

Savitch, Hank V., David Collins, Daniel Sanders, and John P. Markham. "Ties that Bind: Central Cities, Suburbs, and the New Metropolitan Region." *Economic Development Quarterly* 7, no. 4 (1993): 341–357.

Scott, Allen J., editor. *Global City-Regions: Trends, Theory, Policy*. New York: Oxford University Press, 2001.

Searle, Glen and Raymond Bunker. "Metropolitan Strategic Planning: An Australian Paradigm?" *Planning Theory* 9, no. 3 (2010): 163–180.

Shanghai Municipal Government. *Shanghai Master Plan: 1999–2020*. 1998.

Solecki, William D. and Robin M. Leichenko. "Urbanization and the Metropolitan Environment: Lessons from New York and Shanghai." *Environment: Science and Policy for Sustainable Development* 48, no. 4 (2006).

State Government of Victoria. *Plan Melbourne Fact Sheet*. Victorian State Government, 2013.

Steiner, Frederick. "Green Regions, Green Regionalism." In *Regional Planning in America: Practice and Prospect* 29, edited by Ethan Seltzer and Armando Carbonell. Cambridge, MA: Lincoln Institute of Land Policy, 2011.

Swanstrom, Todd. "Ideas Matter: Reflections on the New Regionalism." *Cityscape* 2, no. 2 (1996): 5–21.

Teitz, Michael B. "Rationality in Planning and the Search for Community." In *Rationality in Planning*, edited by Michael Breheny and Andrew Hooper. London: Pion, 1985.

Teitz, Michael B. "Regional Development Planning." *Planning Ideas that Matter: Livability, Territoriality, Governance, and Reflective Practice* (2012): 127–152.

United Nations. "The future we want." *General Assembly*. 2012. Accessed January 10, 2014. www.un.org/ga/search/view_doc.asp?symbol=A/RES/66/288&Lang=E.

Vejre, Henrik, Hans Skov-Petersen, and Katja Lizia Henschel. "The Copenhagen 1948 Finger Plan—a Comprehensive Plan for Urban Growth." Forest & Landscape, University of Copenhagen. Accessed January 20, 2014. www.plurel.net/images/MURI_Vejre.pdf.

Voith, Richard. "Do Suburbs Need Cities?" *Journal of Regional Science* 38, no. 3 (1998): 445–464.

Weaver, Clyde. *Regional Development and the Local Community, Planning, Politics, and Social Context*. Chichester: Wiley, 1984.

Weir, Margaret, Harold Wolman, and Todd Swanstrom. "The Calculus of Coalitions Cities, Suburbs, and the Metropolitan Agenda." *Urban Affairs Review* 40, no. 6 (2005): 730–760.

Wheeler, Stephen M. "State and Municipal Climate Change Plans: The First Generation." *Journal of the American Planning Association* 74, no. 4 (2008): 481–496.

Willis, Arthur J. "Forum." *Functional Ecology* 11, no. 2 (1997): 268–271.

Wong, Cecilia, Hui Qian, and Kai Zhou. "In Search of Regional Planning in China: The Case of Jiangsu and the Yangtze Delta." *Town Planning Review* 79, no. 2 (May 1, 2008): 295–329.

World Commission on Environment and Development. *Our Common Future*. New York: Oxford University Press, 1987.

Xu, Jiang. "Governing City-Regions in China: Theoretical Issues and Perspectives for Regional Strategic Planning." *Town Planning Review* 79, no. 2 (2008): 157–186.

Xue, Jin, Petter Næss, Yinmei Yao, and Fen Li. "The Challenge of Sustainable Mobility in Urban Planning and Development: A Comparative Study of the Copenhagen and Hangzhou Metropolitan Areas." *International Journal of Urban Sustainable Development* 3, no. 2 (2011): 185–206.

Ye, Lin. "Regional Government and Governance in China and the United States." *Public Administration Review* 69 (2009): S116–121.

Yuzer, Sebnem and Salim Kucuk. *The Growth and Development of Metropolitan Planning Strategies in Istanbul: ERSA Conference Paper*. European Regional Science Association, 1998. Accessed January 25, 2014. http://ideas.repec.org/p/wiw/wiwrsa/ersa98p 304.html.

Part I

Guiding Neighborhood Change in the Region

Introduction

Early in an urban planning history class, students learn about Clarence Perry and the concept of the neighborhood unit (Perry 1929). A sociologist, Perry developed an idea of the neighborhood unit based on observation of Forest Hills Gardens in Queens, New York. The neighborhood unit would serve as the physical and social building block of the city, as well as a mechanism for socializing immigrants. Its size was set by the catchment area of the local elementary school (one half-mile radius on foot), reachable by multiple neighborhoods, with shops at corners, and arterial streets as logical boundaries. Though not widely implemented in the exact form envisaged by Perry, the idea of the neighborhood unit clearly influenced the regulation and development of suburban subdivisions. It also shaped the movement for neighborhood public facilities, particularly schools, as well as New Urbanism, which has advocated for traditional neighborhood design (i.e., more compact, walkable neighborhoods with a mixture of uses) (Fishman 2012).

Jane Jacobs is also known for her focus on neighborhoods: "Take care of the neighborhood and the city will be taken care of, Jacobs suggested. This was the bottom-up view of urban development that came out of the reactions to the broad-sweep urban renewal" (Qadeer 2012: 215). But she was not so taken with the ideas of Perry and his disciples, such as Lewis Mumford, critiquing the ideal of "supposedly cozy, inward-turned city neighborhoods" (Jacobs 1961: 115). She argued instead that "good urbanism requires great cities" (i.e., higher densities) (Fishman 2012: 68). And there is no simple recipe for urbanism:

> My idea, however, is not that we should therefore try to reproduce, routinely and in a surface way, the streets and districts that do display strength and success as fragments of city life . . . But if we understand the principles behind the behavior of cities, we can build on potential assets and strengths, instead of acting at cross-purposes to them.
>
> (Jacobs 1961: 140)

According to Jacobs, the success of neighborhoods and cities is contingent upon preserving the mobility of urban residents around the city, through fostering public contact on streets and mixing land uses.

From the perspective of urban sociology, transformation also starts with the neighborhood. The invasion-succession model of the Chicago School describes a process by which lower-income residents residing in the inner core of the city invade the outer rings and gradually succeed the higher-income residents (Figure I.1) (Burgess 1925). Another version of the ecological model of urban change is the life cycle, in which neighborhoods, and in particular their housing stock, are developed, transition in ownership, decline, thin out, and revive (Hoover and Vernon 1959).

These ideas about how change happens continue to shape our thinking about the future—planners try to recreate urbanism by shaping development in specific neighborhoods; developers, supported by the system of infrastructure finance and mortgage underwriting, continue to create the next neighborhood

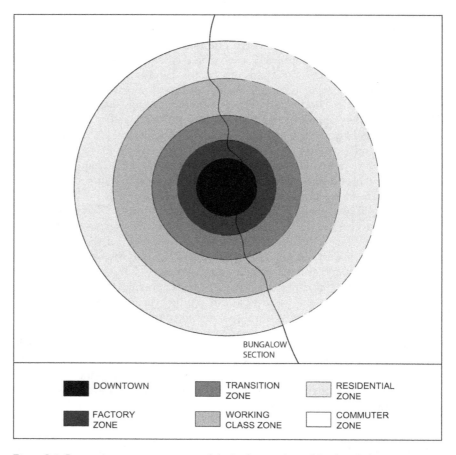

BUNGALOW
SECTION

DOWNTOWN   TRANSITION   RESIDENTIAL
                ZONE   ZONE

FACTORY   WORKING   COMMUTER
ZONE   CLASS ZONE   ZONE

Figure I.1 Burgess' concentric zone model of urban and neighborhood change, 1925
Source: Adapted from Burgess (1925)

out, marketing the higher quality of life; and sociologists see larger societal patterns imprinted on urban neighborhoods over time. Yet, the demographic changes that are creating new market pressures and changing the economics of neighborhoods suggest the need for a new perspective.

Looking forward 30 years, for an entire region this means re-conceptualizing how change occurs. Urbanism may be a bottom-up vision, but it is enabled by a regional perspective: it is not just urban density that facilitates mobility and mixing, but also location and accessibility within the metropolis. We can try to reshape neighborhoods along the principles suggested by Jane Jacobs and advocated by the New Urbanists. But in practice, infill development occurs at a slow pace in the United States: infill sites house just one-fifth of new residential development, and in most regions the majority of construction takes place instead on greenfields (EPA 2012). With the bulk of new development occurring in suburban subdivisions far from transit, not just in the United States but in continents such as Latin America as well, the opportunities to recreate a Jacobean urbanism are few and far between. Even if individual subdivisions are planned to look like diverse and livable neighborhoods, they are located for the convenience of the automobile, not allowing the urbane density and mix of uses prescribed by the New Urbanists.

The composite picture of neighborhood change also looks very different from how sociologists have portrayed it. Whether or not through invasion-succession, the majority of metropolises do end up in a pattern of concentric rings or zones, with the most affluent in the outermost ring (Dwyer 2010). And pockets of concentrated poverty remain. But the population of the urban core is increasing, as is (for the most part) its racial/ethnic integration and economic diversity. In a sense, this is the Jacobean urbanism we were seeking—but absent the happy stable diversity of the 1960s' West Village.

A considerably more complex dynamic is at work than the centrifugal pressure on metropolitan regions we saw in much of the twentieth century. In some ways, U.S. cities are beginning to experience the growth pressures on the core that many developing or newly industrialized countries have long faced. There is still the pressure to move out of the urban core, supported by overbuilding on the urban fringe—itself supported by an array of regulations and institutions, from transportation spending, to underwriting traditions. At the same time, population changes are creating pressure for more housing in more central areas (and, to a lesser extent, businesses as well), just at a time when we cannot build very fast. The sites, buildings, and neighborhoods that will accommodate this new market mostly exist already.

This will entail transformation in multiple dimensions, beyond bricks and mortar. Coping with market pressures to expand space, shift land use, and raise rents will mean changes in how we facilitate infill development, support diversity in the core through affordable housing (defined as housing that costs less than 30 percent of household pretax income), and enable the economy. Though some regions, such as Houston and Detroit, will continue to accommodate growth or population shifts through new subdivisions on the periphery, most of the strong market regions will instead experience competing demands for central land. Thus, they will need to plan for gradual development in existing communities, rather than pop-up subdivisions on the featureless plain. In this context, imposing the neighborhood unit framework—that ghost from another era—is likely to encounter resistance: people do not like planners telling them what their neighborhood is, even if, in reality, change will happen in just a few sites over a 30-year period.

But even more important, with more growth likely to land in existing communities than ever before, the economics of neighborhoods are going to change. High-density infill development will become financially viable in more areas—but not all, and perhaps not even very many. Where job growth occurs, it is not likely to take conventional forms; of course, some growth will take place in office campuses, but much will be dispersed into neighborhoods, changing land use patterns. The influx of more people and jobs without significant new real estate development—and in the face of rising income inequality—means unaffordable rent increases, population shifts (both voluntary and involuntary), and, in some cases, overcrowding and informal housing solutions. It is an even more volatile urbanism than before: new forms of gentrification will emerge, but also more people means more diversity, more integration in the core, and more exposure to difference.

This is not to say that the market will not respond to changing demands—it will, even if it cannot make large-scale infill development work in many regions. But it will not necessarily respond in equitable ways; instead, the development industry will build where it can profit. And because we are still fighting the older battle of suburban growth—and lacking the political will to shift our institutions—we have not armed ourselves with the right tools to win the new war for social equity. This section first examines how neighborhood populations are changing, particularly with regard to income diversity. It then looks at projected demographic changes, the likely developer response, and how well the planners' toolkit is equipped for diversity. Finally, its four chapters explore alternative approaches to equitable growth, in particular how to increase density and diversity.

Neighborhood Change

Macro-level economic change drives the transformation of metropolitan regions. When the regional economy is growing, due largely to external demand for its goods and services, new residents and income flow to it. And during periods of economic decline and adjustment, such as the restructuring of the U.S. economy away from manufacturing, there is a decline in real incomes, housing prices, and ability to maintain the housing stock.

To the Chicago School, it was this influx of immigrants or increase in incomes that spurred the ecological invasion/succession process, as new competition for land caused shifts in land uses and residences in concentric zones. Shifting resulted from both growth and decline: higher land uses would succeed lower in the core, while residents would sort themselves by social-economic status into neighborhoods (Park, Burgess, and McKenzie 1925). This process was not just about displacement, however; the supply of housing also shaped the process. With the core increasingly occupied by high-end commercial uses, developers constructed new neighborhoods on the periphery, attracting higher-income residents ready to leave their aging properties in the urban core (Hoyt 1939). Just as they began to provide a lower quality of shelter, these housing units thus filtered down to lower-income groups, who often overcrowded into the units and hastened their decline.

Observers of metropolitan change suggested some modifications to the concentric zone model over time. Perhaps change occurs in zones that expand outward from the city center, following arterials, in a sectoral model of change. Perhaps some neighborhoods ascend rather than decline, led by the growth of higher-income districts in the core, or by federal place-based policies (Owens 2012). But for the most part, evidence suggests that the concentric zone model and its invasion-succession dynamic accurately depict urban change— or did, until the 1980s. Since then, the rising complexity of urban markets and demographics has reshaped metropolitan structure in as many as half of U.S. metros (Dwyer 2010).

One change that has occurred is the decline of the inner-ring suburbs (Jargowsky 2003; Kneebone 2013; Short, Hanlon, and Vicino 2007; Vicino 2008). However, the concentric zone model nicely predicts this: over time, as housing stock declines, it is expected that the "zone of workingmen's homes" will encroach on the residential zone. Yet, the dynamic of change upsets the model's prediction: rather than resulting from an influx of the urban poor into dilapidated housing, it seems that most suburban decline and poverty is explained by income decreases for existing residents, likely affected by ongoing economic restructuring (Cooke 2010). Moreover, instead of zones of homogeneity, today's inner ring suburbs appear increasingly diverse (Hanlon, Vicino, and Short 2006; Kneebone 2013).

Also unanticipated by the model is the near global rise of the polycentric region (i.e., new concentrations of jobs and housing) in edge cities (or "cosmoburbs," or "metroburbia") (Anas, Arnott, and Small 1998; Garreau 1991; Heikkila et al. 1989; Lang and Knox 2009; Lang and Lefurgy 2007). Although most of these new centers lack the densities of the older urban core, they still tend to replicate the concentric zone pattern, with jobs surrounded by housing. This new centering increases land values in the suburbs and also attracts new upper-income residents, resulting in suburban neighborhood ascent (Owens 2012).[1]

This ascent process (or improvement in neighborhood income) is not restricted to the suburbs, but occurs in the core as well. Although most perceive ascent as gentrification (see Chapter 6), neighborhood renewal may take forms other than the influx of the gentry and their capital. For instance, existing residents may improve the neighborhood in a process of incumbent upgrading, new residents of lower incomes (e.g., artists or younger families) may upgrade the neighborhood, or the public sector may invest in areas (Owens 2012; Van Criekingen and Decroly 2003).

Overall, somewhere between 14 and 29 percent of neighborhoods actually ascend in socioeconomic status each decade, and though the majority of these are white suburbs, diverse (minority and immigrant) core neighborhoods are increasingly likely to improve in income as well (Owens 2012).

Neighborhood change depends not just on individual household choices, but also on the workings of metropolitan housing markets, specifically the amount of housing supplied by developers, and the willingness of landlords to rent to minority and/or poor households. The more housing built on the metropolitan fringe, the more people will be attracted from the urban core and inner rings. This may increase the diversity of the suburbs, but may also result in increasing segregation in core neighborhoods, as George Galster (2012) has shown in the Detroit case (South, Pais, and Crowder 2011). Discrimination also increases neighborhood racial and economic segregation (Levy, McDade, and Dumlao 2010). The more racially segregated a region, the more likely that African Americans move to poor tracts, and the more poor neighborhoods it has, the more likely that poor households will move to equivalent neighborhoods, rather than upgrade (South, Pais, and Crowder 2011). Thus, metropolitan-wide patterns of housing supply and segregation can shape how individual neighborhoods change, resulting in an even more fragmented metropolitan structure. We look next at the relationship between segregation, diversity, and metropolitan form.

Patterns of Income Segregation and Diversity

Before examining the patterns of income segregation and mixing, it is important to define terms. There is no commonly accepted definition of mixed-income neighborhoods in the literature, although definitions do exist for *properties* subject to Housing and Urban Development (HUD) or other guidelines for subsidized housing. In part, this is because most housing policy mechanisms address particular developments, rather than entire neighborhoods.

Income mixing is typically defined by the extent that groups from across the income distribution are present: if a development or place is dominated by one income group, then it has low diversity, but if its population spans the entire range of groups, it offers high diversity (Tach, Pendall, and Derian 2014). The number of income groups used will vary with the context: diversity might be defined as the mix of low-, middle-, and high-income households (three groups), or based on the six income categories that HUD uses to define housing affordability: very low income (less than 50 percent of area median income, or AMI), low income (50–80 percent of AMI), moderate income (80–100 percent of AMI), high-moderate income (100–120 percent of AMI), high income (120–150 percent of AMI), and very high income (over 150 percent of AMI).[2]

Another analytic issue in neighborhood diversity research is the unit of analysis. Because of their dependence on the U.S. Census for data, most researchers rely on tract-level data, though aware that this 15–20-block area, with an average of 4,000 residents, may be too large to represent a neighborhood as perceived on the ground. When tracts are too large, they will be more inclusive and thus give false readings of diversity (Ioannides 2004). Thus, the findings in the literature, which have relied almost exclusively on tract-level measurements of segregation and diversity, may not necessarily lead to robust policy implications.

Income Segregation

Economic segregation has increased steadily since the 1970s, with a brief respite in the 1990s, and is related closely to racial segregation (i.e., income segregation is growing more rapidly among black families than white) (Fischer 2003; Fry and Taylor 2012; Jargowsky 2001; Lichter, Parisi, and Taquino 2012; Reardon and Bischoff 2011; Watson 2009; Yang and Jargowsky 2006). Increases are particularly pronounced in more affluent neighborhoods: between 1980 and 2010, the share of upper-income households living in majority upper-income tracts doubled from 9 to 18 percent, compared to an increase from 23 to 25 percent in segregation of lower-income households in majority lower-income tracts (Fry and Taylor 2012). The rise of rich and exclusive enclaves is neglected in policy, but is a common phenomenon around the world.

The sorting of the rich and poor is even more pronounced between jurisdictions than between neighborhoods in the same city (Reardon and Bischoff 2011). Over time, the poor are increasingly concentrated in high-poverty places, while the non-poor shift to non-poor cities (Lichter, Parisi, and Taquino 2012). Upper-income households in metropolitan areas such as Houston or Dallas are much more likely to segregate themselves than those in denser, older regions such as Boston or Philadelphia or even Chicago (Fry and Taylor 2012). This suggests that segregation is related to metropolitan structure and suburbanization—and, in fact, researchers have observed this relationship in Eastern Europe, Latin America, China, and other regions (Huang 2004; Kok and Kovács 1999; Sabatini 2006). The concentric zone model is particularly strongly associated with the segregation of the affluent. In other words, in metropolitan areas where the affluent are most separated from the poor, they are living on land further from the center.

About half of all U.S. metropolitan areas, including more than 70 percent of the metropolitan population, conform to the concentric zone model (Dwyer 2010). These (e.g., places such as Chicago, Los Angeles, and Philadelphia) tend to be larger and more densely populated metros, often with a higher degree of affluence and inequality, a larger African-American population, and a greater share of population in the suburbs.

In the remaining metropolitan areas, there is greater integration between the affluent and the poor (Dwyer 2010). In these places, such as Seattle, Charleston, and Boulder, the rich concentrate in the urban core, allowing more opportunity for interaction with the poor. Growing racial/ethnic diversity may be reshaping some of these areas, with suburban immigrant enclaves creating more frag-mented, checkerboard patterns of segregation (Coulton et al. 1996).

Why do we have segregation? Public choice theorists, most prominently Charles Tiebout (1956), have long understood economic segregation to result from the preference of consumers for distinct baskets of public goods (services): local jurisdictions provide these services at different levels, attracting residents of similar economic means (Peterson 1981). However, the causality here is un-clear: government policies shape free markets and preferences, as well as respond to them. Thus, as explained so eloquently by Peter Dreier, John Mollenkopf, and Todd Swanstrom in *Place Matters* (2004), transportation policies favor-ing the automobile, discrimination and redlining in early federal home owner-ship policies, mortgage interest tax deductions for homeowners, and other urban policies have actively shaped or reinforced patterns of economic segregation, while severely constraining choices for low-income groups.

But we also now understand that neighborhood income segregation within metropolitan areas is caused mostly by income inequality, in particular higher compensation in the top quintile and the lack of jobs for the bottom quintile (Reardon and Bischoff 2011; Watson 2009). Income inequality leads to income segregation because higher incomes, supported by housing policy, allow certain households to sort themselves according to their preferences—and control local political processes that perpetuate exclusion (Reardon and Bischoff 2011). Other explanatory factors include disinvestment in urban areas, suburban investment and land use patterns, and the practices generally of government and the underwriting industry (Hirsch 1983; Levy, McDade, and Dumlao 2010). But were income inequality to stop rising, the number of segregated neighborhoods would decline (Reardon and Bischoff 2011; Watson 2009).

Income Diversity

Only a few researchers have explored the flip side of the coin, changes in economic diversity, and most of these employ case studies of a single metro-politan area (e.g., Talen 2005, 2006). However, Galster, Booza, and Cutsinger (2008) examine changes in the 100 largest metropolitan areas and find that, consistent with the trend toward increasing economic segregation, there has been a decline in overall neighborhood income diversity since 1970, even as the number of racially and ethnically mixed neighborhoods has been increasing. Still, two-thirds of neighborhoods were highly diverse in 2000—a finding that diversity is the norm, which is shared by other studies as well (Hardman and Ioannides 2004; Ioannides 2004). As the overall share of moderate-income families decreases, due in part to increasing income inequality, and shares of families in the extreme income ranges increase, moderate-income neigh-borhoods are becoming less diverse, while both low- and high-income neighborhoods are becoming more diverse.

Income diversity is thus a moving target. Neighborhood composition is always in flux, not just because of in- and outmigration, but also because of volatility in resident incomes. The notion of the tipping point—the idea that after the neighborhood gains a certain share of African Americans, whites will move out at an accelerating rate—has created a powerful image of neighborhood change (Smith 2010). But the reality in income-diverse neighborhoods is more complex. Neighborhoods, in the process of changing from predominantly high income to low income, may become increasingly diverse, at least momentarily. Thus, the widespread decline of inner-ring suburbs since 1980 has helped to transform them into mixed-income neighborhoods (Lucy and Phillips 2000).

More diverse places tend to have a greater range of housing unit types, housing ages, housing values, and housing tenure types, as well as a smaller proportion of whites (Talen 2006). Rather than planned places, they tend to be planning leftovers, located next to barriers such as interstate highways, adjacent to commercial corridors, and often containing a mix of uses (Talen 2005). Over time, neighborhoods are more likely to become highly diverse by losing middle-aged adults (ages 35–54) and very low-income families, while experiencing both a slack rental market and an active for-sale market (Galster et al. 2005). In other words, diverse neighborhoods may emerge most readily as concentrations of young and/or poor families disappear and the neighborhood offers opportunities for first-time home ownership, rather than hot rental properties.

Income-diverse neighborhoods are particularly susceptible to decline. Less than one-fifth of mixed-income neighborhoods stayed mixed from 1970 to 2000 (Tach 2010). In most cases, income-diverse neighborhoods tend to transition toward homogeneity (Krupka 2008).

Much remains unknown about whether it is possible to maintain income-diverse neighborhoods through policy intervention. The major scholarly contributions in this area look at racial diversity, not income diversity, finding that stable racially integrated communities do exist (Ellen 2000; Nyden, Maly, and Lukehart 1997). Nyden, Maly, and Lukehart (1997) suggest that there are two types of diversity: diversity spread over blocks and small pockets of racial homogeneity within the larger diverse community. Stable diverse communities (discussed in Chapter 4) tend to feature both social seams, or "points in the community where interaction between different ethnic and racial groups is 'sewn' together in some way," and awareness of diversity, or "self-conscious diversity," which spurs social and community groups (ibid.: 507). One example of how community awareness can be important comes from the Cleveland area, where city "affirmative marketing" policies resulted in greater levels of integration than in places lacking an overt policy (Galster 1990). Tach, Pendall, and Derian (2014) also suggest that it may be possible to sustain mixed-income neighborhoods through a combination of subsidies for permanently affordable housing developments and community mobilization. Another path to income diversity may lie in planning and regulation coordinated at multiple levels that encourage diversity of housing types, often using the carrot of infrastructure finance (ibid.).

Despite the emphasis of urban models on change, what is perhaps most startling about this literature is how slow neighborhoods are to change. Over individual decades, the change that researchers are discussing amounts to a few percentage points; neighborhood transformation takes decades to complete. From another perspective, the glass is half full, rather than empty: neighborhoods are remarkably stable. And in fact, overall, Americans have become significantly more rooted over time; just 12 percent of U.S. residents moved in 2008, the lowest rate since 1948 and probably long before (Fischer 2010).[3] Sociologist Claude Fischer credits growing security, as well as technology, for the shift, but adds: "Americans as a whole are moving less and less. But where the remaining movers—both those forced by poverty and those liberated by affluence—are moving is reinforcing the economic and, increasingly, the cultural separations among us" (Fischer 2013).

For many at the lower end of the economic spectrum, stability means imprisonment: even though many families have left, Sharkey estimates that some 70 percent of families in today's ghettos were living there in the 1970s as well (Sharkey 2013). Shaping this neighborhood imprisonment, too, are the actions of city and regional planners, as well as the market and development industry. With the pace of change likely to alter and/or destabilize some of the neighborhoods in the urban core, planners will need a better toolkit to face the challenge of accommodating density and diversity.

Planning and Development in the Neighborhood and Regional Context

Broad economic and demographic trends shape how much a region grows, but planners help shape what gets built where in cities and regions. With the ability to determine where which land use is appropriate and at what intensity, as well as to channel funding over time to capital improvements in roads, parks, schools, and so forth, planners create the rules to which developers respond. How equitable it will be depends on how effective their toolkit is. What actually gets built depends on developer interpretation of market demand, as well as the availability of capital. Developers will build where they anticipate demand and potential for profit from the sale of their developments.

Smart Growth and Infill Development

The push for "smarter" growth patterns—whether walkable neighborhoods, neo-traditional design, transit-oriented development, or simply more compactness—among planners is well known. The movement for New Urbanism may well be the most well known trend in planning in the last 50 years (Grant 2002). The American Planning Association boasts community and regional sustainability as a core value, and its current lobbying efforts focus, in part, on facilitating the new demand for urban living and green infrastructure (American Planning Association 2013). To the extent that smart growth reduces vehicle miles traveled (VMT) and thus greenhouse gas emissions, it is key to regional sustainability. Over time, research has confirmed that smart growth patterns, specifically higher densities, more mixture of land use, and pedestrian-oriented design, indeed reduce auto dependence and VMT, with density playing less of a role than accessibility to destinations and street network design (Cervero and Kockelman 1997; Ewing and Cervero 2010). Households living in central cities have relatively low carbon footprints compared to those in suburbs (Jones and Kammen 2014).

As planners and environmentalists try to encourage development at higher density and in infill locations, they typically can count on the support of developers. Building at higher densities, closer to urban amenities, and with higher intensity land uses may mean more profit. There are increasing indications of market interest (although a gap remains between what people want and what they are able to pay). Are developers and financial institutions responding fully? The evidence suggests not, because of the challenges of implementing smart growth regulations and building infill development economically.

Why have smart growth policies not become more common (i.e., why are planners not changing the rules, despite all the chatter) (Downs 2005)? Most smart growth approaches require two fundamental shifts. Smart growth transforms the status quo of winners and losers: among many known costs and benefits (and not including the unknown), it increases housing prices, helping some and hurting others; it may increase local traffic congestion; and it may decrease the value of land on the metropolitan fringe. In order to limit the outward expansion of new development, it also requires a transfer of power over land use regulation from the local to the regional level. Both barriers make wide-scale implementation of smart growth unlikely without a fundamental change in public attitudes.

Cities have indeed been slow to adopt smart growth regulations (Edwards and Haines 2007; Song 2012; Talen and Knaap 2003). Even when their plans embrace principles of compact development, cities seem unfamiliar with appropriate policies and tools to incentivize it, instead taking a passive approach (Edwards and Haines 2007). Where cities do adopt policies thought to be effective, little progress has been made (Song 2012). It is not entirely clear why change is so slow, though community resistance to change, institutional inertia, the challenge of spurring the market to act, the lack of control that planning departments have over implementation, and the newness of the policies probably all play a role (ibid.). Nonetheless, in states where support for smart growth is strong—as well as some states without smart growth policies—development densities are increasing, land consumption per resident is decreasing, and growth is shifting to more desirable areas from a smart growth perspective (Ingram et al. 2009; Song 2012). Over time, the market may be shifting, with greater impact than any planning tool.

The story of infill development also suggests very slow progress. Because the early years of the smart growth movement focused on limiting greenfield development or reducing its negative effects, developers are only gradually acquiring the skills needed to redevelop urban land. Almost all of the country's

209 metropolitan regions built more housing on greenfields than previously developed areas in the 2000s (EPA 2012). In fact, infill residential development is still relatively rare in Sunbelt cities, although common on the coasts: eight of 10 new homes in San Jose are infill, versus just 7 percent in Austin (ibid.). On the other hand, most large metropolitan areas saw an increase in infill share in the latter part of the decade, suggesting a potential shift in the market (ibid.).

The barriers to infill come from regulation, politics, physical feasibility, infrastructure deficits, land costs, and finance. Inappropriate zoning or parking regulations may need to be changed, and permitting processes may require public hearings that can delay the project, sometimes indefinitely. Local government might not even be supportive if the new development is going to be a net drain on city coffers (Schildt 2011). The greatest physical barrier is that infill lots are often of inappropriate size or shape; a study of California found that about one-fourth of the lots in the infill inventory were less than 0.25 acres in size (Landis and Hood 2005). Many also are contaminated, creating challenges for cleanup. Even the process of acquiring land to assemble a site can defeat a project, as many owners are reluctant to sell.

But in many instances, infill projects simply will not generate enough cash flows or revenues to cover development costs. Construction costs may be prohibitive, particularly for buildings of seven stories and above requiring concrete or steel-frame construction, due mostly to the rising cost of materials, as well as the expense of acquiring large lots (Strategic Economics 2008). Only in the high-end neighborhoods of strong markets are such buildings viable, and additional requirements such as green building or inclusionary housing will make development much less likely (ibid.). Then, this infill may be inequitable: some of the most attractive sites in these neighborhoods are apartment buildings offering affordable housing, whose demolition will exacerbate shortages.

Because of these financial constraints, most regions with substantial infill housing development also have higher home prices. Regions that have invested in rail transit may find infill development more viable, because of the availability of land near stations and the existence of policies encouraging investment (EPA 2012). But most available infill land is not near transit, and may actually be in older urban areas with declining infrastructure, schools, and quality of life (Landis and Hood 2005). Building in these weaker markets lowers revenues for developers who, at the same time, need to cover higher infrastructure costs. This creates a need for significant policies and incentives to facilitate infill.

There is a proven menu of such policies and incentives. To slow down construction on greenfields at the urban fringe, policymakers have an array of zoning and financial tools. At the state level, they can require cities to enact urban growth boundaries and compensate farmers through transfer of development rights programs. City-enacted development impact fees can ensure that greenfield developers pay for the true cost of new development in terms of infrastructure and services. By requiring concurrency, cities can restrict development from areas until adequate infrastructure is in place.

To speed up infill development, cities and regions can target infrastructure spending to priority areas for growth (as Maryland did with its Priority Funding Areas, and the Bay Area is doing now with its Priority Development Areas, or PDAs). Redevelopment programs provide tools for site assembly, such as eminent domain, as well as capital for infrastructure via special districts.[4] States might incentivize infill by relaxing environmental review requirements in priority areas. Many states also have housing trust funds to help support affordable housing.[5]

Given this array of policy options, why is infill not occurring at a faster pace in the United States? Around the world, megacities have seen redevelopment of core areas happen at a dizzying pace, even as suburbanization is occurring (Sorensen and Okata 2011). Meanwhile, in the United States, the major carrot to get projects underway—federal funding for affordable housing and infrastructure—has shrunk significantly. And, most cities and states are enacting policies in a piecemeal fashion. A policy to slow down development on greenfields will not result in infill development unless coupled with incentives to build in the core, and vice versa. Relaxing environmental review will not make a difference if developers cannot assemble parcels. Oregon is the only state to adopt this more comprehensive approach to smarter growth patterns—and the majority of its development is still lower-density housing far from transit.

Shifting to the Regional Scale

Many point to the regional level—councils of government (COGs) and metropolitan planning organizations (MPOs)—as the optimal scale at which to enact infill development policies instead. Though COGs have, if anything, lost power in recent years, MPOs received a major boost in the 1990s after Congress enacted legislation increasing their authority to program federal transportation dollars (Altshuler and Joint Center 1979; Goldman and Deakin 2000; Weiner 1999). However, MPOs and COGS do not actually have authority over local land use decisions.

Thus, the United States fortunately has empowered its regions to guide infrastructure spending. However, regional transportation planning has not evolved to support more equitable development patterns. Traditionally, regions have relied on a standard travel demand forecast model consisting of four steps: trip generation, trip distribution, mode choice, and route choice. MPOs in areas with significant air quality problems rely on these regional transportation models to guide decision-making about infrastructure spending. However, these models fall short, particularly in failing to consider the interaction between transportation and land use.[6] Over time, regions are only slowly shifting to a new generation of integrated transportation and land use models.

At the simplest level, the integrated models explicitly link land use, development, transportation, and economic systems. Based on state and/or national forecasts of population and employment change in the region, MPOs predict where development will occur based on historic trends of land supply, absorption and prices, household and business location or expenditure choices, and present and future transportation accessibility (along with other factors).

However, in many regions, planning for future development is a political process. Rather than letting the model select areas for development based on local land use plans, typically MPO staff work carefully with local cities and counties to determine how many new people or jobs they are willing to accommodate and where. In the end, this results in a forecast that may be politically palatable, but may not conform to model results (Johnston and McCoy 2006). And this is the best case: most U.S. regions still distribute transportation funding based on a transportation model that does not take land use and development patterns into account.

Thus, perhaps the most important carrot for regional sustainability planning, transportation funding, is rarely used to spur smarter growth. In this context, the rise of regional visioning, or blueprint planning, is a welcome addition. Knaap and Lewis (2011) identify several characteristics that most of these regional planning processes share. Most processes begin by identifying goals and objectives through a participatory process and then explore and evaluate alternative scenarios for development in a long-term (20–50 years) time frame. The vision relies on external forecasts of future growth in population and jobs, but stakeholders voice preferences about whether or not to accommodate that growth. The process takes on a broad set of issues, typically including social equity, environmental protection, urban design, health, and other issues. It ends with the stakeholders choosing a preferred development scenario. In regions where these work well, there is significant local government engagement and leadership by a network of stakeholders from local and national nonprofits (Barbour and Teitz 2006; Innes and Rongerude 2013).

One shortcoming of regional visioning processes is that they are rarely integrated well with the modeling behind the scenes—which, in most of the cases to date, again has been the simple four-step transportation model (Knaap and Lewis 2011; Waddell 2011). Stakeholders may develop consensus around a vision for the future, but never learn about the policy tools available—as well as their limits and opportunity costs—for implementation. Thus, it is left to the modelers to assess whether the policies are meeting community goals as intended. And the models, themselves, may be poorly linked to incentives, and thus ineffective in shaping how growth occurs on the ground. Not surprisingly, then, with the exception of Portland, blueprints have little impact. Knaap and Lewis (2011) conclude that significant institutional reform will be necessary to compel local governments and actors to act on these regional visions.

Neighborhood Change, Looking Forward

Thus, how are regions to transform themselves? For the last century or so, planners have concerned themselves with creating good neighborhoods, guided, in part, by principles of diversity. Meanwhile, sociologists and economists have described the organic change occurring in neighborhoods, which, for the most part, consists of increasing income segregation and decreasing racial/ethnic segregation. The trends are related: increasing income segregation is leading to community organizing and policy innovation around income mixing. But at the same time, our ideals for diverse places and the increasing segregation of the affluent and the poor are on a collision course. Given the economics of urbanism and diversity, we are far from achieving our aspirations.

As described in Chapter 1, coming shifts in demographics and housing preferences suggest that the urban core will experience a renaissance in coming years. This could mean an increase in the number of city residents, currently about 85 million across all U.S. metropolitan areas, by about 30 percent.[7] At the same time, the changing nature of work is shifting more jobs into neighborhoods. If preferences continue to shift over the next 30 years, the pressure for urban land will be even more dramatic.

Of course, demographers may have overestimated the extent of the changes. For instance, the Brookings report of a back-to-the-city movement in recent years compared a city annual growth rate of 1.12 percent to a suburban rate of 0.97 percent. For every million metropolitan residents, this means that 11,200 moved to cities and 9,700 to suburbs. An increase of 1,500 urban residents per million is probably not even significant enough for the market to register, unless they concentrate in just a few blocks.

But viewed in light of this literature on neighborhood change and economics, a potential 30 percent change should be taken quite seriously. Occurring just as we are experiencing increasing inequality, an influx of city dwellers would likely accelerate neighborhood change, particularly income segregation. Finally, the market for smart growth has arrived—but potentially at the expense of the city's lower-income residents. And the planner's toolkit of urban growth boundaries, impact fees, redevelopment, and regional transportation funding is, for the most part, ill-equipped to protect social equity.

With redistribution losing favor at the federal level, ensuring equitable growth means developing new tools locally. As markets head back to cities, urban policy has an opportunity to recapture some of the new value created. This will mean shifting focus from the old battles over density and urbanism to developing new mechanisms that enable socioeconomic inclusion and diversity. The following four chapters show the growing irrelevance of the traditional battlegrounds and offer new approaches to accommodate new density—while still equitable—and diversity—without pricing people out. Specifically, we look first at alternative approaches to infill development for housing and jobs, and then housing strategies that sustain income diversity.

Notes

1. This phenomenon is also called "suburban gentrification" (Lees, Slater, and Wyly 2008).
2. Most researchers prefer to use more systematic measures of diversity, computed in either relative or absolute terms (or some combination). Relative measures of diversity, such as the dissimilarity index and the correlation ratio, analyze local

diversity in comparison to a larger geographic area. Researchers have long relied on the dissimilarity index, which measures the proportion of a local group that would have to be redistributed in order to produce a distribution equal to the group as a whole, to measure segregation (or lack of it) (Farley 1977; Stearns and Logan 1986). However, the dissimilarity index only compares two different groups, which makes little sense, given increasing racial/ethnic diversity. Further, the index simply reports the average number of people that would have to move in order to create an even distribution—a measure that does not lead to viable policy recommendations (Denton 2010).

Absolute measures of diversity, such as the coefficient of variation, the entropy index, the Maly index of neighborhood diversity, and the Simpson's index of diversity, generally calculate whether categories (from two to dozens) are equally represented. These measures typically examine patterns within, rather than across, tracts. Though intuitively easier to relate to the neighborhood scale than summary measures such as dissimilarity, these indices abstract diversity from the local context, and thus may be hard to comprehend. For instance, an entropy index measuring low-, medium-, and high-income diversity would measure local conditions against an ideal even distribution of the three groups, regardless of whether in homogeneous rural Iowa or a highly unequal place such as New York City.

3. In any given year, four-fifths of the residents lived in the same house the year before. The mover rate for owner-occupied housing is 5.1 percent versus 24.9 percent for renters (U.S. Census Bureau 2013).

4. Most common in the United States are tax increment finance (TIF) districts, which recapture the incremental increase in property tax that results from new development, using the expectation of this future revenue to issue bonds and finance the development. In California, cities can also enact other types of special districts, special assessment districts to pay for specific improvements that provide a benefit to the affected property owners, or Mello Roos districts to finance infrastructure or community facilities. Special assessment districts require a simple majority vote from property owners, while Mello Roos requires a two-thirds majority within local districts or cities.

5. Housing trust funds are funds established by governments (city, county, state, and national) in the United States to support affordable housing construction and preservation. They are typically funded either through special taxes or bond issues.

6. First, the traditional model does not capture the new development that may result from improving transportation flow—in other words, it is not iterative. Second, these models do not have the ability to evaluate land use measures such as mixing uses. Third, because of the 1994 Environmental Justice Presidential Executive Order, travel models must evaluate the economic impacts of the RTP on different income and minority groups. For a comprehensive review, see Johnston and McCoy (2006).

7. Calculations based on separate studies of primary and small metros: Frey (2012) and Smart Growth America (2012).

References

Altshuler, A. and Joint Center. *The Urban Transportation System.* Cambridge, MA: MIT Press, 1979.

American Planning Association. "APA Mission and Vision." 2013. Accessed August 1, 2013. www.planning.org/apaataglance/mission.htm.

Anas, Alex, Richard Arnott, and Kenneth A. Small. "Urban Spatial Structure." *Journal of Economic Literature* 36, no. 3 (1998): 1426–1464.

Barbour, Elisa and Michael B. Teitz. *Blueprint Planning in California: Forging Consensus on Metropolitan Growth and Development*. San Francisco, CA: Public Policy Institute of California, 2006.

Burgess, Ernest W. "The Growth of the City." In *The City*, edited by Robert E. Park, Ernest W. Burgess, and Roderick S. McKenzie, 47–62. Chicago, IL: University of Chicago Press, 1925.

Cervero, Robert and Kara Kockelman. "Travel Demand and the 3Ds: Density, Diversity, and Design." *Transportation Research Part D: Transport and Environment* 2, no. 3 (1997): 199–219.

Cooke, Thomas J. "Residential Mobility of the Poor and the Growth of Poverty in Inner-Ring Suburbs." *Urban Geography* 31, no. 2 (2010): 179–193.

Coulton, Claudia J., Julian Chow, Edward C. Wang, and Marilyn Su. "Geographic Concentration of Affluence and Poverty in 100 Metropolitan Areas, 1990." *Urban Affairs Review* 32 (1996): 186–217.

Denton, Nancy. "From Segregation to Integration: How Do We Get There?" In *The Integration Debate: Competing Futures for American Cities*, edited by Chester Hartman and Gregory Squires, 23–37. New York: Routledge, 2010.

Downs, Anthony. "Smart Growth: Why We Discuss It More than We Do It." *Journal of the American Planning Association* 71, no. 4 (2005): 367–378.

Dreier, Peter, John Mollenkopf, and Todd Swanstrom. *Place Matters: Metropolitics for the Twenty-First Century*. Lawrence, KS: University Press of Kansas, 2004.

Dwyer, Rachel E. "Poverty, Prosperity, and Place: The Shape of Class Segregation in the Age of Extremes." *Social Problems* 57, no. 1 (2010): 114–137.

Edwards, Mary M. and Anna Haines. "Evaluating Smart Growth: Implications for Small Communities." *Journal of Planning Education and Research* 27, no. 1 (2007): 49–64.

Ellen, Ingrid G. *Sharing America's Neighborhoods: The Prospects For Stable Racial Integration*. Cambridge, MA: Harvard University Press, 2000.

EPA Office of Sustainable Communities. *Residential Construction Trends in America's Metropolitan Regions*. Washington, DC: EPA, 2012.

Ewing, Reid and Robert Cervero. "Travel and the Built Environment." *Journal of the American Planning Association* 76, no. 3 (2010): 265–294.

Farley, Reynolds. "Residential Segregation in Urbanized Areas of the United States: An Analysis of Social Class and Differences." *Demography* 14 (1977): 497–517.

Fischer, Claude. "The Myth that Never Moves." *Made in America*, March 23, 2010. Accessed December 4, 2013. http://madeinamericathebook.wordpress.com/2010/03/23/the-myth-that-never-moves.

Fischer, Claude. "Segregation by Culture." *Boston Review*, December 4, 2013. Accessed December 4, 2013. http://bostonreview.net/blog/fischer-san-francisco-housing-moving-class-gentrification.

Fischer, Mary J. "The Relative Importance of Income and Race in Determining Residential Outcomes in U.S. Urban Areas, 1970–2000." *Urban Affairs Review* 38 (2003): 669–696.

Fishman, Robert. "New Urbanism." In *Planning Ideas that Matter: Livability, Territoriality, Governance, and Reflective Practice*, edited by Bishwapriya Sanyal, Lawrence J. Vale, and Christina Rosan, 65–90. Cambridge, MA: MIT Press, 2012.

Frey, William H. *Population Growth in Metropolitan America Since 1980: Putting the Volatile 2000s in Perspective*. Washington, DC: Brookings Institution Press, 2012.

Fry, Richard and Paul Taylor. *The Rise of Residential Segregation by Income*. Washington, DC: Pew Research Center, 2012.

Galster, George C. "Neighborhood Racial Change, Segregationist Sentiments, and Affirmative Marketing Policies." *Journal of Urban Economics* 27, no. 3 (1990): 344–362.

Galster, George C. *Driving Detroit: The Quest for Respect in the Motor City*. Philadelphia, PA: University of Pennsylvania Press, 2012.

Galster, George C., Jason C. Booza, and Jackie M. Cutsinger. "Income Diversity Within Neighborhoods and Very Low-Income Families." *Cityscape* 10, no. 2 (2008): 257–300.

Galster, George C., Jason C. Booza, Jackie Cutsinger, Kurt Metzger, and Up Lim. *Low-Income Households in Mixed-Income Neighborhoods: Extent, Trends, and Determinants*. U.S. Department of Housing and Urban Development, 2005.

Garreau, Joel. *Edge Cities: Life on the New Frontier*. New York: Random House, 1991.

Goldman, Todd and Elizabeth Deakin. "Regionalism Through Partnerships? Metropolitan Planning Since ISTEA." *Berkeley Planning Journal* 14 (2000): 46–75.

Grant, Jill. "Mixed Use in Theory and Practice: Canadian Experience with Implementing a Planning Principle." *Journal of the American Planning Association* 68, no. 1 (2002): 71–84.

Hanlon, Bernadette, Thomas Vicino, and John Rennie Short. "The New Metropolitan Reality in the US: Rethinking the Traditional Model." *Urban Studies* 43, no. 12 (2006): 2129–2143.

Hardman, Anna and Yannis M. Ioannides. "Neighbors' Income Distribution: Economic Segregation and Mixing in U.S. Urban Neighborhoods." *Journal of Housing Economics* 13, no. 4 (2004): 368–382.

Heikkila, Eric, Peter Gordon, Jae Ik Kim, Richard B. Peiser, Harry W. Richardson, and David Dale-Johnson. "What Happened to the CBD-Distance Gradient? Land Values in a Polycentric City." *Environment and Planning A* 21, no. 2 (1989): 221–232.

Hirsch, Arnold. *Making the Second Ghetto: Race and Housing in Chicago, 1940–1960*. Cambridge: Cambridge University Press, 1983.

Hoover, Edgar Malone and Raymond Vernon. *Anatomy of a Metropolis. The Changing Distribution of People and Jobs within the New York Metropolitan Region*. Cambridge, MA: Harvard University Press, 1959.

Hoyt, Homer. *The Structure and Growth of Residential Neighborhoods in American Cities*. Washington, DC: U.S. Government, 1939.

Huang, Youqin. "Housing Inequality and Residential Segregation in Transitional Beijing." *Restructuring the Chinese City: Changing Society, Economy and Space* (2004): 172.

Ingram, Gregory K., Armando Carbonell, Yu-Hung Hong, and Anthony Flint. *Smart Growth Policies: An Evaluation on Programs and Outcomes*. Cambridge, MA: Lincoln Institute of Land Policy, 2009.

Innes, Judith E. and Jane Rongerude. "Civic Networks for Sustainable Regions— Innovative Practices and Emergent Theory." *Planning Theory and Practice* 14, no. 1 (2013): 75–100.

Ioannides, Yannis M. "Neighborhood Income Distributions." *Journal of Urban Economics* 56 (2004): 435–457.

Jacobs, Jane. *Death and Life of Great American Cities*. New York: Random House, 1961.

Jargowsky, Paul A. "Take the Money and Run: Economic Segregation in U.S. Metropolitan Areas." *American Sociological Review* 61, no. 6 (2001): 984–998.

Jargowsky, Paul. *Stunning Progress, Hidden Problems*. Washington, DC: Brookings Institution Press, 2003.

Johnston, Robert A. and Michael C. McCoy. *Assessment of Integrated Transportation/Land Use Models*. Davis, CA: Information Center for the Environment, University of California, Davis, 2006.

Jones, Christopher and Daniel M. Kammen. "Spatial Distribution of U.S. Household Carbon Footprints Reveals Suburbanization Undermines Greenhouse Gas Benefits of Urban Population Density." *Environmental Science & Technology* 48, no. 2 (2014): 895–902.

Knaap, Gerrit J. and Rebecca Lewis. "Regional Planning for Sustainability and Hegemony of Metropolitan Regionalism." In *Regional Planning in America: Practice and Prospect*, edited by Ethan Seltzer and Armando Carbonell, 176–221. Cambridge, MA: Lincoln Institute of Land Policy, 2011.

Kneebone, Elizabeth. *Job Sprawl Stalls: The Great Recession and Metropolitan Employment Location*. Washington, DC: Brookings Institution Press, 2013.

Kok, Herman and Zoltán Kovács. "The Process of Suburbanization in the Agglomeration of Budapest." *Netherlands Journal of Housing and the Built Environment* 14, no. 2 (1999): 119–141.

Krupka, Douglas J. *The Stability of Mixed Income Neighborhoods in America*. Discussion Paper No. 3370. Bonn, Germany: IZA, 2008.

Landis, John D. and Heather Hood. *The Future of Infill Housing in California: Opportunities, Potential, Feasibility and Demand*. Berkeley, CA: Institute of Urban and Regional Development, University of California, Berkeley, 2005.

Lang, Robert and Paul K. Knox. "The New Metropolis: Rethinking Megalopolis." *Regional Studies* 43, no. 6 (2009): 789–802.

Lang, Robert E. and Jennifer B. Lefurgy. *Boomburbs: The Rise of America's Accidental Cities*. Washington, DC: Brookings Institution Press, 2007.

Lees, Loretta, Tom Slater, and Elvin Wyly. *Gentrification*. London: Routledge, 2008.

Levy, Diane K., Zach McDade, and Kassie Dumlao. *Effects from Living in Mixed-Income Communities for Low-Income Families*. Washington, DC: Urban Institute Press, 2010.

Lichter, Daniel T., Domenico Parisi, and Michael C. Taquino. "The Geography of Exclusion: Race, Segregation, and Concentrated Poverty." *Social Problems* 59, no. 3 (2012): 364–388.

Lucy, William H. and David Phillips. *Confronting Suburban Decline: Strategic Planning for Metropolitan Renewal*. Washington, DC: Island Press, 2000.

Nyden, Philip, Michael Maly, and John Lukehart. "The Emergence of Stable Racially and Ethnically Diverse Urban Communities: A Case Study of Nine U.S. Cities." *Housing Policy Debate* 8, no. 2 (1997): 491–534.

Owens, Ann. "Neighborhoods on the Rise: A Typology of Neighborhoods Experiencing Socioeconomic Ascent." *City & Community* 11, no. 4 (2012): 345–369.

Park, Robert E., Ernest W. Burgess, and Roderick D. McKenzie. *The City*. Chicago, IL: University of Chicago Press, 1967.

Perry, Clarence A. "The Neighborhood Unit, a Scheme of Arrangement for the Family-Life Community." *Monograph One, Neighborhood and Community Planning, Regional Plan of New York and Its Environs* (1929): 2–140. New York: Committee on Regional Plan of New York and Its Environs.

Peterson, Paul E. *City Limits*. Chicago, IL: University of Chicago Press, 1981.

Qadeer, Mohammad A. "Urban Development." In *Planning Ideas that Matter: Livability, Territoriality, Governance, and Reflective Practice*, edited by Bishwapriya Sanyal, Lawrence J. Vale, and Christina Rosan, 207–232. Cambridge, MA: MIT Press, 2012.

Reardon, Sean F. and Kendra Bischoff. "Income Inequality and Income Segregation." *American Journal of Sociology* 116, no. 4 (2011): 1092–1153.

Sabatini, Francisco. *The Social Spatial Segregation in the Cities of Latin America*. No. 3418. Washington, DC: Inter-American Development Bank, 2006.

Schildt, Chris. *Strategies for Fiscally Sustainable Infill Housing Development*. Berkeley, CA: Center for Community Innovation, 2011.

Sharkey, Patrick. *Stuck in Place: Urban Neighborhoods and the End of Progress Toward Racial Equality*. Chicago, IL: University of Chicago Press, 2013.

Short, John Rennie, Bernadette Hanlon, and Thomas J. Vicino. "The Decline of Inner Suburbs: The New Suburban Gothic in the United States." *Geography Compass* 1, no. 3 (2007): 641–656.

Smart Growth America. *City Versus Suburban Growth in Small Metro Areas: Analysis of U.S. Census Data in Metropolitan Statistical Areas Under One Million People*. Washington, DC: Smart Growth America, 2012.

Smith, Janet L. "Integration: Solving the Wrong Problem." In *The Integration Debate: Competing Futures for American Cities*, edited by Chester Hartman and Gregory Squires, 229–246. New York: Routledge, 2010.

Song, Yan. "Suburban Sprawl and 'Smart Growth'." *The Oxford Handbook of Urban Planning* (2012): 418.

Sorensen, André and Junichiro Okata, editors. *Megacities: Urban Form, Governance, and Sustainability*. New York: Springer, 2011.

South, Scott J., Jeremy Pais, and Kyle Crowder. "Metropolitan Influences on Migration into Poor and Nonpoor Neighborhoods." *Soc Sci Res* 40, no. 3 (2011): 950–964.

Stearns, Linda B. and John R. Logan. "Measuring Trends in Segregation: Three Dimensions, Three Measures." *Urban Affairs Quarterly* 22 (1986): 124–150.

Strategic Economics. *Downtown Berkeley Development Feasibility Study*. Berkeley, CA: Strategic Economics, 2008. Accessed September 12, 2013. www.ci.berkeley.ca.us/uploadedFiles/Planning_and_Development/Level_3_-_DAP/FeasibilityReport_Final.pdf.

Tach, Laura Marie. *Beyond Concentrated Poverty: The Social and Temporal Dynamics of Mixed-Income Neighborhoods*. Unpublished dissertation, Harvard University, 2010.

Tach, Laura, Rolf Pendall, and Alexandra Derian. *Income Mixing Across Scales: Rationale, Trends, Policies, Practice, and Research for More Inclusive Neighborhoods and Metropolitan Areas*. Washington, DC: Urban Institute Press, 2014.

Talen, Emily. "Diverse Neighborhoods and How to Support Them." Unpublished paper, 2005.

Talen, Emily. "Design for Diversity: Evaluating the Context of Socially Mixed Neighborhoods." *Journal of Urban Design* 11, no. 1 (2006): 1–32.

Talen, Emily and Gerrit Knaap. "Legalizing Smart Growth: An Empirical Study of Land Use Regulation in Illinois." *Journal of Planning Education and Research* 22, no. 4 (2003): 345–359.

Tiebout, Charles M. "A Pure Theory of Local Expenditures." *The Journal of Political Economy* (1956): 416–424.

U.S. Census Bureau. "About 36 Million Americans Moved in the Last Year, Census Bureau Reports." Washington, DC: U.S. Census Bureau, 2013. Accessed May 29, 2014.

www.census.gov/newsroom/releases/archives/mobility_of_the_population/cb09-62.html.

Van Criekingen, Mathieu and Jean-Michel Decroly. "Revisiting the Diversity of Gentrification: Neighbourhood Renewal Processes in Brussels and Montreal." *Urban Studies* 40, no. 12 (2003): 2451–2468.

Vicino, Thomas J. "The Spatial Transformation of First-Tier Suburbs, 1970 to 2000: The Case of Metropolitan Baltimore." *Housing Policy Debate* 19, no. 3 (2008): 479–518.

Waddell, Paul. "Integrated Land Use and Transportation Planning and Modeling: Addressing Challenges in Research and Practice." *Transport Reviews* 31, no. 2 (2011): 209–229.

Watson, Tara. "Inequality and the Measurement of Residential Segregation by Income in American Neighborhoods." *Review of Income and Wealth* 55, no. 3 (2009): 820–844.

Weiner, Edward. *Urban Transportation Planning in the United States: An Historical Overview.* Westport, CT: Greenwood, 1999.

Yang, Rebecca and Paul A. Jargowsky. "Suburban Development and Economic Segregation in the 1990s." *Journal of Urban Affairs* 28, no. 3 (2006): 253–273.

3 Infill Development and Density

The regional planners found themselves surrounded by signs: "We're being railroaded. No One Bay Area." "Equal justice not social justice." "No stack and pack housing near mass transit." The public meeting quickly erupted into chaos.

The Bay Area's regional agencies (the Metropolitan Transportation Commission, or MTC, and the Association of Bay Area Governments, or ABAG) had embarked on a 30-year planning process, seeking to accommodate the 2 million new residents and 1 million new jobs projected for the region in the next 30 years. As described in Chapter 2, California State Senate Bill 375 requires such agencies to integrate land use, transportation, and housing planning in a Sustainable Communities Strategy that will achieve regional greenhouse gas emission reduction targets (a reduction of 18 percent by 2040). This will mean focusing future growth in core areas near transit and reducing the construction of single-family homes in outlying areas ("sprawl"). The Bay Area plan (now "Plan Bay Area") proposes to channel 80 percent of its future growth into 5 percent of regional land area, using the carrots of transportation funding and streamlining of environmental review to support infill development.

In this region's Sustainable Communities Strategy, each of its 101 cities chose where it wanted growth to go (the PDAs), as well as areas to restrict growth ("planned conservation areas"). Most new growth will go to existing downtowns. Still, some of the exurbs are worried about being overburdened by new residents and congestion. In the core, concerns centered on the potential impacts on housing costs, particularly for low-income communities. An extensive public participation process opened the door to these fears.

The signs disrupting the meeting came from both Tea Party-affiliated and property rights activist members concerned about density and the loss of development rights (Trapenberg Frick 2013). Thus, the protests were not just about protecting local quality of life, but a symptom of a larger societal malaise: the ongoing economic crisis and the failure of the liberal welfare state.[1]

The language from the Citizens Alliance for Property Rights emphasizes the traditional and plays on economic insecurity and fears of change:

YOUR COMMUNITY—YOUR FUTURE
Why Do You Live in Your Town?
Good schools, Suburban lifestyle, Safety
Neighborhood Look and Feel
Unique Character of Your Town
REGIONAL OFFICIALS
(People who do **NOT** live in your town)
WANT TO CHANGE THAT
High Density Housing and Transit Oriented Development
URBANIZES Towns
Puts pressure on the school system
Strains City services
Affects property values
Requires endless PARCEL TAXES to support more people

(CAPR 2013)

But Tea Party/property rights activists are not the only groups fighting the regional agencies. Behind the scenes, fair housing advocates also threatened MTC and ABAG for not analyzing the potential impacts of Plan Bay Area on minority communities. Of particular concern is the plan's attempt to provide more affordable housing in the core cities near transit, as opposed to in the more segregated—but ostensibly opportunity-rich—exurbs. Adding to the chorus is the environmental movement, split between the established interest groups trying to preserve the natural environment and a small-town, quality-of-life environmentalism that borrows language from both the Tea Party/property rights activists and progressives. As Marin progressive environmental activist Bob Silvestri writes in his book *The Best Laid Plans* (2012: 19):

> Working together, their [MTC and ABAG's] One Bay Area Plan proposes planning solutions that would turn our unique small towns into homogenized, Smart Growth, "urban" centers . . . What we really need are solutions that are environmentally sustainable and address our social equity challenges at the same time. We need solutions that make fiscal sense for our cities and financial sense to private capital markets. That is the problem before us. But instead we find ourselves faced with an unappetizing menu of "high density" options and massive bureaucracies trying to force one size fits all solutions down our throats, none of which are sustainable in any real sense of the word. [sic]

Ultimately, there were four lawsuits filed against Plan Bay Area: two affiliated with Tea Party/property rights-related groups fighting high-density development as a violation of property rights (among other objections); one by environmental groups concerned about the lack of transit service funding and the potential for gentrification and displacement; and one by the Building Industry Association of the Bay Area, fighting suburban restrictions on housing growth.

How can we approach infill development to address the concerns of this diverse set of opponents? That these barriers to sustainability are emerging in one of the United States' most progressive and affluent regions suggests that we need a more diverse toolkit of approaches to densification, as well as a clearer understanding and communication of what we can and cannot accomplish via smart growth.

Why Pursue Smart Growth?

> The fact that the neighborhood plays a minor role in people's lives and in their predispositions gives the planner freedom to design neighborhoods as he wishes them to be. At the same time, however, he is less likely to affect the lives of his clients.
>
> (Gans 1968: 23)

So, are Tea Party and property rights advocates correct in fighting density, and is Public Advocates right about the potential impacts on minorities in the Sustainable Communities Strategy? More than 40 years after sociologist Herbert Gans wrote about the futility of changing human behavior through physical planning, academics have converged, more or less, on an understanding about the extent to which urban form can shape travel behavior, especially the reliance on the automobile. In essence, place does matter, but perhaps a little less than planners might wish. But the politics of planning are much more challenging today.

Researchers have struggled to pinpoint the effects of urban form, exactly because of the predisposition problem identified by Gans so long ago, which is a kind of chicken-and-egg problem. People often self-select into certain kinds of places, but it is not clear the degree to which they choose to live in the type of neighborhood that will make it convenient for them to travel in a certain way, and, conversely, the extent to which they travel in a certain way because they live in the type of neighborhood that makes it convenient. If it is not clear how the feedback loops work, it is hard to alter the problem.

It is intuitive that where a family is in the life cycle will affect its choice (if it has one) of neighborhood. Families with children value open space and schools, and often prefer to travel via automobile, rather than transit (Fan and Khattak 2012). Young adults, single-person households, and the elderly may instead choose neighborhoods with nearby amenities and transit. Where we grow up shapes our preferences, but these can also evolve over time based on life experiences (Weinberger and Goetzke 2011). And in fact, demographers are now observing a growth in demand for more urban lifestyles, whether because of the aging of the baby boomers or the gradual exposure of U.S. residents to denser communities, including both traditional urban centers and new smart growth or New Urbanist development. At the same time, the American suburb is far from obsolete. The same forces that Gans observed pushing working-class families to Levittown for a higher quality of life exist today.

Despite these constraints of demography and preference, and the limits of planning, it turns out that urban form does matter; more compact neighborhoods can reduce greenhouse gas emissions somewhere between 10 and 20 percent, depending on context (Echenique et al. 2012; Transportation Research Board 2009). But the impact is through density working together with other factors, primarily the neighborhood's accessibility to employment and its distance from downtown (Echenique et al. 2012; Ewing and Cervero 2010).

Context matters not just in the form of a neighborhood's location within the region, but also in terms of a region's historical density. Increasing compactness in existing or new neighborhoods makes a big difference in regions that are sprawling, but less in areas that are relatively dense already.[2] In other words, a smart growth intervention such as reducing lot size will have an impact of much greater magnitude on greenhouse gas emission reduction in regions that are seeing high population growth consuming vacant land than in slower growth areas, where there also may be little appetite for smaller lots (Pendall 2003).[3]

Another consideration is the costs and benefits of smart growth. Research since the 1970s has established the costs of sprawl, an inefficient land development pattern with costs borne typically by taxpayers (Burchell et al. 1998). Among other impacts, sprawl consumes excessive land and wastes infrastructure (roads, sewers, water, and facilities such as schools). Smart growth in the form of denser or infill development reduces these inefficiencies, but may bring its own costs in the form of higher development costs, leading to higher housing prices. Research to date is mixed on what the precise impact on prices will be; the effect depends on local housing market demand and the design of growth management policies with regard to inclusion (Nelson et al. 2002). And the design of policies depends largely on the local culture (or regime) of land use regulation. The regime prevalent in the San Francisco Bay Area—one in which housing development is not only steered into certain subregions, consistent with smart growth principles, but also heavily regulated *within* those subregions—is clearly associated with high housing prices (Pendall, Martin, and Puentes 2009). These costs, in turn, shape preferences and travel behavior in response to density.

One tool to ensure that affordable housing remains available is *inclusionary housing,* or the local mandate that housing developers provide or financially contribute to below-market housing in return for permission to build market-rate developments (Calavita, Grimes, and Mallach 1997). Because units are often built in higher-income neighborhoods where market-rate housing is profitable, inclusionary housing can also serve as a fair housing strategy, integrating neighborhoods.[4] Studies have shown that inclusionary housing has a modest impact on increasing housing density—and probably prices as well (Knaap, Bento, and Lowe 2008; Pendall 2009; Schuetz, Meltzer, and Been 2009). But inclusionary housing policies are probably insufficient to ensure a broad distribution of housing affordability in a strong market region with strict land use regulation, such as the San Francisco Bay Area.

The opponents of regional sustainability planning thus may have a point. Assessing the evidence, one could easily argue that the costs of increasing density in the PDAs outweigh the benefits. This strategy alone will only reduce greenhouse gas emissions by a slight amount, especially given that it does not use job accessibility and location (the most important factors in reducing emissions) as key criteria for selecting PDAs. In the regional context of the Bay Area, which is already relatively compact, more density will likely have a comparatively minor effect.[5] Since the region is highly regulated, the plan will probably raise housing prices, and thus impact disadvantaged communities.

But we might also assess the research more cautiously. The finding that smarter growth patterns can reduce greenhouse gas emissions, even if just by 10 or 20 percent, is nothing to sneeze at, and the body of work in support has grown to hundreds of studies. The alternative—improved energy technology in buildings and transportation—has not yet emerged, at least not as a cost-effective proposition.

And even if the research findings do not compel action, the crisis of climate change does. As the precedents of medical and safety research show, it is not always necessary for science to complete its work before moving forward.[6] The concern that then arises is, are we asking the right questions? What, exactly, is an urban form that is both sustainable for future generations and politically viable in terms of the daily life of today's residents?[7] And, even before asking about viability, what is actually feasible to build?

The Feasibility of Smart Growth: The Bay Area Case

Builders have long considered infill development challenging in the urban context (Figure 3.1), and it has taken decades for an infill building industry to emerge. Although infill housing development is, in theory, capable of supplying all of California's housing needs through 2025, regulatory and other constraints mean that it will likely proceed at less than 40 percent of its potential level (Landis et al. 2006).

Given these constraints, the form of infill development envisioned by the regional agencies is not exactly "stack and pack housing near mass transit." Most of the new development is anticipated to be in the form of four-story, multifamily dwellings, a type of structure that was common before the 1986 Tax Reform Act eliminated its beneficial tax treatment. Most PDAs would likely see only this modest density, in part because steel frame construction, necessary for buildings over eight stories, does not "pencil" (i.e., is not financially feasible) in a downtown such as Berkeley's (a stable though secondary market in the Bay Area) (Strategic Economics 2008). However, the Sustainable Communities Strategy would concentrate this new, medium-density development in relatively few dense centers served by transit.[8]

But the agencies' own studies of Plan Bay Area's impact conclude that its PDAs cannot accommodate the growth planned—or the affordable housing needed. Assuming modest adjustments to present zoning, the PDAs can

Figure 3.1 Infill development in Oakland, California
Photo credit: Arijit Sen

accommodate just 62 percent of the housing units and jobs proposed to be located there. What if California enacted a stream of both regulatory reforms and funding programs, such as federal financing for affordable housing development?[9] The PDAs would attract more development, but the capture rate increases to just 80 percent (Economic & Planning Systems 2013). The study did not even address the issue of financial feasibility (i.e., what the market can bear). Studies of development potential around new transit stations have shown that outside of downtowns, new housing may not be viable for many years after the new rail line is built (Carlton 2013; Center for Transit-Oriented Development 2010).

Not only is it not going to be feasible, but if it were, the new development is not likely to be affordable to residents. As described in Chapter 4, because of the low wages paid by the majority of the 1 million new jobs anticipated in the Bay Area by 2040, 72 percent of the new housing units built would need to be affordable to households making 120 percent of the area's median income or less. Even with the help of existing programs that help to build affordable housing or provide housing vouchers, the region will be unable to meet 60–70 percent of the demand for affordable housing.[10]

But will people even want this dense, infill housing, even if it is affordable? Planners often argue that if communities were only exposed to denser neighbor-

hoods, they would appreciate them more. Planning academic Peter Marcuse (2010: 366) credits his father, philosopher Herbert Marcuse, with the insight:

> The underlying problem here is an old and well-recognized one: in order seriously to change society, you need individuals seriously committed to real change; but to get individuals seriously committed to a real alternative you need the social experience of alternatives. The two need to be approached together; make the road by walking. Individual consciousness must be changed, but consciousness is a social product.

Gans (1968: 21), again, in language recently echoed by the Tea Party, sees the problem as more intractable, one of planners imposing their own values on the public:

> Generally, however, the planner has advocated policies that fit the predispositions of the upper middle class, but not those of the rest of the population. For example, his advocacy of high-density urban housing has so far found favor only with the cosmopolitan upper-middle class. His proposal for increasing suburban density to cut down urban sprawl is

rejected by people who feel that row housing lacks privacy and that it is less desirable for other reasons than the single-family house.

Even though the growing diversity of U.S. households (e.g., the smaller households and lower birth rates) makes "high-density urban housing" more attractive to many, it is far from the majority preference. Thus, it is interesting that Bay Area planners and developers continue to pick this fight. There are many different ways to achieve higher density—not just stack-and-pack, or even four-story buildings, but also *distributed density*, or infill placed unobtrusively throughout single-family neighborhoods. What if, in pursuing one smart growth alternative so diligently, planners defeat the chance for other, more realistic paths toward the same goals?

Alternative Paths Toward Smarter Growth

One day in 2009, two grad students from Civil Engineering came to my office hours wanting to discuss the economic feasibility of energy-efficient accessory dwelling units (separate small dwellings embedded within single-family house properties). I knew very little about the subject, but jokingly suggested that they use my house and lot in Berkeley for their class project. Just over a year later, based on their design, I had a backyard cottage (Figure 3.2).[11]

The ease of the permitting and building process startled me. Of course, Berkeley is one of a growing number of cities (others include Seattle, Santa Cruz, and Vancouver, BC) that make building backyard cottages relatively straightforward (Dougherty 2013). Backyard cottages fit the low-density vernacular of much of the area's flatlands, the formerly working-class waterfront and downtown areas; in fact, 15 percent of the lots already have cottages or other kinds of secondary units (Chapple et al. 2011). Might we be able to scale up this distributed density to accommodate some of the 2 million new residents (and 660,000 new housing units) anticipated by 2040?

To answer this question, my students and I examined every parcel in the flatlands of the East Bay cities of Berkeley, El Cerrito, and Oakland, comparing the property layout to its host city's zoning regulations for backyard cottages.[12] Under current zoning, the flatlands could accommodate approximately 3,625 backyard cottages (in addition to those already existing) (Chapple et al. 2011). Given that many cities are finding political support for liberalizing their regulations, we also calculated the effects of implementing a set of carefully selected, incremental changes to land use policies, including easing off-street parking requirements, changing building height limits, reducing or eliminating minimum lot size requirements, and reducing or eliminating setback standards. When Santa Cruz relaxed its zoning code in this way, it saw a near tripling of production of backyard cottages and other types of secondary units. With the set of relaxed regulations, the flatlands area could accommodate 8,677 units.

In the flatlands area, the regional agencies have established a goal of 14,323 new units by 2040. The cottage strategy will not meet this goal. Would a

Figure 3.2 My backyard cottage, built under Berkeley's accessory dwelling unit law
Photo credit: Karen Chapple

conventional infill strategy, relying on dense, multifamily housing, fare better? Using the most generous assumptions, our model indicated that 18 percent of the parcels in the flatlands neighborhoods, occupying 1.5 out of 9.5 square miles of the land base (not including street rights of way), are underutilized or vacant. Based on current zoning, these infill parcels could accommodate up to 16,239 units of new housing, in addition to the 60,721 that exist today. Of these, almost half (7,882 units) could be built in buildings of five units or more; due to physical constraints, the remainder would need to be in medium-density, two- to four-unit structures (a rare building type in recent years).

Backyard cottages, then, could yield infill housing production levels (8,677 units), exceeding the results of a high-density infill scenario (7,882 units) and comprising one-third of total potential infill capacity (Figure 3.3). What is more, unlike market-rate, multifamily development, backyard cottage projects require comparatively small injections of capital (frequently under $100,000, as compared to millions of dollars for even a small five-unit project). Backyard cottage development also offers at least the possibility of continuing amid housing downturns, because of the very low capital requirements and minimal construction delay risk, whereas development of multifamily developments tends to grind to a near-halt during down periods. Boosting production to this level, of course, would be challenging. However, cities such as Berkeley and Santa Cruz have increased cottage construction by educating local homeowners and streamlining the permitting process.

The pace of development also favors backyard cottages, which can easily be completed within a year, compared to several years from conception to completion for multifamily projects. Of course, it would likely take decades to

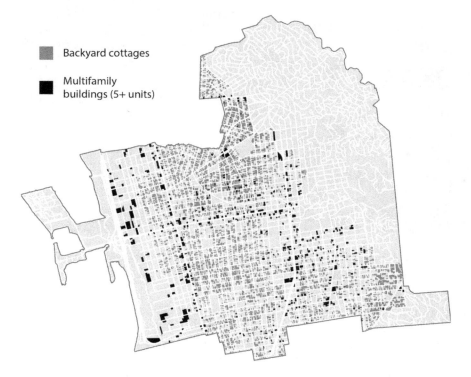

Backyard cottages

Multifamily buildings (5+ units)

Figure 3.3 Potential infill production in the City of Berkeley
Source: Jacob Wegmann

spur construction among homeowners. Yet, the production of high-density housing is not likely to occur at a much faster rate. Historical production levels in these neighborhoods (in the period from 1996 to 2011) vary from a low of 18 in 1996, to a high of 440 housing starts in 2008. At the average pace of 184 housing starts per year in the 1996–2011 period, it would take almost 43 years for the 7,882 infill units to be built. Even in the unlikely event that the maximum yearly pace in the 1996–2011 period was to be sustained, full buildout would still take almost 18 years.

What about affordability? Our analysis of rents for secondary units advertised on Craigslist revealed that they rent for markedly less rent than comparable rental units offered in the same forum. As it turns out, a much higher proportion of secondary units advertised on Craigslist are located in the most affluent tracts (48 percent) than is the case for other types of rental units (11 percent). This evidence supports, therefore, a view of secondary units as likelier to provide rental housing that is affordable within its neighborhood context, whether low or high income, than rental housing in general. Furthermore, a much greater share of secondary units are located in high-income areas, contributing income diversity and suggesting potential as a fair housing strategy.

How would this quantity of added affordable housing stock compare to what would be yielded under a conventional infill strategy? Of the 7,882 units produced via conventional infill, 5,881 would be built in Berkeley, the only city of the three in the flatlands that currently has an inclusionary housing ordinance.[13] Since Berkeley requires reserving 10 percent of all units in rental developments of five units and more for affordable housing, this strategy could result in the production of up to 588 affordable units, much less than the 3,519 new units yielded by the backyard cottage strategy (which, it should be noted, would be constrained in size to studios or one-bedrooms). Given the high construction costs of dense building types suitable for infill development (which, according to the infill model, would have an average density of over 26 units per acre), it is highly unlikely that many, if any, of the non-inclusionary units produced under a conventional infill strategy would be affordable to households earning less than 80 percent of the median income.[14] Distributed density, thus, is a more effective tool to deal with rising land costs on the core.

Backyard cottages are not the solution to global warming. (In fact, our analysis showed that densities would be insufficient to support even bus transit.) But what this analytic exercise shows is that there are multiple paths toward accommodating growth, and we need to pursue all of them simultaneously in order to have impact. "Stack-and-pack" housing is just one of many types of infill development, and given site, market, and political constraints increases in density will occur gradually.

Thus, even in the San Francisco Bay Area, one of the strongest real estate markets in the world, infill development is unlikely to be able to accommodate all of the region's projected growth, at least under current plans. Given the array of implementation challenges—obstructionist politics, onerous regulations, and lack of financial feasibility—it is unlikely that cities will modify their plans to make growth possible. The challenge will only be magnified in weaker markets, both within and outside the United States, where there is very little market for new construction. Many of these regions also liberally allow construction on their outskirts, lessening demand for infill on core land. Given these disincentives, there is an even greater need in these regions to find creative, lower-cost alternatives for infill development.

Especially in newer regions that did not mature around a transit infrastructure, mass transit is just one of the many transportation options we need to explore, as the recent blossoming of transportation alternatives such as Uber and Lyft has underscored. Our regional agencies are often a little too top-down in their thinking, not looking carefully at existing neighborhood character. In the Bay Area, the development mindset is ossified even further by a local building industry with little experience in building diverse types of housing. However, since the benefits of distributed density go to homeowners, rather than developers, there is increasing pressure on cities to liberalize their cottage regulations. Many regions have been slow to catch up.

The regional agencies will settle the lawsuits, and new housing will get built. The most vociferous opponents will get a little less density in their neighborhoods, while the housing advocates will win a few more affordable housing units in theirs. But we will end up with neither enough density nor enough affordability. Ultimately, it may be the planners who are struggling to visualize fundamental change in today's world.

Notes

1. As Peter Marcuse (2010: 365) writes, "The everyday worry and deep discontent that the present crisis has brought to the fore finds its outlet in this form of right-wing activism, by those already suffering from or perceiving an imminent danger of being subjected to unemployment, loss of health care, foreclosure of home or eviction from rental, and loss of even those gains their parents made before them in everyday life. At the ideological level alternatives are discounted, blocked, evicted from serious consideration. The intellectual possibility of visualizing fundamental change vanishes. The repression is often quite unconscious, internally repressed, so that the individual is simply not aware even of the possibility of alternatives."
2. For more in-depth discussion, see Pendall (2012).
3. Reducing building energy use is also critical to reducing emissions. See Kockelman, Thompson, and Whitehead-Frei (2010).
4. Some commentators oppose inclusionary housing, seeing it as a de facto tax on the cost of new housing, which results in a trickle of below-market units available only to a lucky few, while broadly driving up the costs of already-expensive new housing for most others. See, for instance, Powell and Stringham (2005).
5. Ideally, the new housing growth would induce some of the workers who now live in the Central Valley and commute to the region to live within the boundaries. In that case, there is potential for more significant greenhouse gas reductions.
6. As Dowell Myers (2012) puts it: "Here in California, we prefer to act before we have all the evidence, sometimes too hastily, but sometimes ahead of the curve of knowledge accumulation. The California legislature and governor already have enacted a series of climate change/land use planning bills (AB 32, SB 375). In this case, some science accumulated early and, before the matter was totally settled, policy

went forward. In other cases, planning might proceed first, framing issues for public discussion based on preliminary local evidence, and calling on scientists to follow behind and do their normal thing, Kuhn's 'mopping up operations.' But science takes a long time, and our real world will not wait."

7. As Jim Throgmorton (2012) argues: "So, when I see a thoughtful question such as Steve Wheeler's 'How can we move towards more sustainable urban form?', I ask myself, 'How might this question play out in the public arena, right here, right now?' This immediately makes me ask, who is the 'we' in Steve's question? If the answer is 'all the interested officials and public in the locality,' then I'd have to say that it would be foolhardy to rely exclusively on modeling or 'evidence-based decision making.' Why? Partly because the first response I would hear to Steve's question would be: 'Why should we move to a more sustainable urban form?' In fact, 'What the heck does that mean here, now?' And then, 'What would a "more sustainable urban form" mean for me, in terms of my day to day life?' Assuming public discussion got that far, other questions would come from the city manager and other elected officials. Questions such as: 'What would sustainable urban form mean for the revenues and expenditures of the city, and hence for its budget?' And 'What would it mean for its Capital Improvements Program?' "

8. For instance, 86 percent of the new jobs are slated to locate in job centers or dense corridors.

9. The state's major impediments to development include a strict environmental review process that can delay or prevent development, the lack of common redevelopment tools such as eminent domain (to help developers assemble parcels), and the limits on property tax revenue imposed by the taxpayer revolt Proposition 13, which jeopardizes the ability to provide local services.

10. Ironically, the majority of affordable stock, up to 200,000 units, may come from foreclosed homes, which continue to dominate the available housing supply in many U.S. regions. During the recent financial crisis, the Bay Area experienced a sharp increase in the number of residential foreclosures in its nine counties, increasing from 2,098 in 2006 to 37,724 in 2008. While the level of foreclosures has decreased since 2008, it remains far higher than historical levels, with 23,671 in 2011. One recent report suggests that many years, perhaps the remainder of the current decade, will pass before the foreclosure crisis fully recedes (Bocian et al. 2011).

11. The story of the cottage construction is told in articles in the *San Francisco Chronicle*, *Washington Post*, *Daily Californian*, *Diablo Magazine*, and other journals. For more information, see Chapple (2011).

12. A slightly different version of this analysis is published in Wegmann and Chapple (2014).

13. While inclusionary housing ordinances have been actively considered in El Cerrito and Oakland, they have not been implemented to date.

14. Looking at 23 subsidized new construction, multifamily rental projects constructed in Oakland and Berkeley from 2001 to 2011, no project cost less than $199,000 per unit to develop. While these figures pertain only to subsidized multifamily rental housing, total development costs would be expected to be similar for market-rate projects, given the use of the same building types, similar land costs, and a similar regulatory environment, or perhaps even higher, given investor expectations for a return on equity.

References

Bocian, Debbie Gruenstein, Wei Li, Carolina Reid, and Roberto G. Quercia. *Lost Ground, 2011: Disparities in Mortgage Lending and Foreclosures*. Washington, DC: Center for Responsible Lending, 2011.

Burchell, Robert W., Naveed A. Shad, David Listokin, Hilary Phillips, Anthony Downs, Samuel Seskin, Judy S. Davis, Terry Moore, David Helton, and Michelle Gall. "The Costs of Sprawl—Revisited." *Transit Cooperative Research Program (TCRP) Report* 39. Washington, DC: Transportation Research Board, 1998.

Calavita, Nico, Kenneth Grimes, and Alan Mallach. "Inclusionary Housing in California and New Jersey: A Comparative Analysis." *Housing Policy Debate* 8 (1997): 109–142.

Carlton, Ian. *Transit Planning Practice in the Age of Transit-Oriented Development.* Ph.D. Dissertation, University of California, Berkeley, 2013.

Center for Transit-Oriented Development. *Central Corridor TOD Investment Framework: A Corridor Implementation Strategy.* Berkeley, CA: Center for TOD, 2010.

Chapple, Karen. *Second Dwelling Units Can Add Density.* Berkeley, CA: Center for Community Innovation, 2011.

Chapple, Karen, Jake Wegmann, Alison Nemirow, and Colin Dentel-Post. *Yes in My Backyard: Mobilizing the Market for Secondary Units.* Berkeley, CA: Center for Community Innovation, 2011.

CAPR. "Citizens Alliance for Property Rights." Accessed March 3, 2013. www.bay arealiberty.com/libertyblog.

Dougherty, Conor. "The Latest Urban Trend: Less Elbow Room." *The Wall Street Journal,* June 4, 2013.

Echenique, Marcial H., Anthony J. Hargreaves, Gordon Mitchell, and Anil Namdeo. "Growing Cities Sustainably: Does Urban Form Really Matter?" *Journal of the American Planning Association* 78, no. 2 (2012): 121–137.

Economic & Planning Systems. *Draft Bay Area Plan: Priority Development Area Development Feasibility and Readiness Assessment.* Berkeley, CA: Economic & Planning Systems, 2013.

Ewing, Reid and Robert Cervero. "Travel and the Built Environment: A Meta-Analysis." *Journal of the American Planning Association* 76, no. 3 (2010): 265–294.

Fan, Yingling and Asad Khattak. "Time Use Patterns, Lifestyles, and Sustainability of Nonwork Travel Behavior." *International Journal of Sustainable Transportation* 6, no. 1 (2012): 26–47.

Gans, Herbert J. *People and Plans.* New York: Basic Books, 1968.

Knaap, Gerrit-Jan, Antonio Bento, and Scott Lowe. *Housing Market Impacts of Inclusionary Zoning.* College Park, MD: National Center for Smart Growth Research and Education, 2008.

Kockelman, Kara M., Melissa R. Thompson, and Charlotte A. Whitehead-Frei. "Americans' Contributions to Climate Change: Opportunities for Meeting Carbon Targets." *Journal of Urban Planning and Development* 137, no. 2. (2010): 91–100.

Landis, John D., Heather Hood, Guangyu Li, Thomas Rogers, and Charles Warren. "The Future of Infill Housing in California: Opportunities, Potential, and Feasibility." *Housing Policy Debate* 17, no. 4 (2006): 681–725.

Marcuse, Peter. "The Need for Critical Theory in Everyday Life: Why the Tea Parties Have Popular Support." *City* 14, no. 4 (2010): 355–369.

Myers, Dowell. "Re: Do Policy and Planning Follow BEHIND Science?" *Planning Educators Electronic Mail Network* listserv, planet@listserv.buffalo.edu. July 30, 2012.

Nelson, Arthur C., Rolf Pendall, Casey J. Dawkins, and Gerrit J. Knaap. "The Link Between Growth Management and Housing Affordability: The Academic Evidence." In *Growth Management and Affordable Housing: Do They Conflict?*, edited by Anthony Downs, 117–158. Washington, DC: Brookings Institution Press, 2002.

Pendall, Rolf. *Sprawl Without Growth: The Upstate Paradox*. New York: Brookings Institution, Center on Urban and Metropolitan Policy, 2003.

Pendall, Rolf. "How Might Inclusionary Zoning Affect Urban Form?" In *Urban & Regional Policy and its Effects*, edited by Nancy Pindus, Howard Wial, and Hal Walman, 223–256. Washington, DC: Brookings Institution Press, 2009.

Pendall, Rolf. "Simulating Sprawl Reduction: We're Not England." *MetroTrends*, 2012. Accessed August 12, 2013. http://blog.metrotrends.org/2012/08/simulating-sprawl-reduction-england.

Pendall, Rolf, Jonathan Martin, and Robert Puentes. *From Traditional to Reformed: A Review of the Land Use Regulations in the Nation's 50 Largest Metropolitan Areas*. Washington, DC: Brookings Institution Press, 2009.

Powell, Benjamin and Edward Stringham. "The Economics of Inclusionary Zoning Reclaimed: How Effective Are Price Controls." *Florida State University Law Review* 33 (2005): 471–500.

Schuetz, Jenny, Rachel Meltzer, and Vici Been. "31 Flavors of Inclusionary Zoning: Comparing Policies From San Francisco, Washington, DC, and Suburban Boston." *Journal of the American Planning Association* 75, no. 1 (2009): 441–456.

Silvestri, Bob. *The Best Laid Plans: Our Planning and Affordable Housing Challenges in Marin*. Mill Valley, CA: Robert J. Silvestri, 2012.

Strategic Economics. *Downtown Berkeley Development Feasibility Study*. Berkeley, CA: Strategic Economics, 2008.

Throgmorton, James A. "Re: Echenique et al. article." *Planning Educators Electronic Mail Network* listserv, planet@listserv.buffalo.edu. July 30, 2012.

Transportation Research Board, "Driving and the Built Environment: The Effects of Compact Development on Motorized Travel, Energy Use, and CO2 Emissions." *TRB Special Report* 298. Washington, DC: Transportation Research Board and the Board on Energy and Environmental Systems of the National Research Council of the National Academies, 2009.

Trapenberg Frick, Karen. "Actions of Discontent: Tea Party and Property Rights Activists Pushing Back Against Regional Planning." *Journal of the American Planning Association*, 79, no. 3 (2013): 190–200.

Wegmann, Jake and Karen Chapple. "Hidden Density in Single-Family Neighborhoods: Backyard Cottages as an Equitable Smart Growth Strategy." *Journal of Urbanism* (2014): 1–22. doi: 10.1080/17549175.2013.879453.

Weinberger, Rachel and Frank Goetzke. "Drivers of Auto Ownership: The Role of Past Experiences and Peer Pressure." In *Auto Motives: Understanding Car Use Behaviours*, edited by Karen Lucas, Evelyn Blumenberg, and Rachel Weinberger, 121–136. Bingley, UK: Emerald, 2011.

4   Planning for Jobs—and Life

Most days, I walk my daughter four blocks to her school. Then I write at home in the mornings. Sometime before lunch, I bike the three miles uphill to the Berkeley campus to do the rest of my job, teaching, advising, and committee service. At the end of the day, I ride back to the school to pick up my daughter, often stopping at the gym on the way. We walk home and then get in the car and drive to a flurry of evening classes and errands.

My job is far from typical, of course. But my travel pattern is not. Most of the automobile travel we do each day is for purposes other than work (McGuckin 2007). Transportation planners spend a lot of time worrying about peak rush hour congestion, because that is when there is insufficient roadway capacity. But most people are less concerned with *mobility* (i.e., the ease of movement) than *accessibility* (i.e., getting to a variety of locations, from work, to family, to shopping, to play). And unlike me, most do not have the luxury of choosing a different transportation mode to fit each occasion.

When regional planners run their four-step transportation models, they analyze trips generated by different land uses, taking socioeconomic characteristics, population densities, and the availability of cars into account. So, a low-income household is likely to take certain kinds of trips, and a Macy's department store will generate its own activity patterns. The totality of these patterns, viewed in conjunction with trend line projections of how future job and population growth will affect congestion during peak hours, will shape where the regional agencies steer future transportation investment.[1]

Each decision I made about travel was made in the context of my household structure and budget, as well as local land use patterns. Affecting my choices are my own time and budget constraints, the availability of other adults or activities to cover child care, the location of the goods and services I consume, my individual preferences for fitness, and so forth—all of which change continually in the short and long term. But shaping those choices are the system that the government has built to support my journey to work—regional investment to support auto trips, coupled with great bike and transit infrastructure in Berkeley. Also important are the rules that the University of California has established about my salary and hours, as well as the costs of parking. The local weather and violent crime rates also factor into travel decisions. These together decide my bike mode choice, which then determines my subsequent auto mode choice.

And that is just my decision frame and activity space; different households will have their own changeable set of constraints, preferences, and responses to incentives and costs shaped by their geographies. For some, particularly low-income households and women, this activity space will reflect time poverty (i.e., exclusion from the mainstream based on the inability to accommodate multiple demands on the schedule) (Lucas 2012).

The best models—activity-based, dynamic, and integrated transportation-land use models—take much of this complexity into account. Not only do they better recognize our diversity, but they account for the iterative nature of transportation and land use: my travel choices affect those of others, as well as the location choices of businesses, and vice versa.

Through different policies, such as travel demand management, we can also reshape preferences and travel behavior: for instance, we can incentivize employers to provide vanpools, car sharing, or transit passes, or we can raise parking costs or improve transit. But old habits die hard: even in combination, all these policies will only increase the share of transit commuters by a few percentage points.

Thus, many look to regional sustainability plans to reshape travel. Perhaps by shifting transportation investment from roads to transit, and targeting areas with the greatest potential for VMT reduction through transit, we can make a difference. But regional plans may disappoint: most MPOs still depend on much simpler models, focusing not on all the activities in life, but mostly on work-related travel.

In planning for travel between home and work, regional planners throughout the world have coalesced on two key sustainability goals that target job growth in specific places: job centers and jobs–housing balance. Both have demonstrated potential to induce more transit or walk trips and reduce VMT. But both are challenging to implement because we do not have the right tools to ensure equitable development. Businesses may not want to locate near housing or transit, and may not provide the right kind of jobs to match the skills of local residents—or wage levels sufficient to support living nearby. Thus, supporting job centering may decrease job accessibility for those who need it most. Adding jobs to neighborhoods may increase housing prices and displace existing residents, while adding housing to job centers may be prohibitively expensive. Prioritizing job growth in certain areas may reduce the ability to create "complete communities" that accommodate both work and play. For some types of businesses, such as retail, locating near suburban customers is important, rendering location in job centers impossible. We next review the implementation challenges and costs of these smart growth strategies targeting jobs and neighborhoods.

Jobs and Location

The first challenge is inducing jobs to concentrate, or even just to locate, in particular places. A set of studies by the Brookings Institution and others suggests that this will be challenging because of the steady decentralization of jobs in recent decades (Giuliano, Agarwal, and Redfearn 2008; Glaeser and Kahn 2011; Kneebone 2009). At least until the Great Recession, the share of jobs within a three-mile radius of downtown (or the central business district, CBD) was decreasing; by 2006, just 21 percent worked downtown, while 45 percent worked over 10 miles from downtown (Kneebone 2009, 2013). These "edgeless cities" now have as much office space—one billion square feet nationally—as the downtowns (Lang and Lefurgy 2007). The decrease occurred in almost all industries, though manufacturing, construction, and retail jobs are particularly likely to "sprawl" while high-end services remain centralized (Glaeser and Kahn 2011; Kneebone 2009). Large metropolitan areas—those with at least 500,000 jobs—experience more job decentralization, as do those with higher levels of black-white segregation (Kneebone 2013; Stoll 2005). This job sprawl is related to the suburbanization of poverty, but in general, the poor, as well as African Americans, are not benefiting from job-rich suburbs (Galster 1991; Raphael and Stoll 2010; Stoll 2005).

What the narrative of job sprawl misses is that as jobs decentralize, they often form new centers (Giuliano, Agarwal, and Redfearn 2008; Redfearn 2007). Centers are typically defined as contiguous areas (or block groups) with density greater than 20 jobs per acre that have a total number of jobs over 20,000 ("20-20"), or even 10 jobs per acre and 10,000 jobs ("10-10") (Cervero and Wu 1997; Giuliano, Agarwal, and Redfearn 2008). Rather than dispersing evenly across the landscape in a classic pattern of suburban sprawl, jobs cluster. Clustering provides firms with agglomeration economies, reducing costs of production and/or improving efficiency due to the increased ability to share knowledge, markets, labor, suppliers, and so forth (Gottlieb 1995). The literature thus far suggests that this polycentricity is most likely to occur in larger metros, often following location patterns established historically (Giuliano, Agarwal, and Redfearn 2008; Redfearn 2007, 2009).

Which measure is used is not just a matter of preference, but key for sustainability: if jobs are actually clustering in centers, rather than sprawling evenly across the landscape, then it may be possible to support alternative modes of travel and reduce VMT. Among all the different land use factors, location of jobs downtown will have the greatest ability to reduce VMT (Ewing and Cervero 2010; Salon et al. 2012). In general, greater accessibility to job destinations will reduce travel, either by shortening the length of trips or making transit a viable alternative through job proximity (Ewing and Cervero 2010).[2]

The question, then, is which jobs not only prefer to center, but also attract a disproportionate share of transit riders? It turns out that when transit lines and office buildings collocate, the share of transit commuters increases dramatically (Cervero 2006). But it is not just any kind of office building, but those in high job density areas that house government or knowledge-based industries such as professional services, information, and financial services (Belzer, Srivastava, and Austin 2011).

The San Francisco Bay Area exhibits some of the highest levels of job sprawl in the country, according to Brookings, but also offers an example of polycentricity. Overall, our analysis found that there are 29 job centers at the 10-10 level and eight at the 20-20; these smaller centers are continuing to gain jobs, while the larger ones are losing.[3] Using either the distance from CBD or centering measure, over 60 percent of Bay Area jobs are centralized. But combining the two measures (Figure 4.1) shows that it is not just the jobs close to the CBD that center; two-thirds of the jobs from three to 10 miles of the CBD center, as well as 25 percent of the jobs located from 10 to 35 miles out.

A look at Bay Area job densities for sample sectors (Figures 4.2a–d) illustrates the differences in job centering and sprawl among sectors. Overall, jobs are concentrated in the downtown centers of San Francisco, San Jose, Oakland, Berkeley, and the suburban communities along the I-680 corridor. Professional, scientific, and technical services are even more concentrated in specific neighborhoods. But the illustration transforms into a Jackson Pollock painting with healthcare and social assistance establishments; these are much more dispersed because they collocate with residences. Construction jobs concentrate somewhat more because of the big firms downtown, but also tend to collocate because the firms are often home-based.

Thus, there is considerable evidence that the majority of jobs do cluster, though job densities may still be too low to support transit. But many of these

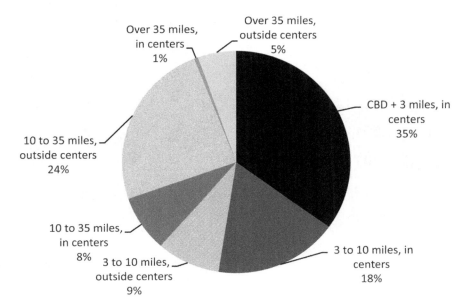

Figure 4.1 Job centering in relation to distance from CBD, San Francisco Bay Area, 2010

Source: Author's calculations

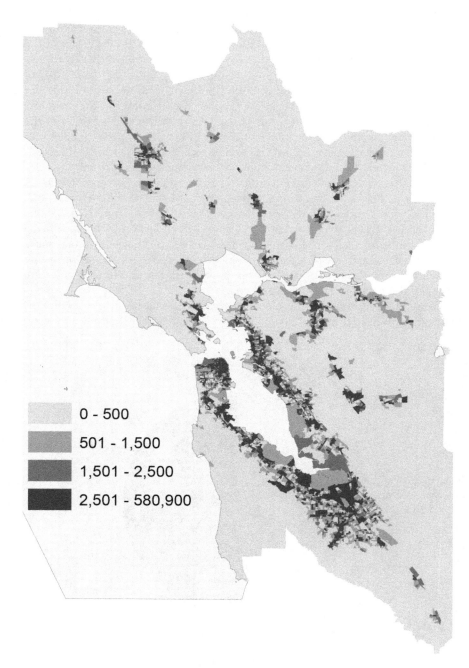

Figure 4.2a Job density in the San Francisco Bay Area, 2010

Source: Author's calculations from Longitudinal Employer-Household Dynamics dataset

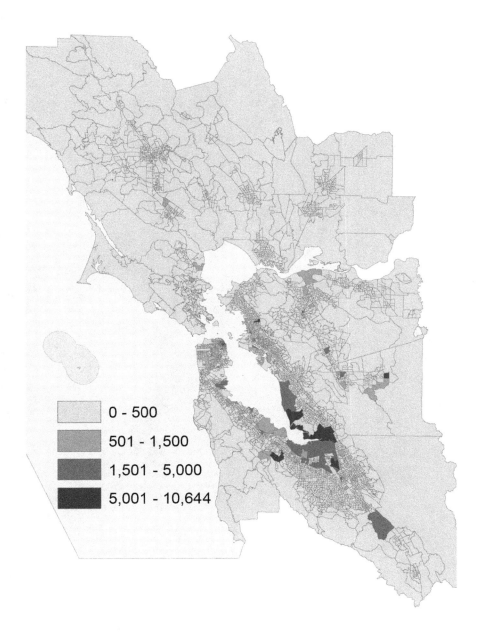

Figure 4.2b Job density: professional, scientific, and technical services, 2010
Source: Author's calculations from Longitudinal Employer-Household Dynamics dataset

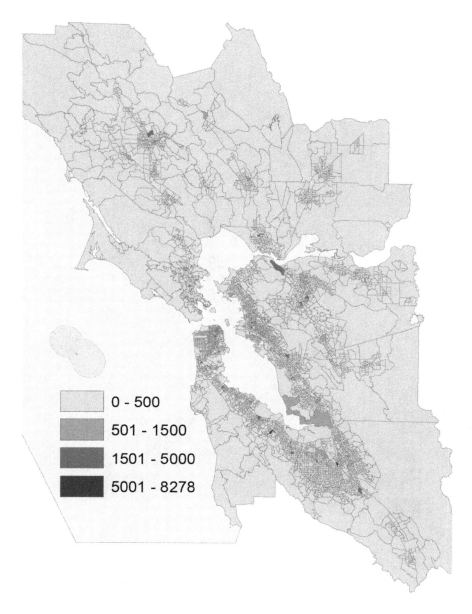

0 - 500

501 - 1500

1501 - 5000

5001 - 8278

Figure 4.2c Job density: healthcare and social assistance, 2010
Source: Author's calculations from Longitudinal Employer-Household Dynamics dataset

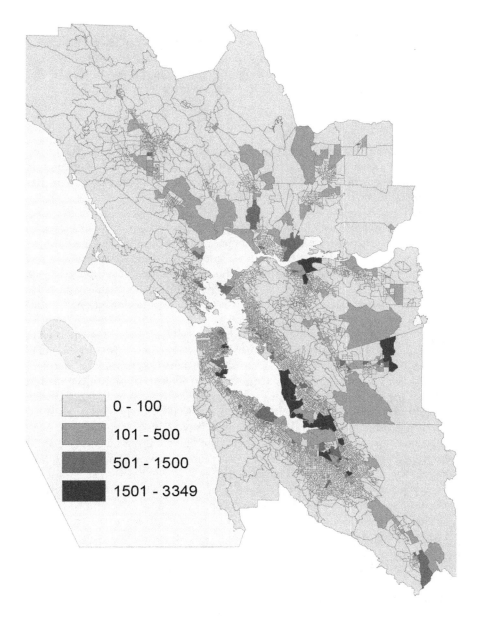

Legend:
0 - 100
101 - 500
501 - 1500
1501 - 3349

Figure 4.2d Job density: construction, 2010

Source: Author's calculations from Longitudinal Employer-Household Dynamics dataset

jobs will be high-wage and high-skill; most of the low-skill jobs in construction, retail, and services tend to locate near residential neighborhoods or in individual homes (i.e., more auto-oriented locations). For instance, in San Diego, rail transit lines and stations provide accessibility to only 20 percent of the city's low-wage jobs (Cervero 2010). Thus, it seems that job centering may promote accessibility mostly for the high-income, and so it is not the answer for equity.

Policies to Support Job Centers

Policies to grow jobs in specific places, especially business incentives, have seen mixed success, as discussed further in Chapter 7. Even if there is some public benefit, such as reduced VMT, from businesses collocating, it is not clear that the benefit is worth the cost of the subsidies.

Further, policies to support the creation of job centers, especially within transit station areas, experience challenges. Many states use redevelopment programs to facilitate the acquisition of land and provide infrastructure finance. Historically, in California and some other states, a dedicated share of the redeveloped space must go to affordable housing. Although many residential projects end up incorporating commercial space, there is no specific requirement, and given challenges with financing and occupying the space, policymakers have been reluctant to mandate job creation as well.

The Bay Area has also benefited from the Metropolitan Transportation Commission setting standards for transit-extension projects. Specifically, MTC requires a minimum threshold for residential density, existing or planned, before approving the extension (Metropolitan Transportation Commission 2005).[4] Originally, the idea was to include job densities as well, but that was gutted from the policy before it was enacted, due to implementation challenges.

Why are there barriers to linking sustainability planning to jobs? One issue is that businesses follow a locational logic based on their products, and even if government attempts to shift that logic with subsidies, it may simply not make sense in the market. Large or chain businesses may also operate at a national or international scale, reducing the sway of local incentives. As Chapter 7 describes, businesses are just not as footloose as commonly thought.

Other barriers specific to transit corridors have to do with the structure of transit funding. New transit systems have to meet cost-effectiveness criteria. As a result, they often end up locating in freight corridors without direct access to job centers. Although the criteria for New Starts funding—the primary federal funding source for transit investments—take potential to leverage joint development into account, there is no analysis of economic development potential beyond the simple availability of land (Federal Transit Administration 2013). To facilitate more job centering, criteria would need to shift focus to job creation potential (which would likely differ with transit type, from heavy rail, to bus rapid transit).

This suggests that it is possible to support some job centering through regional planning, though some sectors will continue to disperse in order to collocate with suburban housing. Then, how important (and feasible) will it be to add housing to these centers?

Jobs–Housing Balance

> For all the implications of "sprawl"—from job loss and economic decline, to alarming obesity, asthma rates and segregation, to the loss of habitat and global warming, to our dangerous dependence on foreign oil—all of them are driven by one fundamental problem: the mismatch between where we live and where we work. Whatever else we do to address these problems, America must find a way to connect housing to jobs. Today, the average household spends more than half of its budget on housing and transport-ation . . . The impact of this mismatch goes straight to our competitiveness as a nation.
>
> (Donovan 2010)

As Secretary Donovan suggests here, the basic premise underlying jobs–housing balance is that by collocating jobs and housing, we allow more people to live near work, reducing driving and commute costs (for both households and governments) and increasing quality of life. Of all the land use approaches available to reduce VMT—including residential density, land use mixing, job centering, and street network connectivity and design—jobs–housing balance is one of the most effective (Cervero and Duncan 2008; Salon et al. 2012). For every 10 percent increase in the number of jobs in the same occupational category within four miles of one's residence, there is a 3 percent decrease in daily work-related VMT—nearly double the impact of nearby retail and service location on shopping VMT (Cervero and Duncan 2008). In particular, jobs–housing balance seems to encourage walking, while diversity of land uses and population and job densities have only a weak effect on travel behavior (Cervero and Duncan 2008; Ewing and Cervero 2010). Moreover, travel to work, particularly outside of the local community, is the main cause of traffic con-gestion (California Planning Roundtable 2008).

But orchestrating working close to home is challenging. Workers change jobs frequently and may not be willing to change residences as well; many, in fact, do not have the choice to move because of affordability constraints. Most households have more than one wage earner, and with the increase in adult children living at home, as many as four or five. Many jobs, such as those in construction, have multiple locations. Even if possible to balance the number of jobs and housing, it will be challenging to match the job skills required to those of local residents. Finally, households typically make their residential location choices based on a number of different factors, such as the quality of schools and neighborhoods, the proximity of friends and family, and so forth.

Because it is a moving target, jobs–housing balance may not work as a definitive goal, though it may effectively indicate the direction to move in (California Planning Roundtable 2008). Even if we cannot build one unit of housing for every 1.5 jobs in a job center, as suggested by the COG in Chapter 1, we can still seek jobs–housing balance within a regional commute shed. A ratio of jobs to employed residents within the commute shed can help shed light on the amount of in- and outcommuting to and from the region, without putting the onus for balance on small individual cities, which have little power to reshape labor markets by inducing locals to work within city boundaries. This then shifts the burden to regional planning to steer transportation investment to commute sheds and specific areas, particularly where new jobs (or housing) are needed for balance. Still, this will not guarantee that the types of jobs locating in centers are appropriate for the skill sets of local residents. Since it is particularly difficult to shape business location (as discussed further in Chapter 7), it may be more feasible for regional agencies to ensure that the housing will be affordable to low-wage workers within the commute shed, as discussed next in the case of San Francisco.

Another complicated and understudied issue is the economics of jobs and housing in close proximity. The fluctuations of the business cycle, particularly pronounced in recent years, mean that the regional economy gains and loses jobs at a rate that is relatively rapid compared to housing (Figure 4.3). To add jobs, businesses can either rearrange their existing space or acquire more spacious quarters. But adding housing units means a slow process of obtaining financing and permits, and then finding a market.[5] Rapid changes in business

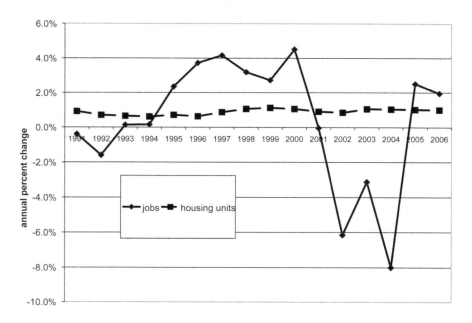

Figure 4.3 Jobs and housing grow at different rates: San Francisco Bay Area, 1991–2006
Source: Author's calculations

space needs, coupled with slow changes in the housing stock, make it hard to create balance: as new job centers arise and disappear, housing will be slow to respond, and changes in the economy can quickly eradicate balance. This is a particular challenge in high-tech regions, since rapid job growth in innovative and/or high-wage sectors can create highly localized spikes in housing prices (Chapple et al. 2004; Kolko 2011).

Finally, there is the issue of how to collocate jobs and housing physically. When there is a balanced distribution of people heading in and out of stations, as in the Tyson's Corner corridor, it is possible to achieve significant VMT reduction benefits (Cervero 2010). These mixed-use corridors have some stations that are dominated by housing and others by jobs, but in total, there is subregional jobs–housing balance along the corridor—horizontal mixed use (a mixture of uses along a street), rather than TOD-level mixed use. This tool for jobs–housing balance may not only be more effective for VMT reduction, but also more viable for developers, who have struggled to build and market mixed-use buildings (as discussed in Chapter 9).

From Theory to Practice

In its Sustainable Communities Strategy, the ABAGs began a new experiment with jobs–housing balance, even naming its approach the Jobs–Housing Connection Strategy. In essence, this approach augmented the region's transportation-land use model by determining the type of housing demand likely to be generated by new jobs in each county, a proxy for the commute shed.

Based on the forecast of job growth in the next 30 years, ABAG determined the number of new residents, the number of households they would form, and their demand for housing. In combination with regional demographic trends, such as the aging of the baby boomers and the continued influx of immigrants with relatively large household sizes, the future of the regional economy shapes local housing demand.

Next, in order to balance this future job growth better with housing demand, ABAG had to determine what type of job growth would occur in which of the region's counties. Unfortunately, job growth in such subregions is very difficult to predict, especially in a long-term time frame: too many factors, from the business cycle, to the availability of real estate, to labor force trends, shape the location of jobs on a micro-scale. However, forecasts of job growth by industry sector and county are relatively robust.

The industry sectors expected to lead job growth in the future are comprised of various occupations that pay a range of wages.[6] The analysis translates the wages paid into household incomes by assuming an average number of workers per household.[7] Because of low wages in growing sectors, particularly retail, transportation, entertainment, hotels, and even construction, it turns out that 72 percent of all households in the future (from 2010 to 2040) will require affordable housing.[8]

Traditionally, in California cities, the fair share housing program (the Regional Housing Needs Assessment (RHNA)) means that suburbs are asked to provide (voluntarily) land zoned appropriately to provide their fair share of regional housing, including affordable units. The jobs–housing connection strategy means a shift in priority to focus on job accessibility. If a county is creating low-wage jobs that require its workers to find affordable housing, then that new housing should be available within that commute shed, within every city in the county. By assigning affordable housing production to low-wage job centers, this strategy gives new workers the opportunity to live nearby their jobs. It also forces counties to deal with the economic consequences of creating mostly low-wage jobs, rather than forcing low-wage workers to look for affordable housing in outlying areas.

By balancing job growth in a commute shed with its related housing demand, ABAG ended up adding the greatest number of new units to the urban core, while outer suburbs still experience the greatest increase in share of affordable housing. This means that the greatest number of affordable housing opportunities remain near jobs, but at the same time the suburbs will continue diversifying. Figure 4.4 maps this distribution of household growth by income category for very low-, low-, and moderate-income groups at the city level. Figure 4.5 shows the 2010–2040 percent growth in these same income categories.

This approach finally incorporates jobs–housing balance—or connection—in regional sustainability planning: the transportation models will have to be adjusted to assume that more low-income households are locating in core areas in transit-accessible locations. Still, fair housing advocates threatened to sue the regional agencies because of the reconcentration of poverty: the argument (discussed further in Chapter 12) is that the ability to live a high quality of life in the suburbs is more important than the accessibility of the urban core.

Yet, the jobs–housing connection approach falls far short of equitable development. It ignores the region's existing residents, who may already have unmet affordable housing and accessibility needs, or might be impacted by future economic shifts. And it fails to account for the possibility that in-migrants may crowd out existing jobseekers and thus lower their wages, creating even more demand for affordable housing (as discussed in the Introduction to Part II).

Planning for Jobs, Sustainability, and Equity—and Life

Both job centering and jobs–housing balance are key goals in regional sustainability planning. Yet, they both raise serious equity issues, mostly because of their potential for raising land prices. The firms that hire low- or medium-skilled workers—trucking firms, grocery stores, nail salons, etc.—need cheap space, and are unlikely to arise in areas with high land costs. At the same time, land costs will make housing prices prohibitively expensive; even job centers in suburban areas tend to attract professional workers to high-priced housing nearby (Cervero and Wu 1998). Thus, job centers may attract new housing and thus help facilitate jobs–housing balance, but in the process, defeat social

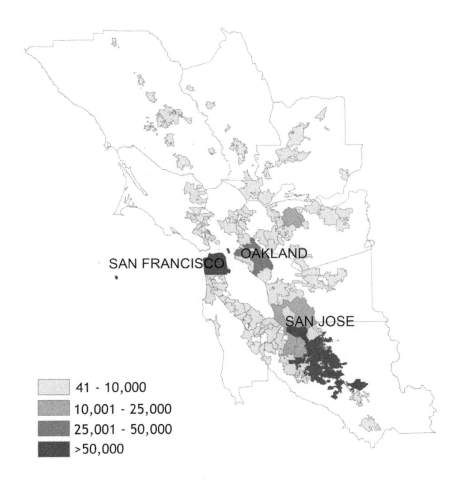

Figure 4.4 Growth in very low-, low-, and moderate-income households, 2010–2040
Source: Author's calculations

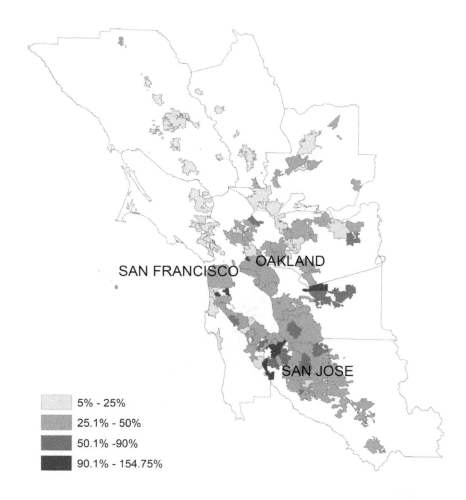

5% - 25%
25.1% - 50%
50.1% -90%
90.1% - 154.75%

Figure 4.5 Percent growth in very low-, low-, and moderate-income households,
2010–2040
Source: Author's calculations

equity goals. At the same time, helping jobs concentrate in residential neighborhoods may destabilize local housing markets and raise prices. These processes are most likely to occur in strong markets, but they may also occur in hot neighborhoods within weak market regions around the world.

One alternative in planning for both job centers and jobs–housing balance is to focus on a larger scale, such as a district (i.e., a group of adjacent neighborhoods, or a small city) or county. For instance, instead of conceptualizing job centers or jobs–housing balance within transit-oriented development, we might spread the footprint of a job center beyond the station area (i.e., to the transit neighborhood or district). Job centers and jobs–housing balance near transit are important sustainability goals, but they do not have to be met adjacent to transit stations. In fact, given that many rail transit systems offer relatively few stops, one way to improve accessibility significantly would be to augment that stop with shuttles and buses that simplify the travel along the "last mile" to the transit stop. While land costs will be high near the station, they will diminish in this zone of influence. This then makes it easier to provide affordable housing, and also to tie transit funding to economic development outcomes such as job creation.

There are logistical and legal issues in shifting from a development to a district scale, as well as coordinating across different agencies that manage land use, rail transit, bus transit, economic development, and so forth. But ultimately, just as in the case of smart growth and income diversity (Chapters 3 and 5), equity goals may be better served by shifting scale. Not only can more families be helped by avoiding high-cost areas, but particularly in the case of jobs and housing, other goals can be met as well: relatively cheap space will make it easier to spur entrepreneurship in home-based businesses, and location further from rail transit stations will likely facilitate access to the elements of complete communities, such as parks and schools. The advent of regional sustainability planning may be the occasion to propel such a shift in focus.

The district is also a more appropriate geographic scale for considering the activity space of life, in particular for alleviating the time poverty of low-income households. The original thinking behind the neighborhood unit was that it would accommodate all of life (except, perhaps, the male head of household's trip downtown to work!). The Ahwahnee Principles, developed by the Local Government Commission in 1991 as the core tenets of New Urbanism, state that: (1) "all planning should be in the form of complete and integrated communities including housing, shops, workplaces, schools, parks and civic facilities essential to the daily life of the residents"; and (2) "community size should be designed so that housing, jobs, daily needs, and other activities are within easy walking distance of each another" (Pivo 2005: 1). The idea of these "complete communities" has been adopted by the movement for healthy land use and communities (Zuk 2013). Complete communities include:

> a quality education, access to good jobs, an affordable roof over our heads, access to affordable healthy food and health services, the ability to enjoy

artistic, spiritual and cultural amenities, access to recreation and parks, meaningful civic engagement, and affordable transportation choices that get us where we need to go ... Complete communities are inclusive, measured by how residents and workers benefit and not necessarily the shape or form they take, and may likely require other supportive assets.

(Brooks et al. 2012: 3)

To be so complete and inclusive, a community may be best off extending beyond neighborhood boundaries. A community that is a city as well will benefit from municipal administrative powers. As described more in the next chapter, planning at the district scale also permits diverse communities to access the same resources, while still maintaining the enclaves that provide social support to unique groups.

All of these aspects of life, and how they are used by locals, can be measured and incorporated into sustainability planning. But in practice, most transportation models are only just beginning to link transport investment to activity patterns, and thus are not yet at the point of considering what helps low-income communities thrive.

Notes

1. SCAG (2007) indicates that work trip patterns essentially determine transportation investment decisions.
2. Note, however, that there is still considerable debate about whether job centering in peripheral areas will lengthen commutes (the position of Cervero and Wu 1998) or decrease them (Gordon, Richardson, and Jun 1991).
3. Our analysis of Longitudinal Employment Dynamics data found that, in 2002, there were 26 10-10 centers with 44 percent of the jobs and 11 20-20 centers with 22 percent. By 2010, there were 29 10-10s with 41 percent and eight 20-20s with 20 percent.
4. Betty Deakin (personal communication) suggests these densities are too low to support sufficient levels of transit ridership.
5. Households in strong markets such as the California coastal regions have adjusted to space constraints by rearranging their existing space (i.e., putting more people in every unit), and residential vacancy rates are very low. Consequently, population growth has continued in spite of slow housing growth.
6. The model uses a multi-step process that translates industry sector-level employment forecasts by county (in turn, based on national forecasts) (see Levy 2012) into estimated growth in households in four income groups: very low (less than 50 percent of median county household incomes), low income (50–80 percent), moderate income (80–120 percent), and above moderate income (greater than 120 percent). It links ABAG's sector-level employment forecasts with occupational characteristics: sectors are translated into industries (at the three-digit NAICS level), which are then linked to occupations (at the three-digit SOC level) and then median wages.
7. Disclosure: conducted by the author.
8. Note that this 2040 analysis complements the affordable housing analysis done by the region for RHNA; RHNA only extends to 2022, but the Sustainable Communities Strategy had to look at housing needs until 2040.
   Based on this analysis, up to 72 percent of new households may fall into the very low-, low-, and moderate-income categories, all of which qualify for affordable housing

today. Together, very low- and low-income households could represent up to 57 percent of new household growth. Of course, this is assuming that only wage and salary income, rather than all forms of income, is available to spend on housing.

By comparison, only 58 percent of households today fall into the very low-, low-, and moderate-income groups. Although this may suggest that there is a heightened need for affordable housing in the future, several caveats must be kept in mind. First, the income of existing households appears relatively higher because ACS data include all sources of income, not just wage and salary income. Second, the universe of existing households includes a wide range of households, not just worker households, including those suffering from unemployment or underemployment, empty-nester or retiree households, and so forth.

References

Belzer, Dena, Sujata Srivastava, and Mason Austin. *Transit and Regional Economic Development*. Berkeley, CA: Center for Transit-Oriented Development, 2011.

Brooks, Allison, Gloria Ohland, Abby Thorne-Lyman, and Elizabeth Wampler. *Are We There Yet? Creating Complete Communities for 21st Century America*. Oakland, CA: Reconnecting America, 2012.

California Planning Roundtable. *Deconstructing Jobs–Housing Balance*. Sausalito, CA: California Planning Roundtable, 2008. Accessed June 3, 2013. www.cproundtable. org/media/uploads/pub_files/CPR-Jobs-Housing.pdf.

Cervero, Robert. "Office Development, Rail Transit, and Commuting Choices." *Journal of Public Transportation* 9, no. 5 (2006): 41–55.

Cervero, Robert. "Destinations Matter." Presented at TOD and Social Equity Conference, Center for Community Innovation, Berkeley, California, June 1, 2010. Accessed July 5, 2013. http://communityinnovation.berkeley.edu/presentations/Cervero_Destinations_ Matter.pdf.

Cervero, Robert and Michael Duncan. "Which Reduces Vehicle Travel More: Jobs–Housing Balance or Retail-Housing Mixing?" *JAPA* 72, no. 4 (2008): 475–490.

Cervero, Robert and Kang-Li Wu. "Polycentrism, Commuting, and Residential Location in the San Francisco Bay Area." *Environment and Planning* 29 (1997): 865–886.

Cervero, Robert and Kang-Li Wu. "Sub-Centering and Commuting: Evidence from the San Francisco Area, 1980–90." *Urban Studies* 36, no. 7 (1998): 1059–1076.

Chapple, Karen, John V. Thomas, Dena Belzer, and Gerald Autler. "Fueling the Fire: Information Technology and Housing Price Appreciation in the San Francisco Bay Area and the Twin Cities." *Housing Policy Debate* 15, no. 2 (2004): 347–383.

Donovan, Shaun. "Prepared Remarks for Secretary of Housing and Urban Development Shaun Donovan." Remarks presented at the 9th Annual New Partners for Smart Growth: Building Safe, Healthy and Livable Communities Conference, Seattle, Washington, February 4, 2010. Accessed January 12, 2013. http://portal.hud.gov/hudportal/ HUD?src=/press/speeches_remarks_statements/2010/Speech_02042010.

Ewing, Reid and Robert Cervero. "Travel and the Built Environment: A Meta-Analysis." *Journal of the American Planning Association* 76, no. 3 (2010): 265–294.

Federal Transit Administration. *Capital Investment Program FY 2013 Annual Report Evaluation and Rating Process*. San Francisco, CA: Federal Transit Administration, 2013.

Galster, George C. "Black Suburbanization: Has it Changed the Relative Location of Races?" *Urban Affairs Review* 26, no. 4 (1991): 621–628.

Giuliano, Genevieve, Ajay Agarwal, and Christian Redfearn. *Metropolitan Spatial Trends in Employment and Housing*. Los Angeles, CA: University of Southern California, 2008.

Glaeser, Edward L. and Matthew E. Kahn. "Decentralized Employment and the Transformation of the American City." *Brookings-Wharton Papers on Urban Affairs* 2 (2011): 1–63.

Gordon, Peter, Harry W. Richardson, and Myung-Jin Jun. "The Commuting Paradox Evidence from the Top Twenty." *Journal of the American Planning Association* 57, no. 4 (1991): 416–420.

Gottlieb, Paul D. "Residential Amenities, Firm Location and Economic Development." *Urban Studies* 32, no. 9 (1995): 1413–1436.

Kneebone, Elizabeth. *Job Sprawl Revisited: The Changing Geography of Metropolitan Employment*. Washington, DC: Brookings Institution Press, 2009.

Kneebone, Elizabeth. *Job Sprawl Stalls: The Great Recession and Metropolitan Employment Location*. Washington, DC: Brookings Institution Press, 2013.

Kolko, Jed. "Job Location, Neighborhood Change, and Gentrification." San Francisco, CA: Public Policy Institute of California Working Paper, 2009.

Lang, Robert E. and Jennifer B. Lefurgy. *Boomburbs: The Rise of America's Accidental Cities*. Washington, DC: Brookings Institution Press, 2007.

Levy, Stephen. *Bay Area Job Growth to 2040: Projections and Analysis*. Palo Alto, CA: Center for the Continuing Study of the California Economy, 2012.

Lucas, Karen. "Transport and Social Exclusion: Where Are We Now?" *Transport Policy* 20 (2012): 105–113.

McGuckin, Nancy. *Analysis of Future Issues and Changing Demands on the System. Part A. Demographic Changes: Impacts on Passenger Travel. Commission Briefing Paper 4A-02: Implications of an Aging Population on Passenger Travel Demand for Different Modes*. Washington, DC: National Surface Transportation Policy and Revenue Study Commission, 2007.

Metropolitan Transportation Commission. *MTC Resolution 3434 Transit-Oriented Development (TOD) Policy for Regional Transit Expansion Projects*. Oakland, CA: Metropolitan Transportation Commission, 2005.

Pivo, Gary. *Creating Compact and Complete Communities: Seven Propositions for Success*. Practicing Planner Case Study. Chicago, IL: American Institute of Certified Planners, 2005.

Raphael, Steven and Michael A. Stoll. *Job Sprawl and the Suburbanization of Poverty*. Washington, DC: Brookings Institution Press, 2010.

Redfearn, Christian L. "The Topography of Metropolitan Employment: Identifying Centers of Employment in a Polycentric Urban Area." *Journal of Urban Economics* 61, no. 3 (2007): 519–541.

Redfearn, Christian L. "Persistence in Urban Form: The Long-Run Durability of Employment Centers in Metropolitan Areas." *Regional Science and Urban Economics* 39, no. 2 (2009): 224–232.

Salon, Deborah, Marlon Boarnet, Susan Handy, Steven Spears, and Gil Tal. "How Do Local Actions Affect VMT? A Critical Review of the Empirical Evidence." *Transportation Research Part D* 17 (2012): 495–508.

Southern California Association of Governments. *The State of the Region 2007*. Los Angeles, CA: SCAG, 2007.

Stoll, Michael A. *Job Sprawl and the Spatial Mismatch Between Blacks and Jobs*. Washington, DC: Brookings Institution Press, 2005.

Zuk, Miriam. "Health Equity in a New Urbanist Environment: Land Use Planning and Community Capacity Building in Fresno, CA." Ph.D. Dissertation, University of California, Berkeley, 2013.

5   The Challenge of Developing and Sustaining Mixed-Income Neighborhoods

The conference was at the San Francisco Federal Reserve Bank; the questioner, the chief financial officer of a large Midwestern community development financial intermediary. "Karen, what is the right mix in mixed income?" I stared at her, trying in my head to parse a two-hour lecture into a sentence that would be meaningful for her. She explained, "We are trying to develop some guidelines to help us decide what to fund."

There were so many problems with the formulation of this question that it was hard to know where to start. She funds housing developments, but the success of a mix in a particular building will depend, in part, on the mix in the surrounding neighborhood, so it is important to consider multiple scales. And in some contexts, such as redevelopment areas, she might have tools to reshape mix in a bigger area, too. But in any case, we do not have a good understanding of the most effective scale at which to achieve a particular impact: for instance, are the "bridging" or weak ties, the connections that are most effective at helping access to the labor market, best found next door or at the local park?

The "right" mix could depend on any of a number of factors: most importantly, the amount of money available to build affordable housing, but also the strength of the regional housing market, the income diversity of the city, the size and layout of the site, and the stability of the neighborhood. But what makes the question so challenging is that even though we know that economic segregation has pernicious effects—and is growing throughout the world—we have not figured out how to promote and sustain income diversity effectively. And even if we had, it is a moving target: income categories are not set in stone, but change with the life cycle of families and the business cycle. With retirement, affluence can turn into just getting by, and at the economy's peak, households in poverty turn into the working class. Most importantly, as described in the Introduction to Part I, national trends in income inequality dominate local patterns of segregation (Reardon and Bischoff 2011; Watson 2009).

Why Integrate Neighborhoods?

The interest in promoting income-diverse neighborhoods comes from the notion, advanced originally by Jane Jacobs (1961), that a mixture of household types, tenures, and incomes is vital to neighborhood character. Such an income mix can also serve to break up or prevent concentrations of poverty that are viewed as generators of neighborhood decline (Jencks and Mayer 1990).

In the United States, income segregation is highly correlated with racial/ethnic segregation. Thus, diversifying by income can break up racial concentrations as well. Residential racial segregation has its own impacts: it weakens educational attainment and earnings, hurts residents' health, and, ultimately, stifles local housing values (Carr and Kutty 2008). Segregation also contributes to poverty in more indirect ways: the depletion of financial, information, and human resources hinders the development of human capital and the transmission of information about job opportunities, and increases discriminatory barriers as well (Galster 1996). These effects, in turn, have adverse societal impacts, including lowering property tax revenues, creating fiscal stress, and reducing service quality (Turner and Rawlings 2009).

Good social services, especially education and safety, are easier to provide in communities with more fiscal capacity to pay for such services (Dreier, Mollenkopf, and Swanstrom 2004). Everyone in the community benefits from better services: low-income families gain, just as middle-class families, from reductions in crime rates, and their children benefit from access to higher-quality education (Varady and Walker 2003). Were segregation to decrease, so would the poverty rate, the high school dropout rate, the unemployment rate, and the homicide rate (Cutler and Glaeser 1997; Galster 1991; Galster and Keeney 1988; Peterson and Krivo 1993). The more racially diverse a neighborhood, the less prejudice its residents feel (Ihlanfeldt and Scafidi 2002). Perhaps the best-established benefit of diversity is in schools, where racial diversity helps minorities learn how to function and compete in majority-white environments (Crain and Wells 1994).

Integration and Regional Sustainability Planning

The issue of how to integrate communities most effectively is critical for planning sustainable regions for several reasons. Integration shapes the accessibility of economic opportunity, albeit in complicated ways, as discussed further in Part III. Mixing incomes in a community with transit may also reduce greenhouse gas emissions—the more affluent the household, the more VMT, so it may be possible to diversify neighborhoods in a way that reduces travel.[1] There are also political considerations at play, since the diversity of communities affects how they vote. In particular, to the extent that the affluent concentrate away from the poor, they may be able and inclined to form a power bloc, which could thwart sustainability efforts.

As Peter Marcuse has pointed out, when advocating for deconcentration of existing segregated neighborhoods, we need to distinguish between the ghetto and the enclave (Marcuse 1997). The spatial cluster that forms the ghetto is a community in which society segregates residents involuntarily in a process of exclusion—not by force, but by a variety of regulations and programs (e.g., zoning, redlining, the location of public housing and infrastructure) that work in concert with the market. In contrast, the enclave is a spatial cluster where residents choose to congregate in order to achieve economic goals (such as Chinatown) or social cohesion (such as Hasidic Williamsburg, Brooklyn).[2] The urban enclave may strengthen social groups or subcultures and more effectively provide the resources to prosper than an integrated neighborhood does (Fischer and Merton 1984).

When we support integration, we often confuse the end with the means. Even if diversity is an important goal among urban planners, it is equality that matters from a civil rights perspective. If the enclave supports equality, policy should facilitate it.

Another consideration is the new hypersegregation of the affluent, often in fortified areas (gated communities)—a third type of spatial cluster that Marcuse calls the citadel. The rich are considerably more segregated from the non-rich than the poor are from the non-poor, many in neighborhoods that are mostly white (Denton 2010; Massey 1996; Reardon and Bischoff 2011). The segregation of the affluent is most pronounced in regions with extensive suburbanization; in contrast, the more concentrated the rich in the urban core, the greater the level of integration with the poor (Dwyer 2010).

Finally, it is important to consider how ongoing demographic change has reshaped segregation, given the increasing diversity of the population. As immigrants (the foreign-born and their children) will comprise 30 percent of the population by 2040, they will increasingly locate not just in gateway communities, but a variety of places, from the urban core, to suburbs (Denton 2010). The new diversity of the population is already being felt across a variety of metropolitan areas and their neighborhoods, reducing segregation in all but the most isolated pockets. In many cases, neighborhoods may already feel integrated, despite the racially concentrated poverty areas elsewhere. This then may reduce popular support for deliberate integration initiatives.

All these points raise the question of how aggressively to pursue integration, at what scale, and where. As Nancy Denton (2010: 31) points out, "'perfect evenness' is an ideal, not a policy." Given how enclaves may function as an incubator for the upward mobility of the disadvantaged, integration efforts will need not to destroy them (as sometimes occurs, for instance, with the widespread demolition of public housing) (Goetz 2013). The desirability of preserving enclaves—and infiltrating citadels—also suggests the possibility that low-income homogeneous neighborhoods (i.e., racially concentrated areas of poverty) may not be the right target for policy. In *The Just City* (2010: 68), Susan Fainstein argues (based on the ideas of Iris Marion Young) that rather than pursue an even distribution of the population across neighborhoods, it may be more just to preserve homogeneous areas but work to ensure that they have "porous boundaries," so that they do not function as isolated ghettos.

But before considering alternative approaches, what do we know about the function of mixed-income developments and neighborhoods?

How Mixed-Income Developments Work

There is no specific formula that is used for mixed-income developments (Levy, McDade, and Bertumen 2013). In practice, mixed-income properties have typically combined market-rate, affordable housing, and traditional public housing with the exact mix depending on the funding source (typically, inclusionary zoning, Low Income Housing Tax Credits (LIHTC), or Housing Opportunities for People Everywhere (HOPE VI)) (Joseph and Gress 2013). In inclusionary programs, the majority of units will be market rate, in order to subsidize the affordable units; commonly employed ratios of market rate to affordable housing are 80/20 or 85/15. The proportions are typically reversed in development subsidized via federal housing programs, with only a small share of units at market rate. Either way, it would be a stretch to describe mixed-income developments as income diverse.

Despite the lack of precision about what diversity is, policymakers do expect certain outcomes from mixing income groups in a development and its surrounding neighborhood. The standard for evaluating the success of mixed-income development comes from a classic article by Joseph, Chaskin, and Webber (2007) that described four potential positive impacts: improved social networks, social control, individual behavior, and political power. Most of the studies have looked at HOPE VI or similar mixed-income developments, where a redeveloped project houses both oldtimers—the original low-income residents—and newcomers—typically new renters or owners of moderate or high income.

Social Interaction and Networks

In theory, living in the same development (or neighborhood) as people from other income groups should improve the chances of making "bridging" or "weak" ties, or the acquaintances from other walks of life who lead most effectively to job opportunities (discussed further in Chapter 11). Though evidence is still accumulating, it seems that in the new developments social interaction is rare and low-income residents have realized few social and economic benefits (Joseph, Chaskin, and Webber 2007). The reluctance to connect seems to come from both the low-income oldtimers and higher-income newcomers: the oldtimers maintain their connections with their former neighbors instead of reaching out to the new, and the newcomers resist interaction out of mistrust for their new neighbors (Briggs 1998; Tach 2009). Where interaction does occur, it is between individuals who share characteristics: they both have children, or are homeowners, or are long-term community residents (Chaskin and Joseph 2010, 2011; Kleit 2005; Pattillo 2008; Tach 2009, 2010). Over an extended period of time, some may form connections, but it is just as likely that less interaction will occur, especially if the lower-income residents feel stigmatized or excluded because of how management enforces social control (Chaskin and Joseph 2010; Graves 2010; Pattillo 2008; Tach 2009, 2011).

Social Control

It is possible that the level of formal and informal social control increases in mixed-income developments. Formal social control might take the form of an organization meant to maintain community cohesion, such as a neighborhood watch group; informal social controls mean the willingness of neighbors to intervene in public conflicts. Although residents of mixed-income developments report improved social control, some experience it as surveillance and harassment (McCormick, Joseph, and Chaskin 2012). In general, the evidence is mixed about whether trust and community cooperation will increase with diversity (Tach, Pendall, and Derian 2014). Sociologist Laura Tach (2009) points out that residents have different neighborhood interpretive frames, and their preconceptions about a place (negative in the case of higher-income newcomers, more positive for oldtimers) may shape their responses to the neighborhood.

Individual Behavior

One of the most cherished hopes for mixed-income developments is that they will alter the behavior of low-income residents, especially those trapped in a "culture of poverty" (Lewis 1966; Wilson 1987). If the new higher-income residents are going to work or attending school regularly, and have stable family situations, they might be able to act as role models for youth without such examples.[3] There is, however, little evidence that this is occurring in mixed-income developments, in part because of the lack of social interaction and community cohesion (Chaskin and Joseph 2010, 2011). In fact, the proximity to upper-income neighbors may actually have a detrimental effect on low-income residents, increasing stress and decreasing psychological well-being (Tach, Pendall, and Derian 2014; Wilkinson and Pickett 2014).

Political Power

As higher-income residents move into a mixed-income development, it is possible that the area will gain higher-quality amenities. To the extent that higher-income residents have political clout, the neighborhood may see new resources and services from local government. And indeed, the experience in mixed-income communities to date has shown that residents, particularly those of low income, are happy with the physical quality of units and improvements in the neighborhood (Chaskin and Joseph 2010; HUD 2013; Popkin et al. 2004). However, residents of different income groups vary in preference for amenities and services, and the new one-size-fits-all facilities and services, as well as new retail stores, may not serve the low-income residents well (Freeman 2006; Graves 2010; Tach 2011).

The inability to meet these goals suggests that we either need to invest much more in design and management practices in mixed-income developments (as suggested by Joseph and Gress 2013), or we need to look elsewhere for policy mechanisms in support of diversity. Perhaps it would be more effective to focus on fostering diversity at higher scales, while letting individual developments remain low-income (Vale 2006).

Scaling up Diversity: Districts and Jurisdictions

The focus of policy to date has been on mixed-income development, while that of research has been on income-diverse neighborhoods. Thus, there is little written on fostering diversity at larger scales, such as the district (an agglomeration of neighborhoods, such as a school district) or jurisdiction (but see Tach, Pendall, and Derian 2014). Yet, given the inexorable increases in neighborhood income segregation, as well as the challenges of developing a policy that breaks up ghettos and citadels yet supports enclaves, focusing on a larger scale may be more effective. And indeed, there is some evidence at least for racial/ethnic segregation that the distribution of population (African Americans and whites) across a metropolis' subregions impacts segregation at the neighborhood level (Lee et al. 2008).

Researchers have not yet examined whether integration at the district or jurisdiction level can meet some of the goals of income mixing. What seems likely is that large-scale integration might improve both accessibility to higher-quality goods and services, and individual well-being and social networks. Although it is important that retail stores, parks, and social agencies be close by, they need not be across the street or even within neighborhood boundaries, à la Clarence Perry. What is most important is that there are enough higher-income residents nearby that the market and government respond by providing higher-quality goods and service levels. This becomes even more salient at the level of the jurisdiction (or school district). Since local governments receive tax revenues and control how they are spent and space is regulated, their decisions can impact quality of life and access to opportunity in a way that does not occur at the neighborhood level. The place level is where political coalitions protect existing property owners and exclude certain interests from having a say in the distribution of resources (Lichter, Parisi, and Taquino 2012).

Income integration at the district level may also be a more effective way to help people thrive. Specifically, research suggests that both poor and rich people are happier when they live in an affluent neighborhood—but in a poor region (for reasons having to do with the importance of relative happiness): "it appears that individuals are happier when they live among the poor, as long as the poor do not live too close" (Firebaugh and Schroeder 2009: 805). Similarly, someone living next door may not be the right connection to bridge into the labor market, given the dynamics of resentment and stigma at play in some mixed-income developments and neighborhoods. But it will be easier to access that weak tie from an individual project if the larger area is integrated.

Thus, though there may be an optimal scale, there is no optimal mix: the appropriate mix depends on the goal of mixing, whether it is improved accessibility (i.e., social interaction and political power) or quality of life (specifically, social control and individual behavior). It also depends on the surrounding context, whether the surrounding region is replete with resources or also poor. And the optimal mix depends also on how a resident experiences the mixture, which, in turn, will depend on his or her particular interpretive frame (Tach 2009). If the appropriate mix is so relative, contextual, and changeable, then it presents a serious challenge to shape it through policy or even good management.

Toward Integration: Alternatives to Mixed-Income Development

My questioner from the community development bank was working on financing mixed-income housing developments. She did so by patching together funding from myriad sources, relying heavily on LIHTCs from the federal government. These developments tend to concentrate in cities, but are less likely to locate in concentrated poverty neighborhoods than traditional public housing was (see Appendix). At HUD, the other major policy approach to mixing incomes has been the HOPE VI program, which redevelops public housing projects as new mixed-income developments. Most of the negative reviews of income mixing come from experiences in these two programs. When mixed-income development house greater numbers of low-income residents, the potential for stigma is greater: management rules may target behavior particular to the low-income (such as hanging out on stoops), and neighborhood police presence may lead to harassment (Graves 2010).

Yet, not only will the poor thrive more when surrounded by the non-poor, but also the segregation of the affluent is growing most rapidly—and may be the better policy target. Might we do better by focusing on integrating suburbs and low-poverty neighborhoods? Or, given that there is more integration in metropolitan areas where the affluent are concentrated and centralized, would it be more effective to focus efforts in the core? Or, should we abandon the idea of creating income-diverse neighborhoods, allowing enclaves, ghettos, and citadels to emerge—but providing social seams that can serve as porous boundaries between neighborhoods? The following looks at each possibility in turn.

Mixing Up the Suburbs: Fair Share Housing and Inclusionary Zoning

Regional fair share housing strategies attempt to integrate communities by shifting more affordable housing provision to the outer suburbs (Bollens 2003; Listokin 1976). Typically, the approach relies on a formula for assigning affordable housing obligations to regional sub-areas, most frequently individual municipalities within a single metropolitan area. The "fair share" formulae can take different forms, pinning the obligation to either the lack of low-cost housing currently, or the future need based on population and job growth.[4]

In the early 1970s, shortly after passage of the Fair Housing Act, the U.S. Department of Housing and Urban Development supported the creation of fair share strategies in metro areas around the country. Regional authorities in a number of areas created programs aimed at producing a more equitable distribution of subsidized housing between cities and their suburban satellites. These efforts, and HUD's interest in supporting them, were short-lived. They were designed at a time of greater federal subsidies for affordable housing, and without that support, quickly lost their potency as a tool. Further, the lack of political appetite for subsidized housing in the suburbs has been an insurmountable obstacle to implementation of fair share schemes (Basolo and Hastings 2003; Goetz 2003).[5]

One of the few programs to endure was the court-ordered effort in New Jersey. A product of the 1975 Mt. Laurel I and 1983 Mt. Laurel II rulings, the State of New Jersey produced a system of regional fair share housing that imposes an affirmative obligation on communities within urban regions to create affordable housing. Over 40,000 units of housing have been subsidized to date (Massey et al. 2013). However, an early study showed that an escape clause long allowed municipalities to pay other cities to build their affordable units, with the result that a disproportionate share of these units is concentrated in lower-income cities. Most units built in the suburban areas of metro regions are occupied by families who already lived in the suburbs. Only 6.8 percent of units are occupied by African-American families who moved out of a central city and into a suburb (Wish and Eisdorfer 1997).

Despite these shortcomings, the states with fair share housing legislation have experienced much greater success at integrating the suburbs. A study I did comparing the San Francisco Bay Area with the Philadelphia region is

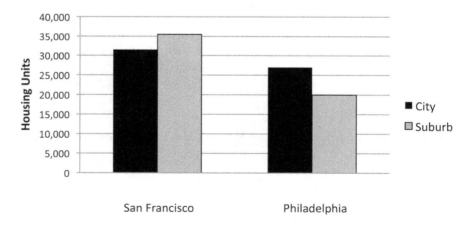

Figure 5.1 Affordable housing production in city versus suburb, San Francisco and Philadelphia

Source: Author's calculations

instructive. California has a Regional Housing Needs Assessment process, which, though lacking any real carrots or sticks to increase affordable housing production, at least asks municipalities to provide space for higher-density housing in their general plans (with the power to delay certification of the general plan, and thus related funding, if goals are not met) (Calavita, Grimes, and Mallach 1997). Pennsylvania has no program, although, of course, builders receiving federal funding are subject to criteria that often favor low-poverty locations. Overall, the geography of production has diverged widely between the two regions (see Figure 5.1). Why?

In San Francisco, entrepreneurial officials in many suburban municipalities aggressively pursued affordable housing. They were met by a network of nonprofit housing developers eager to build, using a combination of federal housing funds, state bond funding, and, most importantly, local redevelopment money. As one urban nonprofit developer told me:

> We made a strategic decision to start working in Contra Costa in the mid-'90s. Contra Costa County was starting to put more money into CDBG [Community Development Block Grants] and redevelopment. At the time, projects out there were a requirement for our organizational survival [because of the increasing cost of urban infill sites].

When affordable housing is built, it is due to expertise and capacity at multiple levels of government and throughout the regional affordable housing industry.

In the Philadelphia metro area, housing is mostly built through serendipity—a combination of land availability, zoning appropriateness, and relationships between cities and nonprofits. Ironically, one criterion for siting—LIHTC scoring systems—weights access to services and transit so highly that it is difficult to build in other areas that may be appropriate for, or in need of, affordable housing.[6] But without the push from multiple levels of government—and in the face of persistent and ubiquitous local opposition to family housing—there will never be any significant effort to build affordable housing in the region. Developers resist the idea of building a new market where there is community resistance: said one, "They [the Zoning Board] are essentially a panel of neighbors that decide what they want and no affordable housing developer can afford a five-year zoning battle."

Figures 5.2 and 5.3 show the results: recent federally subsidized affordable housing concentrated more in suburbs than cities in the Bay Area, but in older central cities (Philadelphia, Chester, Camden) in the Philadelphia region.

The development process depends heavily on relationships between cities and nonprofits, and thus a culture of affordable housing construction gets embedded in certain places and not in others. In California, the best case redevelopment set-asides have meant some dispersal of affordable housing throughout the region, but some suburbs remain slow to build. Ironically, more

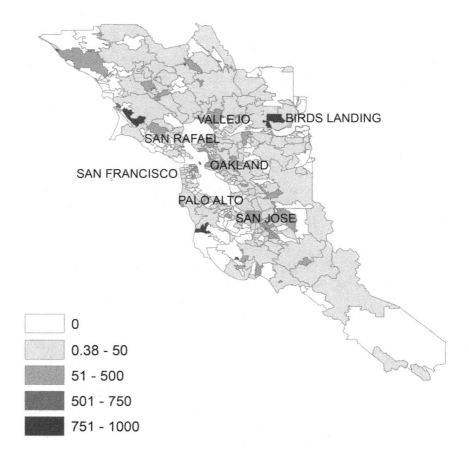

Figure 5.2 LIHTC and Section 8 housing units by zip code in the San Francisco Bay
        Area, 2008

Source: Author's calculations

units have become affordable just through age and depreciation than through
one of the strongest fair share laws in the country, suggesting the potential for
a strategy that focuses on the preservation of affordability.[7]

Would inclusionary zoning (IZ) be more effective in integrating the suburbs?
First enacted in the 1970s, inclusionary zoning requires or encourages developers
to provide a certain proportion of affordable housing units within the new
development or at another site (or in some cases, pay a fee in lieu). There were
some 500 inclusionary policies across the country in 2007 (the majority
mandatory), located in 17 states plus the District of Columbia, and almost all
survived the economic downturn (Calavita and Mallach 2010; Hickey 2013).
Notable successes in inclusionary zoning, at least in volume, have occurred in

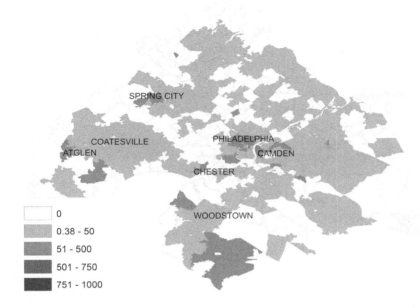

Figure 5.3 LIHTC and Section 8 housing units by zip code in the Philadelphia
metropolitan area

Source: Author's calculations

Montgomery County, Maryland; Fairfax County, Virginia; New York City; and
Chicago (HUD 2013; Center for Transit-Oriented Development 2013).

IZ programs have experienced remarkable success in dispersing units across
jurisdictions, with a large majority in low-poverty neighborhoods—and have
helped children attend schools with better performance than other parts of the
city (Schwartz et al. 2012). Mandatory programs—some still offering compensation for developers such as density bonuses or expedited approval—are
typically more effective than voluntary, and more units will be built if the local
housing market is strong. On the downside, IZ units may not be permanently
affordable, and because they usually cater to homeowners, may not serve the
more disadvantaged population (ibid.). Further, in order to provide the units,
developers may raise the price of market-rate units.

However, most IZ programs are enacted at the level of the individual
municipality, which means that it is not an effective tool to integrate the suburbs
if they are unwilling to participate. One exception at the subregional (county)
level is Montgomery County's Moderately Priced Dwelling Unit Ordinance,
which mandates that 15 percent of the units in new subdivisions be affordable,
and further makes one-third of these available for purchase by the county's public
housing authority. Unlike fair share housing programs, the Montgomery County

ordinance is widely considered successful, though small-scale (with just 13,000 units built) (Montgomery County Department of Housing and Community Affairs n.d.).

But most programs are much smaller. Calavita and Mallach (2010) estimate that IZ may have resulted in the production of up to 150,000 affordable units, mostly concentrated in three states and the Washington, DC metropolitan area; they point out that the policy is more accepted in other countries. Over the 40 years of the policy's existence, this comes to almost 4,000 units per year across the United States. In comparison, the Bay Area alone needs to produce about 17,000 affordable housing units per year to keep pace with new growth. If IZ is to have an impact, it would need to increase in scale at least 100-fold, which would require more systematic implementation. Although it may be the optimal tool to facilitate income diversity in a high-income neighborhood, it can only serve as a small part of a larger strategy. In any case, the experience with fair share housing is instructive: it will be more effective to combine local IZ action with a state mandate and federal funding.

Integrating the Core

Though integrating suburbs and low-poverty areas may, in some ways, be optimal, it is probably the most challenging approach politically. This is not least because as metropolitan regions evolve, they tend to exhibit the most integration when the affluent are concentrated in the core. So, targeting cities may be less of an uphill battle—while also meeting sustainability goals— although there may be severe economic constraints because of high land prices. To create and maintain income diversity in cities, policymakers will need different options depending on whether they are working in strong or weak markets. To illustrate the different goals and tools needed in different places, we look here first at value capture in San Francisco, to help make it possible for the low-income to stay, and then at market-rate development in Richmond, to make concentrated poverty areas more diverse.

Value Capture in San Francisco

Development—whether new buildings, transit stations, or redeveloped parcels—brings new value to an area, conferring new locational advantage. If public investment is involved, the increase in value is essentially a windfall for property owners. Thus, the public sector might consider "capturing" or recovering that private value through a tax or other mechanism. This capital then might be used to fund (or issue bonds for) the public investment or other public benefits. Value capture strategies are typically most successful in areas with strong real estate markets, a clear increase in property values, and an engaged private sector (Center for Transit-Oriented Development 2013).

One early example of linking transportation investment to development is the development of streetcar systems, which leveraged the new accessibility they created to tap into a new financial source. A very common type of value capture is used in redevelopment when it relies on tax increment finance (TIF), which recaptures the incremental increase in property tax that results from new development, using the expectation of this future revenue to issue bonds and finance the development. Alternatively, the city might enact special assessment districts, which assess property owners within a designated district approved by a simple majority vote. Assessment districts have been used for areas around new transit lines in Portland, Seattle, Tampa, Los Angeles, Virginia, and Washington, DC, with more planned (Center for Transit-Oriented Development 2008). However, because assessments are based on benefits landowners will receive from the district, the funds must generally be used to fund public improvements such as parks or street lighting, rather than affordable housing, making them less appropriate as a tool for preserving income diversity in a district. Unlike the other mechanisms, these districts do not depend on new real estate development. They also can work at the jurisdiction level, through simple increases in land taxes or utility fees (which also have the advantage of continuing indefinitely, in contrast to TIF districts, which are time-limited) (Center for Transit-Oriented Development 2013).

Value capture tools (except for redevelopment) have been employed mostly in conjunction with transit investment, within a limited area, not for mixed-income neighborhoods. These approaches have experienced considerable success: although redevelopment (discussed further in Part II) may not generate enough value to pay for itself, at least the redeveloped areas increase in value faster than areas without the activity.[8] The impact of transit investment is similarly positive, though the transit premium varies widely depending on the specific context.[9]

How might value capture tools be used to create and maintain mixed-income neighborhoods that are at risk of losing affordability as investor interest rises? Although redevelopment is probably the most appropriate tool, because it allows for bond financing on a large scale, another potential approach is to create a developer impact fee based on the windfall from publicly created value. For instance, if a city upzones an area, this creates enough of a private windfall to support significant fees, which could then contribute to a housing trust fund to preserve and build affordable housing. In setting the fee, cities must show the nexus between the proposed fee and the city need, whether the fee is for transit impact, affordable housing, or infrastructure construction. The City of San Francisco enacted such a developer impact fee for its Public Benefits Program for the Eastern Neighborhoods. Calculating that zoning changes (allowing new residential development, higher densities, and higher heights, along with streamlined environmental review) would increase land values up to 20 percent on some parcels, the city established fees ranging from $6 to $16 per square foot to fund improvements and affordable housing (Schildt 2011). Although the district has not yet seen any completed development (and thus revenues), it should generate about $25 million in the next five years, covering almost one-third of the cost of capital improvements (ibid.).

Given the need for a strong real estate market with consistent value increases, San Francisco provides a near-ideal context for experimenting with value capture. Housing prices in the San Francisco metropolitan area have increased 250 percent in the past 25 years, beyond inflation.[10] San Francisco property consistently appreciates at the highest rates in the region, losing little value even during recessions. At the same time, about half of San Francisco's housing units are price-controlled, mostly through rent control, but also through public housing programs (Welch 2013).

The public sector investment in HOPE VI provides a great example of how value capture might be used for income diversity. The HOPE VI program made 515 grants ($6.4 billion) in 40 states, with plans to demolish and replace about 83,000 units; only half would be subsidized, meaning a net loss of public housing units (McCarty 2005). Although the promise of HOPE VI development was to eliminate concentrations of poverty in public housing by mixing incomes, it has had side benefits that were not properly anticipated by policymakers. When the new development significantly improves the built environment, the surrounding neighborhood may experience a boost in property value. To analyze this, we picked three HOPE VI redevelopments in San Francisco and matched them with similar public housing projects nearby that were not slated for redevelopment (Figure 5.4 shows the sites).

Then, we looked at all the residential property sales within 0.25 miles of each development from 1997 (as the planning began) to 2007 (a couple years after completion). We found a property value premium conferred in each case by the HOPE VI redevelopment, compared to the comparison site. In all, the premium ranged from 13 to 43 percent of the original value per square foot (Figure 5.5).

Had the city thought to enact some kind of value capture mechanism similar to what it did in the Eastern Neighborhoods, it could have generated some sort of affordable housing fund that tapped into the new value created by public investment. This might make it possible to create the permanent affordability that will keep the area mixed income as property values increase. It is not clear what mechanism would work best here: given that individual homeowners and apartment building landowners are the primary beneficiaries and are unlikely to redevelop their properties, the developer impact fee used in the Eastern Neighborhoods example would probably not work. Perhaps the optimal mechanism would be some kind of real estate transfer tax that recaptures some of the premium upon resale.

Of course, there are drawbacks to value capture mechanisms, in addition to the concern that they may not be viable in markets with weak real estate appreciation. Context shapes their effectiveness: appreciation will be higher in areas with more amenities and higher quality of infrastructure. Historically, value capture projects have varied widely in the amount of revenue raised (Government Accountability Office 2010). Implementation may be challenging in the absence of appropriate financing tools or expertise, and there are political

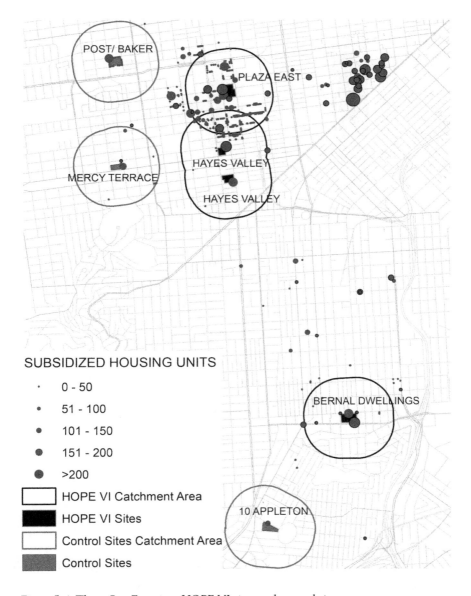

POST/ BAKER

PLAZA EAST

MERCY TERRACE

HAYES VALLEY

HAYES VALLEY

SUBSIDIZED HOUSING UNITS

·   0 - 50

●   51 - 100

●   101 - 150

●   151 - 200

●   >200

☐   HOPE VI Catchment Area

■   HOPE VI Sites

☐   Control Sites Catchment Area

■   Control Sites

BERNAL DWELLINGS

10 APPLETON

Figure 5.4 Three San Francisco HOPE VI sites and control sites

Source: Author's calculations

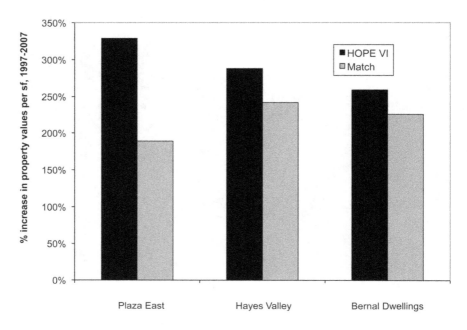

Figure 5.5 Ten-year increase in property values per square foot, HOPE VI and match
          sites

Source: Author's calculations

challenges to enacting new legislation: for instance, single-family homeowners
may not support the assessment.

But without value capture, this is a missed opportunity to preserve a mixed-
income area; the experience in strong markets such as San Francisco has
typically been a rapid influx of affluent residents around HOPE VI redevelop-
ments.

*Income Diversity in a Low-Income Segregated Community: The Case
of Richmond, California*

Across the bay, the City of Richmond provides a stark contrast. A vibrant
industrial center and port through World War II, the city saw its population
drop by over 40 percent when the shipyards closed down. It became increasingly
segregated, both racially and economically. In recent years, an influx of
immigrants has restored Richmond's population almost to its post-World War
II peak, while making it one of the most diverse places in the Bay Area. Still,
it remains income segregated, particularly in the downtown Iron Triangle
neighborhood, which contains many pockets of concentrated poverty. Although
a transit village with mostly market-rate units was planned for its rapid transit

station area in the early 2000s, only the first phase has been built due to poor market conditions.

A development strategy, which would build more market-rate housing and thus bring in upper-income residents, might reduce the concentration of poverty in the Iron Triangle. Depending on the housing construction rates in Richmond, as well as the land supply, it might be possible to build enough new housing to establish new mixed-income neighborhoods. The goal here would be simply to increase diversity in each of Richmond's block groups so that it is as diverse as the Bay Area median.

To evaluate this possibility, we looked first at historic housing construction rates and available land supply (vacant and underutilized sites). Overall, Richmond has gained about 1 percent of all units constructed in the Bay Area for the last 15 years, at 241 units per year, a rate that lags the Bay Area overall.

Another factor shaping Richmond's development is the availability of infill sites. Here, we used the improvement-to-land (IL) ratio to identify vacant and underutilized parcels: we used an IL of 1 for commercial and multifamily residential parcels, and 0.5 for single-family residential parcels (Landis et al. 2006). Based upon existing zoning, approximately 9,000 units can be built in Richmond.

We next determined how many new market-rate households Richmond would need in each block group in order to raise it to the diversity level of the median Bay Area block group. Since Richmond is a highly segregated (and low-income segregated) area, it would take a considerable influx of upper-income households to diversify. Figure 5.6 shows the existing concentration of households in the lowest two (low-income and moderate-income) income categories, while Figure 5.7 shows the new households needed to make Richmond neighborhoods as diverse as the rest of the Bay Area. Overall, two of every three new households in Richmond has to pay market rate in order to make Richmond diverse. Of about 11,000 units that would need to be built, just 3,500 would have to be affordable. This ratio of approximately 67/33 is a level typical of Richmond, which is one of the Bay Area's top performers in affordable housing production in the last five years (Bay Area Council 2006). But interestingly, 11,000 new units for Richmond is nearly exactly what the Plan Bay Area sustainability plan proposes to be built in the city by 2040.

In order to accommodate this growth, about 70 percent higher than the historic construction rate, there would need to be some upzoning and redevelopment of the Iron Triangle area, in order to bring in more market-rate households. At present, there are about 20 housing units per block in this area of Richmond. To bring the typical diversity level in the Bay Area to every block group in Richmond through new development, we would need to add 30–40 units per block in this area.

Building so much new market-rate housing is likely to increase property values in the surrounding area. Though property owners will benefit (and again value capture may be possible), local renters may be at risk of displacement over the

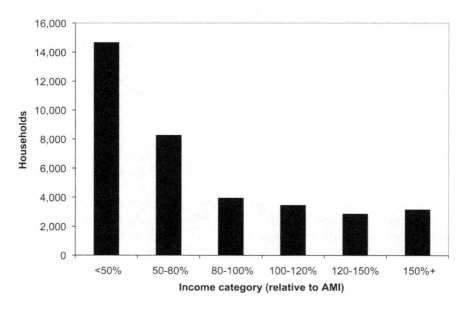

Figure 5.6 Existing household income distribution in Richmond, 1999
Source: Author's calculations

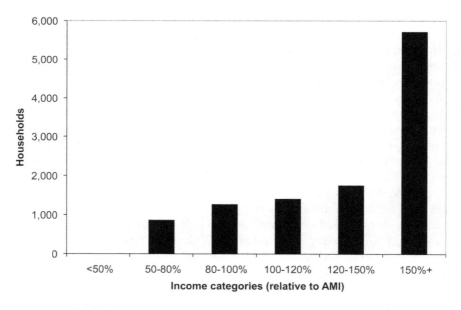

Figure 5.7 New households needed to make Richmond as diverse as the Bay Area
Source: Author's calculations

long-term as rents rise. This, then, will create a need to preserve affordable housing at the same time as developing the new market-rate units.

Since it is politically infeasible to upzone so much of Richmond, and unlikely that the city will sustain a housing construction rate of that high above average without significant incentives, an alternative approach to becoming mixed-income would be to lift some low-income households out of poverty, using income-boosting strategies to push them into the next income category up. If economic development strategies such as job set-asides, job training, and living wage strategies (or, better yet, federal strategies) were able to lift some 3,800 low- and moderate-income households up one category, a growth rate of only 5 percent above average would be required, along with substantially less upzoning. In any case, what this exercise shows is that Richmond cannot build itself into (let alone sustain) income diversity without significant policy intervention and incentives.

Using Social Seams to Create Porous Boundaries

Social seams, or grocery stores, parks, schools, religious institutions, and commercial strips, may be a significant factor in the ability of neighborhoods to maintain a stable mixed-race or mixed-ethnic population, and may influence the stability of mixed-income communities as well due to the public consciousness of diversity that they reinforce (Nyden, Maly, and Lukehart 1997). If social seams can help keep neighborhoods stable, then they can supplement permanent affordability mechanisms. Likewise, if they actually work to facilitate interaction between groups, then they may meet key goals of integration more effectively than diversifying developments. To investigate these questions, we conducted a study of a park in the Mission District, one of the most income-diverse areas of San Francisco (Munekiyo and Chapple 2009).

One city block, comprising approximately 3.5 acres of land, Garfield Square was one of 28 parks that existed in San Francisco before 1910. It includes a playground area, an indoor swimming pool, a staffed recreation center, an artificial turf soccer field, a multipurpose court, and open grassy areas. A 1982 study found that the park was heavily used by "all kinds of people" (Marcus 1982). Garfield Square is a great test case to examine social seams and interaction in a mixed-income neighborhood because of the diverse character of the neighborhood, the presence of an adjacent HOPE VI development, and the recent renovations and high use of the park.

We began with a mail survey of residents in the surrounding blocks (with 233 respondents) to determine the location of social seams overall (Figure 5.9). This showed, perhaps not surprisingly, that the street was the primary arena for interaction in the neighborhood, but that of all the other potential social seams (restaurants, stores, schools, community centers, and apartment buildings), the park was the most likely place to meet people.

Another set of inquiries employed surveys and observation of park users in order to determine whether people interact and whether interaction takes place

Figure 5.8 Garfield Square Park
Photo credit: Tessa Munekiyo

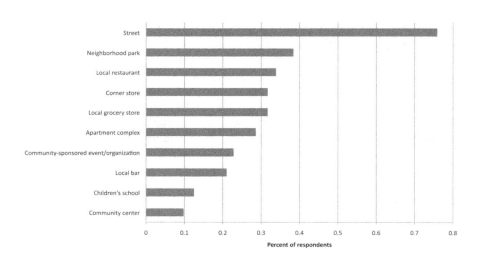

Figure 5.9 Where residents meet people in the neighborhood
Source: Munekiyo and Chapple (2009)

across socioeconomic groups. No matter what the socioeconomic background, the degree to which people recognize others at Garfield Square and their perception of friendliness of others at the park are similar. Despite the friendliness of a majority of park users, many do not interact with others beyond a casual level, making it unlikely, for instance, the contact will lead to job leads. However, several factors increase the likelihood of extended interaction. The longer residents live in the neighborhood, the more likely they are to recognize, be greeted by, and have conversations with others at the park. In addition, middle-income residents ($40,000–$80,000) are more likely to greet others at Garfield Square. More than anything else, the presence of children (and, to a certain extent, dogs) facilitates interaction at Garfield Square. Furthermore, park visitors with children are more likely to know the tenure (renter versus owner) of the last person they met, suggesting more in-depth interaction.

Social seams can work to stabilize neighborhoods and facilitate interaction. Garfield Square functions as a place that helps people of diverse backgrounds find commonalities—a key goal of integration. Residents of the HOPE VI development next door may actually feel safer interacting with each other in the context of the park than within their development. In creating these types of porous boundaries, planners are creating the institutional density (Chapter 12) that makes integration work—in the terms of Iris Marion Young (1990: 240), "the being together of strangers."

The Integration Debate and Regional Sustainability Planning

Decades of efforts to promote integration have focused on residential neighborhoods, usually areas of concentrated poverty. Despite the effort, and even as racial segregation has declined, income segregation has increased. In the face of increasing income inequality, local policies can do little. To integrate the suburbs requires more supportive state and federal policy. Increasing and maintaining diversity in the core would mean a concerted effort to capture value while preserving affordable housing.

Leading the increase in income segregation is the withdrawal of the (primarily white) affluent to their citadels, in Marcuse's term. As Reardon and Bischoff (2011: 1340) point out, this withdrawal has serious implications:

> The segregation of these high-income households in communities spatially far from lower-income households may reduce the likelihood that high-income residents will have social, or even casual, contact with lower-income residents. This in turn may make it less likely that they are willing to invest in metropolitanwide public resources that would benefit residents of all income levels, such as transportation networks, utilities, parks, services, and cultural amenities. Moreover, the spatial separation of the affluent and poor implies that there will be few opportunities for disadvantaged families to benefit from local spillover of public goods. The distance between affluent and lower-income communities makes it unlikely that disadvantaged

families will be able to take advantage of the local schools, parks, and services in which affluent communities invest.

To the extent that this segregation occurs at the place level, rather than in neighborhoods, the impact will be even harsher, because affluent families will not be contributing taxes to the jurisdiction.

Integrating affluent suburbs is probably the most challenging policy problem; it may be more effective to pursue remedies for income inequality at the national level. Integrating the urban core may be more feasible, given the pre-existing income diversity. Though high land prices may present a challenge, preserving diversity may be possible by ensuring that the large stock of subsidized housing in the urban core becomes permanently affordable.[11] But most intentional efforts to mix incomes have not succeeded in meeting integration goals, even if they have created better places.

This chapter suggests the potential for two different approaches. The first is to shift the policy focus from the development and neighborhood level to the district. This avoids the problem of breaking up enclaves, while still promoting accessibility to higher-quality goods and services and diverse social networks. Complementing this strategy is a shift to "complete communities," or places that support full lives—home, work, and play (Brooks et al. 2012). In practical terms, this means thinking beyond narrow housing policy to places, and then ensuring that those places have the porous boundaries or social seams that facilitate mixing. Supporting this approach is the increasing ethnic diversity of regions both in the United States and Europe, which is helping to diversify these seams.

Regional sustainability planning creates an opportunity to move away from failed approaches to integration. For instance, in the fair housing assessments many regions are conducting as HUD sustainability grantees, many are using a regional or municipal lens to look at diversity, rather than neighborhood. The focus has shifted to regional disparities, rather than racially concentrated poverty areas. A regional perspective also makes it possible to then support the seams between segregated jurisdictions. Asking cities to support their fair share of social seams may be more politically viable than asking for the fair share of housing, as does California's RHNA. It is not a panacea, but we should take advantage of the chance to move on from a housing policy that does not meet its own goals.

Notes

1. Lower-income households are more likely than upper-income households to use transit when it is nearby. This would suggest the importance of preserving low-income housing near transit to boost ridership. However, to lower vehicle miles traveled, it may be more effective to locate higher-income households near transit and lower income on the periphery (since they will not travel as much on the periphery as will the higher-income households).

2. Marcuse distinguishes here between a more transitory immigrant enclave, such as a Koreatown, where members of a community locate as they seek to assimilate, versus a cultural enclave, such as Hasidic Williamsburg, where members are staking a claim to a territory.

3. As Tach, Pendall, and Derian (2014) point out, the assumption that low-income neighborhoods lack role models may be false: for instance, Harding (2007) found higher exposure to behavior models among lower-income than higher-income youth.

4. Typical elements of fair share formulae are existing population in sub-areas, estimated population growth, and the (inverse of) relative availability of low-cost or subsidized housing. More sophisticated models incorporate constraints on development such as jobs, job growth, and transportation accessibility.

5. In Minnesota's fair share housing program, we found that a lack of funding, political will, and planner savvy meant that just five acres of every 100 acres set aside for affordable housing in the program actually had new low- or moderate-income housing 20 years later (Goetz, Chapple, and Lukermann, 2003).

6. The Low Income Housing Tax Credit (LIHTC) supports the development of rental housing in qualified areas by allowing credits against federal income taxes.

7. Of about 870,000 housing units built in the Philadelphia metropolitan area (2010 Combined Statistical Area) before 1960, most are relatively affordable, with both median value and rent lower than the region's. For the Bay Area, older homes do not generally depreciate enough to add to the affordable stock, but rental units do—with some 426,000 units at median rent lower than the region's.

8. In a matched-pair analysis, Mike Dardia (1998) found that two-thirds of 38 redevelopment areas in California grew faster than their matches, on average twice as fast. On the other hand, they did not grow fast enough that the new property tax that they generate pays for the public investment (i.e., the increment diverted away from schools, etc.).

9. The Center for Transit-Oriented Development's (2008) review shows a range from a low of 2 percent to a high of 45 percent for residential property, and from 9 percent to 120 percent for commercial property.

10. For more information, see the Case-Shiller Index, http://us.spindices.com/indices/ real-estate/sp-case-shiller-20-city-composite-home-price-index.

11. For a description of this in Boston, see Tach, Pendall, and Derian (2014).

References

Basolo, Victoria and Dorian Hastings. "Obstacles to Regional Housing Solutions: A Comparison of Four Metropolitan Areas." *Journal of Urban Affairs* 25, no. 4 (2003): 449–472.

Bay Area Council. *Bay Area Housing Profile.* San Francisco, CA: Bay Area Council, 2006.

Bollens, Scott. "In Through the Back Door: Social Equity and Regional Governance." *Housing Policy Debate* 13, no. 4 (2003): 631–657.

Briggs, Xavier. "Brown Kids in White Suburbs: Housing Mobility and the Many Faces of Social Capital." *Housing Policy Debate* 9, no. 1 (1998): 177–221.

Brooks, Allison, Gloria Ohland, Abby Thorne-Lyman, and Elizabeth Wampler. *Are We There Yet? Creating Complete Communities for 21st Century America.* Oakland, CA: Reconnecting America, 2012.

Calavita, Nico, and Alan Mallach, editors. *Inclusionary Housing in International Perspective: Affordable Housing, Social Inclusion, and Land Value Recapture.* Cambridge, MA: Lincoln Institute of Land Policy, 2010.

Calavita, Nico, Kenneth Grimes, and Alan Mallach. "Inclusionary Housing in California and New Jersey: A Comparative Analysis." *Housing Policy Debate* 8 (1997): 109–142.

Carr, James and Nandinee Kutty. *Segregation: The Rising Costs for America.* New York: Routledge, 2008.

Center for Transit-Oriented Development. *Capturing the Value of Transit.* Oakland, CA: Center for Transit-Oriented Development, 2008.

Center for Transit-Oriented Development. *Value Capture Strategies for Public Transit.* Oakland, CA: Center for Transit-Oriented Development, 2013.

Chaskin, Robert J. and Mark L. Joseph. "Building 'Community' in Mixed-Income Developments: Assumptions, Approaches, and Early Experiences." *Urban Affairs Review* 45, no. 3 (2010): 299–335.

Chaskin, Robert J. and Mark L. Joseph. "Social Interaction in Mixed-Income Developments: Relational Expectations and Emerging Reality." *Journal of Urban Affairs* 33, no. 2 (2011): 209–237.

Crain, Robert L. and Amy S. Wells. "Perpetuation Theory and the Long-Term Effects of School Desegregation." *Review of Educational Research* 64, no. 4 (1994): 531–555.

Cutler, David M. and Edward L. Glaeser. "Are Ghettos Good or Bad?" *The Quarterly Journal of Economics* 112, no. 3 (1997): 827–872.

Dardia, Michael. *Subsidizing Redevelopment in California.* San Francisco, CA: Public Policy Institute of California, 1998.

Denton, Nancy. "From Segregation to Integration: How Do We Get There?" In *The Integration Debate: Competing Futures for American Cities*, edited by Chester Hartman and Gregory Squires, 23–37. New York: Routledge, 2010.

Dreier, Peter, John Mollenkopf, and Todd Swanstrom. *Place Matters: Metropolitics for the Twenty-First Century.* Lawrence, KS: University Press of Kansas, 2004.

Dwyer, Rachel E. "Poverty, Prosperity, and Place: The Shape of Class Segregation in the Age of Extremes." *Social Problems* 57, no. 1 (2010): 114–137.

Fainstein, Susan S. *The Just City.* Ithaca, NY: Cornell University Press, 2010.

Firebaugh, Glenn and Matthew B. Schroeder. "Does Your Neighbor's Income Affect Your Happiness?" *American Journal of Sociology* 115, no. 3 (2009): 805–831.

Fischer, Claude S. and Robert K. Merton. *The Urban Experience. 2nd Edition.* New York: Harcourt Brace Jovanovich, 1984.

Freeman, Lance. *There Goes the 'Hood: Views of Gentrification from the Ground Up.* Philadelphia, PA: Temple University Press, 2006.

Galster, George C. "Housing Discrimination and Urban Poverty of African-Americans." *Journal of Housing Research* 2, no. 2 (1991): 87–122.

Galster, George C. "Polarization, Place, and Race." In *Race, Poverty, and American Cities*, edited by John C. Boger and Judith W. Wegner, 1421–1462. Chapel Hill, NC: University of North Carolina Press, 1996.

Galster, George C. and W. Mark Keeney. "Race, Residence, Discrimination, and Economic Opportunity Modeling the Nexus of Urban Racial Phenomena." *Urban Affairs Review* 24, no. 1 (1988): 87–117.

Government Accountability Office. *Federal Role in Value Capture Strategies for Transit is Limited, but Additional Guidance Could Help Clarify Policies.* GAO-10-781. Washington, DC: U.S. Government Accountability Office, 2010.

Goetz, Edward G. *Clearing the Way: Deconcentrating the Poor in Urban America.* Washington, DC: Urban Institute Press, 2003.

Goetz, Edward G. *New Deal Ruins: Race, Economic Justice, and Public Housing Policy.* Ithaca, NY: Cornell University Press, 2013.

Goetz, Edward G., Karen Chapple, and Barbara Lukermann. "Enabling Exclusion: The Retreat from Regional Fair Share Housing in the Implementation of the Minnesota Land Use Planning Act." *Journal of Planning Education and Research* 22, no. 3 (2003): 213–225.

Graves, Erin M. "The Structuring of Urban Life in a Mixed-Income Housing 'Community'." *City & Community* 9, no. 1 (2010): 109–131.

Harding, David. "Cultural Context, Sexual Behavior, and Romantic Relationships in Disadvantaged Neighborhoods." *American Sociological Review* 72, no. 3 (2007): 341–364.

Hickey, Robert. *After the Downturn: New Challenges and Opportunities for Inclusionary Housing*. Washington, DC: Center for Housing Policy, 2013.

Ihlanfeldt, Keith R. and Benjamin P. Scafidi. "The Neighbourhood Contact Hypothesis: Evidence from the Multicity Study of Urban Inequality." *Urban Studies* 39, no. 4 (2002): 619–641.

Jacobs, Jane. *Death and Life of Great American Cities*. New York: Random House, 1961.

Jencks, Christopher and Susan Mayer. "Residential Segregation, Job Proximity, and Black Job Opportunities." In *Inner-City Poverty in the U.S.*, edited by Laurence Lynn and Michael McGeary, 187–222. Washington, DC: National Academics Press, 1990.

Joseph, Mark L., Robert J. Chaskin, and Henry S. Webber. "The Theoretical Basis for Addressing Poverty Through Mixed-Income Development." *Urban Affairs Review* 42, no. 3 (2007): 369–409.

Joseph, Mark L. and Taryn H. Gress. *State of the Field Scan #1 Social Dynamics in Mixed-Income Developments*. Cleveland, OH: National Initiative on Mixed-Income Communities, Case Western Reserve University, 2013.

Kleit, Rachel Garshick. "HOPE VI New Communities: Neighborhood Relationships in Mixed-Income Housing." *Environment and Planning A* 37, no. 8 (2005): 1413.

Landis, John, Heather Hood, Guangyu Li, Thomas Rogers, and Charles Warren. "The Future of Infill Housing in California." *Housing Policy Debate* 17, no. 4 (2006): 681–726.

Lee, Barrett, A., Sean F. Reardon, Glenn Firebaugh, Chad R. Farrell, Stephen A. Matthews, and David O'Sullivan. "Beyond the Census Tract: Patterns and Determinants of Racial Segregation at Multiple Geographic Scales." *American Sociological Review* 73, no. 5 (2008): 766–791.

Levy, Diane K., Zach McDade, and Kassie Bertumen. "Mixed-Income Living: Anticipated and Realized Benefits for Low-Income Households." *Cityscape* 15, no. 2 (2013): 15–28.

Lewis, Oscar. "The Culture of Poverty." *Scientific American* 215, no. 4 (1966): 19–25.

Lichter, Daniel T., Domenico Parisi, and Michael C. Taquino, "The Geography of Exclusion: Race, Segregation, and Concentrated Poverty." *Social Problems* 59, no. 3 (2012): 364–388.

Listokin, David. *Fair Share Housing Allocation*. New Brunswick, NJ: Center for Urban Policy Research, Rutgers University, 1976.

McCarty, Maggie. "HOPE VI: Background, Funding, and Issues." *Congressional Research Service Report*. Washington, DC: Library of Congress, 2005.

McCormick, Naomi J., Mark L. Joseph, and Robert J. Chaskin. "The New Stigma of Relocated Public Housing Residents: Challenges to Social Identity in Mixed-Income Developments." *City & Community* 11, no. 3 (2012): 285–308.

Marcus, Clare Cooper. "Garfield Square Park." Unpublished class project, University of California, Berkeley, 1982.

Marcuse, Peter. "The Enclave, the Citadel, and the Ghetto: What Has Changed in the Post-Fordist US City." *Urban Affairs Review* 33, no. 2 (1997): 228–264.

Massey, Douglas S. "The Age of Extremes: Concentrated Affluence and Poverty in the Twenty-First Century." *Demography* 33, no. 4 (1996): 395–412.

Massey, Douglas S., Len Albright, Rebecca Casciano, Elizabeth Derickson, and David N. Kinsey. *Climbing Mount Laurel: The Struggle for Affordable Housing and Social Mobility in an American Suburb.* Princeton, NJ: Princeton University Press, 2013.

Montgomery County Department of Housing and Community Affairs. "Number of MPDUs Produced Since 1976." Accessed October 6, 2013. www.montgomery countymd.gov/DHCA/housing/singlefamily/mpdu/produced.html.

Munekiyo, Tessa and Karen Chapple. *Social Seams in Mixed-Income Neighborhoods: A Case Study of Garfield Square Park.* 2009. Accessed October 12, 2013. http://communityinnovation.berkeley.edu/reports/SocialSeamsMixed-IncomeNeighbor hoods.pdf.

Nyden, Philip, Michael Maly, and John Lukehart. "The Emergence of Stable Racially and Ethnically Diverse Urban Communities: A Case Study of Nine U.S. Cities." *Housing Policy Debate* 8, no. 2 (1997): 491–534.

Pattillo, Mary. *Black on the Block: The Politics of Race and Class in the City.* Chicago, IL: University of Chicago Press, 2008.

Peterson, Ruth D. and Lauren J. Krivo. "Racial Segregation and Black Urban Homicide." *Social Forces* 71, no. 4 (1993): 1001–1026.

Popkin, Susan J., Bruce Katz, Mary Cunningham, Karen D. Brown, Jeremy Gustafson, and Margery Turner. *A Decade of HOPE VI: Research Findings and Policy Challenges.* Washington, DC: Urban Institute Press and Brookings Institution Press, 2004.

Reardon, Sean F. and Kendra Bischoff. "Income Inequality and Income Segregation." *American Journal of Sociology* 116, no. 4 (2011): 1092–1153.

Schildt, Chris. *Strategies for Fiscally Sustainable Infill Housing Development.* Berkeley, CA: Center for Community Innovation, 2011.

Schwartz, Heather L., Liisa Ecola, Kristin J. Leuschner, and Aaron Kofner. *Is Inclusionary Zoning Inclusionary?* Santa Monica, CA: RAND Corporation, 2012.

Tach, Laura. "More than Bricks and Mortar: Neighborhood Frames, Social Processes, and the Mixed-Income Redevelopment of a Public Housing Project." *City & Community* 8, no. 3 (2009): 273–303.

Tach, Laura. "Beyond Concentrated Poverty: The Social and Temporal Dynamics of Mixed-Income Neighborhoods." Doctoral dissertation, Harvard University, 2010.

Tach, Laura. "Imagined Communities, Contested Realities: How Stakeholders Understand and Negotiate Space in Mixed-Income Developments." Paper presented at the annual meeting of the Urban Affairs Association, New Orleans, Louisiana, March 16–19, 2011.

Tach, Laura, Rolf Pendall, and Alexandra Derian. *Income Mixing Across Scales: Rationale, Trends, Policies, Practice, and Research for More Inclusive Neighborhoods and Metropolitan Areas.* Washington, DC: Urban Institute Press, 2014.

Turner, Margery A. and Lynette Rawlings. *Promoting Neighborhood Diversity.* Washington, DC: Urban Institute Press, August 2009.

U.S. Department of Housing and Urban Development (HUD). "Inclusionary Zoning and Mixed-Income Communities." *Evidence Matters.* Washington, DC: U.S. Department of Housing and Urban Development, 2013.

Vale, Lawrence. *Reclaiming Public Housing.* Cambridge, MA: Harvard University Press, 2006.

Varady, David P. and Carole C. Walker. "Using Housing Vouchers to Move to the Suburbs: How Do Families Fare?" *Housing Policy Debate* 14, no. 3 (2003): 347–382.

Watson, Tara. "Inequality and the Measurement of Residential Segregation by Income." *Review of Income and Wealth* 55 (2009): 820–844.

Welch, Calvin. "Assessing and Preventing Displacement in Bay Area Communities." Presentation at A Just Bay Area Conference, Oakland, CA, October 30, 2013.

Wilkinson, Richard and Kate Pickett. "How Inequality Hollows Out." *New York Times*, February 2, 2014.

Wilson, William J. *The Truly Disadvantaged: The Inner City, the Underclass, and Public Policy*. Chicago, IL: University of Chicago Press, 1987.

Wish, Naomi B. and Stephen Eisdorfer. "The Impact of Mount Laurel Initiatives: An Analysis of the Characteristics of Applicants and Occupants." *Seton Hall Law Review* 27 (1997): 1268–1337.

Young, Iris Marion. *Justice and the Politics of Difference*. Princeton, NJ: University Press of Princeton, 1990.

6   Regional Growth, Gentrification, and Displacement

"I don't know what the difference is between gentrification and displacement." "I keep wondering if the whole Bay Area is going to gentrify." I had arrived a little early at the class for the Boards and Commissions Leadership Institute, where I was to give my talk on the early warning gentrification toolkit. Urban Habitat, a regional nonprofit that advocates for social equity and environmental justice, launched the Institute a few years ago to help low-income people and people of color assume positions on local-appointed or -elected bodies. Each year, a dozen students, nominated mostly from local progressive nonprofits, go through a remarkable 80-hour program that trains them to be effective commissioners, grasp planning issues, understand local power dynamics, and network with officials. The majority graduate and quickly gain office. Classes are lively, so it is not surprising that the fireworks began before I said a word.

"If you remember one thing from my talk today, I want you to think of gentrification as an opportunity, not a problem." I looked around at puzzled faces. "Gentrification is the biggest opportunity we have to enact redistributive policies at the local level. Gentrification means that capital is actually coming into the neighborhood. We just need to figure out ways to spread the benefits." But they would need to be proactive to capture a piece of the pie, as the gentrification that thus far had reached just a few neighborhoods in the region was likely to accelerate rapidly as implementation of the policies in support of regional sustainability progressed.

What are Gentrification and Displacement?

The term "gentrification" first appeared in the 1960s, coined by sociologist Ruth Glass (1964), who was describing the influx of the middle class into poor London neighborhoods. Since then, the debate over its meaning and impact has only intensified. Who are the gentry, and who is benefiting from the changes? Clearly the newcomers have higher incomes than the long-term residents of the neighborhood, plus, often, equity to invest in local housing. That probably means higher levels of educational attainment, too, given that income and schooling are highly correlated. But can there be "positive" gentrification, especially in weak market places such as Detroit? When it is an influx of middle-class African-American professionals, as in parts of Atlanta, Washington, DC, and Cleveland, is it still gentrification (Kennedy and Leonard 2001)?

Gentrification is a phenomenon of not just the in-migration of families and businesses, but also investment, whether from private capital or the public sector. This investment can transform a neighborhood nearly overnight, in a shocking contrast with the normally protracted pace of neighborhood change. For some, particularly in weaker markets, gentrification means revitalization that can benefit the entire neighborhood's population by bringing more resources to the area. But in other cases, it results in the displacement of existing residents who most often are people of color.

The neighborhoods that epitomize gentrification—the Village or Soho or Harlem in New York City, the Mission District in San Francisco, the South End in Boston, Society Hill in Philadelphia, Dupont Circle in DC—all have witnessed displacement, in both tangible and intangible forms. The first indications are when, in an established neighborhood, newcomers seem incongruous. It may be hard to tell if the new neighbor has more money or a college education, but it becomes really obvious from the new stores popping up (Figure 6.1).

How we understand gentrification matters. In theory, it means invasion, a spatial form of colonization that changes the social character of the neighborhood (Arbona 2014). But as experienced on the ground, this type

Figure 6.1 Commercial gentrification in Berkeley, California

Photo credit: Karen Chapple

of neighborhood change can be positive or negative. If we want to build inclusive places with opportunity for all, should we encourage gentrification, or not?

On the positive side, neighborhood residents may benefit from the influx of new residents. For instance, a group of college-educated artists may arrive. Instead of pushing up rents so that long-term residents cannot afford to stay, these newcomers may be renovating former commercial spaces, creating public art, and offering low-cost art classes in a low-key process of neighborhood ascent (Owens 2012). Perhaps the neighborhood is becoming more affluent, but rather than hipsters with trust funds, it is that more locals are going to college. All residents are benefiting from the presence of new stores and services attracted by the rising neighborhood incomes. And housing price appreciation might finally make it possible for families to sell their homes and upgrade to the neighborhoods of their dreams.

At the same time, these changes may be harmful. As reinvestment occurs and property values rise, the changes potentially may force out existing residents. Able to command higher rents on the market, landlords will raise rents to the extent permitted by law, increasing tenant turnover. While these increases may impact any tenant not residing in permanently affordable housing, they are most likely to displace those already paying a disproportionate share of their income for rent, who are not able to squeeze their transportation or food budget any more to pay for housing. Whether the influx is of affluent homeowners or nontraditional households, the changes are likely to tighten the housing market and make it difficult for new low-income residents to move in. Moreover, the new population will undoubtedly change the neighborhood's essential character, in some areas making it difficult to preserve historic significance and local culture (Kennedy and Leonard 2001).

In *There Goes the 'Hood: Views of Gentrification from the Ground Up* (2006), Lance Freeman explores perceptions of gentrification through the eyes of long-term New York City residents. As their neighborhoods change, locals appreciate the new retail and services, the new identity of the neighborhood as "desirable," the improvements in property value, and even some of the new neighbors. At the same time, there are downsides. The improvements seem to be for the newcomers' benefit, and in the case of improved policing, it may mean new harassment for locals. This, in turn, seems to validate the idea of conspiracy, that "they"—affluent outsiders aided by the authorities—are trying to take over the neighborhood. And even if oldtimers do not personally know of anyone displaced, the threat of displacement hangs in the air.

Freeman concludes that New Yorkers are making sense of gentrification through the bitter lens of urban renewal. Given the history of planners "revitalizing" neighborhoods by evicting the current low-income residents and building large-scale development largely for middle-class newcomers, it is hard not to see current changes as perpetuating that oppression. The narrative of displacement resonates more than a narrative of benefit. Is it based in reality? And how can we make policy without knowing the answer?

The Research Challenges

Although there is a rich literature on gentrification, researchers have generally struggled to show that it causes displacement. In fact, a number of studies have found that rather than displacing low-income households, gentrification induces them to remain in the neighborhood (Ellen and O'Regan 2011; Freeman 2005; Freeman and Braconi 2004; McKinnish, Walsh, and White 2010; Vigdor 2002). At the same time, new low-income households may have a hard time moving into the neighborhood as its identity changes.

First, what is displacement? Direct displacement occurs when new development results in demolition of older housing units, and indirect displacement is when property values in the area increase due to its new desirability, making it less likely that existing residents stay. Indirect displacement may be voluntary, if property owners elect to sell their residences (typically for a profit), or involuntary, occurring in any of three forms: (1) economic, in which housing becomes prohibitively costly (often because of high rent or property tax increases in places without limits); (2) physical, in which the landlord evicts the tenant or induces departure through harassment or persuasion; and (3) exclusionary, in which low-income and/or minority households no longer have the opportunity to move into the neighborhood (Marcuse 1986).

Researchers do not understand the relationship between gentrification and displacement because it is hard to get access to the panel census data that track households as they move from one neighborhood to another, and even those data do not explain whether moves are voluntary or involuntary. Even when survey data on moves are available (as in New York City), it may be inaccurate. For instance, it may understate displacement by not surveying those who have moved out of the city, or not including those who moved because of the threat of a rent increase rather than an actual increase. But it may also overstate displacement by including those experiencing trouble paying the rent due not to rent increases, but personal economic hardship, such as the loss of a job, or landlord–tenant disagreements over who is responsible for building maintenance. Researchers more or less agree that, at most, 10 percent of all moving households are involuntarily displaced each year—but have had trouble linking that displacement explicitly to gentrification (Freeman and Braconi 2004; Lee and Hodge 1984; Newman and Wyly 2006).

Thus, most academic studies have used mobility rates as a proxy for displacement, examining how both exit and entry rates of low-income households change as the neighborhood's household income increases. Looking at neighborhood departures, low-income residents are disproportionately likely to remain in the neighborhoods experiencing income gains (Ellen and O'Regan 2011; Freeman 2005; McKinnish, Walsh, and White 2010; Vigdor 2002). The evidence on entry rates is more suggestive of displacement (of the exclusionary type): higher-income and/or white households tend to be more likely to take up residence in gentrifying neighborhoods (Ellen and O'Regan 2011; Freeman 2005; McKinnish, Walsh, and White 2010).

Why is gentrification not associated with economic or physical displacement in these studies? It is possible that existing residents gain new income from new economic opportunities in the neighborhood, allowing them to stay (Ellen and O'Regan 2011; Freeman 2006). Since low-income residents often desire to stay in the gentrifying neighborhood as it gains new amenities, households may develop coping strategies (such as doubling up), which enable them to stay. A third possibility is that there is displacement, but since it occurs to such a small share of all movers, it does not affect overall mobility rates. What seems clear is that as neighborhoods improve, locals fight harder to stay.

The Dynamics of Neighborhood Change and Gentrification

To understand this better, let us look at the national study of neighborhood change in low-income neighborhoods by Ingrid Gould Ellen and Katherine O'Regan (2011). Looking at the 1990s, they find that one-third of low-income neighborhoods decreased in income (looking at average household income compared to their metropolitan area), while 37 percent gained significant ground in income (which they characterize as gentrification). They compare these "gaining" neighborhoods to "non-gaining" neighborhoods to see how mobility patterns differ. Overall, the gaining neighborhoods were more stable—renters, the poor, and minorities left at higher rates in non-gaining than in gaining neighborhoods. For the most part, the change in neighborhood income in gaining neighborhoods came from the departure of lower-income homeowners (not renters), who likely gained financially themselves from selling, and the arrival of higher-income homeowners (again, not renters). Although local rents increased in these gaining neighborhoods, the original low-income residents also became more affluent and were relatively more satisfied with the neighborhood. Finally, the gaining neighborhoods were more racially stable. In other words, gentrification was an opportunity for most residents.

How does this work? Figure 6.2 shows the low-income neighborhood as it starts out. Let us say there are 26 households, each represented by a parcel in the diagram. Fourteen rent their housing unit, and 12 own.

Now it turns into a gaining neighborhood (Figure 6.3). Nine of the original homeowners and nine of the original renter households stay (eight households move out). But there are three new affluent homeowners (including the conversion of one rental unit), five new affluent renting households, and six existing (incumbent) households that see their incomes rise. Note, however, that new low-income households are not moving in.

What if the neighborhood does not gain (Figure 6.4)? In that case, just eight of the original homeowners remain, along with eight of the original renters (in other words, 10 households move out). Ten new low-income households move in. None of the original households experience any income gains.

According to this picture, change is slow, but the low-income residents who stayed in gaining neighborhoods are clearly better off than the ones who stayed

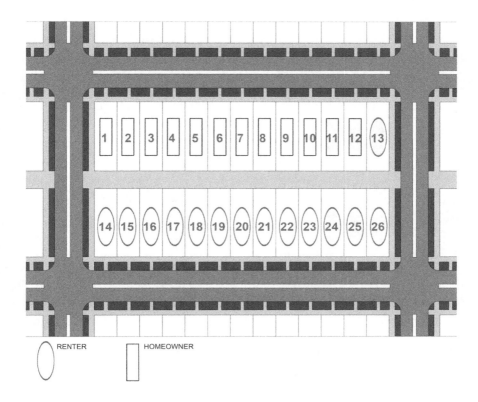

Figure 6.2 Schematic of neighborhood before gentrification's onset
Source: Author's elaboration

in non-gaining: at least six households benefited in these neighborhoods, compared to zero in the non-gaining.

But before we buy into the Ellen-O'Regan argument, it is worth thinking about what they could be missing. First, they look at just one decade, the 1990s. Gentrification is a slow process, and it could take decades for the displacement to occur. In the following decade, if there are no protections for renters, more low-income households will likely move.

Second, this (and much similar research) analyzes gentrification as neighborhood income change, rather than private or public investment. However, an influx of capital into a neighborhood might have much stronger impacts on resident stability than simply higher-income households moving next door. In other words, speculators could be buying up buildings and renovating them slowly over time before evicting tenants.

A final problem is studying neighborhood change across the entire country, grouping gaining neighborhoods in San Francisco with those in Houston and

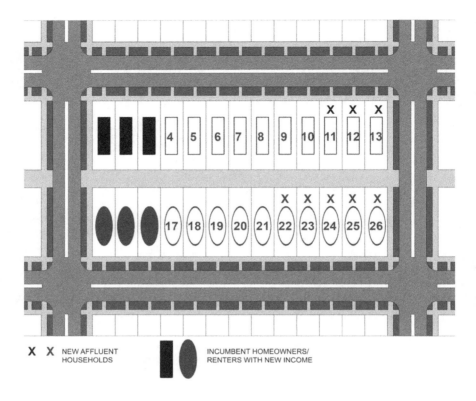

Figure 6.3 Neighborhood gaining in household income
Source: Author's elaboration

Billings. The researchers might find different mobility patterns in individual metropolitan areas, depending on the strength of their real estate markets. The *average* gaining neighborhood may not actually exist anywhere.

Overall, the implication of this research is that on average, gentrification, even as invasion, can revitalize neighborhoods over the short term, except that it reduces housing opportunities for low-income households who can no longer move in—and for middle-income households as well in some extreme cases (as in Manhattan). So, the policy response might be to support neighborhood ascent but provide long-term security of tenure for low-income residents, as well as build some affordable housing to allow room for some low-income in-movers. And in the bigger picture, it remains critical to provide more middle-income housing in core areas to reduce pressure on low-income neighborhoods, as well as to improve the quality of life in other low-income neighborhoods.

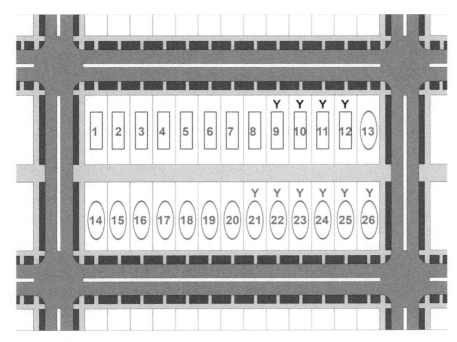

Y Y NEW LOW INCOME HOUSEHOLDS

Figure 6.4 Neighborhood without household income gains
Source: Author's elaboration

What Can Communities Do?

At this point, the Leadership Institute students have had enough of my talk. "But where does that leave the 10 percent of out-movers who are involuntarily displaced?" "That doesn't work for the Mission or the East Village!"

And they are right. Policy based on the average neighborhood does not protect these iconic gentrifying neighborhoods. So how can these community organizers lead?

One approach is to use data to identify the areas that are gentrifying, not so much to pass restrictive regulations in these areas, but to alert community organizers to the need for early intervention. The exact policy put in place will need to vary by the neighborhood and city. So, this analysis must be done region by region, block by block.

This is exactly what we did in a study for the San Francisco Bay Area's regional government, the ABAGs (Chapple 2009). We used the definition of gentrification put forth by Freeman (2005), modified slightly for the Bay Area: a central city neighborhood with housing price appreciation above the regional average, increase in educational attainment above the regional average, and household income at the 40th percentile of regional household income (roughly 80 percent of median income) in the starting year (as the process begins).[1] Then we looked at neighborhood change from 1990 to 2000, identifying six types of change: *gentrifying, becoming bipolar* (with growth of households in both the lowest and highest of the six income groups, at the expense of the four groups in the middle), *becoming more middle income, becoming lower income, becoming upper income,* or other (a mix of patterns).[2]

In the the 1990s, just 7.3 percent of Bay Area tracts (with 5.7 percent of the region's population) were gentrifying, while there were 220 bipolar tracts in the San Francisco Bay Area, about 16 percent of the total (Figure 6.5).[3] Ten percent of Bay Area tracts were becoming more middle income, 32 percent more lower income, and 21 percent more upper income.

What types of neighborhoods are most susceptible to gentrification? To answer this question, we can look at the 102 tracts that gentrified from 1990 to 2000 and examine what they were like in 1990. Using multivariate regression, we can identify different types of factors that make a neighborhood more likely to gentrify.[4] These might be demographic, such as types of families in the neighborhood; income, such as the extent to which local households are experiencing high rent burdens; transportation, such as reliance on transit for the commute; housing factors, such as a large share of rental housing; locational, such as where the neighborhood lies in the region; and amenities, including parks and community facilities.

Availability of amenities and *public transportation* top the list. This is an important finding, because public investment and funding supports these factors, creating an obligation to ensure that the broad public benefits. More than who lived in the neighborhood in 1990, or where it was located within the region, or even the characteristics of the neighborhood, what was most important in attracting change to the area was the proximity of amenities such as youth facilities and public space (and, to a lesser extent, small parks), as well as the convenient location of transit (as evidenced by a high share of transit commuters).

Three *income* variables make a significant difference in whether a neighborhood will gentrify. Income diversity is a very important indicator: if an area is more diverse (i.e., has relatively equal representation across the six income groups), then it is more likely to attract this form of neighborhood change. Likewise, if there is a high share of renters who pay over 35 percent of their income for rent, then the neighborhood is more susceptible.[5] It is easy to envision what occurs in this case: as an influx of newcomers increases area rents, these overburdened renters find themselves unable to pay an even higher share of their income for rent, so they depart, leaving more vacancies for new gentrifiers.

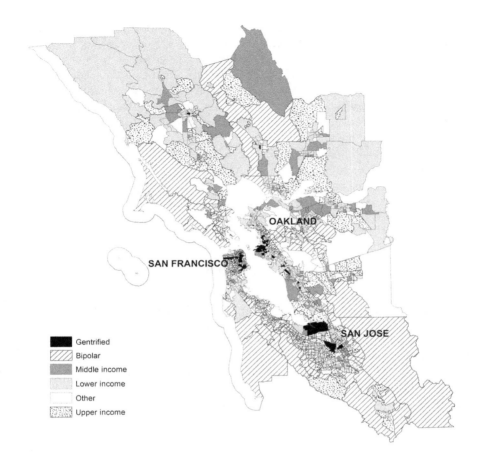

Figure 6.5 Neighborhood change in the San Francisco Bay Area, 1990–2000
Source: Author's calculations

In contrast, neighborhoods with concentrations of overburdened owners are less likely to gentrify, perhaps because the neighborhoods with high concentrations of home ownership tend to be more affluent.

One predictable, but important, *demographic* variable that leads to gentrification is a larger share of non-family households. In contrast, the more non-Hispanic whites are in the area, the less likely it is to gentrify: the most susceptible areas are majority minority. Likewise, the more married couples with children, the less likely the area is to gentrify (though there are some exceptions in areas with concentrations of Latino families, e.g., San Jose).

Finally, four types of *housing* variables, closely related to each other, matter significantly. In particular, the higher the share of multi-unit buildings (with three or more units) and the higher the share of renter-occupied housing, the more likely the area is to gentrify, perhaps because change can occur more rapidly through turnover of rental units.[6] Not surprisingly, the higher the median gross rent, the less likely the area is to gentrify (since it may be affluent already). The higher the number of public housing units, the more likely the area is to gentrify, perhaps because there is often a lot of mobility in neighborhoods adjacent to public housing.[7]

These factors will not be the same everywhere: in fact, a study that attempted to replicate this approach for Houston found that factors such as transit accessibility, nearby amenities, and rent burden did not matter for that area, where transit use is more rare and housing is much more affordable (Winston and Walker 2012). But ideally, such early warning systems would be designed by locals to fit their particular context.

The Case of Lake Merritt/Oakland Chinatown

What can community organizers do with this information? We worked in Oakland's Chinatown to help locals understand how their neighborhood is changing, particularly important right now because of planned redevelopment of the BART station area.

In conjunction with a station area planning process, the ABAGs awarded Asian Health Services and the Oakland Chinatown Chamber of Commerce (along with PolicyLink and my Center for Community Innovation as technical consultants) a small grant to conduct a community engagement process before the planning process started. That engagement process, which included several public meetings, focus groups, and a survey, revealed several community priorities: in particular, preserving and increasing neighborhood open space, reducing crime, and improving pedestrian conditions. But more than anything, it revealed deep bitterness among current and former community members who remembered the displacement that occurred with many previous redevelopment efforts, in particular the construction of the Bay Area Rapid Transit (BART) Lake Merritt station, which demolished three blocks of Chinatown.

Oakland, along with CalTrans and Alameda County, began their urban renewal and highway construction efforts in the 1950s. Early projects, almost all involving the condemnation and acquisition of predominantly residential properties, included the Nimitz Freeway, the Oakland Public Library, the Alameda County Administration Building, and Laney College. The 1960s saw additional acquisition and demolition of residences and community facilities to construct the BART Lake Merritt Station, the BART administration building, the MTC administration building, and the Oakland Museum. By the 1980s, awareness of the loss of housing in Chinatown had grown, and local nonprofits, including the East Bay Asian Local Development Corporation, began building more affordable housing in the area. The pace of large-scale redevelopment slowed in the 1990s, with the exception of the Pacific Renaissance Plaza, which included 200 units of market-rate housing, 50 units of affordable housing, and space for the Asian Cultural Center and Oakland Asian Library. After the landlord evicted the affordable housing tenants, several community groups organized the Stop Chinatown Evictions Coalition, which fought successfully in court to restore the affordable units and construct more affordable units off-site. The Pacific Renaissance experience, compounded by this history and Mayor Jerry Brown's initiative to bring housing back downtown, has made the community very aware of how development pressures are shrinking the boundaries of Chinatown.[8]

In contrast, however, there is less concern about the potential for displacement through gentrification, in part because of the uncertainty over its extent. Local activists are aware that families are leaving for nearby suburbs, but it is unclear whether this is because of high rents, poor schools, rising crime, or some other motive. Whatever the reason, many express a desire to return to the neighborhood.

The gentrification analysis suggests that this area is highly susceptible to gentrification in the future. In particular, it has a high level of amenities, with a large share of transit commuters and small parks, and a very low share of white population.

What, then, might the community learn from the toolkit? First, the high susceptibility level should inform the residents that they will need to remain engaged. The neighborhood is likely to be very attractive to newcomers, and the existing residents will want to manage the change that is likely to happen. This will require a community engagement process that continues well beyond the station area planning process.

From a policy and planning perspective, the most important intervention is to create permanently affordable housing. New development is coming to the area, likely creating a windfall for existing homeowners who can sell to higher-income homeowners or developers seeking to build more density. Policy alternatives (discussed in Chapter 5) in order to fund affordable housing include value capture and inclusionary zoning (though neither has traditionally been used to cope with gentrification-induced displacement). To capture value created by development, cities may enact a special tax assessment district for property owners that are within the spillover area, or, where available under redevelopment law, a tax increment finance district that captures the increase in property values that occurs within a designated area, over a base threshold. The revenue received might then be channeled into a housing trust fund.

Since rent burden does not (yet) seem to be a critical issue, the focus should be on offering more opportunities for low-income homeownership, to slow the pace of residential turnover. Where local property values are rising quickly, cities can exempt long-term homeowners from the rise in property tax assessments (and taxes).[9] One of the community's current strengths that may be slowing the pace of gentrification is the presence of families with children; to ensure that families remain as the neighborhood changes, new housing should include a disproportionate share of large units (with three or more bedrooms). Another strength—but one that may be attracting gentrification—is the concentration of small parks. Over the coming years, as the city and developers enhance existing parks and build new public spaces, these parks should focus on the recreational needs of existing residents (e.g., their need for tai chi space) and celebrate existing culture, rather than provide more generic amenities.

Gentrification, here, is an opportunity. We have identified an area where property values are going up, in large part due to public investment in this transit station, as well as the transit system region-wide. Where public goods create private value, recapture and redistribution to the public is justified. Simply stopping the new development, or slowing the influx of new residents, will not help the existing community as much as letting it happen but preparing and organizing first. The local leaders will have to replace the current narrative of displacement with the new narrative of opportunity.

Some of the most successful community organizing efforts against gentrification have occurred in the face of proposed large-scale development, such as the construction of the Staples Center in Los Angeles, the stadium at the Atlantic Yards in Brooklyn, and the expansion of Johns Hopkins University in Baltimore. In each of these cases, coalitions extracted community benefits from the developer in order to stabilize the surrounding neighborhood against anticipated gentrification. But often the dividing line between newcomers and oldtimers is not that clear.

What happens if there is a false positive (aka a Type 1 error)? In other words, what if the analysis identifies gentrifying areas and the community gets organized, but the change is more complex than the narrative of outsiders coming in and displacing existing residents? This is exactly what happened to my friend Rachel, another Ph.D. city planner who was targeted by the Fifth Avenue Committee's anti-displacement work in Park Slope. Rachel grew up in Park Slope, the product of a working-class family, from whom she was the first to go to graduate school. Upon obtaining her Ph.D., she purchased a townhouse in the Lower Slope, which (unbeknownst to her) was located in what the local community-based organization, the Fifth Avenue Committee, had designated the Displacement Free Zone. Organizers would picket, harass, and, if possible, sue any property owners who evicted existing residents. Rachel renovated the entire building and offered the existing tenants the chance to move back in at below-market rates. Still, the Committee set up camp in front of her building for weeks on end and supported the tenants in court. In the end, Rachel won and the organizers left.

Was she an appropriate target for the Committee? Had somebody else bought the building, the rents would have probably been market-rate. As a planner, Rachel knew to follow the zoning and building codes in renovating her building. She was a local, with longer roots in the neighborhood than any of the community organizers. Later, Rachel and her partner became friends with many of the families on the block, even offering a free and popular summer math camp for neighborhood kids.

The organizers here are guilty of the same mistake the gentrification researchers make, in analyzing the average neighborhood; they targeted a local because she shared characteristics of the average gentrifier. At the very least, before embarking on a campaign such as this, community organizers need to decide who is an outsider/newcomer/gentrifier and who counts as a local. But in the bigger picture, it makes more sense for organizers to fight for an assessment of both new and long-term property owners via a district-wide tax than to harass incomers on a case-by-case basis.

Postscript: Gentrification, Displacement, and Regional Sustainability

Making our regions more sustainable will mean accommodating more growth in some areas (such as core city areas with good existing transit) while also helping others (such as auto-dependent exurbs) densify. Particularly in strong market regions, many of which are experiencing an unprecedented demand for higher-density, transit-oriented communities, this will put gentrification pressures on traditional city neighborhoods, which will not be able to build infill development fast enough. Even if displacement has been slow to date, it will undoubtedly accelerate under this growth pressure. But understanding how these processes unfold, as well as organizing proactive community responses, is critical if we want to take advantage of rare opportunities for more equit-able development. To the extent that regional planning processes involve public participation, they create the opening for engaging the public. And when public investment is involved, it is a moral imperative to seize the opportunity of gentrification.

Notes

1. Freeman's definition also includes a measure of building age (percent of housing units built in the last 20 years), since gentrifiers are often attracted by older, architecturally significant housing stock. However, this variable does not work well in the Bay Area, where gentrifying neighborhoods have seen much new construction.
2. We used the Neighborhood Change Database developed by Geolytics, Inc., a database which allows for the comparison of census tracts over time even when boundaries change. The NCDB provides 1990 census data for normalized 2000 census tract definitions, allowing us to compare 1990 neighborhood characteristics to 2000.

   We chose the six categories to represent categories commonly used by affordable housing programs:
   1. very low income (less than 50 percent of AMI);
   2. low income (50–80 percent of AMI);
   3. moderate income (80–100 percent of AMI);
   4. high to moderate income (100–120 percent of AMI);

     5. high income (120–150 percent of AMI); and

     6. very high income (150 percent of AMI and above).

Galster and Booza (2007) identify neighborhoods that are "bipolar" using a formulation based on the entropy index. The entropy index is based upon the thermodynamic principle that any system will naturally trend toward evenness. The amount of entropy in a system refers to how far along a system is in reaching complete evenness or equilibrium. In the social sciences, researchers have developed an index that varies from 0 to 1, also called the Shannon-Weaver Index, to measure entropy of a population across social categories. In addition to this nominal entropy index, Galster and Booza construct a new ordinal entropy index and use the ratio of the two to measure bipolarity.

3.   Ten of the tracts that were becoming bipolar were also gentrifying, and we classified them as gentrifying. Interestingly, this confirms Galster and Booza's finding that the bipolar category is basically distinct from gentrification.

4.   Since this analysis was attempting to identify systematically which variables did and did not matter, we used a stepwise regression, which starts with a large number of variables and eliminates collinear variables, or those that are highly associated with variables that fit better in the analysis.

5.   We use the 35 percent threshold, rather than 30 percent, to reflect the Bay Area context, where high housing costs have made it customary to pay a higher share of income for housing.

6.   It should be noted that it is not the density itself that is causing gentrification: in fact, the higher share of multi-unit buildings, the less likely the area is to gentrify. Thus, there are several intervening variables that make high-density neighborhoods more susceptible, in particular higher levels of renter occupancy and higher shares of amenities.

7.   Again, however, public housing is negatively correlated with gentrification, suggesting that some other variables are intervening to make the influence of public housing seem positive.

8.   Upon taking office as Oakland mayor in 1998, Jerry Brown launched the 10K initiative, a largely successful program to bring 10,000 new residents to downtown Oakland via the construction of 6,500 market-rate housing units (Sheldon 2008).

9.   Philadelpha has enacted two such programs, the Homestead Exemption and the Longtime Owner Occupants Program.

References

Arbona, Javier. "Happy Fifty Years, Gentrification! Does Gentrification Gentrify without Gentrifiers?" *Polis*. 2014. Accessed February 17, 2014. www.thepolisblog.org/2014/02/happy-fifty-years-gentrification.html.

Chapple, Karen. *Mapping Susceptibility to Gentrification: The Early Warning Toolkit*. Berkeley, CA: University of California at Berkeley Center for Community Innovation, 2009.

Ellen, Ingrid Gould and Katherine M. O'Regan. "How Low Income Neighborhoods Change: Entry, Exit, and Enhancement." *Regional Science and Urban Economics* 41, no. 2 (2011): 89–97.

Freeman, Lance. "Displacement or Succession? Residential Mobility in Gentrifying Neighborhoods." *Urban Affairs Review* 40, no. 4 (2005): 463–491.

Freeman, Lance. *There Goes the 'Hood: Views of Gentrification from the Ground Up*. Philadelphia, PA: Temple University Press, 2011.

Freeman, Lance and Frank Braconi. "Gentrification and Displacement: New York City in the 1990s." *Journal of the American Planning Association* 70, no. 4 (2004): 39–52.

Galster, George and Jason Booza, "The Rise of the Bipolar Neighborhood." *Journal of the American Planning Association* 73, no. 4 (2007): 421–435.

Glass, Ruth Lazarus. *London: Aspects of Change*. Vol. 3. London: MacGibbon & Kee, 1964.

Kennedy, Maureen and Paul Leonard. *Dealing with Neighborhood Change: A Primer on Gentrification and Policy Choices*. Washington, DC: Brookings Institution Press, 2001.

Lee, Barrett A. and David C. Hodge. "Spatial Differentials in Residential Displacement." *Urban Studies* 21 (1984): 219–231.

McKinnish, Terra, Randall Walsh, and T. Kirk White. "Who Gentrifies Low-Income Neighborhoods?" *Journal of Urban Economics* 67, no. 2 (2010): 180–193.

Marcuse, Peter. "Abandonment, Gentrification and Displacement: The Linkages in New York City." In *Gentrification of the City*, edited by Neil Smith and Peter Williams, 153–177. London: Unwin Hyman, 1986.

Newman, Kathe and Elvin K. Wyly. "The Right to Stay Put, Revisited: Gentrification and Resistance to Displacement in New York City." *Urban Studies* 43, no. 1 (2006): 23–57.

Owens, Ann. "Neighborhoods on the Rise: A Typology of Neighborhoods Experiencing Socioeconomic Ascent." *City & Community* 11, no. 4 (2012): 345–369.

Sheldon, Jessica. "The Puzzle of Downtown Development: Housing and Politics in Oakland." Unpublished paper. University of California Berkeley, 2008.

Vigdor, J. "Does Gentrification Harm the Poor?" *Brookings-Wharton Papers on Urban Affairs* (2002): 133–173.

Winston, Francisca and Chris Walker. *Predicting Gentrification in Houston's Low- and Moderate-Income Neighborhoods*. Unpublished paper, November 2012.

Conclusion to Part I

The next 30 years will bring dramatic changes in the U.S. population and economy that our regions and neighborhoods will need to accommodate. The population will be much more diverse, and their jobs will be increasingly dispersed, while paying them less than ever. This, then, will create new patterns of neighborhood change and development. The challenge will be to develop new urban planning and policy tools that soften or even reverse the inequities of new development. The array of mechanisms developed to date—from attracting jobs to transit, to conventional infill development via redevelopment, to mixed-income development, to organizing against gentrification—will help, but they are simply not powerful enough in the fight against growing income inequality. The alternative tools described in the previous chapters are far from a definitive list; examples of other tools that can provide more affordable housing include community land trusts, transferable development rights, and, of course, higher-density infill development (Hickey 2013; Pruetz 2013). Still, these too can only remedy inequity for a few, especially to the extent that they depend on a strong real estate market. Scaling up equitable development—in the absence of state and national action—may be more viable through rent control, housing preservation, or significant public ownership of housing (Keating, Teitz, and Skaburskis 1998).

The specific form of inequitable development will differ across regions, as will the politics of growth and sustainability. Infill development is less challenging in parts of the world without strict environmental regulation and public participation processes. In cities such as Tehran, developers have rapidly transformed traditional single-family neighborhoods into apartment blocks (Madanipour 2011). Copenhagen has seen an increased pace of infill development due partly to its development around rail, but also because of zoning tools, traffic calming, and the provision of amenities that make urban living appealing. High-density infill development pencils out in global cities such as Melbourne, which, like the Bay Area, has chosen to protect most of its suburbs from density and rely on simple planning and zoning tools to encourage infill development. At the same time, it is the regions where infill is most marketable, where the demand for the livable city has taken hold, that will experience the greatest social equity challenges as housing prices rise beyond the means of current low-income residents.

Around the world, regional sustainability plans demonstrate growing awareness of how cities and suburbs can support the complicated lives of their residents. Like Plan Bay Area, Melbourne's plan suggests that we should provide not just affordable housing, but affordable lives. Considering the full cost of living, rather than just housing costs, means supporting location efficiency (i.e., places that provide easy access to transportation, services, and jobs). In Melbourne, this means "20-minute neighborhoods" with easy access to schools, services, and retail—evoking Perry's neighborhood unit, but in practice meaning intervention in a more expansive geography, the district or place. Copenhagen's plan is even more explicit, linking location efficiency to productive and healthy lives and calling for places that minimize time consumption (Capital Region of Denmark 2008).

But the issue of how to approach jobs–housing balance remains complicated. In most developing countries, the informal sector comprises at least half of all employment, making it nearly impossible to plan formally for jobs–housing balance. Metropolitan plans such as Istanbul's do mention the need to support alternative styles of work (Istanbul Metropolitan Municipality 2007). But in Istanbul, Melbourne, Shanghai, and other global cities, the effort to create jobs–housing balance is mostly about accommodating high-skilled workers' desire to live near job centers.

In countries that provide more of a safety net at a national level than the United States does, it is possible to cushion metropolitan income segregation and displacement. At the same time, segregation is a growing issue in almost all metropolitan regions (the possible exception being social democracies such as Denmark). Some regional plans demonstrate awareness of the problem—for example, Melbourne calls for greater diversity of housing types in the suburbs (though failing to identify mechanisms to fund affordable housing). But most seem oblivious. Shanghai calls for the central city to accommodate the skilled workers, while the suburbs are rapidly developed for the relocated urban poor. Much of the new development in Istanbul's polycentric metropolis consists of exclusive office districts and gated communities (Çiraci and Kundak 2000).

Although gentrification (and often displacement) has existed in Europe and the United States for decades, it has only just recently started to impact cities in developing countries (e.g., Santiago, described in Inzulza-Contardo 2012). Its impacts vary widely according to context. Metropolitan areas such as Atlanta that suffer from much higher levels of racial and income segregation and offer few protections for renters may see much higher levels of displacement when gentrification occurs. A mixed-income development can play a catalytic role in changing a neighborhood, and a weak market metro such as Cleveland benefits from gentrification (Swanstrom 2014). But still, the lessons of the Bay Area experience are instructive. The push for sustainability planning is occurring in a context of regional disparities and, without proactive policymaking, will exacerbate them.

The set of tools proposed here is more exploratory and experimental than definitive. Some, such as economy–life balance, are only just emerging. Others, such as value capture, have been used successfully in many other contexts, from Latin America, to the Middle East, to Copenhagen (Knowles 2012; Madanipour 2011; Smolka 2013). Still other possibilities would emerge from careful study of other contexts. But the principles apply widely: given that many of the tools associated with sustainability planning create new winners and losers, we need to re-examine the economics of neighborhoods and create better local tools for redistribution.

This toolkit is also limited to local action, and mostly ignores policymaking at higher levels of government. Were states and countries to take action to reduce inequities within and between regions, such as providing a decent minimum wage, the need for local tools would be reduced. Many have proposed redistributive approaches such as regional tax base sharing or equalization funds (as many states have enacted to ensure balance in spending across school districts). State and federal support for affordable housing, whether through fair share housing or other financial incentives, has also proven effective. Given that income segregation is on the increase between places, these inter-jurisdictional policies are increasingly needed. Arguably, too, they are more effective than any local approach. But politically, there is little prospect of enacting such policies in most states. At least for now, the action is local, block by block.

References

Capital Region of Denmark. *Regional Development Plan: The Capital Region of Denmark—an International Metropolitan Region with High Quality of Life and Growth.* The Capital Region of Denmark, 2008. Accessed January 20, 2014. www.regionh.dk/NR/rdonlyres/D07BBC02-EE45-4FDC-AEF7-0BFCA1ECA99C/0/080904_RUP_UK_net.pdf.

Çiraci, Hale and Seda Kundak. "Changing Urban Pattern of Istanbul: From Monocentric to Polycentric Structure." Paper presented at the 40th Congress of the European Regional Science Association, Barcelona, Spain, 2000.

Hickey, Robert. *The Role of Community Land Trusts in Fostering Equitable, Transit-Oriented Development: Case Studies from Atlanta, Denver, and the Twin Cities.* Cambridge, MA: Lincoln Institute of Land Policy, 2013.

Inzulza-Contardo, Jorge. "'Latino Gentrification'? Focusing on Physical and Socio-economic Patterns of Change in Latin American Inner Cities." *Urban Studies* 49, no. 10 (2012): 2085–2107.

Istanbul Metropolitan Municipality. *The Istanbul Master Plan Summary.* 2007. Accessed January 25, 2014. http://tarlabasi.files.wordpress.com/2009/10/master-plan.pdf.

Keating, W. Dennis, Michael B. Teitz, and Andrejs Skaburskis. *Rent Control.* New Brunswick, NJ: Center for Urban Policy Research, 1998.

Knowles, Richard D. "Transit-Oriented Development in Copenhagen, Denmark: From the Finger Plan to Ørestad." *Journal of Transport Geography* 22 (2012): 251–261.

Madanipour, Ali. "Sustainable Development, Urban Form, and Megacity Governance and Planning in Tehran." In *Megacities: Urban Form, Governance, and Sustainability*, edited by André Sorensen and Junichiro Okata, 67–91. Tokyo: Springer, 2011.

Pruetz, Rick. "Transfer of Development Credits Helps Cities Grow Up." *Built Environment* 39, no. 4 (2013): 502–518.

Smolka, Martim Oscar. *Implementing Value Capture in Latin America: Policies and Tools for Urban Development.* Cambridge, MA: Lincoln Institute of Land Policy, 2013.

Swanstrom, Todd. "Is Gentrification Different in Legacy Cities?" *Legacy Cities*, 2014. Accessed February 25, 2014. http://legacycities.americanassembly.org/is-gentrification-different-in-legacy-cities.

Part II

Growing the Regional Economy through Sustainability

> ... some people continue to defend trickle-down theories which assume that economic growth, encouraged by a free market, will inevitably succeed in bringing about greater justice and inclusiveness in the world. This opinion, which has never been confirmed by the facts, expresses a crude and naïve trust in the goodness of those wielding economic power and in the sacralized workings of the prevailing economic system. Meanwhile, the excluded are still waiting.
>
> Pope Francis, November 24, 2013

That a pope would take a stand on trickle-down economics seems radical in this era, when the working assumption of most industrialized or industrializing countries is indeed that a rising tide will lift all boats. Not surprisingly, the pope's statement quoted above set off a flurry of reaction, both negative and positive, around the world. But he puts forth a challenge: how can economic growth become equitable development?

Sustainable development advocates have long wrestled with the contradictions of sustainable growth. The Brundtland report supports economic growth in order to avert environmental disasters and advance equity goals (Seghezzo 2009). The idea of ecological modernization (i.e., technological progress that addresses environmental problems while also benefiting the economy through productivity improvements) itself suggests the possibility of sustainable growth (Harvey 1996; Krueger and Gibbs 2007). But more typically, economic growth conflicts with environmental goals, and may even use sustainability as a convenient disguise for profit-seeking (Krueger and Gibbs 2008). After all, growth consumes resources that may be finite and irreplaceable, degrades the environment, and may exceed an area's carrying capacity. Yet, equity advocates argue that these may be acceptable trade-offs if they increase life chances for the poor. To the sustainability movement, if new production and jobs grow endogenously out of local context, they may at least be more sustainable than businesses attracted from elsewhere, even if they also harm the environment.

The gradual increase of income inequality since the 1970s belies the claims of the trickle-down theorists. Of course, in the United States, a brief interlude of prosperity, the Clinton decade of the 1990s, reversed the trend. Yet, this is probably due more to a combination of serendipity and progressive policies manifested through taxes and government transfers than a trickle-down dynamic (Hungerford 2008; Stiglitz 2008). And in fact, a growing body of evidence from developing countries suggests that lower levels of inequality, supported by investment in education, increase the amount and duration of growth (Berg, Ostry, and Zettelmeyer 2012; Birdsall, Ross, and Sabot 1995).

This raises the intriguing possibility, explored by Manuel Pastor and his colleagues over the past two decades, that we have been asking the wrong questions about growth and inequality. Instead of examining whether economic growth results in greater inequality, the proposition of interest is whether reducing inequality results in higher economic growth (i.e., equitable regional growth). The preliminary answer seems to be yes: not only do higher levels of inequality mean less per capita income growth, but also reducing inequality means higher growth (Benner and Pastor 2012; Eberts, Erickcek, and Kleinhenz 2006; Pastor et al. 2000).

Yet, the field of regional economic development lacks the tools and even the theories to tackle inequality, just as it is increasing around the world. A vast body of literature explores how economic restructuring has impacted inequality and labor market polarization across regions, and solid research supports the idea that regions grow through increasing their exports, agglomeration, and entrepreneurship. But in practice, with almost no regulatory power over economic development at the regional scale, planners and policymakers have had to turn instead mostly to a bricks-and-mortar approach, relying on two crude tools, real estate development and zoning, as described in the chapters that follow.

The Challenge of Opportunity in Economic Restructuring

As the global economy reinvents itself, regions continually undergo a process of restructuring, or the shift from one economic base from another, adapting with varying degrees of success. Coupled with the retrenchment of government in the neoliberal era, restructuring from manufacturing to services has meant rising income inequality in advanced industrialized countries. This, in turn, has exacerbated disparities between and within regions. Although the economic development toolkit is adapting, it is doing so not quickly enough to facilitate equitable development.

Deindustrialization (defined as a decline in manufacturing's share of national employment) first hit the leading manufacturing regions of the United States and other industrialized countries in the 1970s, and now seems to be impacting other continents such as Latin America as well, albeit for different reasons (Bluestone and Harrison 1982; Brady, Kaya, and Gereffi 2011; Kollmeyer 2009). By the end of the twentieth century, a new phase of restructuring had also led to what Manuel Castells (1996) termed the informational mode of development.

This meant a shift in job quality as well, with a rise in low-wage work accompanied by a loss of middle-income jobs. Scholars have invoked technological as well as institutional explanations for the shift. The skill-biased technological change argument claims that the introduction of new technologies (such as computers) resulted in rising demand for college-educated workers—and wage declines for less-educated workers (Katz and Murphy 1992). The institutional explanation focuses on the transformation of the governance of the labor market. Osterman (1999) shows how the "Fordist era," roughly 1946–1973, had brought rising real wages, productivity growth, oligopolistic competition among large firms, and relative labor peace. Accompanying this was a set of norms held by employers and recognized by a largely unionized industrial workforce that resulted in workplace practices such as internal job ladders and a productivity "dividend" to workers. These institutions broke down in the 1970s, leading to a restructuring of labor market institutions that resulted in rising income inequality. Corporations now shed large portions of their core workforce on an ongoing basis, increasingly relying upon a flexible, contingent pool of workers whose earnings are forced down by stiff competition (Appelbaum, Bernhardt, and Murnane 2003). Coupled with immigration, this has led to the rise of the informal sector, which, though still larger in developing countries, plays a significant and growing role in the United States and other advanced industrialized countries (Nightingale and Wandner 2011). Of course, these changes must be understood in the context of the competitive pressures from rising globalization, although these play a relatively minor role compared to internal labor market dynamics (Katz and Autor 1999).

The following examines the related trends in income inequality, mobility, and opportunity. Given these macro-economic trends, the question arises of what regions can do to promote more equitable economic development.

Income Inequality

The economist Simon Kuznets first introduced the idea (known as the Kuznets curve) that inequality would rise as economic growth accelerates, and then would decrease as average incomes begin gaining from the new prosperity. From his perspective—the developed world in the 1950s—this seemed like a reasonable hypothesis. And, certainly much of continental Europe and Japan has experienced declines in income inequality (Alvaredo et al. 2013). But in reality, the picture has proven more complex. High levels of inequality have persisted in Latin America, Southern Africa, and, most recently, China— although the twenty-first century has brought declining inequality in most Latin-American countries (Economic Commission for Latin America and the Caribbean 2010; Economist 2013). The one notable exception during this period has been the countries of East Asia, where a growing middle class is benefiting from the reinvestment of capital into programs that support equality, such as universal education (Stiglitz 1996).

The United States maintains the highest rates of income inequality in the developed world, accompanied by Israel, Turkey, Mexico, and Chile (Organisation for Economic Cooperation and Development 2013). The rise of income inequality in the United States is not only a well-established fact, but has also entered the public consciousness, as reflected in the sharp increase in the number of those who see a strong conflict between rich and poor (Morin 2012). The most rigorous measures of income inequality take taxes into account, and it is after-tax income that is growing more for highest-income households than for any other group. Between 1979 and 2007, income was redistributed from the bottom to the top, growing by 275 percent for the top 1 percent of households, but just 18 percent for the bottom 20 percent (Congressional Budget Office 2011). After the Great Recession, the trend accelerated, with the top 1 percent seeing 95 percent of all income gains in the recovery (Saez 2013).

Income inequality does not stem simply from technological change, because high-income countries with similar development trajectories have different rates of inequality (Alvaredo et al. 2013). Four factors account for the high inequality in the United States (as well as the United Kingdom): favorable tax rates for the rich, generous executive pay, inherited wealth, and capital (instead of earned) income (ibid.). Because of inherited privilege, the United States is losing its status as the land of opportunity: there is less intergenerational mobility in the United States than in most advanced industrialized countries (i.e., the children of the rich tend to stay rich, while children of the poor stay poor) (Mishel et al. 2012). Intergenerational mobility seems to be related positively to K-12 school quality, social capital, and income growth, and negatively to income inequality, family structure (e.g., divorce rates), and residential segregation, among other factors (Chetty et al. 2013).

Thus, declines in upward mobility have hit low-income households particularly hard. Low-wage workers are simply unlikely to move up: even in the recent interlude of prosperity, only one-fourth of low earners were able to rise above the poverty line for a family of four (Holzer 2004). A study looking at a longer, six-year period found that about 58 percent of low-wage workers experienced earnings gains, while most of the remaining earners had losses (Theodos and Bednarzik 2006).

Most agree that education has become much more important for upward mobility (Bernhardt et al. 2001; McMurrer and Sawhill 1998). But there is no simple recipe for moving up: both the declining returns from working and the job instability that characterize the economy today mean that education alone is not enough to guarantee upward mobility (Bernhardt et al. 2001). Upward mobility also depends on local labor market conditions, corporate culture, union pressure, and other factors; while some employers may choose to increase productivity by investing in worker skills, others compete based upon labor cost (Appelbaum, Bernhardt, and Murnane 2003). Overall, the opportunity to move up will depend on the extent and rigidity of the bipolarization in the labor market.

Opportunity in the Bipolar Labor Market

Economic restructuring is increasing the bipolarization of the labor market, with the growth of both high-skill, high-wage and low-skill, low-wage work. What, then, is low-wage work? There is no international standard, but one way to examine it in the U.S. context is to determine the hourly wage needed to raise a full-time, full-year worker (2,080 hours per year) above the poverty standard for a family of four; by this measure, about 20 percent of working adults are low-wage workers (Osterman 2014). Fully one-third of these workers are in retail or restaurants, with most of the remainder in professional services, manufacturing, education, or healthcare (ibid.).

But it is an open question how much opportunity remains for those without a college education, in particular how many of the low-skill jobs are dead-end rather than offering the potential to lead to middle-skill work. In recent years, all low-skill job growth has occurred in service occupations (such as food service workers, security guards, janitors, gardeners, cleaners, home health aides, childcare workers, and beauticians), while occupations in production, construction, and transportation are in decline. The growth of dead-end service jobs is closely related to the business cycle; most middle-skill job losses occur during recessions, and they fail to reappear during the recoveries (Bernhardt, McKenna, and Evangelist 2012; Jaimovich and Siu 2012). The general consensus now is that skill-biased technological change alone cannot account for all of the increase in low-wage jobs; instead of computers simply replacing human work, they may instead be increasing productivity in certain sectors, thereby creating new consumer demand for services such as restaurant meals and home health (Autor and Dorn 2013). Whatever the cause, if technology is playing a role in wage inequality and job polarization, then the policy remedy is to increase college attendance and invest in infrastructure and R&D (Autor 2010).

There are, however, other explanations for the growth of low-wage work that have different policy implications. First, the 2000s saw little job growth in high-skilled sectors, flattening the U-shaped pattern of bipolarization. Moreover, the wages for college-educated workers have stagnated (Osterman 2014). Second, job polarization has actually been increasing since 1950, while wage inequality only accelerated since the 1970s. This suggests that technology and occupational trends alone do not explain today's low wages (Mishel, Shierholz, and Schmitt 2013). A number of different factors are likely combining to produce the low-wage reality, including offshoring, immigration, labor supply changes (e.g., the entry of women into the workforce), declining unionization, the declining real value of the federal minimum wage, and, most importantly, the transformation of labor market institutions.

There is also some suggestion that demographic and sectoral shifts will continue to support the middle in coming years. Demand remains robust for middle-skilled workers in healthcare, protective services, law, information technology, and some other sectors (Holzer and Lerman 2009). In the coming decade, two-thirds of all jobs will require an associate's degree or higher (Neumark, Johnson, and Mejia 2011). Even if new demand for middle-skilled workers does not materialize, the retirement of baby boomers will create tens of millions of job openings (Bureau of Labor Statistics 2013). The policy implication here is a need for human capital development aimed at helping low-skilled workers move up the ladder (i.e., long-term job training and community college, rather than four-year degrees) (Holzer and Lerman 2009). Even if such changes are implemented, however, the changing nature of work and the lack of negotiating power for labor make it unlikely that the new middle-skill jobs will pay as well as they used to, absent major regulatory changes.

The Geography of Inequality and Opportunity

Economic restructuring has manifested itself in geographic shifts as well; just as some places disproportionately reap the fruits of change, others increasingly experience its downside. Uneven development is a key feature of capitalist industrialization, as capital seeks out greater profits (Storper and Walker 1989). In the last half of the twentieth century, the tremendous number of plant closings and the high unemployment in areas such as the Midwest (e.g., the Rustbelt) helped accelerate a shift in population and employment to the South and West, while new command-and-control centers for the global economy emerged in select metropolitan regions (Sassen 1991). Though both technological change and global trade influenced these shifts, the two forces actually have different regional impacts, with information technology transforming jobs in larger cities such as Chicago, and trade impacting the regions, such as the South Central United States, with more labor-intensive manufacturing plants (Autor, Dorn, and Hanson 2013).

Supply-side forces drive uneven development as well: high-paying service sector jobs in knowledge-intensive, creative industries may be highly concentrated because firms follow an elite workforce (famously termed by Richard Florida "the creative class") to the cities and regions where they choose to live (Florida 2002; Glaeser and Resseger 2010). Taken together, these demand- and supply-side forces are creating what Enrico Moretti (2012) calls "innovation hubs," select metropolitan areas characterized by the growth of innovation sectors, such as information technology or biotechnology.

Innovation might be described as an epistemological transformation, or new knowledge, that combines resources to create new products or services that reach economic fruition. Hubs emerge not just because of the classic pattern of urban agglomeration—firms clustering in order to benefit from shared knowledge, markets, and inputs—but also because of this creative class dynamic. Innovative places attract the very highly educated workers who are in short supply, in turn attracting more firms. As Ed Glaeser (1997) might add here, the more chances that the city gives these new workers to interact (i.e., the denser the city), the greater their learning will be. This type of cluster creates particularly high multiplier effects—in other words, the growth of tradable, export sectors creates new demand for inputs, and also goods and services for the workers and their households.[1] Thus, jobs multiply, particularly in non-tradable sectors, or non-mobile services, such as domestic service, construction, restaurants, and entertainment; the benefits trickle down, creating dead-end jobs. The overall effect is to grow the local economy rapidly, driving up local housing prices and wages—as in strong market regions such as San Francisco. But the metropolitan regions without this innovative upward spiral are left further and further behind.

Uneven development impacts regional opportunity structures as well. Not surprisingly, intergenerational mobility varies across regions, depending on the regional economy and income inequality, but also regional culture, its family structure, and social capital (Chetty et al. 2013). Interestingly, at least at a glance, the regions that facilitate upward mobility look a lot like Moretti's innovation hubs, mostly located in the Northeast, Northwest, Pacific, Midwest, and Southwest of the United States (ibid.).

Restructuring and the evolving geography of sectors and opportunity make equitable approaches to regional sustainability planning even more challenging. What is needed is a toolkit for local and regional economic development (LED) that responds to growing inequality and lack of upward mobility. LED, indeed, is a conscious effort, by means of public policy and action, to increase the level of and capacity for local economic activity, in order to create wealth for local residents. In the United States, it emerged shortly after the post-World War II decades of great prosperity, when rising tides were actually lifting many, if not all, boats, in order to address the unevenness of development across regions. With the labor-management bargain in place, there was little need to address job quality. Thus, even the major theories underlying LED provide little insight into the issue of redistribution, as we discuss next, before turning to specific LED policies.

Theories of Local and Regional Economic Development

Equitable regions will need to create enough jobs (i.e., grow the pie), then ensure that jobs are high enough quality (i.e., pay a living wage), and then, finally, ensure that disadvantaged residents are able to compete for the jobs (i.e., that barriers such as lack of education and discrimination are removed). Theories of how regional economic development occurs suggest significant challenges in each of these areas. We look first at the role of exports, then at agglomeration, and finally at entrepreneurship—all approaches that either grow the pie or increase incomes, but that may struggle at incorporating the disadvantaged into the mainstream.

The Role of the Export Base

As Douglass North argued in 1955, regions grow through new exogenous demand for exports, which instigates a cycle of growth: jobs and production must increase, sales bring revenue to pay the workers and proprietors, and income translates into more local consumption of goods and services from "residentiary" industries (North 1955). In addition, the growth of the export sector spurs the development of related local industries (such as machine tools or agricultural equipment). Regions can influence how growth occurs by helping to reduce production costs (e.g., through investment in transportation or human capital).

There is no real disagreement from North to Enrico Moretti today on the basic principle that growth of exports leads to regional development, mostly because of this cycle of growth and multiplier effects. But major puzzles and contradictions remain. Some regions never become successful exporters, while others export for centuries but become overspecialized, or never manage to diversify and industrialize as predicted. Charles Tiebout (1956) pointed out that the impact of exports is much weaker for larger regions, which can grow on the basis of internal trade (e.g., New York City). As income from exports grows, a regional economy's ability to provide for itself increases, resulting in new processes of import substitution. Though these might then lead to export increases, the cause is not exogenous, but *endogenous* demand.

This, then, suggests that the most important factors behind regional growth might lie within the region (i.e., in its supply side). Within a region, incomes might change because of increases in productivity, government expenditures, changing consumption patterns, non-economic migration (e.g., retirees), and other factors. For instance, more output for export can mean more tax revenues, leading to more government spending, leading to improved services and an influx of labor that can then lower labor costs or improve productivity: export demand matters, but government investment may be the key factor. Supply factors shape how effectively the region can respond to export growth.

The story of the supply side's role in regional growth was best explained by Benjamin Chinitz' classic 1961 study of New York and Pittsburgh. Chinitz sought to solve the puzzle of why the diversified New York metropolitan region grew so much faster than Pittsburgh, highly specialized in the steel industry. Pittsburgh's oligopolistic industry structure led to the suppression of inter-industry relationships. With barriers to entry into the steel industry, there were few opportunities for entrepreneurship. With much work performed in-house, there were few spin-off industries; intermediate goods and services producers failed to emerge. It was not just because of Pittsburgh's small size that it failed to develop external economies (i.e., gains in productivity due to mutual proximity and shared specializations or complementarities among firms), but its very industry structure. Firms in certain types of industries develop closer relationships to other firms.

This leads us to examine the importance of agglomeration in regional growth. But before turning to agglomeration, where does the export base debate leave us in terms of equitable growth? Whether growth stems from the demand or the supply side, it is growing the pie. But there is little guarantee of job quality or fit for disadvantaged residents in a region driven by export demand. Such regions are particularly susceptible to competition from other low-cost regions around the world, the challenges of keeping pace with technological change, and, in the case of resource-based economies, the depletion of natural resources. Although North anticipated that trade would eventually lead to the dispersion of production and equalization of incomes across regions, the flows of labor and capital can be asymmetrical—what Jane Jacobs (1984) called "supply regions," where locals fails to benefit, such as the Amazon. Only those regions that have carefully developed their supply side will be able to meet these challenges.

Agglomeration

As the region grows around its export base, external economies develop to improve its competitive position. With a number of firms in the same industry, or *localization* economies, suppliers begin locating nearby. Related firms emerge to provide ancillary services, such as marketing, access to credit, and legal services. Workers with specific skills migrate to the area. The proximity of this cluster of firms leads to knowledge sharing and spillovers—in the words of Alfred Marshall (1920: 271): "The mysteries of the trade become no mysteries; but are as it were in the air." Michael Porter (1998) later adapted this idea to become his clusters, or geographic concentrations of interconnected companies and institutions that create the specializations that drive regional competitive advantage and growth.

Another form of external economies is *urbanization* economies, in which the higher volume of economic activity in an urban area (i.e., urban size) helps to drive down costs as urban services and infrastructure—as well as the market—expand. The firms that agglomerate to benefit from urbanization economies are those in industries that produce unstandardized goods, experience variable demand, and frequently adapt production processes; this means that investment in fixed capital (buildings and equipment) is inappropriate (as Raymond Vernon's New York study showed in 1960). By relying on outside suppliers and sharing facilities, businesses can cope with uncertainty with minimal risk. Proximity allows greater face-to-face contact with suppliers and customers, thus permitting faster response times. As Jane Jacobs (1969) described in *The Economy of Cities*, it also allows "old work," or traditional production, to morph into "new work" in a nearby field (i.e., innovation). These Jacobean externalities are thus more dynamic than the traditional urbanization economies (shared materials, labor, markets): they are inter- or intra-industry innovations in process (Glaeser et al. 1991). A growing body of evidence suggests that these agglomerations of diverse firms result in higher levels of regional innovation (Feldman and Audretsch 1999; Simmie and Sennett 1999).

Thus, localization economies increase specialization, while urbanization economies increase diversity (Jacobs 1969). The verdict is out on whether specialization or diversity is optimal for equitable economic growth. Some (most notably, Michael Porter) find that more specialization, especially in traded clusters, results in a higher growth rate, while others argue that clusters do not create jobs. Overall, there seems to be slightly stronger evidence that regional economic diversity increases job growth (Dissart 2003; Feser, Renski, and Goldstein 2008; Glaeser 2000; Porter 2003). But, will specialization or diversity bring higher wages? Again, the evidence on per capita income growth is inconclusive and contradictory; if anything, the preponderance of the evidence points to specialization as the means to improving income levels (Dissart 2003; Drennan 2002; Pede 2013; Porter 2003). Most importantly, no research has examined how diversity and specialization reshape the income distribution and income inequality (Dissart 2003).

What is much clearer from the research is that economic diversity leads to reduced unemployment, as regions with a variety of industries are able to protect themselves during cyclic downturns (Dissart 2003; Izraeli and Murphy 2003). Beyond the sheer vulnerability of dependence on the fortunes of one or a few industries, specialization also can suppress activity elsewhere in the economy, as dominant firms monopsonize area resources in ways that suppress entrepreneurship (as Chinitz suggested). The bigger the economy, the more resilient it will be.

Thus, urban agglomerations are able to grow the pie and raise regional incomes. In terms of equitable growth, diverse regions may provide more stability, while specialized regions may succeed better at raising incomes. The higher levels of accessibility and interaction that proximity provides may also reduce the barriers that disadvantaged workers face in competing for jobs. At the same time, the downside of agglomeration is the higher cost of living (as described in Part I); as labor and housing costs rise and congestion increases, firms and workers may experience agglomeration diseconomies.

Entrepreneurship

One last piece of the puzzle comes from the literature on how entrepreneurship occurs and shapes economic growth. Given the role of clusters and agglomeration in regional growth and innovation, it seems that external economies and knowledge spillovers are critical. But the dynamic is not simply one of reducing costs through pooled resources. Instead, it is about how firms are organized in order to allow for rapid learning, experimentation, and adjustment.

AnnaLee Saxenian's *Regional Advantage* (1994) provides the most powerful account of this to date, telling the story of the divergence of Silicon Valley and Route 128-Boston in the 1980s due to differences in the organization of production. Silicon Valley made the shift from vertically integrated firms, doing R&D and most or all phases of production (manufacturing inputs, assembly, final production) in-house, to a network-based system that allowed the transfer of skills and technology. These networks of actors—buyers, suppliers, competitors, and related institutions—are organized loosely, with a changeable configuration, in order to respond to economic changes. Even more importantly, their economic action is not based on individualistic calculation of costs and benefits, but is embedded into larger institutional and social frameworks. Building on the insights of Polanyi (1944) into how markets are socially constructed and Granovetter (1985) on the importance of trust and social relations among firm actors, Saxenian shows how Silicon Valley's culture of openness and collaboration fostered the high-tech sector. Meanwhile, Route 128 stagnated.

What does this mean for equitable development? The horizontal networks of entrepreneurial firms in the Silicon Valley story—and also described by Michael Piore and Charles Sabel (1984) in the district of Emilia-Romagna, or the Third Italy—are comprised mostly of small firms, although Bennett Harrison (1994) and others were quick to point out that larger firms were involved as well. This, along with the pioneering research of David Birch (1979, 1987), suggests that small businesses (with 20 or fewer employees) may dominate job creation. And in fact, in regions dominated by smaller firms, employment grows faster (Acs, Parsons, and Tracy 2008). But it is not just small size that makes the difference; instead, new firm start-ups and young firms generally account for job growth (Haltiwanger, Jarmin, and Miranda 2011; Neumark, Wall, and Zhang 2011).[2] In fact, most new job growth is accounted for by a handful of "gazelle" firms, firms that have increased their sales at a rate many times higher than average (Birch and Medoff 1994; Henrekson and Johansson 2010). Still, large firms, at least in the United States, continue to provide the majority of jobs, pay the highest wages, maintain higher success rates, and are more likely to adopt and implement technology (Harrison 1994).

Whether large or small, entrepreneurial firms clearly create jobs. But these may not be the most equitable. First, start-up firms tend to be undercapitalized and pay relatively low wages; this is particularly true among immigrant communities who may count on low-cost labor from network contacts (Bates 1997; Ong and Loukaitou-Sideris 2006).

And second, there are multiple barriers to entry for lower-income entrepreneurs, including financial insecurity, poor access to credit, low appetite for risk, and low education and training. In particular, inherited wealth and family assets create advantages for entrepreneurship and self-employment (Hurst and Lusardi 2006; Quadrini 2000). In countries with higher inequality, there is much more "necessity entrepreneurship" (i.e., entrepreneurship that occurs because of the lack of other employment prospects) than "opportunity entrepreneurship," where entrepreneurship occurs because of potential market demand (Lippman, Davis, and Aldrich 2005).

Whether looking at the strength of the export base, or the region's diversity, or entrepreneurship, as the source of regional employment growth, there remains one outstanding issue: who will get the jobs? Job growth in a region creates a chain reaction of job shifting within and across regions. First, as Timothy Bartik (1993) has shown, for every 100 new jobs in a metropolitan area, about 80 new workers move in from outside the region; the higher the skills demanded and wages paid in the new job, the more in-migration will occur. The 20 remaining jobs will be taken by local residents, but underemployed residents (in terms of hours, wages, or challenge) will likely be first in line for the new job opportunities, rather than the long-term unemployed. As the workers from both within and outside the region leave their current jobs, they create openings for others, and, presumably down the job chain, the most disadvantaged (or unemployed) worker will gain an opportunity. But chances are that that opportunity will be in another region, because of the attraction of in-migrants to high-growth regions. Because of this job chain effect, the most equitable approach is to focus on increasing regional per capita earnings instead of job creation (Bartik 2011).

The Rise of Regional and Local Economic Development Policy

Although most of the major theories of regional economic development emerged by the middle of the twentieth century, the practice of economic development at the local and regional scale is relatively new. Of course, cities have long engaged in smokestack chasing (the subject of Chapter 7), which follows the logic of the export base in attracting businesses with exogenous markets (such as auto manufacturers). But it is only since the late 1970s' urban fiscal crises, caused by global economic restructuring and government devolution, that cities and regions have strategically tried to increase the level of and capacity for local economic activity. Similar dynamics have led to the rise of local economic development (LED) around the globe. How democratic and participatory the practice of LED is varies around the world according to political context, but the tools of economic development are quite similar.

From the perspective of economists, job creation is most effective at the federal level. Only the federal government can print money, utilize deficit spending, and control trade, providing it with flexibility, relatively cheap currency, and competitive advantage. Without these powers, state and local government action may only shift economic activity from one place to another.

That said, when state and local efforts encourage cluster or agglomeration economies, these do not necessarily come at the expense of other locations, but may create net new jobs. Likewise, local product and technology development can create new jobs, although this will be a long-term process (Basu, Fernald, and Kimball 2004). In the absence of local action, much of this growth would simply not occur. At the same time, developing a cluster of firms and related institutions, or building a physical agglomeration in urban space, is a very complicated endeavor. It is thus not surprising that economic development practitioners have chosen instead, with the encouragement of local politicians, to adopt business attraction or endogenous development strategies with quick and visible outcomes.

Cities and states adopt different types or waves of economic development strategies, each with different implications (albeit rarely spelled out) for equitable development: business attraction, endogenous development, and community economic development and capacity building (Bradshaw and Blakely 1999; Eisinger 1995; Fitzgerald and Leigh 2002; Zheng and Warner 2010). Most use a mix of strategies, though they may revert to business attraction via incentives during times of recession (Osgood, Opp, and Bernotsky 2012).

In the first wave, cities and states try to attract firms to relocate, typically via tax incentives, subsidized loans, or simply marketing (Bradshaw and Blakely 1999). As discussed further in the next chapter, evidence suggests that these strategies rarely create jobs: tax incentives have mixed effects on business location decision-making (Peters and Fisher 2004). On the other hand, business attraction efforts do tend to target relatively high-wage firms, such as high-tech manufacturers and exporters generally. One equitable benefit of the business attraction approach is that economic developers typically work very closely with the businesses, in the process often developing customized training and hiring processes that can ensure that local residents are prepared for jobs.

Endogenous development focuses attention on the entrepreneurial potential of existing firms, often embedded within clusters. Thus, these strategies focus on business start-ups, expansion, and retention, typically via revolving loan funds, business incubators, business management assistance, government procurement, and R&D/innovation support. These might also include various hiring tax credit programs, including those in enterprise zones, which end up benefiting existing firms (again, discussed in the next chapter).

The importance of start-ups, young businesses, and rapid firm expansions in job creation suggests that second-wave endogenous development strategies will be particularly fruitful for equitable development. Yet, there are exceptions. Though innovation policies may grow the pie over the long term, they might also have displacement or at least wage-dampening effects in the short term (Basu, Fernald, and Kimball 2004). Enterprise zone programs underperform in expected job creation and effects disappear quickly (Cray et al. 2011; Greenbaum and Landers 2009). In theory, endogenous development strategies should result in wage increases, since they increase productivity. But in practice, results are likely mixed, as younger firms in particular lack the stability to remunerate workers. Cities and intermediaries may experience challenges in organizing smaller firms to provide equity benefits. There is also no guarantee that local firms will hire locally, and in fact, locals may have prejudices about hiring from certain areas that lead to discrimination (Dewar 2013).

Third-wave strategies build local capacity to participate in the economy, through job training, community empowerment, and improvements in quality of life—in other words, more equitable development. However, recent work suggests that these are still relatively rare in the LED toolkit (Osgood, Opp, and Bernotsky 2012; Zheng and Warner 2010). Although they have not been systematically studied for job creation impacts, their effects are most likely to be felt over the long term. Their benefit is primarily in improving job quality and match for locals.

Growing the Sustainable and Equitable Regional Economy

Serious economic challenges lie ahead. In the United States in particular, most regions are experiencing rising inequality and a restructuring labor market that offers little upward mobility. Even in countries with more of a social safety net, regions have to deal with inequality and the sectoral shifts of the informational mode of development. Labor market polarization, whatever its extent, is creating serious challenges for economic development policy, which needs to shift to more of a focus on the quality of jobs produced.

In the long run, this suggests the need to support agglomerations of economic activity and the entrepreneurship that results. But this may also lead to more uneven development patterns, exacerbating inequality. To achieve per capita income growth that is also sustainable will mean developing a set of complementary economic development policies at the community, local, state, and national levels that address inequality within and between regions. The following chapters start that conversation by looking first at some of the tools available to generate jobs in specific places, then at the types of economic growth that might be considered both equitable and sustainable, and finally at the issue of metropolitan structure (i.e., which uses should locate where within the region to maximize equitable development).

Notes

1. Michael Teitz (2013) points out that in other works, Moretti shows that these multipliers are not statistically significant.
2. But see Acs, Parsons, and Tracy (2008), who found that "high-impact" firms with rapid employment growth tend to be older.

References

Acs, Zoltan, William Parsons, and Spencer Tracy. *High-Impact Firms: Gazelles Revisited.* Washington, DC: Small Business Administration, 2008.

Alvaredo, Facundo, Anthony B. Atkinson, Thomas Piketty, and Emmanuel Saez. "The Top 1 Percent in International and Historical Perspective." *Journal of Economic Perspectives* 27, no. 3 (2013): 3–20.

Appelbaum, Eileen, Annette Bernhardt, and Richard J. Murnane, editors. *Low-Wage America: How Employers are Reshaping Opportunity in the Workplace.* New York: Russell Sage Foundation, 2003.

Autor, David. *The Polarization of Job Opportunities in the U.S. Labor Market: Implications for Employment and Earnings.* Washington, DC: Center for American Progress, 2010.

Autor, David and David Dorn. "The Growth of Low-Skill Service Jobs and the Polarization of the U.S. Labor Market." *American Economic Review* 103, no. 5 (2013): 1553–1597.

Autor, David H., David Dorn, and Gordon H. Hanson. "The Geography of Trade and Technology Shocks in the United States." *American Economic Review* 103, no. 3 (2013): 220–225.

Bartik, Timothy J. "Who Benefits from Local Job Growth: Migrants or the Original Residents?" *Regional Studies* 27, no. 4 (1993): 297–311.

Bartik, Timothy J. "What Works in Job Creation and Economic Development." Paper presented at Transforming Communities Conference of the National Employment Law Project, Flint, MI, June 1, 2011.

Basu, Susanto, John Fernald, and Miles Kimball. *Are Technology Improvements Contractionary?* No. w10592. Cambridge, MA: National Bureau of Economic Research, 2004.

Bates, Timothy. "Entrepreneurship as a Route to Upward Mobility Among the Disadvantaged." In *Race, Self-Employment, and Upward Mobility: An Illusive American Dream*, edited by Timothy Bates, 207–224. Baltimore, MD: Johns Hopkins University Press, 1997.

Benner, Chris and Manuel Pastor. *Just Growth: Inclusion and Prosperity in America's Metropolitan Regions*. New York: Routledge, 2012.

Berg, Andrew, Jonathan D. Ostry, and Jeromin Zettelmeyer. "What Makes Growth Sustained?" *Journal of Development Economics* 98, no. 2 (2012): 149–166.

Bernhardt, Annette, C. McKenna, and M. Evangelist. "The Low-Wage Recovery and Growing Inequality." *National Employment Law Project Data Brief*. New York: National Employment Law Project, 2012.

Bernhardt, Annette, Martina Morris, Mark S. Handcock, and Marc A. Scott. *Divergent Paths: Economic Mobility in the New American Labor Market*. Manhattan, NY: Russell Sage Foundation, 2001.

Birch, David L. *The Job Generation Process*. Cambridge, MA: MIT Program on Neighborhood and Regional Change, 1979.

Birch, David L. *Job Creation in America*. New York: Free Press, 1987.

Birch, David and James Medoff. "Gazelles." In *Labor Markets, Employment Policy, and Job Creation*, edited by Lewis C. Solomon and Alec R. Levenson, 159–168. Boulder, CO: Westview, 1994.

Birdsall, Nancy, David Ross, and Richard Sabot. "Inequality and Growth Reconsidered: Lessons from East Asia." *The World Bank Economic Review* 9, no. 3 (1995): 477.

Bluestone, Barry and Bennett Harrison. *The Deindustrialization of America: Plant Closings, Community Abandonment, and the Dismantling of Basic Industry*. New York: Basic Books, 1982.

Bradshaw, Ted K. and Edward J. Blakely. "What are 'Third-Wave' State Economic Development Efforts? From Incentives to Industrial Policy." *Economic Development Quarterly* 13, no. 3 (1999): 229–244.

Brady, David, Yunus Kaya, and Gary Gereffi. "Stagnating Industrial Employment in Latin America." *Work and Occupations* 38, no. 2 (2011): 179–220.

Bureau of Labor Statistics. "Replacement Needs." Accessed December 19, 2013. www.bls.gov/emp/ep_table_110.htm.

Bureau of Labor Statistics. "Employment by Detailed Occupation." Accessed December 19, 2013. www.bls.gov/emp/ep_table_102.htm.

Castells, Manuel. *The Rise of the Network Society: The Information Age: Economy, Society and Culture Volume I*. Cambridge, MA: Blackwell, 1996.

Chetty, Raj, Nathan Hendren, Patrick Kline, and Emmanuel Saez. "The Economic Impacts of Tax Expenditures: Evidence from Spatial Variation across the US." Unpublished paper. Harvard University and University of California, Berkeley, 2013.

Chinitz, Benjamin. "Contrasts in Agglomeration: New York and Pittsburgh." *American Economic Review: Papers and Proceedings* 51 (1961): 279–289.

Congressional Budget Office. *Trends in the Distribution of Household Income Between 1979 and 2007*. Washington, DC: The Congress of the United States, Congressional Budget Office, 2011.

Cray, Adam, Tram Nguyen, Carol Pranka, Christine Schildt, Julie Sheu, and Erika Rincon Whitcomb. *Job Creation: A Review of Policies and Strategies*. Berkeley, CA: Institute for Research on Labor and Employment, 2011.

Dewar, Margaret. "Paying Employers to Hire Local Workers in Distressed Places." *Economic Development Quarterly* 27, no. 4 (2013): 284–300.

Dissart, Jean Christophe. "Regional Economic Diversity and Regional Economic Stability: Research Results and Agenda." *International Regional Science Review* 26, no. 4 (2003): 423–446.

Drennan, Matthew P. *The Information Economy and American Cities*. Baltimore, MD: JHU Press, 2002.

Eberts, R., G. Erickcek, and J. Kleinhenz. *Dashboard Indicators for the Northeast Ohio Economy: Prepared for the Fund for Our Economic Future*. Working Paper 06-05. Cleveland, OH: The Federal Reserve Bank of Cleveland, 2006.

Economic Commission for Latin America and the Caribbean. *Time for Equality: Closing Gaps, Opening Trails*. Santiago, Chile: ECLAC, 2010.

Economist. "Gini Out of the Bottle." *The Economist Newspaper*, January 26, 2013.

Eisinger, Peter. "State Economic Development in the 1990s: Politics and Policy Learning." *Economic Development Quarterly* 9, no. 2 (1995): 146–158.

Feldman, Maryann P. and David B. Audretsch. "Innovation in Cities: Science-Based Diversity, Specialization and Localized Competition." *European Economic Review* 43, no. 2 (1999): 409–429.

Feser, Edward, Henry Renski, and Harvey Goldstein. "Clusters and Economic Development Outcomes: An Analysis of the Link Between Clustering and Industry Growth." *Economic Development Quarterly* 22, no. 4 (2008): 324–344.

Fitzgerald, Joan and Nancey G. Leigh. *Economic Revitalization: Cases and Strategies for City and Suburbs*. Thousand Oaks, CA: Sage Publications, 2002.

Florida, Richard. "The Economic Geography of Talent." *Annals of the Association of American Geographers* 92, no. 4 (2002): 743–755.

Glaeser, Edward. *Learning in Cities*. Working Paper 6271. Cambridge, MA: National Bureau of Economic Research, 1997.

Glaeser, Edward L. "The New Economics of Urban and Regional Growth." *The Oxford Handbook of Economic Geography* (2000): 83–98.

Glaeser, Edward L. and Matthew G. Resseger. "The Complementarity Between Cities and Skills." *Journal of Regional Science* 50, no. 1 (2010): 221–244.

Glaeser, Edward L., Hedi D. Kallal, Jose A. Scheinkman, and Andrei Shleifer. *Growth in Cities*. No. w3787. Cambridge, MA: National Bureau of Economic Research, 1991.

Granovetter, Mark. "Economic Action and Social Structure: The Problem of Embeddedness." *American Journal of Sociology* (1985): 481–510.

Greenbaum, Robert T. and Jim Landers. "Why are State Policy Makers Still Proponents of Enterprise Zones? What Explains Their Action in the Face of a Preponderance of the Research?" *International Regional Science Review* 32, no. 4 (2009): 466–479.

Haltiwanger, John, Ron S. Jarmin, and Javier Miranda. "Who Creates Jobs? Small vs. Large vs. Young." *NBER Working Paper No. 16300*. Cambridge, MA: National Bureau of Economic Research, 2011.

Harrison, Bennett. "The Myth of Small Firms as the Predominant Job Generators." *Economic Development Quarterly* 8, no. 3 (1994): 3–18.

Harvey, David. *Justice, Nature and the Geography of Difference*. Hoboken, NJ: Wiley, 1996.

Henrekson, Magnus and Dan Johansson. "Gazelles as Job Creators: A Survey and Interpretation of the Evidence." *Small Business Economics* 35, no. 2 (2010): 227–244.

Holzer, Harry. *Encouraging Job Advancement Among Low-Wage Workers: A New Approach.* Washington, DC: Brookings Institution Press, 2004.

Holzer, Harry J. and Robert I. Lerman. *The Future of Middle-Skill Jobs, Center on Children and Families Brief #41.* Washington, DC: Brookings Institution Press, 2009.

Hungerford, T. L. *Income Inequality, Income Mobility, and Economic Policy: U.S. Trends in the 1980s and 1990s.* RS34434. Washington, DC: Congressional Research Service, 2008.

Hurst, Erik and Annamaria Lusardi. "Liquidity Constraints and Entrepreneurship. Household Wealth, Parental Wealth, and the Transition in and out of Entrepreneurship." Paper presented at a conference on savings and entrepreneurship organized by the Hudson Institute, Washington, DC, December, 2006.

Izraeli, Oded and Kevin J. Murphy. "The Effect of Industrial Diversity on State Unemployment Rate and Per Capita Income." *The Annals of Regional Science* 37, no. 1 (2003): 1–14.

Jacobs, Jane. *The Economy of Cities.* New York: Random House, 1969.

Jacobs, Jane. *Cities and the Wealth of Nations: Principles of Economic Life.* New York: Random House, 1984.

Jaimovich, Nir and Henry E. Siu. *The Trend is the Cycle: Job Polarization and Jobless Recoveries.* Working Paper 18334. Cambridge, MA: National Bureau of Economic Research, 2012.

Katz, Lawrence F. and David H. Autor. "Changes in the Wage Structure and Earnings Inequality." In *Handbook of Labor Economics Vol. 3A,* edited by Orley C. Ashenfelter and David Card, 1463–1555. Amsterdam: North-Holland, 1999.

Katz, Lawrence F. and Kevin M. Murphy. "Changes in Relative Wages, 1963–1987: Supply and Demand Factors." *The Quarterly Journal of Economics* 107, no. 1 (1992): 35–78.

Kollmeyer, Christopher. "Explaining Deindustrialization: How Affluence, Productivity Growth, and Globalization Diminish Manufacturing Employment." *American Journal of Sociology* 114, no. 6 (2009): 1644–1674.

Krueger, Rob and David Gibbs, editors. *The Sustainable Development Paradox: Urban Political Economy in the United States and Europe.* New York: Guilford Press, 2007.

Krueger, Rob and David Gibbs. "'Third Wave' Sustainability? Smart Growth and Regional Development in the USA." *Regional Studies* 42, no. 9 (2008): 1263–1274.

Lippman, Stephen, Amy Davis, and Howard Aldrich. "Entrepreneurship and Inequality." *Research in the Sociology of Work* 15 (2005): 3–31.

McMurrer, Daniel and Isabel Sawhill. *Getting Ahead—Economic and Social Mobility in America.* Washington, DC: Urban Institute Press, 1998.

Marshall, Alfred. *Principles of Economics. 8th Edition.* London: Macmillan, 1920.

Mishel, Lawrence, Josh Bivens, Elise Gould, and Heidi Shierholz. *The State of Working America, 12th Edition.* Ithaca, NY: Cornell University Press, 2012.

Mishel, Lawrence, Heidi Shierholz, and John Schmitt. *Don't Blame the Roots: Assessing the Job Polarization Explanation of Growing Wage Inequality.* Washington, DC: Economic Policy Institute, 2013.

Moretti, Enrico. *The New Geography of Jobs.* Boston, MA: Houghton Mifflin Harcourt, 2012.

Morin, Rich. *Rising Share of Americans See Conflict Between Rich and Poor.* Washington, DC: Pew Research Center, 2012.

Neumark, David, Hans Johnson, and Marisol Cuellar Mejia. *Future Skill Shortages in the U.S. Economy.* Working Paper 17213. Cambridge, MA: National Bureau of Economic Research, 2011.

Neumark, David, Brandon Wall, and Junfu Zhang. "Do Small Businesses Create More Jobs? New Evidence for the United States from the National Establishment Time Series." *Review of Economics and Statistics* 94, no. 1 (2011): 16–29.

Nightingale, Demetra Smith and Stephen A. Wandner. *Informal and Nonstandard Employment in the United States: Implications for Low-Income Working Families.* Washington, DC: Urban Institute Press, 2011.

North, Douglass C. "Location Theory and Regional Economic Growth." *The Journal of Political Economy* 63, no. 3 (1955): 243–258.

Ong, Paul and Anastasia Loukaitou-Sideris, editors. *Jobs and Economic Development in Minority Communities.* Philadelphia, PA: Temple University Press, 2006.

Organisation for Economic Cooperation and Development. *Crisis Squeezes Income and Puts Pressure on Inequality and Poverty.* France: OECD, 2013.

Osgood, Jeffery L., Susan M. Opp, and R. Lorraine Bernotsky. "Yesterday's Gains versus Today's Realties: Lessons from 10 Years of Economic Development Practice." *Economic Development Quarterly* 26, no. 4 (2012): 334–350.

Osterman, Paul. *Securing Prosperity. The American Labor Market: How it has Changed and What to Do about It.* Princeton, NJ: Princeton University Press, 1999.

Osterman, Paul. "The labor market context for employment and training policy." In *Connecting People to Work: Workforce Intermediaries and Sector Strategies*, edited by Robert Giloth and Maureen Conway, 21–38. New York: American Assembly, 2014.

Pastor, Jr., Manuel, Peter Dreier, J. Eugene Grigsby III, and Marta Lopez-Garza. *Regions that Work: How Cities and Suburbs Can Grow Together. 1st Edition.* Minneapolis, MN: University of Minnesota Press, 2000.

Pede, Valerien O. "Diversity and Regional Economic Growth: Evidence from US Counties." *Journal of Economic Development* 38, no. 3 (2013): 111–127.

Peters, Alan and Peter Fisher. "The Failures of Economic Development Incentives." *Journal of the American Planning Association* 70, no. 1 (2004): 27–38.

Piore, Michael J. and Charles F. Sabel. *The Second Industrial Divide: Possibilities for Prosperity.* New York: Basic Books, 1984.

Polanyi, Karl. *The Great Transformation: The Political and Economic Origins of Our Time.* Boston, MA: Beacon Press, 1944.

Pope Francis. *Apostolic Exhortation. Evangelii Guadium.* Vatican Press, 2013.

Porter, Michael E. "Clusters and the New Economics of Competition." *Harvard Business Review* 76, no. 6 (1998): 77–90.

Porter, Michael. "The Economic Performance of Regions." *Regional Studies* 37, no. 6–7 (2003): 545–546.

Quadrini, Vincenzo. "Entrepreneurship, Saving, and Social Mobility." *Review of Economic Dynamics* 3, no. 1 (2000): 1–40.

Saez, Emmanuel. "Striking it Richer: The Evolution of Top Incomes in the United States 2013." Unpublished paper. University of California, Berkeley, 2013.

Sassen, Saskia. *The Global City: London, New York, Tokyo.* Princeton, NJ: Princeton University Press, 1991.

Saxenian, AnnaLee. *Regional Advantage: Culture and Competition in Silicon Valley and Route 128.* Cambridge, MA: Harvard University Press, 1996.

Seghezzo, Lucas. "The Five Dimensions of Sustainability." *Environmental Politics* 18, no. 4 (2009): 539–556.

Simmie, James and James Sennett. "Innovative Clusters: Global or Local Linkages?" *National Institute Economic Review* 170, no. 1 (1999): 87–98.

Stiglitz, Joseph E. "Some Lessons from the East Asian Miracle." *The World Bank Research Observer* 11, no. 2 (1996): 151–177.

Stiglitz, Joseph. "Turn Left for Growth." *The Guardian*, August 6, 2008.

Storper, Michael and Richard Walker. *The Capitalist Imperative*. Oxford: Blackwell, 1989.

Teitz, Michael B. "The New Geography of Jobs, by Enrico Moretti." *Berkeley Planning Journal* 26, no. 1 (2013): 211–213.

Theodos, Brett and Robert Bednarzik. "Earnings Mobility and Low Wage Workers in the United States." *Monthly Labor Review* 129, no. 7 (2006): 34–47.

Tiebout, Charles M. "Exports and Regional Economic Growth: Rejoinder." *Journal of Political Economy* 64, no. 2 (1956): 69.

Vernon, Raymond. *Metropolis 1985. An Interpretation of the Findings of the New York Metropolitan Region Study*. Cambridge, MA: Harvard University Press, 1960.

Zheng, Lingwen and Mildred Warner. "Business Incentive Use Among US Local Governments: A Story of Accountability and Policy Learning." *Economic Development Quarterly* 24, no. 4 (2010): 325–336.

7 Incentivizing Businesses to Help People and Places

> We can succeed with the right policies. Last week, Twitter told the city that if the payroll tax exclusion passes, it will stay in San Francisco and move into the Art Deco-style San Francisco Mart building on Market Street between Ninth and Tenth streets. Twitter will contribute to the revitalization of struggling neighborhoods and keep 21st century jobs in San Francisco where they belong.
>
> Mayor Edwin M. Lee and Supervisor David Chiu, *San Francisco Chronicle*, March 22, 2011

Why should the city where every tech firm wants to locate pay firms to stay? The Twitter tax break, referred to in the quote above, will cost San Francisco $56 million in lost revenue just in the next few years (Temple 2013). And Twitter did not even need the cash, having at that point already received over $1 billion in investment (Story 2012). The city argued that it was not responding to blackmail, but seizing an opportunity to catalyze the redevelopment of a long-troubled area, Mid-Market.

The ability to steer development to certain areas (i.e., to use incentives to target neighborhoods for revitalization) is cherished by policymakers. Targeting places is key to achieving equity goals, because it means that businesses locate in places where the local residents are more likely to benefit, either from new job opportunities or improved access to goods. Luring a new business can have a catalytic effect on a neighborhood, reversing a spiral of decline. Politicians buy into the strategy because of its visible impact. Incentivizing business location, especially by getting more jobs to locate near transit, is also a fundamental strategy in many plans for regional sustainability (see Chapter 4).

But even with generous incentive packages, it is challenging to persuade business to relocate. Businesses make decisions based upon their own balance sheets and bottom lines. Policy is a post hoc consideration: once a business has decided on a location that will optimize its business, it might then look at whether it can benefit from any government policies (such as tax breaks) as well. The liberal idea that government can meaningfully shape where businesses choose to locate is not just misguided, but wasteful as well: many targeting policies shift jobs from one place to another without leading to any job growth—

and possibly leading to longer commutes and more vehicle miles traveled (VMT). We are giving away the "candy store" (LeRoy and Healey 1997).

The targeting toolkit varies little throughout the world. Most countries use some form of redevelopment, acquiring land through eminent domain, issuing bonds (often based on the promise of future revenue) to build infrastructure, and attracting businesses through incentives such as land giveaways. Some, such as China, are aggressive, displacing and relocating millions of businesses and households. Others are limiting their use of the tool altogether (California eliminated redevelopment in 2011).

The other major tool is enterprise zones, which provide incentives (such as tax credits for new equipment or hires) to businesses who locate in underdeveloped areas. In developing countries, these often take the form of free trade or export promotion zones, which reduce trade barriers and provide tax breaks in order to stimulate exports. If anything, the use of zones is increasing (although California, again, recently began phasing out its program). Can they work for equity and sustainability?

The Theory of Business Attraction and Local Economic Growth

The chase after businesses arguably began with the Romans, who built 50,000 miles of roads to facilitate trade (Weisbrod 2006). In the United States, the idea was to lure new economic activity to developing areas on the frontier, with the carrot of new infrastructure, the railway station. Boosters, often the local chamber of commerce, promoted the advantages of their communities in terms of land, labor, transportation access, and low taxes. Quickly, it became standard practice to negotiate and then reward business for bringing new jobs, and of course tax base, to a city. Most coveted were manufacturing firms, which would export to other areas, bringing in new revenue. Famously, based on its low cost and hospitable climate, the U.S. Sunbelt lured tens of thousands of firms from the Rustbelt (Raitz 1988).

How productive is this strategy? In the big picture (i.e., thinking about growth in the aggregate), not very. In most cases, job growth in one place means job loss—and disinvestment—in another. In other words, economic activity is simply transferred from place to place. In the best-case scenario, however, the new location would make the firm more productive, so that it could pay higher wages or expand operations. There are also potential equity benefits, if the firm relocates to (and recruits from) an area with disadvantaged jobseekers (Bartik 2007).

The alternative is growing local economic activity instead of attracting it from elsewhere. But even then, there is likely to be job displacement some-where.[1] This suggests the importance of endogenous development strategies focusing on the entrepreneurial potential of existing firms. The most productive growth engines will be start-ups and young businesses that might potentially become the rapidly growing "gazelles" (Haltiwanger, Jarmin, and Miranda

2011; Neumark, Wall, and Zhang 2011). These will benefit from urban agglomeration, which offers the concentrations of skilled labor, specialized services, markets, capital, and other factors that help to facilitate rapid growth. Understanding these business location patterns is key to devising policies to bring new business activity to declining areas.

Why Businesses Locate Where They Do

Traditionally, businesses located where they could minimize costs, with the most sensitive factor being transportation of inputs and products (Weber 1909). This meant locating in central areas for those with specialized markets and low transportation costs, and dispersing across the region for firms with high demand and transport costs; location choice would vary depending on stage in the production process (Hoover 1948). To maximize revenues, firms identified the maximum market areas in which to locate, which then led to the emergence of cities (Lösch 1954). But by the 1970s, global cost differentials led to the reorganization of the production process and sourcing of production throughout the world.

Within the United States, the decentralization of residences, along with improvements in transportation infrastructure and information technology, has made peripheral areas competitive with the urban core (Fujita, Krugman, and Venables 1999). But some firms continue to agglomerate in urban centers, benefiting from knowledge spillovers, the availability of both skilled and immigrant labor pools, and proximity to suppliers and markets (Gottlieb 1995).

Increasingly, it is not just the external economies of urban agglomeration that attract firms, but intangible factors, sometimes called "psychic income," or the non-monetary satisfaction that a location provides (Greenhut 1956). Local and regional networks of relationships—both personal and professional—shape the locational behavior of firms (Stam 2007). An increasing number of independent studies have shown that for entrepreneurial and high-tech firms, which tend to be locally and regionally grown, the most important location factors are executive preferences, quality of life, and access to skilled labor (Bartik 1991; Buss 2001; Fulton and Shigley 2001; Gottlieb 1995; Haug 1991; McLoughlin 1983; Stam 2007). According to current conventional wisdom, proximity to this "talent" has become the *sine qua non* of business location decision-making (Florida 2002). Yet, these talented employees, and the amenities they prefer, need not be local: what matters is that the *region* offers workers a high quality of life, while the neighborhood hosting the firm does not suffer from *disamenities* such as crime and traffic (Gottlieb 1995).

Underlying much of the discussion on firm location is the assumption that firms are perfectly mobile, making ongoing rational economic decisions about where to locate. If relocation is essentially frictionless, then globalization and technology should facilitate increasing mobility of capital. Of course, firms making products often rely on global sourcing: as they reach the mass production phase of the product cycle, they relocate production to low-cost regions, typically outside advanced industrialized countries (Vernon 1966).[2] Yet, business relocation is actually relatively rare; typically, no more than about 10 percent of businesses relocate in their lifetime, and then they do not move far, typically staying in the same city or region (Brouwer, Mariotti, and van Ommeren 2004; Neumark, Zhang, and Wall 2005; Webber 1984).

Why the inertia? Imperfect information coupled with high sunk costs, social ties, and labor at the existing site, plus the costs for a site search, facilities move, and employee rehiring, makes moving unattractive (Blair and Premus 1993; Brouwer, Mariotti, and van Ommeren 2004). In relocation, external factors (such as firm position in the global production network) matter more than internal factors (such as firm size or stage in the product cycle) or location (Brouwer, Mariotti, and van Ommeren 2004). Firms rarely conduct comprehensive searches prior to relocation, and decisions may be subject to a larger corporate planning process involving mergers and acquisitions (Brouwer, Mariotti, and van Ommeren 2004; Hayter 1997).

Our study of business location in California (Chapple and Makarewicz 2010) illustrates these location and relocation patterns.

Business Location in California

At any given time in California, there are about 1.5 million firms with at least two employees. About two-thirds of these firms are located in greater San Francisco (the nine-county Bay Area) or greater Los Angeles (Los Angeles, Orange, and Ventura counties), and only 2 percent are in rural areas.[3]

Job growth comes from business start-ups, expansions, and relocations (in that order). For instance, in California, from 1990 to 2005, the largest source of business growth by jurisdiction (accounting for 60 percent of new firms and 47 percent of new employees) was start-ups. The second largest contributor to growth was expansions (29 percent of firms and 36 percent of employees). The relocation of firms—either from within California or from other states— generates only a small share of growth (about 11 percent of firms and 17 percent of employees).

Start-ups are concentrated in California's most populous regions, and central cities. The availability of affordable rental housing, infrastructure (airports and highways), and immigrant labor contribute the most to a new firm's location decision. In every sector except agriculture, a newly formed firm is more likely to locate where there is at least a highway or interstate, as well as a major airport. Concentrations of immigrants in central cities lead to a disproportionate share of start-ups (relative to suburbs), perhaps since immigrants provide inexpensive labor for business start-ups, often start small businesses themselves, and provide a large consumer base for other start-ups.

Expanding firms follow a similar locational logic, basing their decisions to grow on the availability of housing and immigrants. They are concentrated mostly just outside core urban areas, and the most rapidly growing firms tend to be in infrastructure-rich areas: for instance, almost three-fourths of the new jobs that result from expansion in the manufacturing, wholesale, and FIRE sectors concentrate near highways and airports.

When firms do relocate, they almost always move to the same type of place (i.e., from a central city to a central city, or from a suburb to a suburb), and the vast majority stay within the same city or county. Firms that relocate to central cities often do so because the cities are closer to more rental housing, which can support a younger or lower-wage workforce. Firms moving to the suburbs, by contrast, will have increased proximity to owner-occupied housing and lower residential densities, which may help them meet their employees' housing and lifestyle preferences. In our study, only 7 percent of relocating firms moved to a different region, and only 4 percent left California altogether. So, very few regions see their economies suffer because firms move out, and still fewer see their regional economies gain because firms moved in. In most of California's local jurisdictions, fewer than 5 percent of the existing businesses are the result of relocations. Only in a small handful of rural towns does relocation account for a greater share of businesses.

Thus, factors such as the preferences of the CEO, the concentration of skilled and immigrant labor, and the regional quality of life dictate business location overall, and relocation is rare. What, then, is the role of policy, specifically incentives to increase business presence in specific places?

Incentives and Targeting

In the U.S. landscape of corporate subsidy packages, the Twitter deal was relatively minor. The *New York Times* recently documented $80 billion per year given to companies, some by cities and counties, but mostly by states, given the size of the deals (Story 2012).[4] Many of these are megadeals of $75 million or more; the nonprofit advocate Good Jobs First estimates that the cost per job for these deals is $456,000 (Mattera, Tarczynska, and LeRoy 2013). (In comparison, most of the endogenous development approaches discussed below cost well under $100,000 per job.)

One high-profile example illustrates how the process works (at its worst). Curt Schilling, a famous Boston Red Sox pitcher, started a video game company in Massachusetts but began talking to public officials in nearby Rhode Island about new space for expansion. The state guaranteed $75 million in loans to the company, which had yet to release a game. It never did. And when it went bankrupt, it laid off 400 workers. Rhode Island was left with the loan (Story 2012).

At the very least, do incentives make a difference? In terms of affecting where businesses locate, again, businesses will decide which region to locate in based on factors internal to the firm, such as the preferences of executives. But within that region, an incentive package might induce the firm to choose a particular site. In terms of regional growth, these deals may spur net new job creation, but because of their cost, they are likely to shrink tax revenues (Markusen and Nesse 2007). There is also increasing evidence that to pay for these subsidies, cities and states are making cuts in public services, such as schools (ibid.). Ironically, these very public services may be more likely to lead to residential economic health (as measured by household income, unemployment, and poverty) than incentives (Reese 2013).

Despite the evidence, a complex array of actors supports incentive packages: the growth coalition of local real estate interests, newspapers, utilities, banks, and cultural institutions, all with vested interests in regional growth, and, most importantly, a growing site location industry that lobbies governments (LeRoy 2005). In some cases, incentives exacerbate urban sprawl, by subsidizing business moves from older urban sites to greenfields (LeRoy, Hinkley, and Tallman 2000). In response, some states have enacted reforms that slow the giveaways. Most involve either increased transparency (e.g., analysis of costs and benefits), new standards (especially for wages), or clawbacks (contractual restrictions that allow governments to recover funds from the firm if they do not meet agreed-upon standards for jobs and earnings) (LeRoy 2007). In addition to ensuring that benefits are captured for locals, effective incentive programs will target firms that are actually creating jobs with high wages and multiplier effects (Bartik 2007).

Since incentive packages typically involve the state, they target specific businesses, without necessarily requiring location in specific places. They can create more equitable outcomes by requiring job creation or training for disadvantaged workers, but will not necessarily help places reverse the spiral of decline. Two other tools, common throughout the world, allow governments to attract businesses to specific areas in need of revitalization: redevelopment and enterprise zones.

Redevelopment

Redevelopment is a tool through which the public sector assists the private sector, typically with the assembly of land and finance, in the development of underutilized or vacant property in the urban core. Urban regeneration through redevelopment is a legacy policy. Federal and state urban renewal programs were enacted in the post-World War II climate of white flight to the suburbs and gradual devastation of the central city tax base. In the 1980s, cities throughout advanced industrialized countries began to redevelop their older central cities to facilitate economic restructuring, particularly from manufacturing to office uses. By the 1990s, redevelopment was more commonly associated with the new trend toward urban consumption. Still targeting declining or blighted areas, cities around the world started using redevelopment tools to construct convention centers, shopping malls, aquariums, museums, waterfront or festival marketplaces, hotels, and, most prominently, sport stadia.

In terms of its ability to catalyze market interest in declining or stagnant areas, redevelopment is, more or less, a proven success. Numerous accounts document how cities such as London, New York, San Francisco, Chicago, Baltimore, Boston, and Philadelphia have brought back neighborhoods through large-scale redevelopment projects (Fainstein 2001; Frieden and Sagalyn 1989; Willie 1998). The impact of redevelopment is due to not just the symbolic effect of a new building in the neighborhood, but the positive externalities created by the related investment in infrastructure, such as roadway and streetscape improvements. Redevelopment, with its associated financing mechanisms such as tax increment and infrastructure finance districts, provides a much-needed source of pre-development capital to build supportive infrastructure.[5]

Overall, redevelopment areas grow faster than comparable neighborhoods. However, they rarely generate enough new growth to repay the public investment (Dardia 1998).[6] What is unclear is whether this development is equitable. Cities justify these projects in the name of economic development (i.e., the jobs and taxes they will create); the theory seems to be that benefits will trickle down to middle- and low-income city residents (Fainstein and Fainstein 1986). But how? The implicit theory works as follows. First, redevelopment projects will attract businesses. If these are new establishments, either start-ups or new branches of existing firms, they will create jobs. Of course, if the businesses have simply transferred from another area, there will be no job gain, at least in the big picture, unless their new facilities allow them to operate more efficiently and/or expand.

Second, the businesses will need to have job openings for which local residents are qualified. In order to maximize benefits, the redevelopment program will need to include some sort of local hire provision that gives preference to local residents. Or, it will create jobs at the top of the job chain, opening up positions at the bottom. Again, these openings may be transfers, or they may attract in-migrants from elsewhere. Still, redevelopment is serving a public purpose if it is improving accessibility to job openings for local disadvantaged jobseekers.

Ideally, the businesses would be in economic sectors that offer living wage and/or middle-skill jobs. However, in part because new development is so costly, the majority of redevelopment projects house either high-end office uses or hotel, entertainment, and retail venues that primarily offer low-wage jobs.

A third way that locals might benefit is indirectly, via local spending: the firm and its employees might buy goods and services locally, which creates new demand for low-wage workers and generates new tax revenue. But again, this new revenue is offset from the diversion of tax revenue to fund the redevelopment: typically, these funds come from the property taxes that support the schools, law enforcement, fire protection, libraries, parks, and other local services that heighten quality of life and life chances for locals. However, some states mitigate this loss of property tax revenue by requiring developers to set aside some percentage (typically 15–20 percent) of new tax revenue for affordable housing.

Perhaps the most inequitable aspect of redevelopment is its lack of transparency and accountability. Most cities can dedicate funding to redevelopment without any voter approval; in many cases, redevelopment agencies even operate as semi-autonomous entities, independent of city government.

Overall, redevelopment is an effective tool for catalyzing revitalization, but not for equitable development. Cities often try to use redevelopment as a substitute for an urban economic development policy. But property development plays a supportive, rather than a determining, role in local economic growth.

Enterprise Zones

Progressives have generally supported enterprise zones because they actually target the disadvantaged as beneficiaries, rather than relying on a trickle-down effect. Enacted in the United States and United Kingdom as a response to 1970s-era economic restructuring, enterprise zones designate areas where local firms can receive tax and regulatory relief. Including free trade zones, most EZ programs are enacted at the federal level, but most U.S. states have their own as well. At the federal level, incentives might include tax deductions for capital equipment, capital gains tax relief, accelerated real property depreciation, and, most importantly for equity, the employment tax credit, which reimburses employers for hiring workers who live within the EZ. States often also provide property and income tax abatements, as well as job training assistance, permit streamlining, infrastructure improvements, and access to capital (Greenbaum and Landers 2009).

Overall, there are 43 states with 3,000 designated EZs (ibid.). Evaluations of EZ programs are mixed; about one-half of studies have found positive employment impacts and the other half negative or ambiguous effects (Cray et al. 2011). At best, employment effects are modest in size and only last a few years (Cray et al. 2011; Greenbaum and Landers 2009). Barriers include lack of familiarity with the program, the cost of completing the paperwork (relative to the minor tax benefit), and the challenges of finding qualified employees who live within the EZ (Cray et al. 2011).

It is unclear whether EZs are actually spurring job creation. Just as with the redevelopment program, firms may take advantage of the incentives by simply transferring into the zone, without creating any new jobs.[7]

In addition, firms might be taking tax credits for employees that they would have hired anyway. In many states, firms are allowed to collect tax credits not just for new hires, but also retroactively, and tax-service companies, or tax credit farms, have emerged to assist with the claims (Neumark 2013). Because of the role of this intermediary industry, the beneficiaries of enterprise zone policy are mostly large firms with a large share of eligible workers and high turnover rates (i.e., retail employers).[8]

We could make EZs more effective with some minor reforms, such as disallowing retroactive credits, targeting smaller firms or more industrial areas, and providing better information about the credits to firms. With the employment tax credit at a few thousand dollars per worker, they are relatively low cost. Still, it is possible that we could create more jobs and make firms more productive by addressing quality of life issues instead. Low-cost programs to revitalize commercial corridors, such as business improvement districts, are demonstrably effective at creating low-cost jobs through interventions focusing on quality of life, crime, and marketing (Sideroff 2011). Another approach is a sustainable economic development strategy, discussed in the next chapter.

Targeting Places by Targeting Businesses: The Endogenous Development Alternative

The strategy of targeting places in the hopes that economic benefits will trickle down to residents has had mixed effects on aggregate growth, generally positive impacts on places, and negligible results for social equity. This is not surprising, since businesses make their location decisions based on economic rationale: using a place or people rationale will not necessarily make the business flourish.

Targeting strategies seem to be in decline in California, and perhaps even in the United States as a whole. However, the incidence of incentive megadeals is increasing in the United States (Mattera, Tarczynska, and LeRoy 2013), and redevelopment and free trade zones are increasingly popular globally.[9] Still, reforms could make place targeting more effective by reconfiguring programs to focus on endogenous economic development, specifically identifying new or untapped economic resources and supporting the entrepreneurial capacity needed to take advantage of these economic opportunities. This, then, should support sustainability goals more effectively as well.

The logic here draws from our understanding of business location patterns. The most dynamic firms want to locate in urban agglomerations near major infrastructure that has been in place long enough to attract other city amenities, an ample labor force, and appropriate housing for their workers. Our research shows that if we compare central cities and suburbs that have the same level of highway and airport infrastructure, growing firms (whether expanding in place, starting up, or relocating) are three times more likely to locate in central cities than suburbs.

Thus, by supporting productive firms, economic development programs will, in effect, target more urban places, since these are preferred by the firms that are growing. Firms may not locate in the areas in most need of revitalization, particularly if they suffer from disamenities such as crime, and they will not solve the more recent poverty problems of the inner-ring suburbs, but they will at least be nearby. The most important strategy, then, is to ensure that the denser areas of regions offer not just high quality of public services, but varied housing options to support a growing workforce.

Endogenous development strategies continue to be the most popular tool used by cities, even if more funding goes to business attraction and incentives (Zheng and Warner 2010). These approaches include technical assistance, access to capital, tax incentives targeted to existing businesses, innovation, and infrastructure. Typical programs include networking events, training in business management, access to capital, business incubators, technology transfer, marketing, or quality-of-life improvements.

Endogenous approaches can be more equitable than targeting places to the extent that they are job-centered, as Bob Giloth (1995, 1998) has written. To center economic development on jobs means to prioritize the hiring of low-income or low-skilled workers, rather than count on job creation to trickle down through job chains or spending multipliers. The idea emerged in the 1990s when it became clear that even tight labor markets would not create opportunities for many of the unemployed without explicit targeting strategies.

One example is the Bay Area's Economic Prosperity Strategy, which complements Plan Bay Area.[10] Rather than target specific places, the strategy identifies the industries that are most likely to provide the middle-skill jobs so crucial to a region with rapidly growing income inequality. The goal is to support those industries that tend to locate close to transit or low-income communities.

Some of the most promising endogenous approaches right now focus on the entrepreneurial capacities of low-income communities. The idea is not so much that potential million-dollar businesses are lurking in the ghetto, but that enterprise can supplement the benefits of more formal jobs (a process often called "income patching") (Edgcomb and Armington 2003). Already, there are 20 million micro-entrepreneurs in the United States (defined as a business with five or fewer employees without access to traditional banking), with almost 2 million new sole proprietorships per year (Edgcomb and Klein 2005; Schweke 2011). Surprisingly, about half of microenterprises, even owned by the low-income, create jobs (Edgcomb and Thetford 2013). There is an established network of microlenders, such as ACCION, who provide microloans and training to individual entrepreneurs who need less than $50,000 in financing.[11] Although there are mixed results from evaluations around the world, some of the U.S. programs have been startlingly successful, with low loss rates and a return of 1.3–1.4 times the program investment, with a cost per job of about $6,000 (Banerjee et al. 2013; Edgcomb and Klein 2005; Edgcomb and Thetford 2013). Microenterprise as an economic development strategy can reach into low-income neighborhoods through local intermediaries. Or, to scale up microenterprise to reach more of the self-employed, the government could offer assistance through the tax code (such as Schedule C preparation) (Schweke 2011).

One opportunity to support this entrepreneurial capacity in place is leveraging the resources of large anchor institutions (such as universities and hospitals), as well as government purchasing. Anchor institutions are fixed assets in communities and are unlikely to relocate out of regions. They purchase an array of goods and services—such as food, laundering, record disposal, and recycling—which open up opportunities for entrepreneurship. One of the best-known examples is the Evergreen Cooperative, a worker-owned and -managed cooperative that supplies goods and services to local hospitals (Dubb and Howard 2012). Likewise, almost $100 billion of federal procurement dollars goes to small businesses each year, by government mandate (U.S. Small Business Administration 2011). Economic inclusion strategies that shift government spending to disadvantaged enterprises do not create more jobs, but may provide a net benefit by reducing the need for expenditure on public services (Treuhaft and Rubin 2013). For example, a set of social enterprises employs people with severe disabilities and sells their goods and services—about $2 billion worth— to federal agencies through the AbilityOne network, providing jobs to more than 100,000 individuals with severe disabilities (Javits 2013). This occurred through a combination of procurement incentives, business assistance, and support services (ibid.).

Endogenous development strategies such as these are readily scalable. By targeting population groups—low-income entrepreneurs, or disabled individuals —they reach disadvantaged people, many in declining places. Again, they may simply transfer jobs from one group to another, but entrepreneurship in particular brings the possibility of eventually expanding the pie. In building on local context, institutions, and markets, these strategies create more sustainable economic development.

Targeting places for economic development remains important. Drawing investment to declining areas can catalyze transformation, with a virtuous spiral of ascent. But the policy toolkit has long been flawed, with subsidies wasted on businesses who would have located in the area anyway. Perhaps Twitter did need an incentive to locate in Mid-Market. But the numerous tech firms that have subsequently clustered around Twitter did not.

At $80 billion per year just in the United States, incentives will remain part of the policy toolkit around the world, even if the use of endogenous development strategies is increasing (Zheng and Warner 2010). In the long term, the answer lies in getting the incentive structure right. Redevelopment and enterprise zones offered essentially free money to cities. If cities had to assume responsibility for more of the costs, they would have more of an incentive to support the most effective projects. This would, by definition, be more sustainable, as the most effective projects will build on existing assets, residents, and businesses.

To meet regional sustainability goals, it would make most sense to entrust regional agencies with the money. To obtain incentives, cities would have to show that projects met sustainability goals as well.[12] This would allow businesses more leeway to choose their optimal location to maximize revenues within the region. Ideally, cities would share tax revenue too, through a regional redistribution system, as occurs in Minneapolis-St. Paul (see Part III). But politically, this is a hard sell.

Notes

1. If job growth comes from supply-side factors (lower costs of production), less efficient firms will shed jobs; if it comes from new markets, older products (and perhaps firms and workers) will become obsolete; and if jobs come from expanding exports, the regions importing the goods will lose their own local production.
2. Not everyone agrees that the firms are operating according to the logic of the product cycle (see Webber 1984), or that the departure of mass production from core areas or the United States is inevitable. There are ongoing debates about the impact on

cities of policies that lower trade barriers and heighten global economic competition (e.g., see Ranney and Cecil 1993). Others have pointed to the difficulty in empirically studying the relationships between location, trade, and specialization (Storper, Chen, and DePaolis 2002).

3. This analysis uses the National Establishment Time Series (NETS) data, based on the Dun & Bradstreet dataset, from 2000 to 2005. Of the firms active in 2005, a slight majority, 56 percent, were in the state's 91 central cities, while 41 percent were in suburbs or other non-central city parts of metropolitan areas. Only 2 percent of the firms were not in an MSA and not in a central city (some central cities are not in metropolitan areas).

4. They include property tax abatements, sales tax exemptions and credits, corporate income tax exemptions, payroll tax holidays, cash grants, loan guarantees, free services, and job tax credits tied to the number of workers hired.

5. By increasing local bonding capacity, TIF helps local governments raise large amounts of crucial pre-development capital from private sources. Notably, most of this debt does not count against general obligation debt limits.

6. Only a handful of projects generate enough revenues to compensate for lost tax revenues; on average, projects pay back about one-half of the public investment.

7. One notorious California example was the VWR distribution firm, which relocated from the Bay Area to the Central Valley, receiving $3 million in tax credits for job creation by firing their Bay Area employees and hiring Central Valley replacements (who were not unionized) (PR Newswire 2013).

8. A study of a similar credit, the Work Opportunity Tax Credit, found that two-thirds of the total credit claimed went to large companies, with gross annual receipts of $1 billion or more, and more than half of the total credits went to employers in retail trade (General Accounting Office 2001).

9. The International Labour Organization (2003: 2) estimated that in 2002, there were 3,000 export processing zones in 116 countries.

10. At the writing of this book, this strategy was still a work in progress.

11. FIELD has identified 700 microenterprise programs (Edgcomb and Klein 2005).

12. Various versions of this approach, "Redevelopment 2.0," are under discussion at the California state legislature.

References

Banerjee, Abhijit V., Esther Duflo, Rachel Glennerster, and Cynthia Kinnan. *The Miracle of Microfinance? Evidence from a Randomized Evaluation.* Cambridge, MA: MIT Department of Economics, 2013.

Bartik, Timothy J. *Who Benefits from State and Local Economic Development Policies?* Kalamazoo, MI: W. E. Upjohn Institute for Employment Research, 1991.

Bartik, Timothy J. "Solving the Problems of Economic Development Incentives." In *Reining in the Competition for Capital*, edited by A. Markusen, 103–139. Kalamaoo, MI: W. E. Upjohn Institute for Employment Research, 2007.

Blair, John P. and Robert Premus. "Location Theory." In *Theories of Local Economic Development: Perspectives from Across the Disciplines*, edited by Robert Mier, 3–27. Thousand Oaks, CA: Sage, 1993.

Brouwer, Aleid E., Ilaria Mariotti, and Jos N. van Ommeren. "The Firm Relocation Decision: An Empirical Investigation." *The Annals of Regional Science* 38, no. 2 (2004): 335–347.

Buss, Terry F. "The Effect of State Tax Incentives on Economic Growth and Firm Location Decisions: An Overview of the Literature." *Economic Development Quarterly* 15, no. 1 (2001): 90–105.

Chapple, Karen and Carrie Makarewicz. "Restricting New Infrastructure: Bad for Business in California?" *Access* 34 (2010): 14–21.

Cray, Adam, Tram Nguyen, Carol Pranka, Christine Schildt, Julie Sheu, and Erika Rincon Whitcomb. *Job Creation: A Review of Policies and Strategies*. Berkeley, CA: Institute for Research on Labor and Employment, University of California, Berkeley, 2011.

Dardia, Michael. *Subsidizing Redevelopment in California*. San Francisco, CA: Public Policy Institute of California, 1998.

Dubb, Steve and Ted Howard. "Leveraging Anchor Institutions for Local Job Creation and Wealth Building." Unpublished paper. The Democracy Collaborative, University of Maryland, 2012.

Edgcomb, Elaine and Maria Medrano Armington. *The Informal Economy: Latino Enterprises at the Margins*. Washington, DC: FIELD (Microenterprise Fund for Innovation, Effectiveness, Learning and Dissemination), Aspen Institute, 2003.

Edgcomb, Elaine and Joyce Klein. *Opening Opportunities, Building Ownership: Fulfilling the Promise of Microenterprise in the United States*. Washington, DC: FIELD (Microenterprise Fund for Innovation, Effectiveness, Learning and Dissemination), Aspen Institute, 2005.

Edgcomb, Elaine and Tamra Thetford. *Microenterprise Development as Job Creation*. Washington, DC: FIELD (Microenterprise Fund for Innovation, Effectiveness, Learning and Dissemination), Aspen Institute, 2013.

Fainstein, Susan. *The City Builders: Property Development in New York and London*. Lawrence, KS: University Press of Kansas, 2001.

Fainstein, Susan S. and Norman I. Fainstein. "Regime Strategies, Communal Resistance, and Economic Forces." In *Restructuring the City: The Political Economy of Urban Redevelopment*, edited by Susan S. Fainstein, 245–288. New York: Addison-Wesley Longman, 1986.

Florida, Richard. "The Economic Geography of Talent." *Annals of the Association of American Geographers* 92, no. 4 (2002): 743–755.

Frieden, Bernard and Lynn Sagalyn. *Downtown Inc.: How America Rebuilds Cities*. Cambridge, MA: MIT Press, 1989.

Fujita, Masahisa, Paul R. Krugman, and Anthony J. Venables. *The Spatial Economy: Cities, Regions and International Trade. Vol. 213*. Cambridge, MA: MIT Press, 1999.

Fulton, William and Paul Shigley. "Little Chips, Big Dreams." *Governing Magazine*. May, 2001.

General Accounting Office. *Work Opportunity Tax Credit: Employers Do Not Appear to Dismiss Employees to Increase Tax Credits*. GAO-01-329. Washington, DC: U.S. General Accounting Office, 2001.

Giloth, Robert P. "Social Investment in Jobs: Foundation Perspectives on Targeted Economic Development During the 1990s." *Economic Development Quarterly* 9, no. 3 (1995): 279–289.

Giloth, Robert P. *Jobs & Economic Development: Strategies and Practice*. Thousand Oaks, CA: Sage, 1998.

Gottlieb, Paul D. "Residential Amenities, Firm Location and Economic Development." *Urban Studies* 32, no. 9 (1995): 1413–1436.

Greenbaum, Robert T. and Jim Landers. "Why are State Policy Makers Still Proponents of Enterprise Zones? What Explains Their Action in the Face of a Preponderance of the Research?" *International Regional Science Review* 32 (2009): 468.

Greenhut, M. L. *Plant Location in Theory and Practice*. Chapel Hill, NC: University of North Carolina Press, 1956.

Haltiwanger, John, Ron S. Jarmin, and Javier Miranda. "Who Creates Jobs? Small vs. Large vs. Young." *NBER Working Paper No. 16300*. Cambridge, MA: National Bureau of Economic Research, 2011.

Haug, Peter. "The Location Decisions and Operations of High Technology Organizations in Washington State." *Regional Studies* 25, no. 6 (1991): 525–541.

Hayter, Roger. *The Dynamics of Industrial Location: The Factory, the Firm, and the Production System*. Chichester: Wiley, 1997.

Hoover, Edgar M. *The Location of Economic Activity*. New York: McGraw-Hill, 1948.

International Labour Organization. *Employment and Social Policy in Respect of Export Processing Zones (EPZs)*. GB.286/ESP/3. Geneva: International Labour Office, 2003.

Javits, Carla. "A Market Solution to Job Creation and Opportunity: Social Enterprise." Unpublished paper. San Francisco, CA: Roberts Enterprise Development Fund, 2013.

LeRoy, Greg. *The Great American Jobs Scam*. San Francisco, CA: Berrett-Koehler, 2005.

LeRoy, Greg. "Nine Concrete Ways to Curtail the Economic War Among the States." In *Reining in the Competition for Capital*, edited by Ann Markusen, 183–198. Kalamazoo, MI: W. E. Upjohn Institute for Employment Research, 2007.

LeRoy, Greg and Richard Healey. *No More Candy Store: States and Cities Making Job Subsidies Accountable*. Washington, DC: Institute on Taxation and Economic Policy, 1997.

LeRoy, Greg, Sara Hinkley, and Katie Tallman. *Another Way Sprawl Happens: Economic Development Subsidies in a Twin Cities Suburb*. Washington, DC: Good Jobs First, 2000.

Lösch, A. *The Economics of Location*. Translated by W. H. Woglom. New Haven, CT: Yale University Press, 1954.

McLoughlin, P. J. "Community Considerations as Location Attraction Variables for Manufacturing Industry." *Urban Studies* 20, no. 3 (1983): 359–363.

Markusen, Ann and Katherine Nesse. "Institutional and Political Determinants of Incentive Competition." In *Reining in the Competition for Capital*, edited by Ann Markusen, 1–41. Kalamazoo, MI: W. E. Upjohn Institute for Employment Research, 2007.

Mattera, Phil, Kasia Tarczynska, and Greg LeRoy. *Megadeals: The Largest Economic Development Subsidy Packages Ever Awarded by State and Local Governments in the United States*. Washington, DC: Good Jobs First, 2013.

Neumark, David. "Spurring Job Creation in Response to Severe Recessions: Reconsidering Hiring Credits." *Journal of Policy Analysis & Management* 32, no. 1 (2013): 142–171.

Neumark, David, Brandon Wall, and Junfu Zhang. "Do Small Businesses Create More Jobs? New Evidence for the United States from the National Establishment Time Series." *Review of Economics and Statistics* 94, no. 1 (2011): 16–29.

Neumark, David, Junfu Zhang, and Brandon Wall. *Employment Dynamics and Business Relocation: New Evidence from the National Establishment Time Series*. San Francisco, CA: Public Policy Institute of California, 2005.

PR Newswire. "Visalia VWR Employees Vote to Join Teamsters Union." *PR Newswire*, February 15, 2013.

Raitz, Karl. "Advantages of Place as Perceived by Sunbelt Promoters." *Growth and Change* 19 (1988): 14–29.

Ranney, David C. and William Cecil. *Transnational Investment and Job Loss in Chicago: Impacts on Women, African-Americans and Latinos.* Chicago, IL: University of Illinois at Chicago, Center of Urban Economic Development, 1993.

Reese, Laura A. "If All You Have is a Hammer: Finding Economic Development Policies that Matter." *The American Review of Public Administration* (2013): 1–29. doi: 10.1177/0275074013483166.

Schweke, Bill. "Leveraging the Federal Tax Code to Encourage Self-Employment and Jobs." Unpublished paper. Institute for Research on Labor and Employment, University of California, Berkeley, 2011.

Sideroff, Desiree. *Building Community through Economic Development.* San Francisco, CA: Local Initiatives Support Corporation, 2011.

Stam, Erik. "Why Butterflies Don't Leave: Locational Behavior of Entrepreneurial Firms." *Economic Geography* 83, no. 1 (2007): 27–50.

Storper, Michael, Yun-chung Chen, and Fernando DePaolis. "Trade and the Location of Industries in the OECD and European Union." *Journal of Economic Geography* 2, no. 1 (2002): 73–107.

Story, Louise. "As Companies Seek Tax Deals, Governments Pay High Price." *New York Times*, December 1, 2012.

Temple, James. "'Twitter Tax Break' Could Cost SF Tens of Millions More after IPO." *The Tech Chronicles*, October 27, 2013. Accessed November 1, 2013. http://blog.ctnews.com/techblog/2013/10/27/twitter-tax-break-could-cost-sf-tens-of-millions-more-after-ipo.

Treuhaft, Sarah and Victor Rubin. "Economic Inclusion: Advancing an Equity-Driven Growth Model." Unpublished paper. Oakland, CA: PolicyLink, 2013.

U.S. Small Business Administration. *Small Business Procurement Data Shows Significant Progress Toward 23 Percent Federal Contracting Goal.* San Francisco, CA: U.S. Small Business Administration Press Office, 2011.

Vernon, Raymond. "International Investment and International Trade in the Product Cycle." *The Quarterly Journal of Economics* 80, no. 2 (1966): 190–207.

Webber, Michael John. *Industrial Location.* Beverly Hills, CA: Sage, 1984.

Weber, Alfred. *Über den Standort der Industrie [The Theory of the Location of Industries].* Translated by Carl J. Friedrich. Chicago, IL: University of Chicago Press, 1909.

Weisbrod, Glen. "Evolution of Methods for Assessing Economic Development Impacts of Proposed Transportation Projects." Presentation at the 3rd International Conference on Transportation and Economic Development (TED 2006), Orlando, Florida, March 13–16, 2006.

Willie, Lois. *At Home in the Loop: How Clout and Community Built Chicago's Dearborn Park.* Carbondale, IL: SIU Press, 1998.

Zheng, Lingwen and Mildred Warner. "Business Incentive Use Among US Local Governments: A Story of Accountability and Policy Learning." *Economic Development Quarterly* 24, no. 4 (2010): 325–336.

8 The Power of Local Markets

Right now, exports are one of the brightest spots in our economy. Thanks in part to new trade deals that we signed with countries like Panama and Colombia and South Korea, we now export more goods and services than ever before. And that means jobs right here in the United States of America. Last year, every $1 billion in exports supports nearly 5,000 jobs, including jobs right here at this port. So we're working on new trade deals that will mean more jobs for our workers, and more business for ports like this one, And, by the way, when I travel around the world, I'm out there selling. I'll go anywhere in the world to make sure that . . . those products stamped with those words, "Made in America" . . . that we can open up those markets and sell them anywhere.

President Barack Obama, New Orleans, November 8, 2013[1]

Every president trumpets the growth of exports, the engine of regional development per Douglass North, as Barack Obama did in the speech quoted above. A chorus of supporters, from Enrico Moretti, to Bruce Katz of the Brookings Institution, elaborate how export sectors boost income growth for metropolitan regions.

The policy implications of the argument are clear. If exports are the genesis of growth, then local-serving or residentiary businesses are derivative; in other words, demand for exports creates demand for local goods and services, rather than vice versa. So, regions need to target exporting firms, and, since it is too challenging to spur local firms to export, they need to attract big exporters, such as auto manufacturers, from outside the region.

Proponents of sustainable economic development put forth a different narrative. First, a definition:

Sustainable economic development enhances equitable local income and employment growth without endangering local fiscal stability, degrading the natural environment, or contributing to global climate change. It challenges the model of growth based on pure consumption rather than human happiness, takes into account long-term goals as well as short-term needs and is sensitive to local context and history.

(Gage and LoPresti 2012)

A regional economy that depends on people in faraway lands to consume goods and services, the production of which endangers local environmental and fiscal viability, is not a sustainable growth model. Instead, achieving lasting income growth means prioritizing development that a place can support—economic activity that grows out of and celebrates local assets, particularly the skills, passions, and needs of residents, while not undermining a place's long-term chances. This means a different portfolio of policies to support locally owned businesses that pay workers well, support the city's sense of place, incorporate sustainable processes, innovate new products and services, and yet are diverse enough to withstand economic downturns.

As noted previously, sustainability advocates question whether economic growth can be reconciled with environmental goals. A new market that appreciates quality of life and livability is emerging, but it has not been accompanied by a major change in consumption habits, meaning that resources will continue to be depleted at more or less the same rate (Haughton and Counsell 2004; Krueger and Gibbs 2008; Krueger and Savage 2007). Evidence suggests that although there is widespread support for environmental goals, individual preferences for material consumption are even stronger (Leiserowitz, Kates, and Parris 2006). Although consumption may degrade the environment, it is also an opportunity to institute more sustainable growth patterns. It is thus worth revisiting the arguments for an economy driven by consumption, rather than exports, most eloquently described by regional economist and planner Ann Markusen.

The Argument for Consumption-Driven Economic Growth

The conventional wisdom is that the cycle of job growth begins with export or tradable sector jobs because of their multiplier effects on residentiary or non-tradable sector jobs. Moreover, non-tradable sector jobs have little chance for productivity growth, and hence income growth, because they do not really change: the technology behind a haircut has not transformed enough to accelerate the number of haircuts per hour (Moretti 2012).

However, there are multiple reasons to challenge this premise, both on its validity and merits. First, researchers have questioned the very relationship between exports and output (i.e., the chicken-and-egg question raised years earlier by Tiebout). Though exports seem to be the source of growth in countries such as Germany, the relationship is reversed in others such as the United States, the United Kingdom, and many developing countries (Ghartey 1993; Jung and Marshall 1985; Sharma and Dhakal 1994; Sharma, Norris, and Cheung 1991). In other words, when a country's output grows, it then exports more; research has misinterpreted the causality (Ahmad 2001). Second, the multipliers produced by the export base seem to be inflated; the anticipated job growth often does not materialize (Drucker 2013).

But also, local consumption may drive regional growth by creating new markets, intensifying local impacts, or enhancing a region's attractiveness

(Markusen and Schrock 2009). Building new markets is not just about the process of import substitution, whereby regions reduce dependence on exports by learning how to produce goods and services for themselves. Rather, it is the growth of expenditures on new goods and services, as innovation and even marketing present different consumption possibilities (e.g., a new type of bicycle or a theater production that is only produced locally) (ibid.). In some cases, the market may simply shift from one type to another, resulting in no net gain for the region. But in others, it is actually growing, as people spend money (presumably from debt or savings, or even taking on new employment) on the newly appreciated good or service.

There are reasons to believe that these purchases from new consumption sectors will have a greater impact on the local economy than do export sectors. Local retailers and services such as healthcare are highly labor-intensive, and their workers tend to live and spend locally (ibid.). Locally based cultural workers have particularly strong connections to the local arts economy (ibid.). Local ownership of businesses will keep relatively more revenues within the region. To the extent that new local-serving activity also relies on underutilized land or labor, it will also increase overall productivity (Bartik 2004). Services such as childcare can also grow the economy by increasing local output and worker productivity, not just by making it possible to participate in the labor force, but also by boosting regional human capital attainment over the long term (Bartik 2011; Warner and Liu 2005).

Ultimately, the new consumption activity may result in exports of its own. One obvious example is local cultural activity, which can draw tourists from far away (as have New Orleans and Austin) (Markusen and Schrock 2009). Even sectors typically classified as local-serving may actually be exporting, as in the case of hospitals that attract patients from other areas (Nelson 2009). New types of services, such as innovations in ride sharing, have also grown from a local to a national or global market, generating significant numbers of new jobs.

As new local-serving consumption sectors emerge and grow, they begin a virtuous circle of growth: the region becomes a more attractive place to live, thereby attracting more skilled workers or retirees, both with disposable income to support more local consumption. Interestingly, the cities that most aggressively pursue sustainability policies tend not only to have larger creative classes, but also experience higher levels of income growth (Portney 2013). Florida (2002) argues that the preference of talented workers to live in places where they can meet their consumption needs is increasingly driving local economic development, although others have found that it is not creativity per se, but human capital and industry structure generally that matters (Donegan et al. 2008). Such workers are willing to bear higher rents in exchange for living near concentrations of amenities and services (Bartik 2011; Glaeser, Kolko, and Saiz 2001). Indeed, the growing share of job growth in consumption-oriented occupations provides evidence that this dynamic is at work (Markusen and Schrock 2009).

This suggests that in practice, cities and regions should be focusing on strategies that help build new markets, increase local spending, or improve local quality of life. And in fact, a new movement for sustainable economic development, focused not so much on consumption-driven growth, but more narrowly on "buying local," is emerging.

Sustainable Economic Development in Practice

Localist movements, which support locally owned, independent organizations, became prominent in the 2000s.[2] Over 130 Buy Local organizations are members of the two major national networks (Businesses Alliance for Local Living Economies and American Independent Business Association), and in addition there are numerous community finance organizations, local farms and community gardens, and municipal utilities that could be characterized as localist (Hess 2012).[3] Much of the localist network's focus is protecting locally owned businesses from the onslaught of big box and chain stores, but some also are interested in issues of social responsibility and environmental sustainability (ibid.). Although they have not been systematically studied, local organizations seem to be effective in increasing local purchases (Hess 2009).

The evidence in support of the impact of local markets and spending is substantial. One set of studies, by Civic Economics, shows that the multipliers of locally owned businesses are substantially higher than those of national and multinational chains. When residents support local firms, a greater share of the revenues will circulate back to local suppliers (as well as charitable nonprofits), and it is more likely that profits will produce more investment in the local economy as well. The counties with a higher density of small, locally owned businesses experience greater per capita income growth (Fleming and Goetz 2011). When Wal-Mart or other big box retailers come to town, there is net job and business loss, as well as decreases in retail wages (though, as noted above, small local entrepreneurs may not compensate workers well either) (Dube, Lester, and Eidlin 2007; Ficano 2012; Haltiwanger, Jarmin, and Krizan 2010; Neumark, Zhang, and Ciccarella 2008). They not only create significant negative externalities in the form of increased traffic and wasteful infrastructure, but may even impact the level of health, safety, and social welfare in nearby communities (Blanchard, Tolbert, and Mencken 2011; Goetz and Rupasingha 2006; Vivian 2006).

Yet, even in cities that are marketing themselves as sustainable, policies and regulations may not be in place to support local and/or sustainable businesses. Research by the Institute of Justice has shown how regulation run amok has dampened local entrepreneurship (Kregor 2013). For instance, often at the behest of existing professionals wishing to limit competition, many states enact burdensome licensing requirements that restrict entry into professions (Kleiner 2006). One example is mandating hundreds of hours of training and a cosmetology license for braiders who specialize in African-American hair (Kregor 2013). Despite the importance of residences as an incubator space for businesses (see Chapter 9), zoning often restricts the operations of start-up businesses, forcing them to waste precious start-up capital on commercial space. In addition, local restaurants and retailers fight to restrict the locations of vendors and food trucks. Ironically, local businesses may come under much more scrutiny than national chains.

Still, buying goods and services that are produced locally may not necessarily result in sustainable economic development. As Born and Purcell (2006) point out, local production methods may not be sustainable: choosing to deplete and degrade local resources, rather than transport goods from places with more abundant resources, may actually have greater environmental impact. From an economic perspective, there may not only be opportunity costs in using local resources to produce goods, but also these goods may be produced more efficiently elsewhere, or improve the well-being of more disadvantaged communities (as is the case with food produced locally versus imported from developing countries). Locally produced goods and services are often expensive relative to those sold in chain stores, and out of reach of lower-income households. The higher prices of local stores likely offset any gains to the local economy from more local purchasing (Egan 2014).

Despite the growing popularity of "buy local," relatively few cities and regions have adopted the more comprehensive sustainable economic development strategies that adopt a consumption-based approach. One exception is Santa Monica, California (Earthvoice Strategies 2009). Santa Monica's plan for sustainable economic development combines fiscal and place-making strategies. To stabilize the tax base, it targets high revenue sectors such as accommodation and retail, and promotes reinvestment in the local economy, but also seeks economic diversity. To build Santa Monica's reputation as a center for sustainable business, it aims to grow businesses that add to the city's sense of place and also adopt sustainable production processes. Enabling the accomplishment of these goals are close partnerships with businesses, dissemination of information about sustainability, the greening of new and existing commercial buildings, and, of course, marketing campaigns for "buy local" and a "sustainable Santa Monica" image. But what stands out about the Santa Monica effort is its adoption of broader endogenous development strategies for sustainability. By sharing resources and information across businesses, the plan sees the possibility for building more sustainable businesses through both supply chains, with local and regional sourcing, and markets, via shared market research. And in fact, focusing on local markets may well be key to more sustainable growth, as the case of the green economy shows next.

Local Markets Case

Local green businesses offer products or services that reduce energy use and/or improve environmental quality. Supporting the green economy offers the potential to grow an export sector by first developing new local markets. It may also intensify impacts on the local economy and even help market the region.

Our study for the U.S. Economic Development Administration explains how the green economy produces regional innovation and economic growth in California (Chapple et al. 2010).[4] As part of our project, we surveyed 650 businesses and compared traditional and green firms. We found numerous examples of new green products, such as compostable packaging, green supply chain consulting, carbon footprint calculators, building deconstruction and recycling, net zero energy houses, hybrid electric bicycles, solar water purifiers and heaters, and native gardens.[5]

The survey was conducted during the height of the Great Recession, when green businesses were continuing to grow despite the overall slowdown. Thus, not surprisingly, green firms expected to grow faster than traditional firms. But what is most interesting is how they operate: the green firms are much more closely tied to the region and the state than are traditional firms, and rely heavily on local markets and networks. They also view local and state public policy and regulation much more favorably than do other businesses.

Local quality of life and the location of the executives' residence currently play a deciding role in a firm's location (as described in Chapter 7), and for green businesses, location decision-making is no different, except that there is one other decisive factor—having a local market for the product. Because California offers the desired quality of life and market, green companies are disproportionately likely to want to remain in the state.

In part because they are relatively new, green firms are more embedded in both local and regional networks and markets than traditional firms. This orientation is also an important factor in the innovation of green products and services, since local markets provide feedback about new products and spur demand. Green companies are thus more likely than other types of businesses to serve markets within their cities or regions (Figure 8.1). Traditional companies have a very different customer base, catering to private firms in

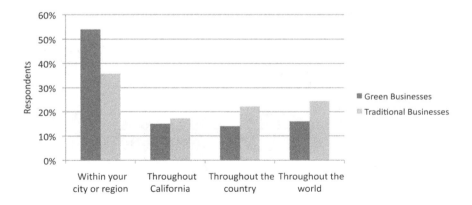

Figure 8.1 Primary market location by business type

Source: Author's calculations

national and world markets more than regional or local markets. But private households constitute the largest market for green businesses.

Firm innovation and growth depend on business networks with competitors, partners, suppliers, and support organizations such as trade associations within and outside the home region. Green businesses report making greater use of several types of local networks compared to other firms, including local nonprofits, local government, and similar businesses in the local area. For green businesses, competitors, suppliers, and partners are also more likely to be located within the home city or region of the firms.

The survey asked businesses about their interactions with different types of organizations, providing further evidence of the local and regional nature of many green businesses. Almost two-thirds of green businesses reported weekly or monthly interactions with similar businesses in the region. Green businesses have, in general, more frequent interactions with other organizations, local governments, and nonprofits than traditional businesses (Figure 8.2), and differ from other business types in their reliance upon networking forums, such as conventions, for information about their trade.

Green businesses are much less likely than traditional to object to the costs of doing business (and high taxes). Instead, they ask for more government incentives, not only for businesses (financial incentives), but also to increase

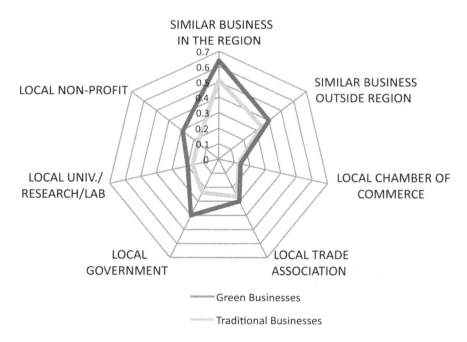

Figure 8.2 Weekly/monthly interactions with organizations by business type
Source: Author's calculations

the demand for green products among consumers (market incentives/market education). For instance, a soil remediation and restoration company based in Silicon Valley says, "there needs to be significantly more education on sustainable landscaping and soil management practices," while a green construction company in the East Bay suggests: "offer incentives to be a green business that are tangible. While it is becoming mainstream, green business is still as much a personal ethical choice of the management, as it may be market driven." A green architecture firm with more than 100 employees located in Silicon Valley suggests, "provide more energy conservation financial incentives for lower to middle income families and businesses." Other types of incentives mentioned include tax credits for buying "green," utility rebates, subsidies for energy-efficient equipment installation, low-cost loans for home improvement, and fast-track permitting for green projects.

Green companies seem to be relatively more affected by local policies and less by state policies than traditional companies. But our respondents in green firms perceived policies at all levels as having a much more positive impact in their business than those at traditional companies did. Some respondents from green companies saw opportunities in regulations: a green architecture company from the East Bay suggested, "zoning, building codes, energy efficiency standards, difficult city approval processes create a demand for our services."

Growing the local green economy is textbook sustainable economic development. Because rapidly growing green businesses are tied to place, they support local fiscal stability and cultural context. By definition, green businesses do not degrade the environment or contribute to climate change. And though the businesses depend on consumption, their products also have an educative function and are likely to become export goods in the near future.

But the sector also provides important lessons about the power of local markets, the role of planning and regulation, and the shortcomings of a simplistic "buy local" approach. At present, buying local essentially means substituting goods and services from locally owned businesses for those from national chains, rather than trying out new innovations. But because it may be inefficient to produce those goods locally, they may be overly expensive. Because of their lack of originality and their high cost, they may never be suitable for exporting—and thus, these businesses may never be sustainable.

In contrast, by innovating new goods and services, green business is driving both regional growth and sustainability. Innovation depends on building relationships with actors and markets that are not just local, but throughout the region. In many cases, these businesses are also adopting a holistic approach that takes into account the sourcing of inputs via a local (or regional) supply chain. Local and state government is playing a pivotal role in building this market, both via environmental regulations that force businesses to innovate new production processes, and through energy conservation programs that subsidize costs for consumers.

Whether or not sustainable economic development is an effective tool to address income inequality is an open question. As local businesses begin to export, they may grow the pie. To the extent that they can increase productivity, they may bring higher wages. The involvement of government in nurturing the sector creates an opportunity to match new job opportunities to local disadvantaged jobseekers. Though sustainable economic development is not a panacea for inequality, it does offer hope.

Notes

1. www.whitehouse.gov/blog/2013/11/08/president-obama-talks-exports-big-easy.
2. American Independent Business Alliance defines a local independent business as one that is in either private or cooperative ownership, is at least 50 percent locally owned, with local management, and has a limited number of venues within a local geography (see www.amiba.net/about_ibas/social-media).
3. Only including members of the American Independent Business Alliance and the Business Alliance for Local Living Economies.
4. U.S. Economic Development Administration Award #99-07-13863.
5. The survey sampled three types of firms—those defined as green by the product or service offered (n = 351), and a sample of traditional firms (n = 299), including a strategic random sample of firms that do not offer green products or services, and a sample of firms that report their toxic chemical releases and waste management activities to the U.S. Environmental Protection Agency's Toxic Release Inventory due to their high environmental impact (n =72, hereafter referred to as TRI firms). We developed the green survey sample from the National Establishment Time Series (Dun & Bradstreet) data combined with the Build It Green database of California green building businesses. For the traditional business survey, we developed a parallel or matched set of businesses not identified as green: for instance, we sampled a variety of regular construction and manufacturing firms, as well as other traditional sectors likely to be affected by environmental regulations, such as transportation and agriculture. The sample covered firms throughout the state, providing a rich picture of the variations among and within the case study regions, different green and other industry sectors, and among small and large green and non-green firms. Because of an oversampling of metropolitan areas, the survey represents, broadly, California's largest metropolitan areas, as well as its inland valley, but likely underrepresents its central coastal areas, mountain regions, and the far northern counties.

References

Ahmad, Jaleel. "Causality Between Exports and Economic Growth: What Do the Econometric Studies Tell Us?" *Pacific Economic Review* 6, no. 1 (2001): 147–167.

Bartik, Timothy J. "Economic Development." In *Management Policies in Local Government Finance. 5th Edition*, edited by J. Richard Aronson and Eli Schwartz, 355–390. Washington, DC: International City/County Management Association, 2004.

Bartik, Timothy J. *Investing in Kids: Early Childhood Programs and Local Economic Development*. Kalamazoo, MI: W. E. Upjohn Institute for Employment Research, 2011.

Blanchard, Troy C., Charles Tolbert, and Carson Mencken. "The Health and Wealth of US Counties: How the Small Business Environment Impacts Alternative Measures of Development." *Cambridge Journal of Regions, Economy, and Society* 5, no. 1 (2011): 149–162.

Born, Branden and Mark Purcell. "Avoiding the Local Trap Scale and Food Systems in Planning Research." *Journal of Planning Education and Research* 26, no. 2 (2006): 195–207.

Chapple, Karen, Malo Hutson, Cynthia Kroll, T. William Lester, Larry Rosenthal, Emilio Martinez de Velasco, Ana Mileva, Sergio Montero, Anita Roth, and Laura Wiles. *Innovating the Green Economy in California Regions.* Berkeley, CA: Center for Community Innovation, UC Berkeley, 2010.

Donegan, Mary, Joshua Drucker, Harvey Goldstein, Nichola Lowe, and Emil Malizia. "Which Indicators Explain Metropolitan Economic Performance Best? Traditional or Creative Class." *Journal of the American Planning Association* 74, no. 2 (2008): 180–195.

Drucker, Joshua. "Assessing Economic Impacts Amid Rapid Change: Examples from Defense Communities." Unpublished paper. University of Illinois at Chicago, 2013.

Dube, Arindrajit, T. William Lester, and Barry Eidlin. *A Downward Push: The Impact of Wal-Mart Stores on Retail Wages and Benefits.* Berkeley, CA: UC Berkeley Center for Labor Research and Education, 2007.

Earthvoice Strategies. *City of Santa Monica: Strategy for a Sustainable Local Economy.* North Vancouver, BC: Earthvoice Strategies, 2009.

Egan, Ted. *Expanding Formula Retail Controls: Economic Impact Report.* San Francisco, CA: Office of Economic Analysis, 2014. Accessed February 19, 2014. http://sfcontroller.org/Modules/ShowDocument.aspx?documentid=5119.

Ficano, Carlena Cochi. "Business Churn and the Retail Giant: Establishment Birth and Death from Wal-Mart's Entry." *Social Science Quarterly* 94, no. 1 (2013): 263–291.

Fleming, David A. and Stephan J. Goetz. "Does Local Firm Ownership Matter?" *Economic Development Quarterly* 25, no. 3 (2011): 277–281.

Florida, Richard. "The Economic Geography of Talent." *Annals of the Association of American Geographers* 92, no. 4 (2002): 743–755.

Gage, Alea and Anthony LoPresti with Cecilia Estolano, Karen Chapple, and Michelle Wilde Anderson. *Sustainable Economic Development Policy Overview.* Berkeley, CA: Institute of Urban and Regional Development, 2012.

Ghartey, Edward E. "Causal Relationship Between Exports and Economic Growth: Some Empirical Evidence in Taiwan, Japan and the US." *Applied Economics* 25, no. 9 (1993): 1145–1152.

Glaeser, Edward, Jed Kolko, and Albert Saiz. "Consumer City." *Journal of Economic Geography* 1 (2001): 27–50.

Goetz, Stephan J. and Anil Rupasingha. "Wal-Mart and Social Capital." *American Journal of Agricultural Economics* 88, no. 5 (2006): 1304–1310.

Haltiwanger, John, Ron Jarmin, and Cornell John Krizan. "Mom-and-Pop Meet Big-Box: Complements or Substitutes?" *Journal of Urban Economics* 67, no. 1 (2010): 116–134.

Haughton, Graham and Dave Counsell. "Regions and Sustainable Development: Regional Planning Matters." *The Geographical Journal* 170, no. 2 (2004): 135–145.

Hess, David J. *Localist Movements in a Global Economy: Sustainability, Justice, and Urban Development in the United States.* Cambridge, MA: MIT Press, 2009.

Hess, David J. "An Introduction to Localist Movements." Paper presented at the annual meeting of the American Sociological Association, Denver, Colorado, August 17–20, 2012.

Jung, Woo S. and Peyton J. Marshall. "Exports, Growth and Causality in Developing Countries." *Journal of Development Economics* 18, no. 1 (1985): 1–12.

Kleiner, Morris M. *Licensing Occupations: Ensuring Quality or Restricting Competition?* Kalamazoo, MI: W. E. Upjohn Institute for Employment Research, 2006.

Kregor, Elizabeth. "Space to Work: Opening Job Opportunities by Reducing Regulation." Unpublished paper. Chicago, IL: Institute for Justice, 2013.

Krueger, Rob and David Gibbs. "'Third Wave' Sustainability? Smart Growth and Regional Development in the USA." *Regional Studies* 42, no. 9 (2008): 1263–1274.

Krueger, Rob and Lydia Savage. "City Regions and Social Reproduction: A 'Place' for Sustainable Development?" *International Journal of Urban and Regional Research* 31, no. 1 (2007): 215–223.

Leiserowitz, Anthony A., Robert W. Kates, and Thomas M. Parris. "Sustainability Values, Attitudes, and Behaviors: A Review of Multinational and Global Trends." *Annual Review of Environmental Resources* 31 (2006): 413–444.

Markusen, Ann and Greg Schrock. "Consumption-Driven Urban Development." *Urban Geography* 30, no. 4 (2009): 344–367.

Moretti, Enrico. *The New Geography of Jobs*. Boston, MA: Houghton Mifflin Harcourt, 2012.

Nelson, Marla. "Are Hospitals an Export Industry? Empirical Evidence From Five Lagging Regions." *Economic Development Quarterly* 23, no. 3 (2009): 242–253.

Neumark, David, Junfu Zhang, and Stephen Ciccarella. "The Effects of Wal-Mart on Local Labor Markets." *Journal of Urban Economics* 67, no. 1 (2008): 1–168.

Portney, Kent E. "Local Sustainability Policies and Programs as Economic Development: Is the New Economic Development Sustainable Development?" *Cityscape* 15, no. 1 (2013): 45–62.

Sharma, Subhash C. and Dharmendra Dhakal. "Causal Analyses Between Exports and Economic Growth in Developing Countries." *Applied Economics* 26, no. 12 (1994): 1145–1157.

Sharma, Subhash C., Mary Norris, and Daniel Wai-Wah Cheung. "Exports and Economic Growth in Industrialized Countries." *Applied Economics* 23, no. 4 (1991): 697–708.

Vivian, Georgiena M. "Trip Generation Characteristics of Free-Standing Discount Superstores." *ITE Journal* 76, no. 8 (2006): 30–37.

Warner, Mildred E. and Zhilin Liu. "Economic Development Policy and Local Services: The Case of Child Care." *International Journal of Economic Development* 7, no. 1 (2005): 25–64.

9 The Challenge of Mixing Uses and the Secret Sauce of Urban Industrial Land

The UC-Berkeley hall was packed with local officials and grad students eager to hear Bruce Katz, Vice President of the Brookings Institution, pitch his new book, *The Metropolitan Revolution*. Key to the revolution is the innovation district: "Innovation Districts cluster and connect leading edge anchor institutions and cutting-edge innovative firms with supporting and spin off companies, business incubators, mixed-use housing, office and retail and 21st century amenities and transport" (Katz and Bradley 2013: 114). For instance, the 22@Barcelona mixed-use innovation district is redeveloping a 200-acre industrial area as a cluster of media, medical technologies, information technology, energy, and design businesses, along with housing, retail, and parks.

A planner from the City of Oakland raised her hand. "You've described this innovation district in Barcelona that shifted zoning from industrial to mixed use. We've discussed that for West Oakland, too—we have some similar businesses to Barcelona. But what we can't figure out is, what happens when the new businesses in IT can pay more for rent and the existing manufacturers get pushed out? You can't sustain the mix." Katz explained that Barcelona was a little different from the United States because of all the public funding available to finance infrastructure and development. But the question about industrial displacement and the impermanence of mixed use was just too tough to tackle.

Even if the theories of regional and sustainable economic development outlined in previous chapters suggest we should foster existing industrial businesses, why should we protect those in the region's core? The line of argument typically put forward by the local Chamber of Commerce is that these businesses are mostly heavy manufacturers who have been leaving the city for decades anyway, or distributors who are using the land inefficiently, mostly for parking. With resistance to infill development in urban neighborhoods, and high land costs downtown, the industrial land near the core becomes the low-hanging fruit for developers.

Often, an odd growth machine coalition in support of converting industrial land emerges, armed with ideas such as innovation districts. This might include not just the Chamber and developers, but nonprofit housing developers concerned about the need for affordable or workforce housing downtown, planners interested in more housing to achieve jobs–housing balance, politicians seeking retail and the sales tax revenue it brings, environmental justice advocates concerned about pollution from productive businesses in high-density areas, and economists advocating export-based regional growth based on high-tech.

At the same time, a broad movement is supporting the preservation of industrial land in the urban core of regions across the country. Driving the movement are organizations working to preserve and promote urban manufacturing, such as the Urban Manufacturing Alliance, as well as entrepreneurial city agencies. They share the recognition that industrial businesses (or, more broadly, production, distribution, and repair firms) support both the residential sector and other businesses, that they need to be located close by their customers downtown, and that the availability of affordable land is key to maintaining these businesses (Dempwolf 2010). These businesses play a vital role in the local economy, but are almost invisible.

San Francisco, where ongoing pressure for rezoning to residential has diminished its industrial land supply to just 4.5 percent of its land (from 14 percent in 1948), provides many great examples of the interconnectedness of its industrial and commercial districts. When the San Francisco Opera, located in the Civic Center, incurs damage to a tree on its set in the middle of a performance, how does it get a replacement? Its own building is too small to store its sets, but it needs them nearby for rapid access. So, it has a storage warehouse just minutes away in the Potrero industrial district. A civic use such as the opera cannot afford storage space in the urban center, but it can maintain trucks to fetch props in an emergency.

And there are other equity-related reasons to support industrial land as well, ranging from its positive fiscal impacts to the high-quality jobs it provides, often for local residents. Cities often turn to mixed-use (or now, innovation) districts as a compromise that will accommodate the different interests. But that diversity is not sustainable.

The Tension Between Mixed-Use and Industrial Land

In the industrial city, industrial land is typically located near the urban core, for easy transport of goods and access to labor. Over time, competing uses, such as office and high-end residential, that could pay more for centrally located land, outbid industrial uses, and these businesses moved out. Still, many core industrial districts remained intact, particularly if they were located on less desirable land, next to railroad tracks or freeways that prevented direct access to the central business district. By the 1970s, many of the industrial businesses had departed for the suburbs or overseas. Thus, when artists, young families, and soon, investors, began seeking out unique live-work spaces in non-residential areas, they quickly gravitated toward these neighborhoods. Their transition to mixed use was part of a larger trend.

The Advent of Mixed-Use Districts

Most credit Jane Jacobs with illustrating most effectively the value of mixing uses. Her critique of urban renewal contrasted single-use residential tower superblocks with the vibrancy of blocks containing a fine-grained mix of diverse uses. But in reality, most North American cities relied on an entrenched system of single-use zoning that would prove hard to modify. The 1917 Zoning Code in New York City had introduced the notion of the hierarchical zone— with housing at the top, then commercial, then industrial—and little or no mixing in order to protect higher uses. These reflect societal ideals of order and privacy, with homogeneous residential districts placed at a distance from the chaos of commercial development (Boyer 1983; Hirt 2007; Perin 1977). Arguably, these single-use districts subsequently shaped not only American culture, but also its construction industry, which separated into home builders, office developers, retail developers, and industrial developers (Hirt 2007). This, then, made it more expensive to construct developments that would mix uses.

By the 1980s, community acceptance of mixed use had grown, to the point where today a majority (53 percent) of U.S. residents prefer to live close to restaurants, shops, and offices (Urban Land Institute 2013). From the 1980s to today, mixed use gradually became integrated into planning (Grant 2002). Cities have modified zoning regulations to permit and intensify the mixture of uses— residential, commercial, open space, institutional, and, less frequently, industrial (ibid.). New Urbanists, particularly its transit-oriented development advocates, are strong proponents of mixed use for sustainability reasons, citing its ability to maximize efficient use of infrastructure and reduce VMT through collocation of diverse uses (ibid.). Proponents of traditional neighborhood design focus more on its impacts on the quality of life, with the mixing of home and work in the dense and diverse European city as their model (Foord 2010). But even planners who have embraced mixed use see challenges in including industrial businesses in the mix (Grant 2002).

Mixed-use proponents generally support both horizontal mixed use (i.e., walkable clusters of different uses) and vertical mixed use (i.e., a mixture within a specific building or development). The ideal is to mix at the finest grain possible, what Constance Perin (1977) called the "bathtub in the kitchen"—though even advocates admit that it may be challenging to generate market demand (Ewing 1996). But the context also shapes the character of mixed use: a vertically mixed-use development within a single-use district may not be particularly vibrant, while a horizontally mixed-use district may also not be very lively if different types of uses are dispersed and not within a short walking distance.

Despite the gradual institutionalization of mixed-use zoning codes, in practice, communities do not always embrace them. NIMBYism, the not-in-my-backyard movement, often occurs in response to attempts to mixed use in residential areas by adding public facilities or high-density housing (or even parks!) (Grant 2002). The benefits of mixed-use communities are clearer for workers

Figure 9.1 Industrial district, Oakland
Photo credit: Katherine Rife

in high-consumption lifestyles than, say, families with children, which might benefit more from socially cohesive communities (Foord 2010). Retail, restaurants, and nightlife can create impacts (or "negative externalities") such as noise and trash that make life challenging for local residents (Foord 2010). Even if community residents prefer mixed-use in principle, they have not yet proved willing to get out of their cars. As Jill Grant and Katherine Perrott (2011: 192) point out: "The kinds of cultural changes necessary to save the café and transform the retail landscape of suburbia into an urban form require more than mixed-use policies can deliver."

The greatest implementation challenges for both mixed-use developments and districts lie in the market. Although multiple examples of successful large-scale mixed-use developments now exist, they are still relatively high risk. The legacy of separate commercial and residential construction industries means that mixed use requires collaboration, incurring new costs. Residential and retail components may have different leasing requirements, and project phasing can also bring complications, since the retail needs the residential population to be established for it to survive (Grant and Perrott 2011). As high ground-floor retail vacancy rates attest, mixed-use requirements have led to an oversupply of retail space (Foord 2010; Grant and Perrott 2011). Large chain stores and Internet retail have absorbed much of the mom-and-pop market, and even if gentrifying neighborhoods bring new markets for boutique small-format retail, the market is generally slow to respond to neighborhood change (Chapple and Jacobus 2009; Grant and Perrott 2011). At the district scale, increasing the mix can paradoxically also decrease diversity, particularly in formerly industrial areas: as residential and commercial uses paying higher rent move in, existing industrial users will gradually be displaced (Grant and Perrott 2011).

Industrial Districts: To Mix or Not to Mix

What type of district helps industrial users thrive? In principle, we might encourage zoning land to exclusively industrial use for two reasons. Hierarchical

zoning, separating lower (agricultural, industrial) uses from higher (commercial, residential), prevents the impacts of production from affecting other, less noxious uses. Zoning can also help the market understand the land's highest and best use, or the types of development that would be most appropriate (and able to pay rent) on the site.

The problem is that zoning designations often remain in place while the market shifts, and zoning can be very hard to change. Since it may appear to be obsolete, pressure builds on cities to revisit its designations. Across the United States, over 20 municipalities and counties have recently undertaken studies of industrial land supply, typically in response to developer pressures to convert the land to residential, commercial, or mixed use. It is mostly the strong market regions that are re-evaluating how much industrial land they need.

As studies show, industrial areas contribute to the regional economy in multiple ways: as job and tax revenue generators; providers of supplies and services, such as back-office functions or automobile repair, to businesses and households; and reservoirs of low-cost space that can incubate start-up businesses (Howland 2011). Land that generates employment, whether in industrial or commercial uses, tends to have net positive fiscal benefits (Strategic Economics 2004). Many sites house large buildings with potentially flexible use: many industrial sites can accommodate not just production, but also back-office functions, storage, loading, parking, and even research and development (Figures 9.1 and 9.2). They can also be subdivided when firms decrease in size. In contrast to more modern office buildings, this type of space offers firms the flexibility they seek in today's economy, with the ability to shift between vertical and horizontal organization, and to easily add or shed employees.

More recently, advocates for the preservation of industrial land have argued that this land is most likely to support the coveted middle-skill jobs. Production, distribution, and repair (PDR) businesses locate in many different types of buildings on industrial land and typically provide jobs in industries that pay well over a living wage, such as auto repair, construction, landscaping, and utilities (San Francisco Planning Department 2002). The rise of sustainable and

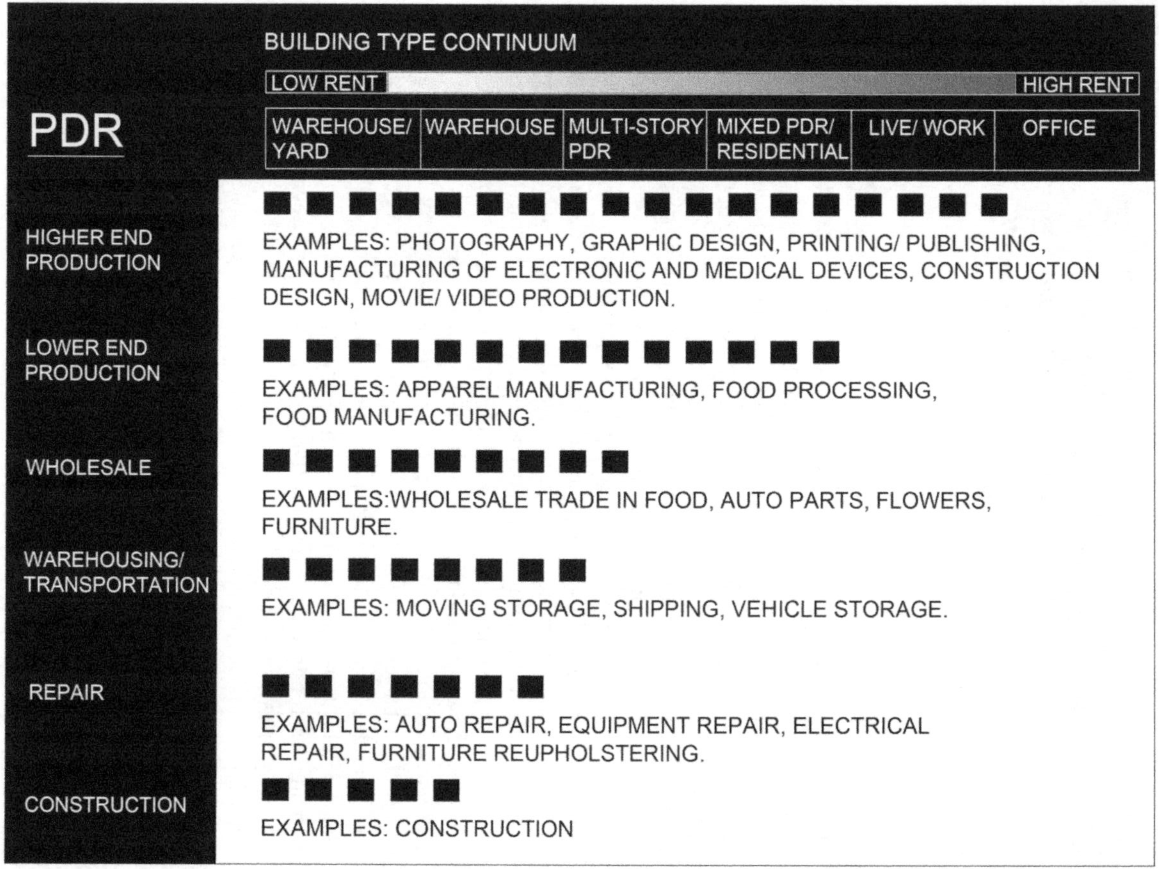

BUILDING TYPE CONTINUUM

LOW RENT   HIGH RENT

WAREHOUSE/ YARD	WAREHOUSE	MULTI-STORY PDR	MIXED PDR/ RESIDENTIAL	LIVE/ WORK	OFFICE

PDR

HIGHER END PRODUCTION

EXAMPLES: PHOTOGRAPHY, GRAPHIC DESIGN, PRINTING/ PUBLISHING, MANUFACTURING OF ELECTRONIC AND MEDICAL DEVICES, CONSTRUCTION DESIGN, MOVIE/ VIDEO PRODUCTION.

LOWER END PRODUCTION

EXAMPLES: APPAREL MANUFACTURING, FOOD PROCESSING, FOOD MANUFACTURING.

WHOLESALE

EXAMPLES: WHOLESALE TRADE IN FOOD, AUTO PARTS, FLOWERS, FURNITURE.

WAREHOUSING/ TRANSPORTATION

EXAMPLES: MOVING STORAGE, SHIPPING, VEHICLE STORAGE.

REPAIR

EXAMPLES: AUTO REPAIR, EQUIPMENT REPAIR, ELECTRICAL REPAIR, FURNITURE REUPHOLSTERING.

CONSTRUCTION

EXAMPLES: CONSTRUCTION

Figure 9.2 Businesses and building types on industrial land

Source: Adapted from San Francisco Planning Department (2002)

niche manufacturing, along with the relatively strong performance of manu-facturing during the economic recovery—due largely to changing production costs (rising transportation costs, falling energy costs), a weak dollar, and competitive wages—has suggested the continued importance of industrial zoning in the core (Christopherson 2011).

The location of production, distribution, and repair businesses within the region also has important implications for smart growth and regional sustain-ability (Leigh and Hoelzel 2012). Locating logistics businesses in particular (e.g., wholesale distributors) in the urban core, near major trading ports, helps ensure the efficient movement of goods. Displacing these firms from the core into peripheral areas—a trend that is already occurring—would mean a significant increase in VMT from trucks (Hausrath Economics Group and Cambridge Systematics 2008).

However, critics continue to raise the issue of inefficiency, arguing that the benefits are not high enough to warrant the cost to the city of subsidizing the land. From their perspective, policies that slow the relocation of these businesses to more appropriate areas may actually impede regional economic growth (Hills and Schleicher 2011). Moreover, rezoning to the highest and best use—often thought to be commercial office or apartment buildings—might yield higher returns in terms of business attraction and local tax revenues—with these higher density uses more likely to be occupied by transit users. And in many cities, "industrial chic" is valued for its potential to attract innovative entrepreneurs—the fabric of these new innovation districts of the "metropolitan revolution."

Not surprisingly, council meetings over the rezoning of industrial land attract hundreds of stakeholders on both sides of the issue. The battle is playing out in New York City, Boston, San Francisco, Chicago, Los Angeles, Denver, Baltimore, Minneapolis, Charlotte, Portland, Seattle, much of the DC metropolitan area, and many other smaller cities. How can we bolster the regional sustainability argument for preserving industrial land?

The Secret Sauce of Messy Industrial Land

Support Integrity of Industrial Zones
for Industry, Artisans, & Artists
Support Housing In Allowable, Mixed Use Residential & S.Pablo Zones,
NOT Industrial Zones Where City Admits Housing Pressures Industry
& Arts OUT
∫∫∫∫∫∫∫∫∫∫∫
Nation, Obama Support Manufacturing Renaissance While
City Proposes 1,304+ residential units in Mixed Use Light Industrial
Zone
West Berkeley Artisans and Industrial Companies
(WEBAIC) Newsletter (WEBAIC 2012)

WEBAIC's plea to save crafts manufacturing from an influx of high-end residential could have come from any of these strong-market regions: residential buildings bring in new residents, and new retail and residential construction and conversion follow. Given the shortage of land and the perceived chic of much of the industrial building stock, this raises rents and may displace long-standing PDR users. The city looks at the district and sees underutilized land and obsolete buildings where WEBAIC sees a renaissance. Even Enrico Moretti (2012: 175) has weighed in: "One of the most extreme cases is the city of Berkeley, which in an effort to protect 'good blue-collar jobs' has effectively stunted high-tech growth in the entire west side of the city." Is this vibrant local economy invisible to the experts?

The East Bay of the San Francisco Bay Area, specifically Oakland, Berkeley, Richmond, and Emeryville, early developed its own distinct and diversified economy, with strengths in transport, logistics, and manufacturing located on its abundant waterfront industrial land. Despite the decline and decentralization of goods-producing industries throughout the latter half of the twentieth century, the cities still maintained steady rates of growth and job creation, mostly through a rapid transition to a service economy with niches in healthcare and education, but also via steady employment in small PDR businesses, typically housed in aging industrial buildings. Growth in recent decades has put pressure on industrial landowners to convert prime areas along the waterfront to residential and office uses, despite vacancy rates of just 5 percent. Overall, 38 percent of industrial land in the region is already planned for new office, residential, or mixed uses (Hausrath Economics Group and Cambridge Systematics 2008).

The East Bay economy has about 400,000 jobs, and the majority of its businesses (83 percent) are located in its commercial and residential zones. It gets

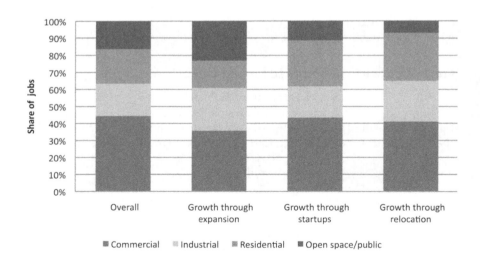

Figure 9.3 Jobs by zone in the East Bay: start-ups versus expansions versus relocations
Source: Author's calculations

much of its dynamism from start-ups and small firms, as the studies have found for other areas: in recent decades, about 45 percent of net new jobs in a given year come from new firms, and overall, 94 percent of firms have fewer than 20 employees. These start-ups most often are in high-end services such as professional, scientific, and technical services or information. Jobs from start-ups are disproportionately concentrated in residential zones (not surprisingly, as many firms start up at home) (Figure 9.3).

However, over half of net new jobs come from existing firms expanding, and businesses in the industrial zones, no matter what the sector (both PDR and services), are much more likely to expand than those in other zones, adding employees at four times the rate of commercial zones and nine times the rate in residential zones.[1] Residential and industrial land also gains disproportionately from firm relocations into the region, though these accounted only for about 5 percent of net new jobs in the region each year.

What lies behind firm expansion? Factors internal to the firm, particular mergers and acquisitions, of course play an important role, but these are hard to measure with secondary data (Brouwer, Mariotti, and van Ommeren 2004). So, let us look instead at local factors and firm characteristics. No matter what industry sector a firm is in, which neighborhood it is located in, or where the economy is in the business cycle, three factors predict job creation by existing firms: firm size (measured in terms of both employees and sales), building square footage, and industrial zoning.

Firm size matters: in other words, the smaller a firm is in terms of employment at the initial point in time, and the larger its sales, the more likely it is to expand. Thus, there is an inverse relationship between firm employment and sales: firms with high sales but low employment tend to expand (i.e., they are "gazelles"), while those with both high sales and employment are more static or actually losing jobs.

But most importantly, these results suggest the importance of actual sites— location on industrially zoned land, regardless of neighborhoods, in a relatively large building. While start-ups, as low-overhead, home-based businesses, benefit from the ability to locate in residential zones, firms that expand—whether in production, distribution, and repair or information-based services—need the flexibility to spill into available space in large buildings. Industrial zones seem to facilitate this slightly more effectively than commercial zones, perhaps because they have more of the "flex" space that allows firms to grow and shrink readily (Figure 9.4). Confirming this finding, a related survey of 88 firms in the East Bay found that when businesses are expanding, office firms are more likely to move all operations to a larger site, while industrial uses either acquire more square footage at their current site or increase their hours of operation. The major barriers to creating new jobs are labor costs, space costs, and access to capital (Meigs and Wiles 2010).

Industrially zoned land comprises just a small share of the region, typically around 10 percent. But it plays an outsize role because its low cost and flexible set-up allows firms to experiment, to shift focus from production, to distribution,

Figure 9.4 "Messy" industrial space in West Berkeley
Photo credit: Karen Chapple

to R&D as need be. Once firms reach a certain size, they might move some operations: management can work downtown, and production can take place in another country. But most do not reach that size, and in fact, most add and subtract jobs several times during their lifespan. This type of space makes it possible—and invisible. Rather than stunting high-tech growth, these low-cost districts are indirectly supporting it, by providing this messy space. Meanwhile, the high-tech businesses can still locate in transit-friendly locations with the amenities that creative workers covet.

The pressure on industrial land occurs because of its location, predominantly near the core. This is not just a result of historic development patterns, but also of the need for goods movement. Many of the PDR businesses—from construction support, to manufacturing, to wholesale—depend on the region's ports and highways to support frequent freight trips. But although demand from these businesses is steady or growing, the amount of warehouse and manufacturing space in central areas is declining: in a recent five-year period in the East Bay, about 7 percent of building space was lost or converted (Hausrath Economics Group and Cambridge Systematics 2008). With land use plans already in place calling for reuse of much remaining industrial land, cities are no longer maintaining the infrastructure in many of these older areas (ibid.). Even if this land remains industrial, the supply will still be insufficient to house demand by 2035 (ibid.). This will cause many PDR businesses to shift location to the region's periphery, or even adjacent lower-cost regions (in this case, the Central Valley), with increasing VMT and its implications for greenhouse gas emissions.

Strong market regions around the world are losing their messy industrial land near the core to office, residential, and mixed-use development—often in the name of creating new innovation districts. The idea of cross-fertilization between sectors, as in the Barcelona case, is exciting and may well yield interesting new ideas. But most innovation does not occur in cafés in expensive new mixed-use districts; the garage where HP started is a much more accurate image of Silicon Valley. Innovation is not just about developing new ideas or scientific discoveries, but introducing them into the marketplace or implementing them into production processes. It is thus highly experimental and variable. In spatial terms, it benefits from low land costs and sites that permit different business configurations, but also proximity to inputs and markets. For businesses that are just starting up or expanding, redeveloped space in a branded mixed-use innovation district brings a premature formality—quite different from the bathtub in the kitchen. Thus, how can we preserve the existing messy, but productive spaces?

Policy and Planning

Industrially zoned land contributes to the regional economy by providing flexibility, specifically offering a reserve of relatively large sites that accommodate uses from storage to R&D. But many cities have opened up their industrial land to a variety of uses, including commercial and residential, risking unsustainable rent increases that will gradually displace PDR businesses. Other cities, while preserving their land as industrial zones, open it up to many types of industrial users. In the face of competition for land from higher rent-paying office uses, rents will escalate beyond the means of some of the firms that are contributing more jobs to the economy.

Policy recommendations for the preservation of industrially zoned land generally follow three tactics: regulation, penalties, and incentives. Regulatory tools are the most powerful; they include restricting the types of uses that can locate within a zone, instituting criteria for land conversion, and rezoning land.

Policies that preserve industrial zoning are essential "exclusionary zoning"; they prohibit higher uses despite market interest (Heikkila and Hutton 1986). This policy has costs, in that it may mean inefficient use of resources, slowdown of the transition away from industrial uses, and impacts on the local tax base in ways that are rarely made explicit. However, it may be appropriate to pursue exclusionary zoning under certain conditions, in particular: (1) when the industrial district is economically viable, functioning as a business incubator or housing businesses linked to other local clusters; (2) when there is a high level of structural unemployment; or (3) negative externalities are an issue (ibid.). Exclusionary zoning can not only keep rents low for businesses, but also provides certainty to developers about city intentions.

Figure 9.5 New live-work lofts in mixed-use industrial zone, south of Market neighborhood, San Francisco
Photo credit: Arjiit Sen

In practice, exclusionary zoning for industrial use has existed in a few cities since the 1980s, due to fears that demand from commercial and residential uses was displacing viable industrial businesses (Fitzgerald and Leigh 2002). Some of these districts—called Planned Manufacturing Districts in Chicago, Industrial Protection Zones in San Francisco, and Industrial Business Zones in New York—permit the mixture of uses in the districts, but limit land availability for non-industrial users.

The case of San Francisco is notable for defining PDR so narrowly as to exclude office, which includes new media businesses. In the late 1990s, almost 2,800 acres, or 12.6 percent of land in the city, was available for industrial use—though in reality, this included the port and buffer zones where most businesses cannot locate, so the total was closer to 5 percent. In any case, zoning in most of these areas allowed various types of office and, with a conditional use permit, housing, as well as, of course, heavy and light industrial and commercial. Housing moved into industrial areas, the "Eastern Neighborhoods," because it was cheaper to build, there was less neighborhood opposition, and the zoning permitted it. At the same time, tech start-ups were attracted to the low-cost, flexible space. As developers built live-work lofts in the area (Figure 9.5), mostly for a market interested more in living in a chic industrial area than actually producing anything, businesses were displaced and jobs lost. Meanwhile, the new residents complained about the lack of neighborhood services and the nuisances and noise from the PDR firms.

But in the 2000s, after a public planning process, the city acted to preserve its industrial land. To accommodate housing, it ceded over half of its industrial

land near downtown to mixed-use zoning, with housing, and preserved the rest in industrial protection zones. The most transit-accessible areas were opened up to a variety of uses, but a short distance away, still within a mile of the downtown, the city protects its PDR uses. To maintain the dynamism of industrial districts, which often provide valuable low-cost incubator space, these zones also encourage start-up firms, but only in a few industry sectors such as cleantech and digital media, and only in lab, not office, space.

Another zoning tool currently in vogue is form-based zoning. These codes regulate urban form, rather than land use, detailing requirements for both buildings and the surrounding built environment (Woodward 2013). By controlling form, rather than use, the zoning allows the market to select the optimal user for the space. Despite the buzz, however, very few cities have enacted form-based codes (Hirt 2013). And by lifting use restrictions, this form of zoning actually threatens industrial use: if a developer were to build an industrial-style building, it might attract higher-end users who appreciate the industrial chic—and can outbid true industrial users for the space.

Key among incentives for industrial land preservation is the industrial land trust or bank, an approach in which the public sector acquires industrially zoned land and leases it to qualifying uses; examples include the Marine Industrial Park in Boston, the Brooklyn Navy Yard, and the Cleveland Industrial-Commercial Land Bank (Hausrath Economics Group and Cambridge Systematics 2004). Other specific incentives may include brownfield remediation or site assembly.

Industrial Land Preservation as a Regional Sustainability Strategy

Older industrial areas near the urban core are coveted by non-industrial users because of their proximity to the center and their built fabric. The pressures to convert core industrial land occur because of higher land prices at the center— a phenomenon that even occurs in "donut-hole" metros such as Detroit as they are hollowing out.

From a regional sustainability and equity perspective, there are several key reasons to preserve this land for PDR uses. Low-cost land permits firms to add jobs faster, and often the jobs are of higher quality, paying a living wage. Letting industrial uses locate near the core reduces truck VMT.

What, then, of the innovation district? There is probably room for both in our cities, as San Francisco has shown. Redeveloped areas of the district, preferably those nearer to transit, could house the creative high-end firms that comprise today's urban innovators, using either form-based or permissive mixed-use zoning. If PDR users are displaced, developers can be required to replace the square footage. At a short distance away would be the messy low-cost land preserved in exclusionary industrial zones. And zoning, that much-maligned tool of planners, can make all this possible.

Note

1. Over each three-year period from 1995 to 2008, they added an average of 0.72 employees, compared to 0.19 in commercial zones and 0.08 in residential zones. For more detail, see Chapple (forthcoming).

References

Boyer, M. Christine. *Dreaming the Rational City: The Myth of American Planning.* Cambridge, MA: MIT Press, 1983.

Brouwer, Aleid E., Ilaria Mariotti, and Jos N. van Ommeren. "The Firm Relocation Decision: An Empirical Investigation. *The Annals of Regional Science* 38 (2004): 335–347.

Chapple, Karen. "The Highest and Best Use? Urban Industrial Land and Job Creation." *Economic Development Quarterly* (forthcoming).

Chapple, Karen and Rick Jacobus. "Retail Trade as a Route to Neighborhood Revitalization." *Urban and Regional Policy and Its Effects, Volume II*, edited by Howard Wial, Nancy Pindus, and Harold Wolman, 19–67. Washington, DC: Urban Institute Press and Brookings Institution Press, 2009.

Christopherson, Susan. "Riding the Small Wave in Manufacturing to a More Diverse Economy and More Good Jobs." Unpublished paper. Cornell University, 2011. Accessed June 30, 2012. www.bigideasforjobs.org/wp-content/uploads/2011/09/Christopherson-Full-Report-PDF1.pdf.

Dempwolf, Scott C. "An Evaluation of Recent Industrial Land Use Studies: Do Theory and History Make Better Practice?" Unpublished paper. University of Maryland, College Park, 2010. Accessed June 15, 2012. www.academia.edu/319809/An_

Evaluation_of_Recent_Industrial_Land_Use_Studies_Do_Theory_and_History_Matter_In_Practice.

Ewing, Reid. *Best Development Practices: Doing the Right Thing and Making Money at the Same Time*. Chicago, IL: APA Planners Press, 1996.

Fitzgerald, Joan and Nancey G. Leigh. *Economic Revitalization: Cases and Strategies for City and Suburbs*. Thousand Oaks, CA: Sage, 2002.

Foord, Jo. "Mixed-Use Trade-Offs: How to Live and Work in a Compact City Neighbourhood." *Built Environment* 36, no. 1 (2010): 47–62.

Grant, Jill. "Mixed Use in Theory and Practice: Canadian Experience with Implementing a Planning Principle." *Journal of the American Planning Association* 68, no. 1 (2002): 71–84.

Grant, Jill and Katherine Perrott. "Where is the Café? The Challenge of Making Retail Uses Viable in Mixed-Use Suburban Developments." *Urban Studies* 48, no. 1 (2011): 177–195.

Hausrath Economics Group and Cambridge Systematics. *MTC Goods Movement Study Phase 2, Task 11 Working Paper: A Land Use Strategy to Support Regional Goods Movement in the Bay Area*. Oakland, CA: Hausrath Economics Group, 2004.

Hausrath Economics Group and Cambridge Systematics. *MTC Goods Movement/Land Use Project for the San Francisco Bay Area*. Oakland, CA: Hausrath Economics Group, 2008. Accessed August 21, 2013. www.mtc.ca.gov/planning/rgm/final/Final_Summary_Report.pdf.

Heikkila, Eric and Thomas A. Hutton. "Toward an Evaluative Framework for Land Use Policy in Industrial Districts of the Urban Core: A Qualitative Analysis of the Exclusionary Zoning Approach." *Urban Studies* 23 (1986): 47–60.

Hills, Jr., Roderick M. and David Schleicher. "The Steep Costs of Using Noncumulative Zoning to Preserve Land for Urban Manufacturing." *University of Chicago Law Review* 77, no. 1 (2010): 249–273.

Hirt, Sonia. "The Devil is in the Definitions: Contrasting American and German Approach to Planning." *Journal of the American Planning Association* 73, no. 4 (2007): 436–450.

Hirt, Sonia. "Form Follows Function: How America Zones." Paper presented at AESOP-ACSP Joint Congress, Dublin, Ireland, July 16, 2013.

Howland, Marie. "Planning for Industry in a Post-Industrial World." *Journal of the American Planning Association* 77, no. 1 (2011): 39–53.

Katz, Bruce and Jennifer Bradley. *The Metropolitan Revolution: How Cities and Metros are Fixing Our Broken Politics and Fragile Economy*. Washington, DC: Brookings Institution Press, 2013.

Leigh, Nancey Green and Nathanael Z. Hoelzel "Smart Growth's Blind Side: Sustainable Cities Need Productive Urban Industrial Land." *Journal of the American Planning Association* 78, no. 1 (2012): 87–103.

Meigs, Nina and Laura Wiles. *How Place Affects Business Expansion in the East Bay*. Masters Professional Report, Department of City and Regional Planning, University of California, Berkeley, 2010.

Moretti, Enrico. *The New Geography of Jobs*. New York: Mariner Books, 2012.

Perin, Constance. "Everything in its Place: Social Order and Land Use in America." *Michigan Law Review* 77, no. 3 (1977): 925–931.

San Francisco Planning Department. *Industrial Land in San Francisco: Understanding Production, Distribution, and Repair*. San Francisco, CA: San Francisco Planning

Department, 2002. Accessed September 10, 2013. http://sf-planning.org/Modules/ShowDocument.aspx?documentid=4893.

Strategic Economics. *Building San Jose's Future: Jobs, Land Use, and Fiscal Issues in Key Employment Areas, 2000–2020*. Berkeley, CA: Strategic Economics, 2004. www3.sanjoseca.gov/clerk/Agenda./03_30_04docs/03_30_04_4.7.attG.pdf.

Urban Land Institute. *America in 2013: A ULI Survey of Views on Housing, Transportation, and Community*. Urban Land Institute, 2013.

West Berkeley Artisans and Industrial Companies. *Support Integrity of Industrial Zones for Industry, Artisans, & Artists*. Proposal presented at the Planning Commission Meeting on Master Use Permits, Berkeley, California, March 7, 2012. Accessed August 21, 2013. www.webaic.org/webaic/Newletters/Entries/2012/3/7_Planning_Commission_Mtg_on_Master_Use_Permits.html.

Woodward, Katherine A. "Form Over Use: Form-Based Codes and the Challenge of Existing Development." *Notre Dame Law Review* 88, no. 5 (2013): 2627–2653.

Conclusion to Part II

Given the likely increase in income inequality in coming decades, the economic development toolkit is woefully inadequate. Existing approaches to growing the regional economy through exports, agglomerations, and entrepreneurship pay little heed to the need to develop high-quality jobs that match the skills of local residents, particularly the disadvantaged. Both business incentives and endogenous development strategies tend to fall short in remedying inequity.

It is interesting that California is not only leading much of the world in terms of environmental regulation, but also in the reform of economic development. Ironically, it is forging a new path by eliminating minimally effective tools such as redevelopment and enterprise zones, relying on tried and true tools such as zoning (for industrial uses), and stimulating the green economy through regulation. To deal directly with growing inequality, the state (along with San Francisco and San Jose) has raised its minimum wage above the federal level.

All of the approaches described herein further sustainability goals. Targeting businesses through endogenous development strategies such as creating new worker-owned businesses that supply anchor institutions means using underutilized local resources—a much more efficient strategy than shifting jobs from one place to another through redevelopment or enterprise zones. Building local markets for innovative local businesses that are saving the environment creates the possibility of exporting sustainability globally. Preserving low-cost, messy space near the metropolitan core will not just help PDR business with well-paying jobs expand, but also will help keep the core accessible and thus reduce VMT. All these tools ultimately foster exports, but via tapping into local assets and supporting existing location preferences, rather than looking to attract outside businesses.

There are many other approaches that deal even more effectively with issues such as job quality. Proven effective are labor demand policy, including customized training and technology transfer services for small and medium-sized businesses (e.g., the Manufacturing Extension Program in the United States), and wage subsidy programs to encourage hiring the unemployed (Bartik 2001).

Further research is needed to understand whether these approaches actually mitigate inequality, or whether national and state action is necessary to level the playing field. But what is already clear is that the old economic development toolkit, with its corporate subsidies and bricks-and-mortar solutions, did much to reinforce uneven development patterns.

One ingredient these strategies all imply is the strengthening of the urban agglomerations that are so fundamental to regional growth. In general, sustainable economic development strategies will create the types of places that will attract "talent." But they also call for the continued growth of agglomerations, in order to benefit from the proximity of markets and skilled workers. This, then, suggests that to create economic development, we might best focus on housing, places, and people, as Parts I and III also argue. At the same time, this livability comes at a cost, making equitable development policies even more imperative.

Weak market regions often prefer the old economic development toolkit to sustainable economic development strategies; the Rustbelt and Texas dominate the map of U.S. regions that rely heavily on incentives (Story 2012). Interestingly, business tax incentives, often ineffective, are common around the world (Klemm 2010). Even Denmark recently relaxed its ban on the use of incentives by subnational actors (Halkier 2009). Redevelopment also remains popular around the world.

Yet, at the same time, it seems that weak market regions, and many developing countries as well, support endogenous development policies more systematically. For instance, it is cities such as Cleveland and Baltimore that are most enthusiastically pursuing the anchor institution-entrepreneurship connection, and small business development is at the heart of the industrial policy in many Latin-American countries (Alburquerque 2004). La Araucanía is trying to attract investment, but in emerging and established economic sectors such as secondary wood industry, tourism, aquaculture, and agriculture (Regional Government of La Araucanía 2010). South Transdanubia sees economic development potential in involving the long-term unemployed in the labor market, supporting microenterprise, connecting SMEs to university R&D, and developing its urban areas (which itself creates jobs) (Government of the Republic of Hungary 2007).

Around the world, strategic planning for the location of industry and jobs is still weak. Many metropolitan plans, from Copenhagen to Shanghai, focus on attracting the creative class by creating more livable cities. But at least in strong markets, there is little awareness of the need to preserve core areas for industry, and in fact cities such as Istanbul are working actively to facilitate economic restructuring and decentralize industry (OECD 2008).

Where regional sustainability planning lags most is in conceptualizing what sustainable economic development looks like. Regions from South Transdanubia to Melbourne see economic opportunities in the green economy, recognizing that environmental management and education will not just improve local quality of life, but also increase the region's economic competitiveness (Government of the Republic of Hungary 2007). But the idea of export-led development still prevails, with few answers to the question of how to reduce income inequality.

References

Alburquerque, Francisco. "Local Economic Development and Decentralization in Latin America." *CEPAL Review* 82 (2004): 151–171.

Bartik, Timothy J. *Jobs For the Poor: Can Labor Demand Policies Help?* New York: Russell Sage Foundation, 2001.

Government of the Republic of Hungary. *South Transdanubia Operational Programme 2007–2013*. National Development Agency, Hungary, 2007.

Halkier, Henrik. "Policy Developments in Denmark: Regional Policy, Economic Crisis and Demographic Change." *EoPRA Paper* 9, no. 2. European Policies Research Centre, 2009. Accessed January 21, 2014. http://vbn.aau.dk/files/18793928/EoRPA_Denmark__16_July_2009_HH_1_.pdf.

Klemm, Alexander. "Causes, Benefits, and Risks of Business Tax Incentives." *International Tax and Public Finance* 17, no. 3 (2010): 315–336.

Organisation for Economic Cooperation and Development. *OECD Territorial Reviews*. Istanbul, Turkey: OECD, 2008. Accessed January 25, 2014. http://browse.oecdbookshop.org/oecd/pdfs/free/0408051e.pdf.

Regional Government of La Araucanía. *Final Report: Regional Development Strategy 2010–2022*. 2010. Accessed January 14, 2014. www.sernam.cl/sistema_gt/sitio/integracion/sistema/archivos/file/pdf/a%C3%B1o%202010/erd%20IXregion.pdf.

Story, Louise. "As Companies Seek Tax Deals, Governments Pay High Price." *New York Times*, December 1, 2012. Accessed January 10, 2014. www.nytimes.com/2012/12/02/us/how-local-taxpayers-bankroll-corporations.html.

Part III

Addressing Poverty, Opportunity, and Accessibility in the Region

Regions are a patchwork of places, some thriving, some declining, and some just getting by. A complex array of individual choices, market barriers, and public policies sorts residents over time, generally yielding more homogeneous communities. As a consequence, neighborhood economic segregation, which is also a reflection of growing income inequality and poverty, is increasing in the United States, as well as in many other countries, both developing and industrialized (Massey 1996; Musterd and Ostendorf 2013; Reardon and Bischoff 2011; Sabatini 2006).[1] This then hinders opportunity and accessibility for the region's less-advantaged residents.

While all regions experience at least economic segregation, the pattern may be most extreme in southern regions such as Houston and Memphis that experience high regional income inequality (Acs 2013; Booza, Cutsinger, and Galster 2006). Segregation of high-income households is happening most rapidly, especially in developing countries, but most regions also have a significant and growing number of low-income segregated neighborhoods, and cities as well (Pendall et al. 2011; Sabatini 2006; Tach, Pendall, and Derian 2014). These are often neighborhoods marked by concentrated poverty (with poverty rates over 30 percent), places that hinder the life chances of their residents because of lack of economic opportunity, high crime rates, disinvestment, poor institutional capacity, and other factors (Carr and Kutty 2008; Ellen and Turner 1997).

These regional disparities are a drag on the economy: as we read in Part II, regions and countries with more equality grow faster (Benner and Pastor 2012). But inequality also presents regions with opportunities for redistribution, and the increasing influence of regional sustainability planning creates an opening to rethink how to build more equitable places. The question is, how best to share the resources of the more advantaged communities with the less advantaged? Before turning to the policy tools available for redistribution, we first examine the poverty of today—and tomorrow.

The Nature of Metropolitan Poverty

Reversing the prosperity of the 1990s, poverty, the state in which money income (before taxes) is insufficient to meet basic needs, has increased steadily in recent years, with 47 million U.S. residents living in poverty in 2011. From a peak of 15.1 percent in 1993, the poverty rate decreased to 11.3 percent in 2000, only to rise again to 15 percent in 2011, due to a sharp increase in unemployment during the Great Recession (Center on Budget and Policy Priorities 2013). Poverty spared few places in the 2000s, growing in 86 percent of U.S. metropolitan areas in the 2000s (Pendall et al. 2011).

Along with this increase in poverty (and segregation of the affluent) has come a steady rise in concentrated poverty, neighborhoods where 30 percent or more live in poverty (as noted above). While most people in the Global North recognize this as a trend that occurs in developing countries, where rapid urbanization has resulted in the growth of slums (UN-Habitat 2003), it is perhaps less well-known that concentrated poverty is growing rapidly in metro areas in the middle of the United States—in states such as Texas, Oklahoma, and Arkansas—while big cities such as New York, Los Angeles, Chicago, and Miami are, for the most part, eluding it (Jargowsky 2013; Pendall et al. 2011). Those living in concentrated poverty, one in 11 U.S. residents, are disproportionately likely to be African American, Latino, or Native American. These increases in concentrated poverty are closely tied to the metropolitan poverty rate: in the 100 largest metro areas, each time the poverty rate increases by one percentage point, the share of residents living in concentrated poverty increases by 1.8 percent (Pendall 2011a).

Though recent research has called attention to the suburbanization of poverty, growing suburban poverty is correlated with increases in national and metropolitan poverty rates (Pendall 2011b). Suburban poverty rates remain much lower than urban poverty (an average of 11 percent versus 21 percent), in part because of the ability of the new immigrants in these areas to rise out of poverty, and in part because of measurement inconsistencies: the construct "suburb" includes many types of places, from Gary, Indiana, to Gaithersburg, Maryland (Chapple 2013). But it is interesting to note the gradual convergence between U.S. and developing country metropolitan areas, where suburban poverty has long been part of metropolitan structure, and the suburban middle class is currently growing.

What, then, will poverty look like in 2040? Job forecasts suggest growth in low-skill, low-wage jobs, which will exacerbate inequality and poverty, thus increasing both suburban and concentrated poverty. Of course, a return to the economic growth patterns of the 1990s could conceivably lower poverty again. But declining relative wages and a shrinking social safety net make it less likely that a rising tide will lift all boats. In the absence of major policy shifts, metropolitan poverty is with us to stay.

Addressing Equity via Regionalism and Sustainability

Recently, the advent of sustainability approaches has renewed the focus on poverty and equity at the regional level. Yet, in some ways, this is just more of the same. Both regional planning and sustainability have long offered opportunities to address disparities: what Pastor et al. (2000) call *equity regionalism*, or regional policies to address poverty, dates back to the 1960s. Whether these strategies are effective at reducing poverty is an open question, in part because, to date, most policies to advance equity have been small-scale federal experiments or approaches implemented on an ad hoc basis by cities and states.

Equity Regionalism

The equity regionalist program grew out of the initial awareness of urban-suburban disparity powerfully articulated by the Kerner Commission in 1968, with its warning that "Our nation is moving toward two societies, one black, one white—separate and unequal." The primary cause, as supported by research by John Kain, was the shift of new employment opportunities to the suburbs and the lack of federal policies to counter suburban housing discrimination and connect urban residents, particularly African Americans, to jobs; the major remedy was to be opening up the suburbs to the disadvantaged (Kain 1968, 1992).

This early framing of the urban poverty problem as connected to urban-suburban disparities quickly became the prevailing wisdom. By the mid-1990s, researchers were framing the problem in terms of the "geography of metropolitan opportunity," referring to the actual prospects that the opportunity structure (as governed by markets, institutions, and social systems) offers based on geography (Galster and Killen 1995). In a memorable analogy, David Rusk (1999) compared the landscape of metropolitan opportunity to the game of basketball, prescribing a focus on the outside game as the way to solve the problems of the inside game. This inside-outside dichotomy of uneven development results from institutional structures and rules of the game that are specific to the United States (i.e., the embrace of home rule, the reliance on the property tax for funding local services, and the use of government subsidies for the development of low-density suburbs). Although intra-regional disparities are common throughout the world, they usually take other forms (e.g., in many megacities, the dichotomy is reversed, with an affluent core surrounded by impoverished suburbs).

Regional strategies to remedy unequal opportunity include reducing tax or service disparities (typically either via new regional governing or taxation strategies, or place-based programs that bring new affordable housing or other opportunities) or changing the spatial distribution of population (for instance, through moving inner-city residents to the suburbs or transporting city residents to suburban jobs). The first two (regional and place-based approaches) are common around the world, while the latter two (dispersal and mobility approaches) are more peculiar to the United States (Kearns 2002). Federal government monies, initiatives, and/or guidelines underlie most of these approaches, yet together they do not constitute a concerted, coordinated attempt to improve metropolitan poverty. Planners at the municipal level manage efforts to deconcentrate poverty through mostly federal funds. Regional or county-level agencies, empowered by the devolution of some transportation and social welfare programs from the state and federal level, typically handle programs to improve metropolitan accessibility. Cities, for the most part, administer the place-based incentive and tax-credit programs that are funded by both states and the federal government. Overall, the policy context is fragmented and underfunded, resulting in little to no impact.

Regional Strategies for Opportunity

Of the four strategies discussed here, most had appeared in the United States by the mid-1970s. Regional government—an equity strategy to the extent to which it evens out service and fiscal disparities—was the first to appear, in the form of the councils of government (COGs) and metropolitan planning organizations (MPOs), as well as ongoing government consolidations among cities and counties. Multiple states in the 1970s addressed opportunity in place via either community development strategies or fair share housing programs (including inclusionary zoning), which required developers to provide low- or moderate-income housing units in exchange for development permission (Listokin 1976). The 1970s also saw some trials of dispersal and mobility programs, but it was not until the 1990s that the federal government implemented larger-scale experiments. The following provides a brief overview of these policies; the chapters that follow illustrate their successes and failures.

Regional Governance to Reduce Disparities

Regional strategies provide a variety of ways to equalize opportunity across a region, either by changing the spatial distribution of the population through land use planning and growth control or by reducing service disparities through government consolidation, special purpose districts, state equalization aid (typically used to remedy fiscal disparities among school districts), or tax base sharing.

State or metropolitan land use planning can help create a more even landscape of opportunity. By requiring cities and counties to prepare comprehensive plans, as well as specific plans for neighborhoods, states give local governments a tool to create more local diversity. Some states also push local governments to zone for more high-density housing (e.g., by enacting growth boundaries). However, unless regions incentivize affordability at the same time as encouraging density, such growth control may be associated with increases in housing prices (Nelson et al. 2002).

Government consolidations typically unify the city and county governments (e.g., Miami-Dade County). There have been just 22 approved in the United States since 1921, perhaps, in part, because of the difficulty of gaining both city and suburban voter approval (Altshuler et al. 1999). In theory, a single general-purpose regional government should eliminate both tax and service disparities by centralizing government taxing powers and service delivery. However, in practice, individual cities often retain their taxing authority, undermining the idea of revenue sharing, and studies have shown that cities, as well as consolidated metros, consistently underserve their minority and low-income neighborhoods and/or dilute minority voices (ibid.). Special districts (e.g., for water or sewer services) function in much the same way, with their own taxing and service functions, but have rarely been evaluated in terms of their ability to remedy inequities (ibid.).

State and federal equalization aid, which takes the form of either general revenue sharing grants or special grants (e.g., for education) from higher levels of government, helps to remedy fiscal disparities among cities. These generally reduce differences in per capita spending, but rarely actually equalize it, due to both the inequality in other sources of funding and the variation in need (ibid.).

Tax base sharing, which originated in Minnesota's 1971 Fiscal Disparities Act, exists in just nine urban areas, with the Minneapolis-Saint Paul metropolitan area as the most famous example (Summer 2000). Local governments in that region have been sharing 40 percent of the new commercial/industrial tax revenues and reallocating those resources within the region. In general, donor municipalities are on the metropolitan periphery and recipients in the urban core; however, because Minneapolis has a rich commercial property base, it has occasionally been a donor city (Altshuler et al. 1999). The program reduces disparities in the commercial/industrial tax base from what would be a 12 to 1 per capita ratio to a 4 to 1 ratio between cities (Metropolitan Council 2008).

Regional governing strategies may well be more effective ways to address regional disparities than the place-based, dispersal, and mobility approaches discussed next and in the chapters that follow. Yet, there is currently little or no discussion of these approaches in the United States, perhaps because of the political challenges of implementation. Special districts and equalization have proved easiest to enact; however, they typically address just one aspect of opportunity (such as education or environmental quality), rather than regional income disparities per se (Altshuler et al. 1999). Thus, we do not pursue these further in this volume.

Place-Based Approaches

The vast majority of recent federal and state housing and anti-poverty programs have helped to improve neighborhoods, whether in city or suburb. These approaches are premised on reducing disparities by increasing opportunity in place, as opposed to directly transferring resources to the people living in that place. The vast majority provide subsidies for affordable housing, but a few programs support economic opportunity or community development more generally. They fall into three basic categories: flexible grants for neighborhood revitalization, programs to spur neighborhood investment, and project-based programs (Appendix I provides more detail). A fourth category, which is described in the next section, is dispersal strategies, which assist the poor in more affluent areas.[2] We return to place-based or place-conscious strategies at the end of this section, in Chapter 12.

Dispersal Approaches

The 1968 Kerner Commission report called for the integration of the suburbs via the elimination of discrimination and the construction of affordable housing. The Fair Housing Act subsequently supported enforcement, albeit weak, against discrimination. With the federal government increasingly out of the business of constructing affordable housing itself, dispersing the poor from the ghetto to the suburbs would need to involve either moving to existing housing via the use of housing choice vouchers, or constructing new housing via local governments or other intermediaries.

The former approach is reflected in three major policy initiatives, the Gautreaux program, Moving to Opportunity, and the HOPE VI program (see also Appendix I). The key mechanism underlying all three is the Tenant-Based Rental Assistance program, which provides housing choice vouchers that subsidize units found via the market-rate housing market.

The construction alternative is facilitated via the Low Income Housing Tax Credit (LIHTC), state fair share housing initiatives, and local inclusionary zoning (to the extent that they increase affordability in the suburbs). The HUD-funded programs (and to a certain extent, the fair share and inclusionary programs as well) build on a set of site selection rules that comply with fair housing law by not concentrating new housing in areas with existing concentrations of minorities and/or poverty. According to fair housing advocate Phil Tegeler, the assumption underlying these standards is "that *balanced development across a region should be a policy goal*" (Tegeler et al. 2011: 3, original emphasis). The effectiveness of dispersal programs is discussed at length in the next chapter.

Mobility Approaches

Another major approach to concentrated poverty is to connect jobseekers to opportunities throughout the metropolitan region through transportation, under the assumption that job accessibility is a major barrier to employment. Most funding to link low-income urban residents to suburban jobs has supported reverse commuting via transit or vanpooling; more recently, programs have experimented with low-income auto ownership (for more detail, see Appendix I). Chapter 11 discusses mobility in more detail.

Equity in Sustainability Planning

The last 50 years have seen the implementation, albeit relatively small-scale, of what might be called equity regionalist strategies: regional governance strategies to remedy disparities, community development strategies that increase housing and other opportunities in place, dispersal strategies that encourage the relocation of the poor to the suburbs, and mobility programs that help the dis-advantaged connect to suburban job opportunities. At the same time, conditions have changed: for instance, communities in both city and suburb have become more diverse and the suburbs no longer offer a clear advantage over the city in terms of opportunity. The legacies in urban planning and policy, such as the fight for fair housing or against displacement, have taken on new meaning even as their proponents are fighting the old battles. Given current political condi-tions, the prospects for regional governance strategies look ever dimmer.

The approaches for improving opportunity through equity regionalism have been slow to enter the conversation about sustainable development. Advancing sustainability means thinking about problems more holistically, so that as we develop our cities and regions, we improve quality of life for all, while living within our limits. In practice, though, to the extent that cities and regions have embraced sustainability, it is more for its environmental and economic benefits, than equity; for example, the implementation of bike lanes brings an amenity that likely reduces greenhouse gas emissions and attracts young skilled workers, but may not enhance mobility for low-income populations. A variety of envir-onmentally friendly programs, from Ciclavia, to assistance in building green, emerge more from the desire to attract and retain high-educated residents than to promote equity (Zavestoski and Agyeman 2014). Indeed, these approaches often heighten the conflict between environment and equity, as new residents receive the environmental benefits of sustainability programs while creating affordability problems for locals.[3]

Yet, as we saw in Chapter 2, the U.N. has called for eliminating poverty and hunger as a precondition for sustainable development. In the United States, Housing and Urban Development's (HUD) recent grand experiment in sustainability planning (the SCI-RPG program described in Chapter 2) has brought equity to the fore once more by forcing its grantees to address issues of fair housing, displacement, and economic opportunity, albeit "through the back door."

The following chapters illustrate the issues with traditional urban anti-poverty policy. Chapter 10 reviews the experience with the dispersal approach and analyzes what it would look like if it were a fully funded, scaled-up urban policy. Next, by looking at how job accessibility really works for low-income jobseekers, Chapter 11 shows the shortcomings of mobility strategies. Finally, because much of the equity regionalist approach is premised on cer-tain assumptions about what and where opportunity is, Chapter 12 revisits those assumptions and offers an assessment of what they mean for development strategies. This, then, points to alternatives, both back and front door means to incorporate equity into sustainable development.

Notes

1. Europe seems to lag the United States, but segregation is growing there too. Although little systematic quantitative analysis is available on segregation in

Latin-American cities, it is clear that new forms of segregation, particularly high-income enclaves in the suburbs, have arisen across the continent in recent years.
2. Not included here are an array of programs for childcare, food, health, and schools, such as Head Start and Consolidated Health Centers, some of which serve needy places and others that target individuals based on income.
3. Godschalk (2004) calls this the "gentrification conflict."

References

Acs, Gregory. "Examining Income Inequality in America's Largest Metros." *MetroTrends*, 2012. Accessed August 12, 2013. www.metrotrends.org/commentary/Income-Inequality.cfm.

Altshuler, Alan, William Morrill, Harold Wolman, and Faith Mitchell, editors. *Governance and Opportunity in Metropolitan America*. Washington, DC: National Academies Press, 1999.

Benner, Chris and Manuel Pastor, Jr. *Just Growth: Inclusion and Prosperity in America's Metropolitan Regions*. New York: Routledge, 2012.

Booza, Jason, Jackie Cutsinger, and George Galster. *Where Did They Go? The Decline of Middle-Income Neighborhoods in Metropolitan America*. Washington, DC: Metropolitan Policy Program, Brookings Institution, 2006.

Carr, James H. and Nandinee K. Kutty, editors. *Segregation: The Rising Costs for America*. New York: Routledge, 2008.

Center on Budget and Policy Priorities. "By the Numbers." Accessed June 4, 2013. www.cbpp.org/research/index.cfm?fa=topic&id=36.

Chapple, Karen. "Confronting Suburban Poverty—or Celebrating Suburban Resilience?" *MetroTrends*, 2013. Accessed June 15, 2013. http://blog.metrotrends.org/2013/06/confronting-suburban-poverty-celebrating-suburban-resilience.

Ellen, Ingrid G. and Margery A. Turner. "Does Neighborhood Matter? Assessing Recent Evidence." *Housing Policy Debate* 8 (1997): 833–866.

Galster, George and Sean Killen. "Geography of Metropolitan Opportunity: A Reconnaissance and Conceptual Framework." *Housing Policy Debate* 6, no. 1 (1995): 7–43.

Godschalk, David R. "Land Use Planning Challenges: Coping with Conflicts in Visions of Sustainable Development and Livable Communities." *Journal of the American Planning Association* 70, no. 1 (2004): 5–13.

Jargowsky, Paul. *Concentration of Poverty in the New Millennium: Changes in the Prevalence, Composition, and Location of High-Poverty Neighborhoods*. Washington, DC: The Century Foundation, 2013.

Kain, John F. "Housing Segregation, Negro Employment, and Metropolitan Decentralization." *Quarterly Journal of Economics* 2, no. 2 (1968): 175–197.

Kain, John F. "The Spatial Mismatch Hypothesis: Three Decades Later." *Housing Policy Debate* 3, no. 2 (1992): 371–469.

Kearns, Ade. "Response: From Residential Disadvantage to Opportunity? Reflections on British and European Policy and Research." *Housing Studies* 17, no. 1 (2002): 145–150.

Listokin, David. *Fair Share Housing Allocation*. New Brunswick, NJ: Center for Urban Policy Research/Transaction Publishers, 1976.

Massey, Douglas S. "The Age of Extremes: Concentrated Affluence and Poverty in the Twenty-First Century." *Demography* 33, no. 4 (1996): 395–412.

Metropolitan Council. "Fiscal Disparities: Tax Base Sharing in the Twin Cities Metropolitan Area," 2008. Accessed May 5, 2009. www.metrocouncil.org/metroarea/FiscalDisparities/index.htm.

Musterd, Sako and Wim Ostendorf, editors. *Urban Segregation and the Welfare State: Inequality and Exclusion in Western Cities.* New York: Routledge, 2013.

Nelson, Arthur C., Rolf Pendall, Casey J. Dawkins, and Gerrit J. Knaap. "The Link Between Growth Management and Housing Affordability: The Academic Evidence." In *Growth Management and Affordable Housing: Do They Conflict?*, edited by Anthony Downs, 117–158. Washington, DC: Brookings Institution Press, 2002.

Pastor Jr., Manuel, Peter Dreier, J. Eugene Grigsby III, and Marta Lopez-Garza. *Regions that Work: How Cities and Suburbs Can Grow Together.* Minneapolis, MN: University of Minnesota Press, 2000.

Pendall, Rolf. "To Reduce Concentrated Poverty, Reduce Poverty for Everyone." *MetroTrends*, 2011a. Accessed June 10, 2013. http://blog.metrotrends.org/2011/03/to-reduce-concentrated-poverty-reduce-poverty-for-everyone.

Pendall, Rolf. "When Poverty Grows in the Metro, it Grows in Both Cities and Suburbs." *MetroTrends*, 2011b. Accessed June 10, 2013. http://blog.metrotrends.org/2011/08/poverty-grows-metro-grows-cities-and-suburbs/.

Pendall, Rolf, Elizabeth Davies, Lesley Freiman, and Rob Pitingilo. *A Lost Decade: Neighborhood Poverty and the Urban Crisis of the 2000s.* Washington, DC: Joint Center for Political and Economic Studies, 2011.

Reardon, Sean F. and Kendra Bischoff. "Income Inequality and Income Segregation." *American Journal of Sociology* 116, no. 4 (2011): 1092–1153.

Rusk, David. *Inside Game/Outside Game: Winning Strategies for Saving Urban America.* Washington, DC: Brookings Institution Press, 1999.

Sabatini, Francisco. *The Social Spatial Segregation in the Cities of Latin America.* Inter-American Development Bank, 2006.

Summer, Anita A. "Regionalization Efforts Between Big Cities and Their Suburbs: Rhetoric and Reality." In *Urban-Suburban Interdependencies*, edited by Rosalind Greenstein and Wim Wiewel, 181–204. Cambridge, MA: Lincoln Institute of Land Policy, 2000.

Tach, Laura, Rolf Pendall, and Alexandra Derian. *Income Mixing Across Scales: Rationale, Trends, Policies, Practice, and Research for More Inclusive Neighborhoods and Metropolitan Areas.* Washington, DC: Urban Institute Press, 2014.

Tegeler, Philip, Henry Korman, Jason Reece, and Megan Haberle. *Opportunity and Location in Federally Subsidized Housing Programs: A New Look at HUD's Site & Neighborhood Standards as Applied to the Low Income Housing Tax Credit.* Washington, DC: Poverty & Race Research Action Council, 2011.

UN-Habitat. *The Challenge of Slums.* Sterling, VA: United Nations Human Settlements Programme, 2003.

Zavestoski, Stephen and Julian Agyeman, editors. *Incomplete Streets: Processes, Practices and Possibilities.* London: Routledge, 2014.

10 Dispersing Poverty
The Nature of Choice

Virginia: They're trying to move everybody off of this hill. [Mayor Willie] Brown has something to do with it. They give you Section 8 to move you out of the city; they're trying to spread us out.

Toni: My auntie bought a house in Antioch. It was so peaceful. I would want to move there. Or Pittsburg.

Residents of San Francisco's Bayview-Hunter's Point neighborhood, quoted in Chapple (2000: 208)

In recent years, the United States demolished some 200,000 public housing units, reduced funding for project-based affordable housing, and sharply increased the use of housing choice vouchers, which assist tenants looking for housing in the open market.[1] Justifying these policy approaches is the idea of breaking up concentrations of the poor (i.e., "they're trying to spread us out").

Neighborhoods with high concentrations of poverty may suffer from two types of neighborhood effects: the social externalities that arise from the behavior of some residents (e.g., stigmatization, negative peer influences), and the dearth of resources from outside (such as local jobs and public services) (Galster 2007). Thus, proponents of dispersal policy argue that moving from these neighborhoods will not only shift poverty out of a wider area, but will eliminate many of the obstacles facing the urban poor, ultimately providing a mechanism for rising out of poverty. A second, but related, argument involves access to jobs and resources. Because of job growth and higher-quality public services in the suburbs, moving the poor out of the central cities means relocating to high opportunity.

For almost 50 years, progressive policymakers have sought to improve opportunities for disadvantaged minorities via integration. Fair housing law enforcement was put in place in the late 1960s, and subsequent policies (e.g., housing choice vouchers, LIHTCs, HOPE VI), judicial consent decrees (Gautreaux and subsequent decisions), and experiments (Moving to Opportunity) have all sought to integrate the suburbs.

The appeal of dispersal policies is that they seek to address a variety of neighborhood effects simultaneously: poor quality of services, lack of socialization and role modeling, negative peer influences, the lack of social networks, and exposure to crime (Ellen and Turner 1997). If each of these factors is largely, if not primarily, determined by neighborhood, then it stands to reason that moving to a better neighborhood will dramatically increase one's prospects. If this can be accomplished by moving to a neighborhood that is also in greater spatial proximity to jobs, then spatial mismatch, or the disconnect between poor inner-city residents and suburban job opportunities, can be addressed as well. In short, dispersal, on its face, seems to be a cure-all for those participating.

Setting the Stage

The watershed moment for dispersal policy came in 1976, when the U.S. Supreme Court ruled on *Gautreaux v. Harris*. The court sided with the plaintiff, who had alleged that the Chicago Housing Authority had discriminated in its placement of projects, limiting them to predominantly African-American neighborhoods. In addition to an order that future public housing be built in scattered sites in white neighborhoods, this ruling resulted in a program whereby vouchers were to be offered to 6,000 residents of public housing. These vouchers could be used to move to private apartments, either in predominantly white suburbs or in the city of Chicago. The outcomes of this much-studied program are somewhat muddied by the rigorous screening process that was required of participants, creating a self-selection effect; the results for educational attainment of suburban movers were encouraging enough, however, that the program is widely considered to have been a success.

The housing choice voucher program grew rapidly in the 1970s; over 2 million were issued by 2009, although Congress rescinded funding during certain periods (Schwartz 2010). In theory, vouchers are an efficient means of housing the low-income; they are less expensive than building affordable housing and they provide relatively more choices of neighborhoods to live in (ibid.). However, in practice, voucher holders often fail to find landlords willing to rent to them or vacancies in higher-income neighborhoods; in general, they are not moving to low-poverty, less segregated neighborhoods (ibid.).

The success of Gautreaux helped inspire the Moving to Opportunity Program (MTO), instituted in 1992, and contributed to the conceptualization of HOPE VI. In the MTO experiment, $70 million was authorized to assist families in five cities (New York, Los Angeles, Chicago, Boston, and Baltimore) to move from high-poverty areas (census tracts with a poverty rate greater than 40 percent) to low-poverty areas (census tracts with a poverty rate less than 10 percent). HOPE VI also quickly became a dispersal program when the federal government eliminated the requirement to replace demolished public housing units on a one-for-one basis in 1995. While families are typically given Section 8 vouchers in order to assist rent payment in the private market, the result is nevertheless an involuntary relocation (Goetz 2003). In addition to these initiatives, there are smaller programs in operation in cities across the country, as well as the ongoing "vouchering out" of older HUD-subsidized projects that are demolished or converted to market-rate housing (Varady and Walker 2000).

After 30 years of these dispersal initiatives, dozens of studies have evaluated their impact on family safety, social networks and place attachment, and economic opportunity. As discussed below, in practice the findings are mixed: although arguably dispersal is an effective strategy in the most disadvantaged neighborhoods, such as in Chicago and Baltimore, where almost any change is a change for the better, there is not a strong case for scaling up the program nationally (Sharkey 2013). Overall, it seems that policymakers have over-emphasized the contagion effects of place while underestimating the importance of informal social networks and supports grounded in particular neighborhoods (Chapple 2001; Clampet-Lundquist 2007; Edin and Lein 1997; Gibson 2007; Gilbert 1998; Trudeau 2006).

Safety

Studies consistently show that families that move out of neighborhoods of concentrated poverty report an increased sense of safety including significant declines in drug-related activity, a greater personal sense of safety, and improvements for their children (Gibson 2007; Goetz 2003; Kling, Liebman, and Katz 2007; Petit 2004; Popkin and Cove 2007). Among HOPE VI displacees, those who moved into other public housing reported fewer benefits (Popkin and Cove 2007). However, there were no statistical linkages between these findings and any secondary benefits (improved mental or physical health) among displacees (ibid.).[2]

Despite increased perception of safety, the effect of deconcentration on criminal behavior among program participants is more mixed. MTO moves to lower poverty neighborhoods had different effects on the criminal behavior of girls and boys, with fewer arrests for girls, but increases in property crime among males over time (Kling, Ludwig, and Katz 2005).

Social Networks and Place Attachment

Dispersal programs, especially HOPE VI, have generally failed to integrate displaced families socially. Very few households rebuild social ties in their new neighborhoods, regardless of neighborhood poverty levels (Clampet-Lundquist 2004). Studies of Philadelphia, Fort Worth, Minneapolis, Seattle, and Boston find that youth are more likely to rebuild friendship networks than the adults; however, youth are unlikely to look at their new neighbors as role models, or to interact with other adults in their new neighborhoods (Barrett, Geisel, and Johnston 2006; Clampet-Lundquist 2007; Curley 2006; Gallagher and Bajaj 2007; Goetz 2003; Kleit and Manzo 2006). Smaller children are even less socially connected in their new communities, perhaps because the financial hardships experienced by families who moved to low-poverty neighborhoods had a negative impact on the social connections of smaller children (Petit 2004). These findings from dispersal programs echo those obtained from studies of mixed-income communities that find little social interaction between higher- and lower-income residents (see Chapter 5).

Many involuntarily displaced families are not ready or entirely willing to move out of their existing public housing communities because of place attachment (Kleit and Manzo 2006; Vale 1997). Those who have lived in public housing the longest are the least willing to move because most regarded their particular development as home and had put down roots in the community. For instance, two-thirds of the residents of Columbia Villa HOPE VI project in Portland, Oregon were content in the development and did not want to leave (Gibson 2007). Even after being forced to move, many residents reminisced about the community, mourned the loss of their neighbors, the open space, and the level of comfort they felt at Columbia Villa, and felt their new neighborhoods did not measure up. Only one-third felt their new neighborhood had a better sense of community than their original public housing site.

Employment and Economic Security

As an anti-poverty strategy, dispersal should have, at a minimum, some discernible effect on the earnings, wealth, or economic security of low-income families. Unfortunately, the research evidence is clear and consistent on this; dispersal efforts have not had any demonstrable positive effect on employment, earnings, or income of individuals. As Gautreaux showed, only in comparison to those who moved elsewhere within the city did the suburban movers show better outcomes. There was no increase in rates of employment or wages for any group in the Gautreaux program (Popkin, Rosenbaum, and Meaden 1993). The lack of any effect on economic self-sufficiency is repeated for all forms of dispersal (Clampet-Lundquist 2004; Curley 2006; Goetz 2002; HUD 2004; Kling, Liebman, and Katz 2007; Levy and Woolley 2007; Turney et al. 2006; Vigdor 2007).[3]

The lack of impact on employment or earnings among adults remains years after implementation of the MTO or HOPE VI program (Clampet-Lundquist 2004; Goetz 2002; Kling, Liebman, and Katz 2007; Levy and Woolley 2007). Moving seems not to be effective in increasing employment rates among low-income families in other contexts as well. HUD's own evaluation of the Welfare to Work Voucher program (which provided vouchers to families with a worker making the transition from welfare to a job) documented a negative impact on employment, an effect the evaluators attributed to the disruption caused by moving (HUD 2004). Hurricane Katrina displacees from New Orleans showed no employment, earnings, or income effect from their forced displacement, either (Vigdor 2007).

Various researchers have investigated the reasons for the lack of positive impact, suggesting barriers such as the significant health problems (both physical and mental) of relocatees, the lack of transportation and childcare, the failure of social support services, and the loss of social capital (Barrett, Geisel, and

Johnston 2006; Clampet-Lundquist 2004; Levy and Woolley 2007). In Clampet-Lundquist's study (2004), individuals who had relied on friends or other local connections to gain employment when they lived in the pre-move public housing development did not report using the same techniques after moving to new neighborhoods. Involuntary displacement seems to have actually undermined the social capital strategies of the low-income families.

In fact, more than simply not producing economic improvements for these families, dispersal may actually increase economic insecurity, which, in turn, may lead to greater residential instability. Many relocatees experience difficulty in paying for rent, utilities, or even food (Barrett, Geisel, and Johnston 2006; Gibson 2007; Popkin 2006).

Scaling Up the Dispersal Model

The argument implicit in dispersal policy is that if only we could move enough poor people to the suburbs, there would be equal opportunity for all—in other words, distributing poverty evenly across the landscape. But, even if it were effective, is this even viable? Together with my colleagues Mason Austin and Ed Goetz, I examined the effects of scaling up dispersal in San Francisco, with an analysis of Philadelphia as well for comparison, looking at the year 2000.[4] This analysis examines scaling up dispersal from the simple perspective of physical planning and accessibility: how many people would have to move in order to create an even distribution of poverty, and how much closer would they be to employment once dispersed? Thus, we do not tackle the complexities of the social costs of dispersal (i.e., the costs to society of increasing poverty in some areas and decreasing in others).[5]

Superficially, the cases are similar: the poverty rate stands at 11 percent in the Philadelphia metropolitan area and 9 percent in the San Francisco Bay Area, while both regions have similar suburbanization of concentrated poverty, with 12 percent of the suburban poor in concentrated poverty tracts.

But their economic contexts differ. The Bay Area's thriving economy and tight housing market has resulted in a high degree of "suburbanization" of poverty, with the most tracts in the central city hosting lower levels of poverty than the average for the region. This pattern, coupled with one of the rare cases of a central city with a growing jobs base, means that here, "dispersal" may actually imply moving the poor from high-poverty suburbs back into the central city.

Philadelphia is an example of an older East Coast city, with an economy that has not recovered from the loss of its industrial base in the 1960s and 1970s. It features a high degree of economic inequality and is home both to neighborhoods of deep and concentrated poverty and some of the wealthiest areas in the nation. High levels of vacancy and relatively affordable housing prices are complemented by higher overall levels of poverty and lower prevailing wages.

Scaling up dispersal to achieve spatial equity would mean ensuring that the poverty rate of each tract matches the regional average. To achieve equity, for each census tract, we added or subtracted persons with income below the poverty line until the desired poverty rate was reached; we used fractions of persons where necessary but then rounded populations for each tract to the nearest whole number.

The analysis involved two scenarios. The first of these assumes that incentives and regulations will be directed only at poor residents, and that the flow of moves will be in a single direction: from high-poverty to low-poverty areas. A concern with this method is that although it has the benefit of requiring no action by wealthier residents, it would lead to major shifts in population density throughout the region. The "hollowed-out" central cities would be highly unstable and likely to change rapidly: in some cases, they might attract higher-income persons to replace the now-vacant units and buildings, thus "gentrifying" these areas; in others, no such replacements would come, and the remaining residents would be further disconnected from retail and job opportunities, potentially resulting in an increase in poverty in the long term. To address this problem, we run a second "gentrification" condition, with below-poverty residents replaced by wealthier residents on a one-for-one basis. In this case, there is no change of population in any census tract, only a change of composition. This roughly emulates some of the other goals of HOPE VI, as well as the prevailing local housing policy in many cities: building more market-rate housing in high-poverty areas. It would also require fewer poor residents to move since, mathematically, the "replacement" residents would help to further lower the poverty rate.

In both regions, an enormous share of the population would be required to move in order to achieve equality in poverty. In Philadelphia, depending on the condition, either 5.1 percent (dispersal alone) or 9.1 percent (dispersal plus gentrification) of the population would need to move; in San Francisco, either 2.8 percent or 5.1 percent would move—in other words, hundreds of thousands of people (Figure 10.1).

Though in theory the influx of affluent gentrifiers into tracts should reduce concentrated poverty rates and allow more poor residents to stay, in practice it has minimal impact, just reducing by 11 percent the number of below-poverty residents that would have to move. In fact, because of the huge influx of suburbanites into the city in both regions, the gentrification condition requires more total moves than the pure dispersal condition. Figures 10.2 and 10.3 map the "dispersal only" condition.[6] The conditions that include "gentrification" are identical in proportion to these, producing a similar visual arrangement.

The Bay Area departs somewhat from the expected pattern of the dispersal from core to suburbs because of its many nodes and lack of a traditional suburban/urban divide. Philadelphia also has many "donor" tracts outside of the central core, though this is a reflection of the presence of smaller impoverished cities, such as Chester, Camden, and Trenton, and not of existing regional equity. Nonetheless, it is still largely true that denser areas are exporting their population to less-dense areas. More noteworthy than these patterns is the scale

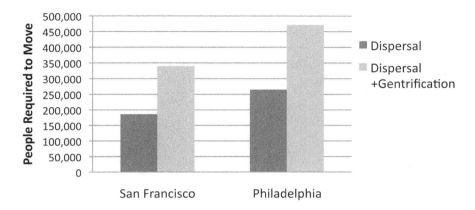

Figure 10.1 Residents required to move in order to create an even distribution of poverty
Source: Author's calculations

of the moves required. In both areas, there are at least a few tracts wherein more than 1,000 residents would need to leave in order to bring that tract to the mean level of poverty for the region. In the Philadelphia metro area, there are 94 such tracts, including one wherein 4,376 residents would need to leave. Given that tracts, on average, have a total population of only 4,000 residents, this represents a vast depopulation of urban neighborhoods.

Equally surprising is the number of below-poverty residents that would need to move to each of the higher-income tracts. One might expect, due to the large number of suburban tracts and the constrained variability of poverty rates below the regional average, that each tract would only need to accept a few dozen low-poverty residents. Again, however, this does not seem to be the case.

These numbers suggest that obtaining this "ideal" redistribution of poverty may be impossible, not only from political or financial standpoints, but also physically. Would there even be room to construct the housing units necessary to accommodate all these new residents? Given how housing densities decline dramatically with distance from the urban core in most U.S. metros, there likely is sufficient land if supportive zoning, the market, transportation infrastructure, and politics are in place. At present, however, these challenges seem nearly insurmountable, at least in the United States (Downs 2005).

What About Jobs?

This experiment thus shows that the number of people required to move in order to achieve these goals, regardless of the economic status or land capacity of a region, is enormous. The model does not yet address, however, whether such programs, even if feasible, would be a good idea, specifically whether access

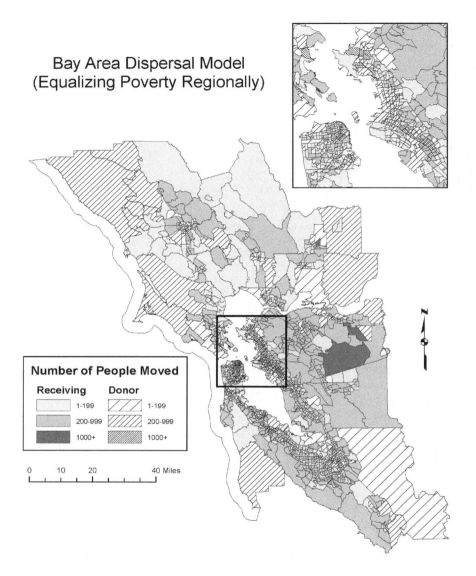

Figure 10.2 Dispersal scaled up in the San Francisco Bay Area
Source: Adapted from Austin (2008)

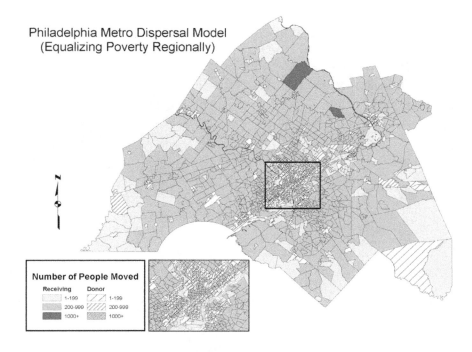

Figure 10.3 Dispersal policy scaled up in the Philadelphia-Camden Metropolitan Area
Source: Adapted from Austin (2008)

to job opportunities will increase for poor residents who move to lower-poverty tracts. As Chapter 11 will show, increased proximity to job opportunities is not a *sufficient* condition for judging dispersal's success, since social connections to employers are vital; however, it is a *necessary* condition.

For this next analysis, only jobs paying near, or below, 80 percent of the median annual earnings were counted; this filter was selected in order to include well-paying but low-skilled jobs and jobs into which workers might be promoted.[7] In the Philadelphia metro area, this income cut-off was $30,000; in the Bay Area, it was $35,000. The radius was a 30-minute drive from home. (The model assumes car ownership in its calculation of accessibility, as the simplest way to compare commutes across space. It is also the most conservative: if transit users were included, the suburbs would look highly inaccessible due to their poor transit access and resultant long-transit commutes).

What is the number of jobs accessible to the average person in poverty for the base condition and for each dispersal condition?[8] In San Francisco (Figure 10.4), of the 450,092 low-skill jobs that were accessible to a person in poverty before the move, 10 percent fewer were accessible afterwards (9 percent in the gentrification condition). In Philadelphia (Figure 10.5), 245,074 jobs were

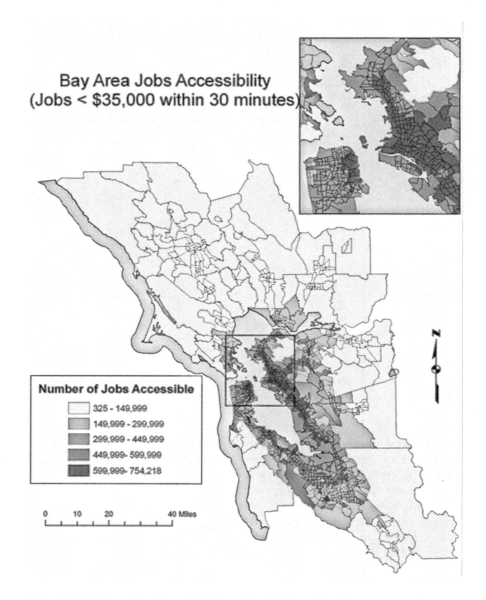

Figure 10.4 Geography of low-skill jobs in San Francisco Bay Area
Source: Austin (2008)

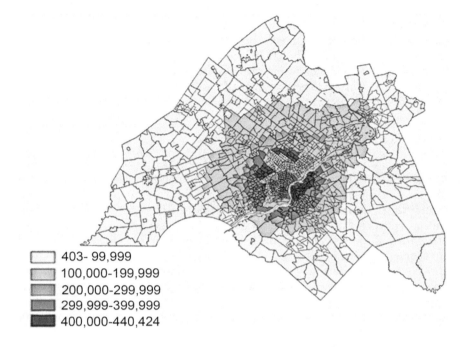

403- 99,999
100,000-199,999
200,000-299,999
299,999-399,999
400,000-440,424

Figure 10.5 Geography of low-skill jobs in the Philadelphia-Camden metropolitan
area

Source: Austin (2008)

available pre-move, with a loss of 26 percent (23 percent under gentrification)
afterwards.

In other words, in both regions, the average number of jobs that are located
within a half-hour drive decreases as a result of the move from high-poverty to
low-poverty areas. In fact, there is a direct relationship in each region between
the number of persons below the poverty line that are moved and the magnitude
of this decrease: the more that move to low-poverty, generally suburban areas,
the greater the decrease in economic opportunity. This suggests that any
"mismatch" between residents and jobs is, at least at the regional level, not
primarily a spatial one—or at least a better spatial match now than it would
be by moving residents to the suburbs.

Of course, it is possible that once the population had dispersed, jobs would
follow them to the suburbs. For example, at least in Chicago, the suburbanization of the poor has improved job accessibility (Hu 2014). But in general, the
jobs and the poor (particularly African Americans) actually tend not to
collocate as they suburbanize (Galster 1991; Raphael and Stoll 2010).

One caveat: this model looks at total jobs, not at vacancies or job growth, each of which might be more closely associated with job accessibility. Yet, these tend to be centralized too, given the overall agglomeration of jobs in metros (Shen 2001). Regardless, the chief finding of this model is important: almost 50 years after the Kerner Commission's findings that inner-city residents were isolated from suburban jobs, there are still more low- and moderate-skilled jobs in or near high-poverty areas than in or near low-poverty areas.

What Next, Then?

This model was developed as a means to test whether, at scale, this set of strategies will yield positive results for poor households. The first part of the simulation demonstrates the magnitude of the commitment, politically and financially, that would be necessary to fully mitigate the negative neighborhood effects of poverty through a dispersal strategy. Of course, although the advocates of housing dispersal are seeking balanced development, they may not be envisioning a program that precisely equalizes poverty across a region. Yet, surely effecting tectonic shifts in population patterns cannot be the core of one's urban housing policy. Moreover, the second part of the simulation suggests that dispersal may be a poor strategy, regardless of scale or attendant policy. The more poor people were moved to the suburbs, the further they were placed from job opportunities.

Studies of dispersal have suggested its inadequacy in improving economic outcomes. This is likely due to both social and structural factors. Movers experience difficulty in constructing new ties, particularly to assist in job search, and miss their social contacts from the old neighborhood; leaving support systems behind creates new space-time constraints in negotiating work and family obligations (Clampet-Lundquist 2004, 2007; Gibson 2007; Kleit 2001; Trudeau 2006). Given the predominance of dead-end, low-skill jobs in the labor market, and the continuing human capital deficit among today's youth, it is not surprising that movers experience little or no improvement in earnings or employment rate. It is similarly unsurprising that after the Gautreaux experiment, the expected improvement in educational outcomes did not materialize for dispersed families: poor schools are no longer limited to inner-city neighborhoods. Dispersal benefits are much more likely for issues of safety and housing quality, factors that vary considerably between neighborhoods, and factors that reflect environmental conditions more directly.

The dispersal policy model has been heavily influenced by a small number of extreme cases. The Gautreaux program resulted from a lawsuit specific to the city of Chicago, a single city with an extremely dysfunctional public housing system. The MTO program was based on the purported successes of Gautreaux. The analysis that resulted in the HOPE VI program indicated that only 6 percent of the national public housing stock was severely distressed enough to require such a degree of demolition and dispersal (Goetz 2013). Most public housing has not deteriorated as much as the notorious examples in Chicago (e.g.,

Cabrini-Green). Compared to these extreme cases, most residents of public housing are not as anxious to leave, may see a functioning social fabric where others do not, and may end up being less likely to see substantial differences between their old neighborhoods and the new ones to which they have been relocated.

HUD's Sustainable Communities Initiative required that grantees conduct a fair housing analysis, identifying areas of racially concentrated poverty, engaging their residents, and addressing disparities in the regional sustainability planning process. Yet, the toolkit available to deconcentrate poverty is a set of dispersal strategies—public housing demolition, HOPE VI, and vouchering out—rather than strategies that provide the information or skills necessary to connect residents to opportunities to which they are already near. By increasing the incomes of residents, such a framework may foster a "deconcentration of poverty," and a concomitant diminution of negative neighborhood effects, *without* necessitating a population change.

Expanding opportunities for low-income residents to access a full range of neighborhoods, whether through vouchers, project-based assistance, reforming land use regulations, or a combination of all three, is laudable. However, these measures cannot be taken at the expense of the need for lower-income residents to maintain their access to economic opportunity, or the networks and support systems that make working in the mainstream economy possible. The potential of regional sustainability planning is to look at where such systems are in place, and to ensure that these neighborhoods are sustainable as the region continues to grow.

Notes

1. Project-based assistance (programs such as Section 8, 208, etc.) typically comes in the form of developments funded by the public but built by the private or nonprofit sector. The number of households receiving project-based housing assistance is relatively stable, while the number of households receiving tenant-based assistance doubled to 1.6 million from 1984 to 1998, with growth slowing in the budget cuts of the 2000s (Quigley 2000).
2. The improved sense of safety is not universal; Gibson (2007) reports that 30 percent of displaced households in Portland's Columbia Villa HOPE VI project thought their new neighborhoods were safer, while 18 percent felt they were less safe in their new neighborhoods.
3. The only study, to my knowledge, to identify an employment benefit for dispersed public housing families is an analysis of the Yonkers scattered site program (Briggs 1998).
4. The region was defined as the area served by the local Metropolitan Planning Agency (the Metropolitan Transportation Commission for the Bay Area and the Delaware Valley Regional Planning Authority for Philadelphia).
5. George Galster (2003) finds that a large number of dispersed city dwellers would need to move to low-poverty tracts in order to achieve significant societal benefits.
6. The conditions that include "gentrification" are identical in proportion to these, though with slightly smaller numbers of moves in each direction.
7. This analysis uses jobs data from the 2000 Census Transportation Planning Package.

8. For each tract, the number of jobs within a half-hour radius was multiplied by the number of people in poverty; this was summed for all census tracts and divided by the total number of people in poverty in that metro area. This was repeated, with jobs multiplied by the number of people in poverty that would result from each dispersal condition. Through this method, the degree to which people were moved into tracts with a larger or smaller number of jobs within a half-hour radius is reflected in the change in jobs accessible for the average person in poverty.

References

Austin, Mason. "Diaspora as Urban Policy: A Dispersal Simulation Model for Minneapolis-St.Paul, Philadelphia, and the San Francisco Bay Area." Unpublished master's capstone project, University of California, Berkeley, 2008.

Barrett, Edith J., Paul Geisel, and Jan Johnston. "The Ramona Utti Report: Impacts of the Ripley Arnold Relocation Program: Year 3 (2004–5)." Unpublished paper for the City of Fort Worth, Texas, 2006.

Briggs, Xavier de Souza. "Brown Kids in White Suburbs: Housing Mobility and the Many Faces of Social Capital." *Housing Policy Debate* 9, no. 1 (1998): 177–221.

Chapple, Karen Diane. *Paths to Employment: The Role of Social Networks in the Job Search for Women on Welfare in San Francisco.* Ph.D. dissertation, University of California, Berkeley, 2000.

Chapple, Karen. "Time to Work: Job Search Strategies and Commute Time for Women on Welfare in San Francisco." *Journal of Urban Affairs* 23, no. 2 (2001): 155–173.

Clampet-Lundquist, Susan. "Moving Over or Moving Up? Short-Term Gains and Losses for Relocated HOPE VI Families." *Journal of Policy Development and Research* 7, no. 1 (2004): 57–80.

Clampet-Lundquist, Susan. "No More 'Bois Ball: The Effect of Relocation from Public Housing on Adolescents." *Journal of Adolescent Research* 22, no. 3 (2007): 298–323.

Curley, Alexandra M. "HOPE and Housing: The Effects of Relocation on Movers' Economic Stability, Social Networks, and Health." Ph.D. dissertation, Boston University, 2006.

Downs, Anthony. "Smart Growth: Why We Discuss it More than We Do It." *Journal of the American Planning Association* 71, no. 4 (2005): 367–378.

Edin, Kathryn and Laura Lein. *Making Ends Meet: How Single Mothers Survive Welfare and Low-Wage Work.* New York: Russell Sage Foundation, 1997.

Ellen, Ingrid Gould and Margery Austin Turner. "Does Neighborhood Matter? Assessing Recent Evidence." *Housing Policy Debate* 8, no. 4 (1997): 833–866.

Gallagher, Megan and Beata Bajaj. *Moving On: Assessing the Benefits and Challenges of HOPE VI for Children. HOPE VI: Where Do We Go from Here? Brief 4.* Washington, DC: Urban Institute Press, 2007.

Galster, George C. "Black Suburbanization: Has it Changed the Relative Location of Races?" *Urban Affairs Review* 26, no. 4 (1991): 621–628.

Galster, George. "MTO's Impact on Sending and Receiving Neighborhoods." In *Choosing a Better Life? Evaluating the Moving to Opportunity Social Experiment,* edited by John M. Goering and Judith D. Feins, 365–382. Washington, DC: Urban Institute Press, 2003.

Galster, George. "Neighborhood Social Mix as a Goal of Housing Policy: A Theoretical Analysis." *European Journal of Housing Policy* 7, no. 1 (2007): 19–43.

Gibson, Karen J. "The Relocation of the Columbia Villa Community: Views from Residents." *Journal of Planning Education and Research* 27, no. 1 (2007): 5–19.

Gilbert, Melissa. "'Race, Space, and Power': The Survival Strategies of Working Poor Women." *Annals of the Association of American Geographers* 88 (1998): 595–621.

Goetz, Edward G. "Forced Relocation vs. Voluntary Mobility: The Effects of Dispersal Programmes on Households." *Housing Studies* 17, no. 1 (2002): 107–123.

Goetz, Edward Glenn. *Clearing the Way: Deconcentrating the Poor in Urban America.* Washington, DC: Urban Institute Press, 2003.

Goetz, Edward G. *New Deal Ruins: Race, Economic Justice, and Public Housing Policy.* Ithaca, NY: Cornell University Press, 2013.

Hu, Lingqian. "Changing Job Access of the Poor: Effects of Spatial and Socioeconomic Transformations in Chicago, 1990–2010." *Urban Studies* 51, no. 4 (2014): 1–18.

Kleit, Rachel Garschick. "The Role of Neighborhood Social Networks in Scattered-Site Public Housing Residents' Search for Jobs." *Housing Policy Debate* 12, no. 3 (2001): 541–573.

Kleit, Rachel G. and Lynne C. Manzo. "To Move or Not to Move: Relationships to Place and Relocation Choices in HOPE VI." *Housing Policy Debate* 17, no. 2 (2006): 271–308.

Kling, Jeffrey R., Jeffrey B. Liebman, and Lawrence F. Katz. "Experimental Analysis of Neighborhood Effects." *Econometrica* 75, no. 1 (2007): 83–119.

Kling, Jeffrey R., Jens Ludwig, and Lawrence F. Katz. "Neighborhood Effects on Crime for Female and Male Youth: Evidence from a Randomized Housing Voucher Experiment." *The Quarterly Journal of Economics* 120 (2005): 87–130.

Levy, Diane K. and Mark Woolley. *Employment Barriers Among HOPE VI Families, HOPE VI: Where Do We Go from Here? Brief 6.* Washington, DC: Urban Institute Press, 2007.

Petit, Becky. "Moving and Children's Social Connections: Neighborhood Context and the Consequences of Moving for Low-Income Families." *Sociological Forum* 19, no. 2 (2004): 285–311.

Popkin, Susan J. "The HOPE VI Program: What Has Happened to the Residents?" In *Where are Poor People to Live? Transforming Public Housing Communities,* edited by Larry Bennett, Janet L. Smith, and Patricia A. Wright, 68–90. Armonk, NY: M. E. Sharpe, 2006.

Popkin, Susan J. and Elizabeth Cove. *Safety is the Most Important Thing: How HOPE VI Helped Families. Brief 2.* Washington, DC: Urban Institute Press, Metropolitan Housing and Communities Center, 2007.

Popkin, Susan, James Rosenbaum, and Patricia Meaden. "Labor Market Experiences of Low-Income Black Women in Middle-Class Suburbs: Evidence from a Survey of Gautreaux Program Participants." *Journal of Policy Analysis and Management* 12 (1993): 556–573.

Quigley, John. "A Decent Home: Housing Policy in Perspective." *Brookings-Wharton Papers on Urban Affairs* 1 (2000): 53–88.

Raphael, Steven and Michael A. Stoll. *Job Sprawl and the Suburbanization of Poverty.* Washington, DC: Metropolitan Policy Program at Brookings, 2010.

Schwartz, Alex F. *Housing Policy in the United States.* New York: Routledge, 2010.

Sharkey, Patrick. *Stuck in Place: Urban Neighborhoods and the End of Progress Toward Racial Equality.* Chicago, IL: University of Chicago Press, 2013.

Shen, Qing. "A Spatial Analysis of Job Openings and Access in a US Metropolitan Area." *Journal of the American Planning Association* 67, no. 1 (2001): 53–68.

Trudeau, Daniel. "The Persistence of Segregation in Buffalo, New York: Comer vs. Cisneros and Geographies of Relocation Decisions Among Low-Income Black Households." *Urban Geography* 27, no. 1 (2006): 20–44.

Turney, Kristin, Susan Clampet-Lundquist, Kathryn Edin, Jeffrey R. Kling, and Greg. J. Duncan. *Neighborhood Effects on Barriers to Employment: Results from a Randomized Housing Mobility Experiment in Baltimore.* Working Paper #511. Princeton, NJ: Princeton University, 2006.

U.S. Department of Housing and Urban Development (HUD). *Evaluation of the Welfare to Work Voucher Program: Report to Congress.* Washington, DC: U.S. Government Printing Office, 2004.

Vale, Lawrence J. "Empathological Places: Residents' Ambivalence Toward Remaining in Public Housing." *Journal of Planning Education and Research* 16 (1997): 159–175.

Varady, David P. and Carole C. Walker. "Vouchering Out Distressed Subsidized Developments: Does Moving Lead to Improvements in Housing and Neighborhood Conditions?" *Housing Policy Debate* 11, no. 1 (2000): 115–162.

Vigdor, Jacob L. "The Katrina Effect: Was There a Bright Side to the Evacuation of Greater New Orleans?" *The B.E. Journal of Economic Analysis & Policy* 7, no. 1 (2007): 1–40.

11 Unpacking Accessibility

Spatial Mismatch or Social Networks?

> Most new employment opportunities do not occur in central cities, near all-Negro neighborhoods. They are being created in suburbs and outlying areas—and this trend is likely to continue indefinitely.
>
> National Advisory (Kerner) Commission on
> Civil Disorders (1968: 392)

> Latisha: I was already taking my daughter, and her teacher, I just happened to say, if you hear of anything, let me know. And it's amazing, I'm so glad I said that. And she said, you know what, we need a reception here. And that's how I got that job. And I was there almost a whole year.
>
> (Chapple 2001b: 632)

Latisha got her job at the YMCA by chance, during her regular routine of dropping off her daughter for childcare. The teacher who connected her to the job opening was a weak tie—an acquaintance—from her social network. The YMCA, located in her neighborhood, San Francisco's Bayview-Hunter's Point, was part of her daily activity patterns. And in fact, regardless of jobseeker race or ethnicity, gender, or income level, about half of all jobs are obtained via social networks such as this (Granovetter 1995).

Yet, the notion of the isolated ghetto that the Kerner Commission put forth (i.e., the framing of the problem as one of physical, rather than social, proximity) was adopted by decades of researchers and policymakers as the framework for analysis and programs. Looking for a "spatial mismatch," they (beginning with John Kain's 1968 epic article on mismatch) found confirmation of isolation. The further away from the suburbs, the worse the employment outcomes of city residents. This suggested a diagnosis of inaccessibility, and a policy remedy of improved mobility to the suburbs. That social networks might intervene to connect jobseekers to jobs, whether in cities or suburbs, was not considered, perhaps for the simple reason that no data were available to measure network extent, and in any case it was not clear how to design policies to build networks.

The process by which jobseekers get matched to jobs consists of three elements, each building upon the last: personal factors, social strategies, and physical strategies. The importance of each varies by region (with, for instance, physical solutions much more important in large metropolitan areas with high degrees of mismatch), but typically the three combine in some fashion to link jobseekers and employers.

Personal factors consist of issues that shape the initial entry into the labor market, including motivation, physical health, human capital, and reservation wage, or the lowest wage at which the jobseeker is willing to work. With relatively high levels of human capital and motivation and/or a low reservation wage, jobseekers often succeed in the job search by using formal intermediaries, such as newspaper advertisements or the Web. But when one or more of these factors constitutes a serious barrier, jobseekers may turn to social strategies.

Social strategies consist of networks of social contacts (often formed by ethnic groups) and workforce intermediaries. Such resources may help build motivation and human capital, or even substitute for human capital; they also help to overcome barriers such as discrimination and lack of information about job openings.

Urban policy and regional sustainability planning tends to privilege *physical* strategies, such as mobility, dispersal, or development. Once jobseekers have resolved their personal barriers, many will need help getting to the jobs. Yet, bringing jobs and jobseekers in close proximity to each other will have little effect if opportunity structures, such as job information networks to counter discrimination and negative jobseeker perceptions, are not in place (Dickens 1999; Fernandez and Su 2004; Galster and Killen 1995; Kelly 1994). For many, access to jobs is not just about overcoming physical barriers and matching worker skills to employer needs, but is also about strengthening the social institutions that manage connections between employers and jobseekers, a crucial middle step.

In the process of searching for a job, a social contact may assist either by providing information about the opportunity or actually helping to place the jobseeker (Campbell and Rosenfeld 1985; Corcoran, Datcher, and Duncan 1980).[1] Social contacts are effective intermediaries because they improve the quality of information and thus trust in the employment process: they may help to allay employer concerns about the employability and appropriateness of job applicants, sometimes substituting for formal educational credentials (Chapple 2002).

If knowing the right person is one of the best ways to get a job, how is it that we became so focused on spatial mismatch? Part of it is what might be called the Detroit fallacy, the image of a declining inner-city core surrounded by prosperous suburbs. The first research on spatial mismatch centered on Detroit, and the donut-hole image has created a powerful narrative ever since. And in fact, Detroit is characterized by very poor accessibility, with job concentrations located well outside the central business district (Grengs 2010).

But the pictures of San Francisco and Philadelphia in the dispersal vignette above are much more typical of U.S. metropolitan areas: for the most part, jobs concentrate in the core where densities—and productivity—are greatest (Chapter 4). What, then, is the nature of mismatch?

The Mismatch Studies

Poor access to jobs explains much of why some groups experience disproportionately high rates of unemployment. With greater proximity to jobs, unemployment and welfare usage decrease slightly, and earnings increase slightly (Blumenberg and Ong 1998; Carlson and Theodore 1997; Immergluck 1998).

Still, there are several reasons to rethink the notion that the problem is a mismatch of space, or at least of city versus suburb. First, metropolitan spatial structure has changed dramatically since 1970, with the rise of multi-ethnic suburbs, new urban and suburban job centers, and suburban poverty (Frey 2003; Kneebone and Berube 2013; Lang and Simmons 2003). Continued residential segregation does mean that African Americans, in particular, remain relatively isolated from jobs, unless they move near new suburban job centers (Holzer 1991; Ihlanfeldt and Sjoquist 1998; Kain 1992, 2004; Martin 2004; Stoll 2005).[2] But suburban job growth may not constitute an opportunity, because the majority of job openings are vacancies resulting from turnover and thus follow the location of existing, not new, jobs (Shen 2001).

Second, research has shown that race has a much larger impact than space on employment outcomes (Carlson and Theodore 1997; Cervero, Rood, and Appleyard 1999; Ellen and Turner 1997; Ellwood 1986; Holzer 1991; Immergluck 1998). Employers continue to screen out jobseekers based upon their race: matched-pair studies consistently show that minorities, particularly African Americans and foreign-sounding Latinos, are less likely to receive job interviews and offers than whites applying for the same job (Bertrand and Mullainathan 2004; Cross et al. 1990; Holzer 1996; Turner, Fix, and Struyk 1991). Segregation reinforces this discrimination by employers, who may identify race based on neighborhood of residence. Employers also may prefer to hire from outside the neighborhood where their business is located, either to avoid getting involved in local animosities or to target a specific ethnic group (Hanson and Pratt 1995; Kasinitz and Rosenberg 1993; Mier and Giloth 1985; Neckerman and Kirschenman 1991; Newman 1999).

Third, in many cities, the poor employment outcomes may be due to "automobile mismatch": with a car, workers can access many more job opportunities than by relying on transit (Blumenberg and Hess 2003; Blumenberg and Manville 2004; Fan 2012; Grengs 2010; Kawabata 2003; Shen 1998; Taylor and Ong 1995). This is obviously true for the sprawling cities of the American West; more surprising are findings that even in a city such as Detroit, center city workers with a car have greater accessibility than suburban workers without.

Fourth, the extent of mismatch also varies by region, suggesting that planners in metropolitan areas such as Cleveland should be far more concerned than those in, say, Austin. Smaller metros have less mismatch than larger metros, perhaps because of shorter distances between jobs and housing, as well as lower levels of residential segregation (Ihlanfeldt and Sjoquist 1991; Weinberg 2004). The nature of economic restructuring also differs between regions, affecting the impact of mismatch. In some regions, minority residents are overrepresented in suburbanizing industries, while in others minorities are underrepresented; for instance, in New York City, relatively few African Americans were employed in manufacturing, so they were not disproportionately affected by mismatch (Fainstein 1986; Galster 1991).

But perhaps most important is the role of networks, particularly weak ties such as Latisha's, who provide access to more varied sources of job information, from a greater variety of people, than a more dense personal network of family and friends (Granovetter 1995; Lin, Vaughn, and Ensel 1981). By bridging different worlds—diverse neighborhoods, educational and work environments, and racial/gender groups—using a weak tie contact to get a job can lead to upward mobility (Chapple 2001a; Elliot and Sims 2001; Jarrett 1995; Johnson, Bienenstock, and Farrell 1991). For cohesive ethnic or immigrant groups, strong ties of family and friends also play an important role in connecting to job opportunities (Elliot and Sims 2001; Granovetter and Tilly 1988; Green, Tigges, and Diaz 1999; Waldinger 1996). Both strong and weak ties can also help access opportunities for informal or under-the-table work.

In general, the lower the socioeconomic status, the smaller the network, particularly of weak ties (Braddock and McPartland 1987; Fischer et al. 1977; Granovetter 1995). And networks also constrict when living in a segregated neighborhood, because of the reduced opportunities to interact with weak ties (Chapple 2001b; Elliot and Sims 2001). Segregation also reinforces the perception of discrimination by jobseekers, preventing them from capitalizing on job opportunities. Even with perfect information, jobseekers may encounter subtle barriers in unfamiliar areas, such as racial profiling on suburban streets, that dissuade them from pursuing job opportunities (Meiklejohn 2003).

How Networks Function in Places

If opportunity does not come from simple proximity to jobs, how do networks such as Latisha's fill the gap? Regional planners have thought more about how to accommodate more jobs near residential neighborhoods than how to facilitate network connections, yet there are ways to encourage regional development that increases networking opportunities too. First, then, let us consider how networks of strong and weak ties function in places, as found by my ethnographic study of low-income mothers in San Francisco (Chapple 2000).

The strong ties that help build connections to employment are typically friends or family that live in the same community. These provide three forms of valuable assistance: they furnish timely information by monitoring openings on behalf of their friends and families; they provide appropriate opportunities because they understand the constraints that jobseekers face (such as child-rearing responsibilities); and they assist in the application process by offering inside knowledge about what the employer is looking for. They also often provide other forms of support, such as childcare, or car sharing, or informal work opportunities.

For example, Lucy's brother was working at Toys "R" Us for the Christmas season, and told her that they had a shortage of workers. Sonia's friend, an assistant manager at a bank, got her a part-time job as a teller, at a higher wage than the other tellers were making, and with a schedule that could accommodate her childcare needs. Hazel could not get jobs directly through her mother, "because she's in banking, and I'm in nursing. But a couple of her employees that had friends or family that were ill, yes, I've worked for them through my mama like that."

In contrast, using weak ties for assistance in the job search is usually facilitated by interaction in different spheres of life outside the home. The typical weak tie is an acquaintance from school, work, government agencies, the neighborhood, or activities associated with childrearing. In most cases, the weak tie is strategically approached by the jobseeker, but in others, the interaction is initiated by the weak tie and thus is less a strategy than a chance opportunity, a job gained through nonsearch. In general, the more exposed to a variety of people, the more both search and nonsearch opportunities will arise.

Often, those looking for a job will touch base with casual acquaintances who are employed in similar fields, to see if any job openings are available. In my research, many described a practice of cultivating social contacts for the purpose of obtaining jobs. For the women who like to work sporadically, staying in touch with a wide variety of people enables them to move in and out of the workforce at will.

Take June:

> I've got a lot of people. I always tell somebody, if I have a job lead. My circle of people, we do that. I got a lot of people I associate with, some for certain things, some for others, circle who is consistently looking for work, either they're out of work or in between jobs.

But most of the jobs obtained through weak ties come from daily routines.

Daily Activity Patterns

Activity patterns are closely related to finding jobs, whether through a social contact or direct application. When a jobseeker has a daily routine that puts him or her into contact with a variety of people and potential employment situations, an opportunity may arise purely from chance, in the course of daily activities. The success of a direct application strategy is also often related closely to daily activity patterns, as jobseekers walk in and apply at an establishment because of a "help wanted" sign in the window or a flyer posted somewhere. Ann got hired at the local liquor store after the manager got to know her, and many women hear about seasonal job openings, such as at the post office, from neighbors.

Getting a job by walking in often happens at the spur of the moment: typically, while on daily rounds, the jobseeker sees a sign that a store is hiring and walks in to apply. Using the strategy of pounding the pavement is easiest when it can be incorporated into a daily routine. Few make a concerted effort to visit stores or firms to apply (except, for instance, when there is heavy seasonal hiring); instead, they drop in at a few stores when they are at the mall, or apply at the supermarket while there, or take note of openings on their way somewhere else:

> *Penny:* I seen an inquiry on the building. See, my mother lives like a block from there, so one day I was walking to the bus stop or something, no, I was going to the store, and I seen a big inquiry on them walls, so I called and I went in the next day and filled out an application, and then I got the job that next week.

Sometimes appearing in person helps to establish a rapport with the employers: Althea was eating at the Doggie Diner when she asked the proprietor if he had any job openings, and Elena was drinking at her local bar when she got her first bartending job. In this sense, direct application is a way of making new acquaintants, who then become the weak ties that lead to a new job.

However, direct application is less likely to succeed if it takes place at stores owned by members of other racial/ethnic groups, whether in the neighborhood of residence or not. These "family" stores may hire disproportionately from their own racial/ethnic groups.

Apart from visiting retail establishments, the daily rounds of low-income community residents might involve a variety of public and nonprofit institutions, including the school system, the public housing authority, hospitals, and social service agencies, to soup kitchens, to job training programs, to drug recovery programs, to parenting counseling groups. Such institutions often have short-term or part-time jobs available and find it convenient to hire the women who make use of their services. For instance, the Goodwill drug recovery program hires some of its graduates to work in its retail outlet. Churches running soup kitchens typically have several other nonprofit programs that often need workers. In other instances, program participants share job opportunities: for instance, Michelle was taking a computer training class at a local church when one of her classmates told her about a firm desperate for security guards.

Others end up working at the housing development where they live, doing odd jobs in housekeeping or landscaping. In many cases, these jobs are paid under the table. This type of informal work is almost always obtained through a social contact, and usually consists of personal services for relatives, friends, and neighbors who can pay in cash or in kind.

There are 11 million self-employed entrepreneurs in the country, many patching together income from a variety of sources. For most low-income households, the extra income is critical to making ends meet. Further, enjoying the independence that entrepreneurship provides, many decline opportunities to work in the formal low-wage labor market. Working on the side may span a variety of activities, most of which take in the local neighborhood, often in the home: selling crafts or household necessities; providing childcare or home healthcare; landscaping or construction; housecleaning; braiding hair; and so forth.

The availability of informal work through contact networks leads many to work locally. Along with the concentration of strong ties in the neighborhood of residence and the daily activity patterns that help jobseekers learn about job opportunities, it constitutes one of several ways that inner-city residents end up working near home, regardless of where job concentrations lie.

Many also try to work close to home because of family responsibilities or the inconvenience of public transportation. My study of San Francisco found that women without a car tended to look for jobs closer to home. But also, daily activities for low-income mothers take place within a tightly circumscribed area. As a result, many women are unfamiliar with job opportunities outside of the areas where they typically shop, visit with friends, and obtain social services. Some are even unfamiliar or uncomfortable with neighborhoods relatively nearby their own: Rosa applied for a childcare job in Diamond Heights, about two miles from her home in the Mission, but was relieved when she did not get the job: as she says, "because Diamond Heights is way out there, I don't even know how to get out there. And once I got out there, it's like, I'd like to work around here [the Mission]."

Locating jobs next door to poor neighborhoods does not ensure that low-income residents enter the labor market; improving the "match" may not solve the problem. There is, for better or worse, a kind of serendipity that undergirds the labor market, a role played by chance encounters or connections. This seems to come into play when *communities* are dense, giving people more opportunities to interact. But the jobs themselves need not be next door. Since the other chapters in this section focus on the development and dispersal policy options, here we examine the mobility option for connecting jobseekers better to opportunities throughout the metropolitan region—what I call supersizing the labor market.

Policies for the Mobility of the Low-Income

Supersizing strategies are essentially transportation improvements, particularly reverse commuting programs and low-income car ownership programs.[3] Most funding to link low-income urban residents to suburban jobs (for instance, the Jobs Access and Reverse Commute program, which has provided almost $900 million in funding from 1999 to 2009) has supported reverse commuting via transit, rather than auto ownership programs. Yet, historically, such initiatives have had little success, particularly in terms of reducing inner-city unemployment, though they may help those who are already employed (Crain 1970; O'Regan and Quigley 1999; Rosenbloom 1992). One evaluation of a vanpooling experiment called Bridges to Work, which provided job placement and transportation services to help urban low-skilled workers access suburban jobs in five regions, concluded that it was not an effective solution, since the program did not increase employment or earnings (compared to a control group) (Roder and Scrivner 2005). Perhaps because the labor market was relatively tight when the program was implemented, turnover at the suburban jobs was high; given the choice between the low-wage, low-skill jobs in the suburbs or close to home in the city, jobseekers chose the latter. The findings indicated that workforce development, particularly recruitment and job-readiness, is the major policy challenge in improving the employment chances of the disadvantaged, and in any case workers will not take on long reverse commutes if they cannot realize substantially higher wages in return.

Though the poor are disproportionately dependent on transit, it is not well designed to meet their travel needs. Whether living in isolated suburbs or isolated ghettos, the daily activity patterns of low-income families are particularly complex for low-income families, who may suffer from time poverty, or the inability to meet complex multiple responsibilities within a set schedule (Lucas 2012). For instance, low-income workers may live in neighborhoods lacking stores and services or may work alternative shifts when transit is not available (Clifton 2004; Fan 2012). Family sizes are larger, necessitating more trips to more places for education, health, and recreation, and leading to higher levels of auto dependency (Fan and Khattak 2012). Lower-income households, particularly with working mothers, tend to make more trips (Blumenberg 2004). This occurs, in part, because they experience challenges in developing efficient trip chaining strategies, due to their reliance on multiple modes, as well as their fixed work schedules that do not allow for stops to and from work (Bhat 1997; Clifton 2003). Relying on family and friends for assistance (e.g., for childcare or errands) may complicate daily travel further, if they are not local. In any case, the design of new transit systems often neglects to take account of these accessibility issues for low-wage workers.

Public transit may improve employment outcomes, but not as effectively as autos (Cervero, Sandoval, and Landis 2002; Fan 2012; Sanchez 1999). Owning a car typically improves job accessibility and increases employment rates and wages, regardless of whether jobs are nearby or not (Blumenberg 2004; Cervero, Sandoval, and Landis 2002; Fan 2012; Ong 1996, 2002; Ong and Miller 2005; Raphael and Stoll 2001; Shen 1998). However, 30 percent of poor households do not own a car (compared to 8 percent of all households) (Giuliano 2005).

Compared with reverse commuting programs, car ownership programs offer great promise in terms of overcoming the last, physical barriers to work in both city and suburb. They also help support the non-work travel that constitutes the bulk of daily activity and is projected to grow in the future (McGuckin 2007). Evaluation of nonprofit low-income car ownership programs has shown significant and positive effects on wages and probability of employment for a very small sample of participants (Goldberg 2001; Lucas and Nicholson 2003). But they remain small and are difficult to support politically in regional sustainability planning.

But even without owning a car, low-income families often have access to an automobile. Coping strategies to improve mobility include getting rides from others, borrowing cars, or relying on others, often through barter, to run errands or deliver goods (Clifton 2004). The success of these strategies depends on social networks and relationships of trust. Further, if relying on other people's cars, proximity is key: families and friends must live nearby for the strategy to work.

Given the accessibility challenges of a region's low-income residents, as well as the overwhelmingly positive impact of auto ownership on employment outcomes, the most equitable approach to regional sustainability, at least in the short term, might be to improve access to automobiles among the poor. This does not negate the need for strategies that assure the inclusion of the low-income in the urban core as it densifies (Chapter 5), or that invest in places by increasing the density of amenities and institutions (described in the next chapter). All of these are ways that we can help low-income families spend less time traveling (Makarewicz 2013). However, supporting car ownership acknowledges that many will continue to live in less accessible parts of the region. Low-income households are still likely to drive fewer miles than higher-income; if supporting sustainability means reducing vehicle miles traveled (VMT), the primary target should be higher-income drivers. In any case, a VMT tax will be less regressive than other taxes such as the sales tax (Schweitzer and Taylor 2008).

Much of our thinking about accessibility and equity in regional sustainability planning draws from the notion of the isolated ghetto from the 1960s. Planners continue to map suburban job centers and the opportunities they offer for the disadvantaged, without paying heed to the complications of the lives of the poor that make conventional commutes challenging. But supersizing the labor market through long commutes is not a sustainable alternative (in multiple senses of the term). Improving accessibility means building on the existing coping strategies in the informal economy and the role of network contacts in helping the poor navigate the labor market. These systems are sustainable, even if the context of poverty should not be.

Notes

1. See also the review in Granovetter (1995).
2. Although this work does not look at employment outcomes per se, the implication is that physical inaccessibility worsens employment and earnings.
3. Improving labor market information via the Internet is also a supersizing strategy of growing importance, but not enough is known about its effectiveness to evaluate it. Given what we know about the role of networks and discrimination in hiring processes, the Internet may not be the most effective channel to open up job opportunity for low-income jobseekers.

References

Bertrand, Marianne and Sendhil Mullainathan. "Are Emily and Greg More Employable than Lakisha and Jamal? A Field Experiment on Labor Market Discrimination." *American Economic Review* 94, no. 4 (2004): 991–1013.

Bhat, Chandra R. "Work Travel Mode Choice and Number of Nonwork Commute Stops." *Transportation Research* 31B (1997): 41–54.

Blumenberg, Evelyn. "En-Gendering Effective Planning: Spatial Mismatch, Low-Income Women, and Transportation Policy." *Journal of the American Planning Association* 70, no. 3 (2004): 269–281.

Blumenberg, Evelyn and Daniel B. Hess. "Measuring the Role of Transportation in Facilitating Welfare-to-Work Transition: Evidence from Three California Counties." *Transportation Research Record* 1859 (2003): 93–101.

Blumenberg, Evelyn and Michael Manville. "Beyond the Spatial Mismatch: Welfare Recipients and Transportation Policy." *Journal of Planning Literature* 19, no. 182 (November 2004): 132–205.

Blumenberg, Evelyn and Paul Ong. "Job Access, Commute and Travel Burden among Welfare Recipients." *Urban Studies* 35, no. 1 (1998): 77–93.

Braddock, Jomills Henry and James M. McPartland. "How Minorities Continue to be Excluded from Equal Employment Opportunities: Research on Labor Market and Institutional Barriers." *Journal of Social Issues* 43, no. 1 (1987): 5–39.

Campbell, Karen E. and Rachel A. Rosenfeld. "Job Search and Job Mobility: Sex and Race Differences." *Research in the Sociology of Work* 3 (1985): 147–175.

Carlson, Virginia and Nicholas Theodore. "Employment Availability for Entry-Level Workers: An Examination of the Spatial-Mismatch Hypothesis in Chicago." *Urban Geography* 18, no. 3 (April 1997): 228–242.

Cervero, Robert, Timothy Rood, and Bruce Appleyard. "Tracking Accessibility: Employment and Housing Opportunities in the San Francisco Bay Area." *Environmental and Planning A* 31 (1999): 1259–1278.

Cervero, Robert, Onesimo Sandoval, and John Landis. "Transportation as a Stimulus of Welfare-to-Work: Private versus Public Mobility." *Journal of Planning Education and Research* 22, no. 1 (2002): 50–63.

Chapple, Karen. *Paths to Employment: The Role of Social Networks in the Job Search for Women on Welfare in San Francisco*. Ph.D. dissertation, University of California, Berkeley, 2000.

Chapple, Karen. "Time to Work: Job Search Strategies and Commute Time for Women on Welfare in San Francisco." *Journal of Urban Affairs* 23, no. 2 (2001a): 155–173.

Chapple, Karen. "Out of Touch, Out of Bounds: How Job Search Strategies Shape the Labor Market Radii of Women on Welfare in San Francisco." *Urban Geography* 22, no. 7 (2001b): 617–640.

Chapple, Karen. "'I Name it and I Claim it—in the Name of Jesus, this Job is Mine': Job Search, Networks, and Careers for Low-Income Women." *Economic Development Quarterly* 16, no. 4 (2002): 294–313.

Clifton, Kelly J. "Examining Travel Choices of Low-Income Populations: Issues, Methods, and New Approaches." Unpublished paper. Pesented at 10th International Conference on Travel Behaviour Research, 2003.

Clifton, Kelly J. "Mobility Strategies and Food Shopping for Low-Income Families: A Case Study." *Journal of Planning Education and Research* 23, no. 4 (2004): 402–413.

Corcoran, Mary, Linda Datcher, and Greg Duncan. "Information and Influence Networks in Labor Markets." *Five Thousand American Families: Patterns of Economic Progress* 8, no. S1 (1980): 1–37.

Crain, John. *The Reverse Commute Experiment: A $7 Million Demonstration Program*. Washington, DC: Urban Mass Transportation Administration, U.S. Department of Transportation, 1970.

Cross, Harry, Genevieve M. Kenney, Jane Mell, and Wendy Zimmermann. *Employer Hiring Practices*. Washington, DC: Urban Institute Press, 1990.

Dickens, William T. "Rebuilding Urban Labor Markets: What Community Development Can Accomplish." In *Urban Problems and Community Development*, edited by Ronald F. Ferguson and William T. Dickens, 381–436. Washington, DC: Brookings Institution Press, 1999.

Ellen, Ingrid G. and Margery A. Turner. "Does Neighborhood Matter? Assessing Recent Evidence." *Housing Policy Debate* 8 (1997): 833–866.

Elliot, James and Mario Sims. "Ghettos and Barrios: The Impact of Neighborhood Poverty and Race on Job Matching among Blacks and Latinos." *Social Problems* 48, no. 3 (2001): 341–361.

Ellwood, David T. "The Spatial Mismatch Hypothesis: Are There Teenage Jobs Missing in the Ghetto?" In *The Black Youth Employment Crisis*, edited by Richard B. Freeman and Harry J. Holzer, 147–151. Chicago, IL: University of Chicago Press, 1986.

Fainstein, Norman. "The Underclass/Mismatch Hypothesis as an Explanation for Black Economic Deprivation." *Politics and Society* 15, no. 4 (1986): 403–451.

Fan, Yingling. "The Planners' War Against Spatial Mismatch Lessons Learned and Ways Forward." *Journal of Planning Literature* 27, no. 2 (2012): 153–169.

Fan, Yingling and Asad Khattak. "Time Use Patterns, Lifestyles, and Sustainability of Nonwork Travel Behavior." *International Journal of Sustainable Transportation* 6, no. 1 (2012): 26–47.

Fernandez, Roberto M. and Celina Su. "Space in the Study of Labor Markets." *Annual Review of Sociology* 30 (2004): 545–569.

Fischer, Claude, Robert M. Jackson, C. Ann Stueve, Kathleen Gerson, Lynn McAllister-Jones, and Mark Baldassare. *Networks and Places: Social Relations in the Urban Setting*. New York: The Free Press, 1977.

Frey, William H. "Melting Pot Suburbs: A Study of Suburban Diversity." In *Redefining Urban & Suburban America: Evidence from Census 2000*, edited by Bruce Katz, Alan Berube, and Robert E. Lang, 155–179. Washington, DC: Brookings Institution Press, 2003.

Galster, George C. "Black Suburbanization: Has it Changed the Relative Location of Races?" *Urban Affairs Quarterly* 26 (1991): 621–628.

Galster, George and Sean Killen. "Geography of Metropolitan Opportunity: A Reconnaissance and Conceptual Framework." *Housing Policy Debate* 6, no. 1 (1995): 7–43.

Giuliano, Genevieve. "Low Income, Public Transit, and Mobility." *Journal of the Transportation Research Board* 1927 (2005): 63–70.

Goldberg, Heidi. *State and County Supported Car Ownership Programs can Help Low-income Families Secure and Keep Jobs*. Washington, DC: Center on Budget and Policy Priorities, 2001.

Granovetter, Mark. *Getting a Job: A Study of Contacts and Careers. 2nd Edition*. Chicago, IL: University of Chicago Press, 1995.

Granovetter, Mark and Charles Tilly. "Inequality and Labor Processes." In *Handbook of Economic Sociology*, edited by Neil Smelser, 175–221. Newbury Park, CA: Sage, 1988.

Green, Gary Paul, Leann M. Tigges, and Daniel Diaz. "Racial and Ethnic Differences in Job-Search Strategies in Atlanta, Boston, and Los Angeles." *Social Science Quarterly* 80, no. 2 (1999): 263–278.

Grengs, Joe. "Job Accessibility and the Modal Mismatch in Detroit." *Journal of Transport Geography* 18 (2010): 42–54.

Hanson, Susan and Geraldine Pratt. *Gender, Work, and Space*. New York: Routledge, 1995.

Holzer, Harry J. "The Spatial Mismatch Hypothesis: What Has the Evidence Shown?" *Urban Studies* 28, no. 1 (1991): 105–122.

Holzer, Harry J. *What Employers Want: Job Prospects for Less-Educated Workers*. New York: Russell Sage Foundation, 1996.

Ihlanfeldt, Keith R. and David L. Sjoquist. "The Effect of Job Access on Black and White Youth Employment: A Cross-Sectional Analysis." *Urban Studies* 28, no. 2 (1991): 255–265.

Ihlanfeldt, Keith R. and David L. Sjoquist. "The Spatial Mismatch Hypothesis: A Review of Recent Studies and Their Implications for Welfare Reform." *Housing Policy Debate* 9, no. 4 (1998): 849–892.

Immergluck, Daniel. *Neighborhood Jobs, Race, and Skills: Urban Unemployment and Commuting*. New York: Garland, 1998.

Jarrett, Robin L. "Growing up Poor—the Family Experiences of Socially Mobile Youth in Low-Income African-American Neighborhoods." *Journal of Adolescent Research* 10, no. 1 (1995): 111–135.

Johnson, James H., Elisa Jayne Bienenstock, and Walter C. Farrell Jr. "Bridging Social Networks and Female Labor-Force Participation in a Multiethnic Metropolis." *Urban Geography* 20, no. 1 (1991): 3–30.

Kain, John F. "Housing Segregation, Negro Employment, and Metropolitan Decentralization." *Quarterly Journal of Economics* 82, no. 2 (1968): 175–197.

Kain, John F. "The Spatial Mismatch Hypothesis: Three Decades Later." *Housing Policy Debate* 3, no. 2 (1992): 371–469.

Kain, John F. "A Pioneer's Perspective on the Spatial Mismatch Literature." *Urban Studies* 41, no. 1 (2004): 7–32.

Kasinitz, Philip and Jan Rosenberg. "Why Enterprise Zones Will Not Work." *City Journal* 3, no. 4 (1993): 63–69.

Kawabata, Mizuki. "Job Access and Employment Among Low-Skilled Autoless Workers in US Metropolitan Areas." *Environment and Planning A* 35, no. 9 (2003): 1651–1668.

Kelly, M. Patricia Fernández. "Towanda's Triumph: Social and Cultural Capital in the Transition to Adulthood in the Urban Ghetto." *International Journal of Urban and Regional Research* 18, no. 1 (1994): 88–111.

Kneebone, Elizabeth and Alan Berube. *Confronting Suburban Poverty in America*. Washington, DC: Brookings Institution Press, 2013.

Lang, Robert E. and Patrick A. Simmons. "The Urban Turnaround." In *Redefining Urban and Suburban America: Evidence from Census 2000*, edited by Bruce Katz, Alan Berube, and Robert E. Lang, 51–61. Washington, DC: Brookings Institution Press, 2003.

Lin, Nan, John C. Vaughn, and Walter M. Ensel. "Social Resources and Occupational Status Attainment." *Social Forces* 59, no. 4 (1981): 1163–1181.

Lucas, Karen. "Transport and Social Exclusion: Where Are We Now?" *Transport Policy* 20 (2012): 105–113.

Lucas, Marilyn and Charles F. Nicholson. "Subsidized Vehicle Acquisition and Earned Income in the Transition from Welfare to Work." *Transportation* 30 (2003): 483–501.

McGuckin, Nancy. *Analysis of Future Issues and Changing Demands on the System. Part A. Demographic Changes: Impacts on Passenger Travel. Commission Briefing Paper 4A-02: Implications of an Aging Population on Passenger Travel Demand for Different Modes*. Washington, DC: National Surface Transportation Policy and Revenue Study

Commission, 2007. Accessed October 4, 2013. www.transportationfortomorrow.com/final_report/volume_3_html/technical_issues_papers/paperf91e.htm?name=4a_02.

Makarewicz, Carrie. *Examining the Influence of the Urban Environment on Parent's Time, Energy, and Resources for Engagement in their Children's Learning.* Ph.D. dissertation, University of California, Berkeley, 2013.

Martin, Richard W. "Spatial Mismatch and the Structure of American Metropolitan Areas, 1970–2000." *Journal of Regional Science* 44, no. 3 (2004): 467–488.

Meiklejohn, Susan. "'There's No Place Like Home': Suburban Job Search of Urban Workers in Oakland, California." Working Paper. San Francisco, CA: Public Policy Institute of California, 2003.

Mier, Robert and Robert Giloth. "Hispanic Employment Opportunities: A Case of Internal Labor Markets and Weak-Tied Social Networks." *Social Science Quarterly* 66 (1985): 296–309.

Neckerman, Kathryn M. and Joleen Kirschenman. "Hiring Strategies, Racial Bias, and Inner-City Workers." *Social Problems* 38, no. 4 (1991): 433–447.

Newman, Katherine. *No Shame in My Game: The Working Poor in the Inner City.* New York: Knopf and the Russell Sage Foundation, 1999.

O'Regan, Katherine M. and John M. Quigley. "Spacial Isolation and Welfare Recipients: What Do We Know?" Working Paper No. W99-03. Berkeley, CA: Program on Housing and Urban Policy, 1999.

Ong, Paul M. "Work and Car Ownership among Welfare Recipients." *Social Work Research* 20, no. 4 (1996): 255–262.

Ong, Paul M. "Car Ownership and Welfare-to-Work." *Journal of Policy Analysis and Management* 21 (2002): 255–268.

Ong, Paul M. and Douglas Miller. "Spatial and Transportation Mismatch in Los Angeles." *Journal of Planning Education and Research* 25, no. 1 (2005): 43–56.

Raphael, Steven and Michael Stoll. "Can Boosting Minority Car-Ownership Rates Narrow Inter-Racial Employment Gaps?" *Brookings-Wharton Papers on Urban Affairs* 2 (2001): 99–137.

Roder, Anne and Scott Scrivner. *Seeking a Sustainable Journey to Work: Findings from the National Bridges to Work Demonstration.* Philadelphia, PA: Public/Private Ventures, 2005.

Rosenbloom, Sandra. *Reverse Commute Transportation: Emerging Provider Roles.* Washington, DC: Urban Mass Transportation Administration, U.S. Department of Transportation, 1992.

Sanchez, Thomas. "The Connection between Public Transit and Employment: The Cases of Portland and Atlanta." *Journal of the American Planning Association* 65, no. 3 (1999): 284–296.

Schweitzer, Lisa and Brian Taylor. "Just Pricing: The Distributional Effects of Congestion Pricing and Sales Taxes." *Transportation* 35 (2008): 797–812.

Shen, Qing. "Location Characteristics of Inner-City Neighborhoods and Employment Accessibility of Low-Wage Workers." *Environment and Planning B* 25 (1998): 345–365.

Shen, Qing. "A Spatial Analysis of Job Openings and Access in a US Metropolitan Area." *Journal of the American Planning Association* 67, no. 1 (2001): 53–68.

Stoll, Michael A. *Job Sprawl and the Spatial Mismatch Between Blacks and Jobs.* Washington, DC: Brookings Institution Press, 2005.

Taylor, Brian D. and Paul M. Ong. "Spatial Mismatch or Automobile Mismatch—an Examination of Race, Residence, and Commuting in U.S. Metropolitan Areas." *Urban Studies* 32, no. 9 (1995): 1453–1473.

Turner, Margery Austin, Michael Fix, and Raymond J. Struyk. *Opportunities Denied, Opportunities Diminished: Racial Discrimination in Hiring.* Washington, DC: Urban Institute Press, 1991.

Waldinger, Roger. *Still the Promised City? African Americans and New Immigrants in Postindustrial New York.* Cambridge, MA: Harvard University Press, 1996.

Weinberg, Bruce A. "Testing the Spatial Mismatch Hypothesis using Inter-City Variations in Industrial Composition." *Regional Science & Urban Economics* 34, no. 5 (2004): 505–533.

12 The Geography of Opportunity

A progressive coalition called Six Wins, including some 30 social justice, faith, public health, and environmental organizations, emerged to oppose the MTC/ABAG regional sustainability plan. Public Advocates, a law firm that specializes in fair housing, was one of the most vocal opponents, fighting the overconcentration of new growth in Priority Development Areas (PDA), which could create displacement pressures, as well as the insufficient provision of affordable housing in "high-opportunity" suburban neighborhoods. Six Wins won some concessions during the environmental review process, including a plan to incentivize cities to build affordable housing near transit. But funds are too limited to build more than a handful of units, and MTC/ABAG did not shift any of the planned affordable housing to the suburbs per the Six Wins request.

The Six Wins concerns stem from the 45-year battle to integrate the suburbs. The passage of the 1968 Fair Housing Act supported efforts to fight discrimination in suburban housing markets, as well as the disproportionate siting of publicly funded housing in minority-dominated neighborhoods. Progress has been slow: paired-test studies reveal that discrimination still exists, and though neighborhood diversity is increasing in racial/ethnic terms, many concentrated poverty neighborhoods, particularly in cities, are still disproportionately minority. Given the challenge of enacting legislation to force suburban jurisdictions to facilitate the construction of more affordable housing (see Chapter 5), the battle has taken place primarily in two venues: the courts and HUD. Courts can penalize property owners for denying accommodation on the basis of race, as well as cities (in states with fair share housing such as California and New Jersey) for not zoning enough land for higher-density housing. HUD has site selection standards for the LIHTC tax credits that direct them outside areas with concentrations of racial minorities or low-income residents. But by focusing only on the location of disadvantage, not opportunity, these arguably fall short, as Tegeler et al. (2011) argue:

> An alternative allocation model that distributes tax credits equitably across a metropolitan area, using an opportunity-based profile of the region, will have the best chance to achieve civil rights goals and maximize housing choice in the LIHTC program.

The fundamental assumption underlying this fair housing strategy is that there is more opportunity in the suburbs than in cities. Yet, the MTC/ABAG approach, which indeed plans for more affordable housing in core areas (Chapter 4), reflects another set of concerns, specifically that living in the suburbs means taking on disproportionately high transportation costs, because of both the lack of transit alternatives and the higher level of VMT. The awareness of transportation costs stems from the pioneering work of the Center for Neighborhood Technology (CNT), which has mapped the variation in housing and transportation costs combined for all neighborhoods across the country.[1] CNT's analysis shows that primarily because of lower transportation costs and higher accessibility in core areas, they typically remain more affordable than the suburbs.

That MTC/ABAG proposes to concentrate growth, invest resources, and concentrate affordable housing in PDAs threatens to raise land prices and, if insufficient housing is built, spur displacement, as Six Wins suggests (see also Part I). Figure 12.1 shows the relationship between these PDAs (dark gray) and disadvantaged communities (in light gray, called "Communities of Concern" by MTC/ABAG).[2] There is considerable—but far from total—overlap. Yet, MTC/ABAG clearly recognizes the opportunity and accessibility that lies in these core neighborhoods.

In the halls of HUD headquarters, this is called the fair housing-gentrification debate. Returning to the trilogy of anti-poverty policies, it might also be called the dispersal versus community development approach. Which is worse, then, the isolation of the ghetto or the isolation of the suburb? It depends first on what opportunity means, then on where low-income households live relative to opportunity, and finally on how people experience opportunity in their neighborhoods.

What is "Opportunity"?

Opportunities are circumstances that allow us to thrive and succeed in life, typically by helping us change or advance in an endeavor. In the U.S. context, opportunity is the American dream: regardless of origin or socioeconomic status, Americans should be able to achieve prosperity through hard work. This then creates a system of upward mobility: whatever economic status a family starts with, its children are able to move to a higher one.

Despite this expectation, there is relatively little intergenerational upward mobility in the United States, particularly relative to other countries, with even smaller gains for African Americans than for whites (Corak 2013; Hertz 2005). There is a correlation of 0.47 between the earnings of fathers and sons in the United States, as compared to 0.15 in Denmark (a zero correlation would mean that there was no relationship and thus total intergenerational mobility) (Gould 2012). This suggests remarkable stability in economic status, perhaps due to increases in income inequality (Corak 2013).

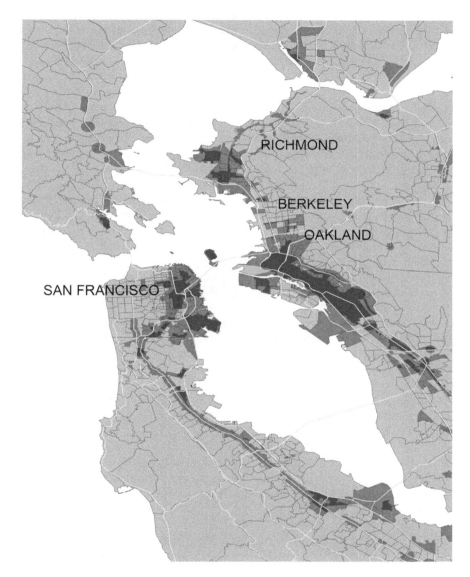

Figure 12.1 Location of existing Communities of Concern (light gray) and proposed
PDAs (dark gray)

Source: Association of Bay Area Governments, http://geocommons.com/maps/199657

Living in a particular neighborhood can affect access to opportunity and thus upward mobility. In particular, concentrations of poverty can create neighborhood effects (Jencks and Mayer 1990). Once the area becomes a high-poverty neighborhood, average educational attainment levels decrease and teenage pregnancy and high school dropout rates may increase dramatically (due to both changes for existing residents and the characteristics of new residents).[3] Neighborhoods can affect economic outcomes through several different mechanisms (Sharkey 2013). They may shape what school a child attends and what other social institutions are available for assistance. They shape access to amenities and resources such as parks and jobs. They can affect the extent and types of contacts in a social network. And, at the most basic level, they determine exposure to hazards such as toxics and crime.

The type of neighborhood also helps explain life trajectories (Datcher 1982). Until recently, the evidence had been quite mixed because of the challenges of compiling a data set that follows families over time.[4] But Patrick Sharkey shows more convincingly that the ghetto is inherited: if parents come from concentrated poverty neighborhoods, and their children do as well, the disadvantages of place seem to accumulate across generations (Sharkey 2013). In particular, living over generations in the ghetto reduces the total number of hours worked, as well as income and wealth. However, it is the family background that determines how much education a child gets. Interestingly, the neighborhood does not so much hinder an individual from moving up as it makes downward mobility much more likely; the gains of one generation are not passed to the next.

This adds up to what Galster and Killen (1995: 10) call the "geography of metropolitan opportunity," or the distribution of markets and institutions across space, and the resultant ability of households to live in the locations of their preference, in terms of housing and labor markets, services, educational systems, and social networks. This distribution does not by itself constitute opportunity, but interacts with local residents' perceptions, as well as their ability to acquire information about these opportunities (e.g., through social networks or simply firsthand experience). Thus, opportunity cannot be mapped, because it is constructed by individuals.

From a policy perspective, the key question about opportunity is whether a positive change in a neighborhood, intentional or not, will positively impact outcomes. Looking at neighborhoods where socioeconomic conditions are improving most rapidly, Sharkey finds that what is changing most significantly for existing residents is earnings and income, not education or social outcomes. The mechanism this seems to work through is the influx of immigrants, making the neighborhood more ethnically diverse. Sharkey's work does not investigate how this process works: it could be that immigrants bring new businesses or form new networks with existing residents, but it could also be about role modeling or even a new competitive dynamic in the neighborhood. But what is interesting is that the greatest success for these core neighborhoods is in creating economic opportunity—in direct contrast to suburban dispersal policies, which fail to improve economic circumstances even though they may improve education or social outcomes after the move to the suburbs.

The challenge, however, is identifying the geography that matters, both in terms of distribution of opportunity and information. Most studies use a very crude proxy, the census tract, to study the neighborhood. Tracts can consist of many city blocks or, in the country, square miles, and thus often include multiple neighborhoods. Though proximity to institutions, jobs, amenities, networks, and social disorganization clearly matters, it is not clear which of these factors matters most. More importantly, it is unclear whether their impact is transmitted at a highly local scale (the house next door), or more of the district level (several adjacent census tracts), or even higher (the county). Measuring distance from opportunity or disorder is not like calculating risks from a toxic spill. If the grocery store or childcare center is in the next tract over, rather than down the street, quality of life and life chances will not change. On the other hand, gun violence on the block can dramatically reshape life outcomes.

Where are the Poor People Today?

As poverty has grown nationally in the 2000s, it has also increased in both cities and suburbs, and in concentrated poverty neighborhoods—but not evenly across and between metropolitan areas. In general, poverty is growing fastest in the suburbs, but their poverty rate remains just over half of the urban poverty rate. When poverty rates change, it is not because of the poor being pushed from one place to another; instead, poverty in both city and suburb follows metropolitan and national fortunes (Cooke 2010; Cooke and Marchant 2006; Jargowsky 1996; Pendall et al. 2011).

Suburbs tend to be more resilient than cities for several reasons. One is that communities are able to absorb poverty that is relatively low and not spatially concentrated. Suburban municipalities, schools, and voluntary associations have enough capacity to cope when just 12 percent of families are impoverished. It is where neighborhood poverty rates persist at 30 percent or higher that systems break down. Another reason is that because suburban poverty is dominated by immigrants, its communities have more coping mechanisms (Pendall 2011b). Not only do immigrant groups rely on networks of extended family, but also they do not experience as much racial discrimination as have African Americans historically. Another explanation is that many suburbs continue to exclude low-income households, whether through zoning or discouraging the construction of affordable housing.

Much research on suburban poverty is problematic because of the limitations of the city-suburb boundaries defined in census data. The most well-known research, by the Brookings Institution, designates almost all places not named in the Census official metropolitan area name as suburbs—meaning that older cities such as White Plains, Gary, and Berkeley are grouped along with Tukwila, Washington, and Lakewood, Ohio (Kneebone and Berube 2013). At the same time, many cities, such as Jacksonville, Florida, are actually more suburban in character (Cooke and Marchant 2006). Including many different types of places in one category turns suburban poverty into a fuzzy concept (Pendall 2011a). With increasingly dilapidated infrastructure and housing, inner-ring suburbs likely resemble core impoverished neighborhoods, but a simple city-suburb dichotomy cannot capture this dynamic. In fact, as shown in Chapter 10, eliminating poverty concentrations means moving from city to suburb in Philadelphia, but may mean moving from suburb to city in the Bay Area.

In general, concentrated poverty neighborhoods remain the biggest policy concern, with over half (22 million) of the country's impoverished residents (Pendall et al. 2011). The poorer a region gets, the more of its residents live in concentrated poverty neighborhoods; but this growth is occurring mostly in the country's weaker markets in the middle of the country. The inhabitants of concentrated poverty neighborhoods have been constant over time: over two-thirds of African-American families living in concentrated poverty neighborhoods are descended from families who lived in similar neighborhoods in the 1970s (Sharkey 2013). Moreover, the areas of racially concentrated poverty from the 1970s have mostly persisted over the decades, losing population and becoming even more impoverished (Pendall et al. 2011). On the other hand, high-poverty neighborhoods are increasingly racially and ethnically diverse: over one-fifth of these tracts have a mix of African-American, Latino, and white non-Latino residents (ibid).[5]

Where is Opportunity?

There has long been a perception that the suburbs offer greater opportunity, with advantages in terms of employment growth, school quality, and safety from violence (Dreier, Mollenkopf, and Swanstrom 2004). However, the suburbs of the metropolitan inner ring are increasingly struggling with the growth of poverty and loss of tax revenue. And, as CNT's work has shown, cities continue to outperform suburbs in terms of accessibility and infrastructure.

Opportunity mapping is one way to show the location of favorable conditions throughout a region. Several regions have developed regional equity atlases that analyze the accessibility of amenities and opportunities across a region relative to concentrations of disadvantage. The Kirwan Institute for the Study of Race and Ethnicity has developed an approach that many regions have used to map either their "impediments" or "conduits" to opportunity (Tegeler et al. 2011: 5). For "Economics and Mobility Opportunity," the indicator averages three economic conduits and two impediments—jobs, commute time, availability of transit, unemployment rate, and rate of dependence on public assistance—to come up with a composite measure of opportunity.[6] "Educational Opportunity" is a composite indicator of class size, test scores, participation in free school lunch programs, and adult educational attainment. "Housing and Neighborhood Opportunity" maps a composite of home value, vacancy rate, gross rent, poverty level, crime level, toxic hazards, and open space.

But because the comprehensive opportunity map is an average of several averages, with all the indicators weighted the same, many distinctions are washed out: opportunity is high both in most cities and nearby affluent suburbs, and generally anywhere near a highway corridor. Economic opportunity is in job centers, educational opportunity is located across the suburbs, and neighborhood opportunity is in the affluent city core and outer suburbs. It seems that nearly any location will offer some advantages for the poor. This finding runs counter to the assumption underlying the dispersalist viewpoint (Chapter 10), which argues for deconcentrating the poor via housing choice vouchers to low-poverty suburbs.

Maps may actually fall short in this case. First, there is no sense of scale. Locating next door to a toxic waste site can be harmful, hindering the ability to thrive and move up in the world. Locating next door to a major corporation is unlikely to affect life chances, because employment opportunity rarely arises through mere proximity. Indicators of opportunity function at multiple geographies, from the parcel, to the block, to the neighborhood, to the district, to the jurisdiction, to the county, to the metropolitan area.

Indicators also may not measure what they purport to. Showing disadvantage gives no sense of the quality of services. Students attend schools in large school districts, not necessarily in the neighborhood. We know that open space matters, but the city park has one kind of meaning while the neighborhood public space has another.

Chapter 11, "Unpacking Accessibility," suggests another way to conceptualize opportunity. Labor market accessibility, in particular, means knowing the right people, so that when jobs open up, or informal work is available, jobseekers are connected. Once the connection is made, the new worker may need a ride, or to borrow a car, in order to access the opportunity. What if we conceptualized and mapped accessibility in terms of social networks, instead of the location of opportunity?

Such a map is likely to be nearly impossible, since some opportunity and/or information comes via the strong ties in the neighborhoods (e.g., an offer to look after the kids), while the information most useful in the job search is most likely to come from the weak-tie network contact located in another neighborhood than the one next door. But the location of the means of access is likely to be more important than the location of the "opportunity" itself. How information about opportunity is transmitted, as well as the perception of that opportunity, cannot be mapped. But if a picture were possible, it would be even more mixed than the equity atlases are showing, with neighborhoods in the city likely outperforming those in suburbs.

Most importantly, there is a geography of opportunity, but neighborhoods matter in a different way than we have thought. Cities and regions provide opportunity, or circumstances that help us thrive. Within a city, it matters little whether a family lives across the street from a park in an area with median income at 120 percent of the regional income, or a few blocks away with median income at 80 percent of the regional income. But neighborhoods do matter in life chances when they contain concentrations of poverty, with all the challenges that creates for daily life. We can help these places by reinvesting in them, particularly if we consider how we can improve access to *people*. An example of how this can work comes from the Family Independence Initiative in Oakland, a nonprofit that helps entire families develop social support systems and peer networks to reinforce goals of self-sufficiency (through employment and savings). The Initiative calls these "opportunity platforms," or investments in the initiative of low-income families in terms of accessing networks and resources. Thus, these investments in places facilitate access to people, who then improve accessibility to opportunity.

Community Development for the Twenty-First Century

Chapters 10 and 11 demonstrate the challenges of scaling up the dispersal and mobility approaches. Thus, here we return to the idea of helping people in places, or community development, as the most viable approach to regional equity. Community development is a collaborative, collective, self-renewing action taken by a group of people to enhance the long-term social, economic, and environmental assets of a place to which they are tied.[7] Typically, in the United States this takes the form not of self-help, but of local organizations acting with federal, state, or city support. These place-based approaches have just as mixed a history as the other strategies do, in part because they have never been fully funded, but also because of the challenge of improving outcomes simultaneously for both a place and the people that live within it.

People versus Place in Community Development

As many have observed, much urban policy has seemingly been dichotomous, focused on either place or people, improving concentrated poverty neighborhoods or enabling people to leave them behind via dispersal or mobility (Crane and Manville 2008; Sharkey 2013). The traditional argument against what John Kain and Joe Persky (1967) called "gilding the ghetto" is that sending resources to racially concentrated areas of poverty is not only an ineffective band-aid approach, but also acquiesces to racism. Moreover, residents may actually prefer to leave the neighborhood. Still, proponents of community development argue for giving people a realistic choice to stay (Shiffman and Motley 1990).

The choices of low-income communities are not well understood. When they do move, are they pulled to other neighborhoods, or pushed out due to disinvestment? A move may reflect a choice to improve location or house quality, or a coping strategy for a financial or family challenge. One of the few studies to track residential mobility, the Urban Institute study of the Annie E. Casey Foundation's Making Connections Initiative (a comprehensive community development approach), found high levels of neighborhood churning due almost equally to one positive and one negative cause—upward mobility and housing instability (Coulton, Theodos, and Turner 2009). Whatever the reason, movers tended to relocate nearby, due, in part, to attachment to the neighborhood.[8] To the extent that the neighborhoods benefited from place-based interventions, the impact was on the upwardly mobile movers; little changed economically for the stayers.

Ironically, what the Making Connections experiment suggests is that when we think we are helping places, we may be assisting people to leave, and when we help people leave, they may actually move just to the next neighborhood over. Would they prefer to move to the suburbs if they could? In the overall population, there is a clear preference for the privacy that single-family houses provide. But this preference is somewhat weaker among low-income families: ethnographic research finds that less than half would prefer to move from their urban neighborhood to less-dense areas (Chapple 2000; Makarewicz 2013). The dispersal experience has also shown the strength of place attachment, particularly when mobility is involuntary. In MTO, given the chance to move from the housing projects, just 25 percent chose to leave (Goering 2003).

When low-income residents do choose to move to lower-density neighborhoods, the primary motive is not the pull of opportunity, but a push factor, the lack of a sense of safety and the desire for a calmer neighborhood (Makarewicz 2013). The poor are disproportionately likely to choose a neighborhood (when choice is available!) based on proximity to friends and relatives, good schools, and low rent, rather than convenience to work—in part because accessibility comes through connections to people (Smith 2010).

Thus, as the Making Connections Initiative shows, even if living in a concentrated poverty neighborhood hurts life chances, it does not mean that policy intervention in place will fix the problem. As Margery Turner (2013) writes:

> Families move back and forth across neighborhood boundaries; break apart and re-form; send their kids to out-of-boundary schools; and engage with religious, cultural, or family networks that transcend place. Increasingly, we're realizing that anti-poverty and family-strengthening initiatives have to be "place conscious" but not myopically "place based."

But enacting such a place-conscious strategy would likely require changing the rules of the development game and the neighborhood scale of community development.

Changing the Rules of the Game

Government investment underlies community prosperity (Galster 2012; Sharkey 2013). The rules of the game have supported suburban prosperity, at the federal government level by underwriting road infrastructure and home ownership, and at the local level by facilitating the unequal funding and provision of services and education. These rules make it less risky to develop new property on the periphery than to infill the core, and also encourage the segregation of the affluent into their own communities. This then creates a self-fulfilling prophecy, where rules set up to support a strong market then suppress other markets from emerging.

In Detroit, George Galster (2012) has shown how local governments, supported by the state and national regulatory and tax codes, have encouraged oversupply of new suburban housing, which then has encouraged the mobility of Detroit firms and residents with the means to leave—and thus the gradual abandonment of the urban core. Neighborhood revitalization has little chance of success in the face of these larger economic and regulatory forces.

What would investment in city prosperity look like? Instead of funding roads, it might support a variety of travel modes. Instead of underwriting single-family homes, it might support diverse types of rental housing; asset building might occur through financial strategies rather than real estate. In addition to subsidizing education, it might invest in various aspects of social organization, including community-based organizations, after-school programs, open space, community policing, and so forth. This kind of *institutional* density then helps to support local activity patterns and increase interaction with a diverse social network that can lead to jobs.

Rethinking Scale in Community Development

Both cities and suburbs are becoming much more diverse—not so much through policy, but demographic change—and opportunity is not so clearly divided between city and suburb. Thus, investing in places of need becomes more of a universal approach, rather than targeting (and stigmatizing) certain types of areas. This suggests a need to rethink the scale of community development, to target places and subregions, rather than neighborhoods.

Long ago, in a study of perceptions of Los Angeles done for the City Planning Commission, Kevin Lynch (1976) showed how Latinos and African Americans exhibit the least spatial familiarity with the region. One way to help disadvantaged urban residents overcome constricted activity patterns is to centralize the location of retail, services, and recreational uses, rather than providing them in each neighborhood (i.e., rethinking the scale of diversity for a complete community) (as described in Chapters 4 and 5).

Institutional density is particularly lacking in the suburbs, suggesting the need for investment. In general, services for the poor are more plentiful in wealthy urban areas than in high-poverty areas, and there is a high degree of spatial mismatch between the location of social service nonprofits and the poor populations that are most in need of services (Allard 2008; Joassart-Marcelli and Wolch 2003; Kneebone and Berube 2013; Reckhow and Weir 2011). But this does not necessarily call for distributing institutional capacity evenly throughout the region. If intermediaries are effective, they can be centralized in location and regional in scope. The key is to ensure first that these intermediaries are not concentrated in disadvantaged neighborhoods, but located throughout the region in transit-accessible locations, and second that a diverse set of providers continues to meet social service needs.[9]

One example of nonprofit expansion to the regional scale is the affordable housing industry (see Chapter 5). In the Bay Area, when builders ran out of affordable sites in the urban core, they shifted to the suburbs. But the expansion of the network in either case did not occur in a vacuum; rather, it was induced by entrepreneurial county government officials, supported by suburban redevelopment agencies obligated by the state to fund affordable housing development.

Other innovations are occurring in regional service provision. For instance, in Montgomery County, Maryland, a partnership between public and nonprofit sectors launched the Neighborhood Opportunity Network, an initiative that reaches out to residents to raise awareness and create connections to social services. A similar example is the United Way SparkPoint Centers, regional financial education centers that also connect clients to a network of county social service providers and legal services. Interestingly, this new regional infrastructure is emerging without a new federal effort, such as the Model Cities program from which so many urban nonprofits originated, in part because of county government structures already in place for social service delivery.

Towards a Place-Conscious Anti-Poverty Strategy

Whatever form it took, a program to invest in places, both city and suburb, would essentially level the playing field. With high-quality environment and services providing the same floor across regions, families would experience a greater level of security from which to make life choices. Part of this security would come from increased accessibility to opportunity: not from locating next door to it, but from joining a support system that facilitates access. This system thus integrates the development, dispersal, and mobility approaches: the options exist, but the choice is up to the family.

In a review of anti-poverty policies, economist Sheldon Danziger (2007) argues that the War on Poverty was based on the idea that there is a positive relationship between economic growth and poverty—an assumption that no longer held true after 1973 because of rising earnings inequality. Policies for the twenty-first century, particularly those focused on education and training, need to shift to address this structural inequality.

Policies to deal with concentrated poverty suffer from obsolescent assumptions as well. In the 1960s, the suburbs were new and apparently overflowing with opportunity, while cities were declining. Struck by the vivid contrast, we tried a variety of approaches to mix the disadvantaged with opportunity. But the suburbs were not thriving because of the proximity of families to opportunity, but because of inflows of capital. And access to those opportunities was facilitated more by social structures than physical infrastructure.

It is by intervening primarily in these arenas that we can have an impact on poverty in place. A government commitment to investment, focusing on both quality of life and social supports, offers sustainability. The structural problems of capitalism will remain, but these cannot be the target of an urban policy, or it will undoubtedly fail. Where it might make a difference, though, is in creating real accessibility to opportunity—through people.

Notes

1. Housing costs are typically considered to be affordable at no more than 30 percent of the household budget (including utilities). CNT argues that combined housing and transportation costs should comprise no more than 45 percent of a household's budget (www.htaindex.org).
2. These are census tracts that include disproportionate shares of minorities, low-income households, low English proficiency residents, no-car households, seniors, persons with a disability, female heads of household with children, and/or cost-burdened renters.
3. Studies from the 1980s and 1990s typically defined concentrated poverty neighborhoods as those with 40 percent or more of their residents in poverty. The threshold used today is generally 30 percent. For the original studies of neighborhood effects, see Corcoran et al. (1987), Crane (1991), and Datcher (1982).
4. See Sharkey (2013). Chetty et al. (2013) compiled such a longitudinal data set, showing that segregation and local income distribution make a difference in intergenerational mobility outcomes, but they do not specifically analyze the neighborhood scale.
5. We should pause here to note that we do not actually know how many concentrated poverty neighborhoods there are at this point, because the data are no longer reliable. In 2005, the U.S. Census Bureau shifted from collecting a large sample of detailed data at the tract level in the decennial census, to collecting much smaller samples each year. Because of the small sample size, most data points come with very large margins of error, making it nearly impossible to track issues such as concentrated poverty. So, for instance, for all 44 concentrated poverty neighborhoods in the Bay Area, sample sizes are too small to come up with reliable estimates, and the data must be viewed with caution. This calculation is based on the coefficient of variation; almost all values fall between 12 percent and 40 percent, the category typically considered "medium reliability."
6. To calculate the index, Kirwan researchers normalize each variable using z-scores and then average the components. "None of the indicators or categories of data are weighted in the index, reflecting the need for strong structures environments in every area represented within the index."
7. I am indebted to my History, Theory, and Practice of Community Development class, Fall 2008, for this definition.
8. Anne Martin's dissertation (2012) on relocation after foreclosure found the same phenomenon: most foreclosed households relocate less than five miles away.
9. Although the evidence certainly points to the importance of "bridging" ties, particularly for African Americans, no studies have compared the effectiveness of concentrated versus dispersed intermediaries. The evaluation of Jobs-Plus, an employment and training program within public housing developments, suggests positive effects for concentrated intermediaries, particularly on earnings (Bloom et al. 2005). However, that program was unique because it included financial incentives to work in the form of continued housing subsidies.

References

Allard, Scott W. *Out of Reach: Place, Poverty, and the New American Welfare State.* New Haven, CT: Yale University Press, 2008.

Bloom, Howard S., James A. Riccio, Nandita Verma, and Johanna Walter. "Promoting Work in Public Housing. The Effectiveness of Jobs-Plus. Final Report." New York: Manpower Development Research Corporation, 2005.

Chapple, Karen. *Paths to Employment: The Role of Social Networks in the Job Search for Women on Welfare in San Francisco.* Ph.D. dissertation, University of California, Berkeley, 2000.

Chetty, Raj, Nathan Hendren, Patrick Kline, and Emmanuel Saez. "The Economic Impacts of Tax Expenditures: Evidence from Spatial Variation across the US." Unpublished paper, Harvard University and UC Berkeley, 2013.

Cooke, Thomas J. "Residential Mobility of the Poor and the Growth of Poverty in Inner-Ring Suburbs." *Urban Geography* 31, no. 2 (2010): 179–193.

Cooke, Thomas J. and Sarah Marchant. "The Changing Intrametropolitan Location of High-Poverty Neighbourhoods in the US, 1990–2000." *Urban Studies* 43, no. 11 (2006): 1971–1989.

Corak, Miles. "Income Inequality, Equality of Opportunity, and Intergenerational Mobility." *The Journal of Economic Perspectives* 27, no. 3 (2013): 79–102.

Corcoran, Mary, Roger Gordon, Deborah Laren, and Gary Solon. "Intergenerational Transmission of Education, Income, and Earnings." Unpublished paper, Ann Arbor, MI: University of Michigan, 1987.

Coulton, Claudia, Brett Theodos, and Margery A. Turner. *Family Mobility and Neighborhood Change: New Evidence and Implications for Community Initiatives.* Washington, DC: Urban Institute Press, 2009.

Crane, Jonathan. "The Epidemic Theory of Ghettos and Neighborhood Effects on Dropping out and Teenage Childbearing." *American Journal of Sociology* 96 (1991): 1226–1259.

Crane, Randall and Michael Manville. "People or Place? Revisiting the Who versus the Where of Urban Development." *Land Lines* 20, no. 3 (2008): 2–7.

Danziger, Sheldon H. "Fighting Poverty Revisited: What Did Researchers Know 40 Years Ago? What Do We Know Today?" *Focus* 25, no. 1 (2007): 3–11.

Datcher, Linda P. "Effects of Community and Family Background on Achievement." *The Review of Economics and Statistics* 64, no. 1 (1982): 32–41.

Dreier, Peter, John Mollenkopf, and Todd Swanstrom. *Place Matters: Metropolitics for the Twenty-First Century.* Lawrence, KS: University Press of Kansas, 2004.

Galster, George. *Driving Detroit: The Quest for Respect in the Motor City.* Philadelphia, PA: University of Pennsylvania Press, 2012.

Galster, George and Sean Killen. "Geography of Metropolitan Opportunity: A Reconnaissance and Conceptual Framework." *Housing Policy Debate* 6, no. 1 (1995): 7–43.

Goering, John. "Comments on Future Research and Housing Policy." In *Choosing a Better Life? Evaluating the Moving to Opportunity Social Experiment,* edited by John M. Goering and Judith D. Feins, 383–407. Washington, DC: Urban Insitute Press, 2003.

Gould, Elise, "U.S. Lags Behind Peer Countries in Mobility." Washington, DC: Economic Policy Institute, 2012. Accessed December 5, 2013. www.epi.org/publication/usa-lags-peer-countries-mobility.

Hertz, Tom. "Rags, Riches and Race: The Intergenerational Economic Mobility of Black and White Families in the United States." In *Unequal Chances: Family Background and Economic Success*, edited by Samuel Bowles, Herbert Gintis, and Melissa Osborne, 165–191. New York: Russell Sage and Princeton University Press, 2005.

Jargowsky, Paul. *Poverty and Place: Ghettos, Barrios, and the American City*. New York: Russell Sage Foundation, 1996.

Jencks, Christoper and Susan E. Mayer. "Residential Segregation, Job Proximity, and Black Job Opportunities." In *Inner-City Poverty in the U.S.*, edited by Laurence Lynn and Michaell McGeary, 187–222. Washington, DC: National Academy Press, 1990.

Joassart-Marcelli, Pascale and Jennifer R. Wolch. "The Intrametropolitan Geography of Poverty and the Nonprofit Sector in Southern California." *Nonprofit and Voluntary Sector Quarterly* 32, no. 1 (2003): 70–96.

Kain, John F. and Joseph Persky. *Alternatives to the Gilded Ghetto*. Cambridge, MA: Harvard University Press, 1967.

Kneebone, Elizabeth and Alan Berube. *Confronting Suburban Poverty in America*. Washington, DC: Brookings Institution Press, 2013.

Lynch, Kevin. *Managing the Sense of a Region*. Cambridge, MA: MIT Press, 1976.

Makarewicz, Carrie. *Examining the Influence of the Urban Environment on Parent's Time, Energy, and Resources for Engagement in their Children's Learning*. Ph.D. dissertation, University of California, Berkeley, 2013.

Martin, Anne J. *After Foreclosure: The Social and Spatial Reconstruction of Everyday Lives in the San Francisco Bay*. Ph.D. dissertation, University of California, Berkeley, 2012.

Pendall, Rolf. "Suburbanizing Poverty: Fuzzy Concepts, Fuzzy Policy," *MetroTrends*, 2011a. Accessed December 2, 2013. http://blog.metrotrends.org/2011/06/suburbanizing-poverty-fuzzy-concepts-fuzzy-policy.

Pendall, Rolf. "W(h)ither the 'Fringe Suburb'?" *MetroTrends*, 2011b. Accessed December 2, 2013. http://blog.metrotrends.org/2011/11/whither-fringe-suburb.

Pendall, Rolf, Elizabeth Davies, Lesley Freiman, and Rob Pitingilo. A *Lost Decade: Neighborhood Poverty and the Urban Crisis of the 2000s*. Washington, DC: Joint Center for Political and Economic Studies, 2011.

Reckhow, Sarah and Margaret Weir. "Building a Resilient Social Safety Net." In *Urban and Regional Policy and its Effects Vol. 4*, edited by Margaret Weir, Howard Wial, Harold Wolman, and Nancy Pindus, 275–323. Washington, DC: Brookings Institution Press, 2012.

Sharkey, Patrick. *Stuck in Place: Urban Neighborhoods and the End of Progress Toward Racial Equality*. Chicago, IL: University of Chicago Press, 2013.

Shiffman, Ronald and Susan Motley. *Comprehensive and Integrative Planning for Community Development*. New York: Community Development Research Center, 1990.

Smith, Janet L. "Integration: Solving the Wrong Problem." In *The Integration Debate: Competing Futures for American Cities*, edited by Chester Hartman and Gregory Squires, 229–246. New York: Routledge, 2010.

Tegeler, Philip, Henry Korman, Jason Reece, and Megan Haberle. *Opportunity and Location in Federally Subsidized Housing Programs: A New Look at HUD's Site & Neighborhood Standards as Applied to the Low Income Housing Tax Credit*. Washington, DC: Poverty & Race Research Action Council, 2011.

Turner, Margery. "Lessons Learned from the Making Connections Initiative." *MetroTrends*, 2013. Accessed May 20, 2013. http://blog.metrotrends.org/2013/05/lessons-learned-making-connections-initiative.

Conclusion to Part III

By all indications, poverty will only increase in coming years, as the country adjusts to globalization, technology, and internal political conflict. But as the chapters in this section show, our policies that attempt to connect the poor to housing and jobs have largely failed to meet their own goals. All operate under the assumption that improving physical proximity to opportunity will remedy poverty, and that opportunity consists primarily of the availability of traditional jobs and education. In this view, measuring and mapping opportunity across a region, in relation to the location of the low-income, should help determine strategies for redistribution. But as Chapter 12 demonstrates, proximity is not solving the problem for either the concentrated urban or suburban poor; even with opportunity available, the poor cannot access it without family and institutional support systems. Even if dispersal programs were effective, Chapter 10 shows how they are impossible to implement at scale. Chapter 11 illustrates the intricate survival systems of the poor—the role of both strong and weak ties in helping the poor navigate both the formal and informal economies. Opportunity is thus not just the existence of nearby assets and services, but the resources families have to thrive.

This adds up to a need for a renewed investment in place, beyond the singular focus on affordable housing of the regional equity advocates in the Bay Area and elsewhere. But this time around, federal money need not narrowly support highways and districts of single-family homes, or target impoverished neighborhoods. These mistakes in the United States should inform development elsewhere. Funding instead could subsidize a diverse array of travel modes and housing types. As suggested in Melbourne, this might mean bringing affordable multifamily housing to the exurbs, but in "20-minute neighborhoods," rather than isolation. In Shanghai, dispersing the urban poor to the suburbs may be creating challenges for job accessibility, and regional planning will need to create more of an integrated network of transit-oriented corridors (Cervero and Day 2008).

Community development, education, and health expenditures might strategically support interventions that provide more opportunities within communities (though not necessarily neighborhoods) to build social networks. And unlike interventions in the market to increase built density and create economic development, this set of policies would be effective equally in weak and strong market regions. Just as in the Bay Area, South Transdanubia is planning to deal with the lack of services in remote areas by supporting centers that integrate various services on-site.

Regions can address social inclusion not just via equitable facilities location, but also at a more basic level, through how their plan expresses the vision for the region. Plan Araucanía stands out for how it promotes social inclusion, calling explicitly for avoiding social polarization through strategies that strengthen personal and collective autonomy, social capital, responsible participation, and respect for human dignity (Regional Government of La Araucanía 2010). Other plans, such as those in Istanbul and Shanghai, have little vision for inclusion, and in reality these metros are displacing massive numbers of low-income residents from the urban core. They have much to learn from the cities that are successfully upgrading slums (Belsky et al. 2013; OECD 2008).

Much anti-poverty policy is not within the purview of regional sustainability planning, in any country. Whether focused on ecological systems, smart growth, or human development, regional authorities rarely have access to all the types of government support necessary for an investment in place. In most countries, in fact, both social and spatial development programs are even more centralized than in the United States. Ultimately, what will be necessary to make this happen will be community organizing, to put pressure on politicians, and multilevel governance, to access resources vertically from state and federal governments (Weir and Rongerude 2007). To date, with the possible exception of some European countries and U.S. regions, regional planning processes have failed to incorporate significant public participation. Ultimately, achieving more equitable development will depend on developing more participatory democratic processes for regional planning.

References

Belsky, Eric S., Nicholas DuBroff, Daniel McCue, Christina Harris, Shelagh McCartney, and Jennifer Molinsky. *Advancing Inclusive and Sustainable Urban Development: Correcting Planning Failures and Connecting Communities to Capital*. Cambridge, MA: Joint Center for Housing Studies of Harvard University, 2013.

Cervero, Robert and Jennifer Day. "Residential Relocation and Commuting Behavior in Shanghai, China: The Case for Transit Oriented Development." *UC Berkeley Center for Future Urban Transport: A Volvo Center of Excellence*, April 1, 2008. Accessed January 9, 2014. http://escholarship.org/uc/item/0dk1s0q5.

Organisation for Economic Cooperation and Development. *OECD Territorial Reviews*. Istanbul, Turkey: OECD, 2008. Accessed January 25, 2014. http://browse.oecdbookshop.org/oecd/pdfs/free/0408051e.pdf.

Regional Government of La Araucanía. *Final Report: Regional Development Strategy 2010–2022*. 2010. Accessed January 14, 2014. www.sernam.cl/sistema_gt/sitio/integracion/sistema/archivos/file/pdf/a%C3%B1o%202010/erd%20IXregion.pdf.

Weir, Margaret and Jane Rongerude. *Multi-level Power and Progressive Regionalism*. Working Paper no. 15. Institute of Urban and Regional Development, 2007.

13 Conclusion: Towards a Just Regional Sustainability Planning

By the end of the twentieth century, urbanists had developed a sophisticated set of theories and tools to understand and foster diversity, economic development, and opportunity. Simultaneously, a new concern with creating development patterns that would be sustainable for future generations was arising globally. As regional sustainability planning has emerged around the world, many regions have looked to established practices to develop a new, inclusive regionalism.

But the targets have been moving, in the United States and around the world. Inequality and segregation are generally rising. The population is becoming much more diverse, both demographically and in terms of housing preferences. Jobs are dispersing and, at least in advanced industrialized countries, paying less. Yet, the role of family and social support systems in navigating this changing world remains as vital as ever.

The world that is evolving will increasingly value proximity, which will create new development pressure on regions' urban cores. Just as cities and regions are trying to prepare for millions of new residents, these pressures will translate into higher land prices and, potentially, more exclusion. As Chapter 2 demonstrated, most regional sustainability plans around the world are ill-prepared for the equitable development that will be needed. While rapidly reconfiguring cities to be more livable, we have failed to take into account the consequences for social equity. We need to open the front door to equity, before it is too late.

Much of the toolkit available to help places grow more dense and diverse—and regions more sustainable—was developed or refined at a time when inequality was declining, and the U.S./U.K. models of planning were dominant (Hall 2002). Tools for infill development, transit-oriented development, inclusionary and fair share housing, business incentives, mobility, and other such approaches were largely based on the assumption of an ever-expanding metropolis with a declining urban core in need of economic revitalization. The demand for suburban homes does continue unabated around the world, but at the same time, whether due to limits on urban expansion or the emergence of a new market, the gaze is turning back to the city. In the absence of significant new—and equitable—development, market pressures will create overcrowding and displacement.

How, then, might we reconfigure these tools for more equitable development? The policy solutions offered in the previous chapters suggest three basic types of approaches. Rather than a new toolkit, these approaches offer a reconceptualization of existing tools.

The first approach is to diversify strategies that have become too rigid. The regional core will need to grow via infill development, but in some places that will mean distributed density, rather than new centers. To retain high-quality jobs that are accessible, regions will also want to plan for low-density industrial land in addition to job centers in the region's core. Economic development and planning should support entrepreneurship and urban quality of life broadly rather than targeting specific places for firms to relocate. Given shifting work patterns, transportation planning needs to take the full array of activity patterns into account.

The second is to shift scales from the parcel, block, and neighborhood to the district, place, and region. Mixing uses at a micro scale is critical to make lively streets, but mixing will only work if policies at the district scale and above simultaneously make it possible for people from all walks of life to enjoy the livable city. Deliberately mixing income in a development has not proven successful, and income integration at the neighborhood scale may hinder the formation of the enclaves so helpful to community stability and mobility. Yet, preserving income diversity where it is occurring naturally is a key opportunity. The most achievable goal of income mixing is improving access to resources, but this need only be at the district scale or above. Social seams between neighborhoods may support income mixing as well or better than providing a diversity of housing types within a neighborhood, and can also provide the kind of institutional density that helps support life chances. Redeveloping sites and neighborhoods might spur revitalization, but is unlikely to create economic development without supportive policies at the macro scale. At the regional level, it will be important to consider the optimal location for industrial land from the perspective of greenhouse gas emissions reduction.

The third concept is value capture. The increase in property value due to public investment in transit, infrastructure, and urban regeneration is one of the unsung opportunities of urban development. Thus far, planners have mostly used value capture to help fund the capital costs of infrastructure or to finance city government as in Tehran (Madanipour 2011). Yet, in certain strong market areas, it might also serve a redistributive function, helping to subsidize affordable housing or even industrial space.

If we can reconfigure our regional planning to support more equitable development patterns, will they be just? The need to level the playing field creates an imperative for regional action; as a National Academy of Sciences committee on metropolitan governance framed it, "A lack of equal opportunity is thus in the most profound sense a 'moral' problem for Americans" (Altshuler et al. 1999). Yet, a growing body of work on the "just city" demonstrates the need to evaluate carefully whether regional strategies address systemic injustices.[1] As shown in Part III, though remedying unequal opportunity is obviously important to regional equity, it may not be possible to satisfy common aspirations and respect human dignity through policy that attempts to construct an even landscape of metropolitan opportunity by rearranging either opportunity or the population. Planners adopting liberal conceptions of justice embrace an abstract principle of equality at the expense of situated ethical judgment that appreciates individual circumstance (Campbell 2006).

Justice and Equitable Development for Regions

The work of John Rawls (1971) provides a useful framework to understand the characteristic beliefs, rooted in the twentieth-century liberal project, that undergird the policy solutions typically advocated for more equitable regions (O'Connor 2001). There are two components of Rawls' theory of justice that are particularly relevant to the equity regionalist argument: the "difference principle" and the idea of "primary goods."

The Difference Principle

In his second principle of justice (the difference principle), Rawls (1971: 72) argues that:

> Social and economic inequalities are to be arranged so that they are both (a) to the greatest expected benefit of the least advantaged and (b) attached to offices and positions open to all under conditions of fair equality of opportunity.

The idea of equality of opportunity is not just that "offices and positions" are open to all, but that all have the opportunity to acquire the skills necessary in order to achieve in a meritocracy. Rawls acknowledges that social and economic inequality is pervasive and does not suggest that the distribution of wealth and income should be equal, but that it should be to everyone's advantage. In remedying inequalities, maintaining some unequal distribution is justifiable, as long as it is to the benefit of all. In order to be just, the more fortunate can benefit disproportionately, so long as the condition of the least well-off improves relative to their previous state.

As in Rawls, the argument for spatial interventions, whether income mixing, neighborhood-based business incentives, or dispersal, starts from the position that the distribution of the economy across metropolitan areas is unjust. Economic restructuring reinforced by public policy exacerbated existing inequalities within metropolitan areas by the end of the twentieth century, with increasing concentrations of poverty in the inner city and affluence in the suburbs (Dreier, Mollenkopf, and Swanstrom 2004). Regionalists seek to establish a more just distribution by breaking up pockets of poverty, creating more housing choice in the suburbs, and revitalizing the old inner-city neighborhoods with an influx of businesses and upper-income residents. They are not so naive as to think this will fully remedy inequality, but they do expect the change to improve the condition of the least well-off by putting them in an environment rich with resources and opportunities; at a minimum, fair governance, coupled with less isolation from the mainstream, should level the playing field. If opportunity depends on the ability of individuals to acquire skills to succeed in the meritocracy, then where you live is key.

As shown in Part III, this strategy has not actually succeeded in providing more equality of opportunity, with the least advantaged all experiencing some improvement. Deliberate policies to mix incomes within the neighborhood are not meeting the intended goals for existing residents. Political constraints have prevented fair share housing programs from achieving their promise. Dispersal and mobility policies are not improving equality of opportunity. In the best case, dispersal policies have successfully helped families in severely disadvantaged neighborhoods, such as in Baltimore and Chicago, to move to residential neighborhoods with lower levels of poverty. But even so, direct benefits to the families are limited, perhaps in part because of the short-term nature of the programs: as Patrick Sharkey (2012: 134) writes, "a temporary change of scenery is unlikely to disrupt the effects of a family history of disadvantage." In other words, these policies are failing even to meet the Rawlsian condition of benefit to all, since life chances are not improving in the new neighborhoods relative to the former neighborhoods.

Primary Goods

In order to realize opportunity, individuals need equality in "primary goods." These are defined as the prerequisites, both social and natural, for rational individuals to achieve their life plans. Social goods include rights, liberties, and opportunities, which confer the capacity to realize goals, but also income and wealth. Natural goods include health, intelligence, and imagination. According to Rawls, these add up to self-respect: a sense of one's own value and confidence in one's ability to carry out one's life plan.

Traditionally, policies from fair housing, to infill development, to business incentives privileged the suburbs, believing that they offer more equality in primary goods than cities do. The suburbs not only improve access to opportunity, but also ostensibly offer a higher quality of life and better business climate (Dreier, Mollenkopf, and Swanstrom 2004). The quality of public services and schools is assumed to be better, neighborhoods are safer and friendlier, and the sense of community is greater; there is no spiral of decline that will hinder the acquisition of primary goods. Businesses also benefit from the lack of crime and the low cost of land. Thus, in many regions, plans preserve suburbs by directing new density elsewhere, while at the same time encouraging businesses to relocate from the urban core to the periphery.

This assumes, of course, that the suburbs do offer enhanced opportunities: that suburban schools are of high quality, jobs (both formal and informal) are plentiful and accessible, businesses can operate more efficiently, and social systems and networks are inclusive. In reality, the quality of life is deteriorating in the suburbs, particularly the places that open their doors to the poor (Kneebone and Berube 2013). As we have seen in Parts II and III, suburban relocation is often disruptive for both the urban poor and industrial businesses with strong ties to people, places, and firms in the urban core.

Alternative Conceptions of Justice

The ideas of equality of opportunity and choice underlie much of urban and regional policy, even if it has had little success at these goals. The psychological literature on values and economic class helps explain why pursuing equality of opportunity alone may not be the most just approach. Critics of urban renewal have shown how the experience of relocation can be traumatic for low-income residents (Fried 1966; Fullilove 2004). People strongly prefer stability to opportunity, given a choice between the status quo and uncertain future earnings (Hacker 2006).

Providing more choice may also not be the most equitable approach. The lower the income, the more choice is associated with fear, doubt, and difficulty: "While the upper and middle classes define freedom as choice, working-class Americans emphasize freedom from instability" (Schwartz, Markus, and Snibbe 2006). Where choices are overwhelming or where one feels unable to make educated choices on issues of importance, "more choices may not always mean more control" (Schwartz 2004: 104). In general, too much choice, and the process of researching and seeking the best possible choice in various arenas, significantly detracts from individual satisfaction and happiness, taking time and energy away from more meaningful pursuits. Instead, individual happiness is closely correlated with having rich social relationships, which, interestingly, often constrain choice.

Perception of opportunity is important; Galster and Killen (1995) argue that the more options that low-income youth have, the more deliberate their decision-making. In theory, it is possible to provide people and firms with more information about all the locational choices available in the region. But in practice, it is challenging to determine all the costs and benefits ahead of time. And as Chester Hartman wrote about housing vouchers in 1975, there is no true free choice if the housing market is not providing a diverse set of options.

One alternative is the capabilities approach, which shifts our focus to what inner-city residents are able to do or be, instead of how much they can achieve in purely economic terms (Nussbaum 2000; Sen 1999). Related to this is the idea that needs differ among groups, so the Rawlsian set of primary goods may not apply uniformly to all, and equal starting points may not mean equal outcomes (Fainstein 2006; Harvey 1973). Another line of argument lies in the concept of a "right to the city," which includes the right to urban life and its centrality, vitality, and visibility (Fainstein 2010; Lefebvre 1996; Mitchell 2003).

Capabilities

The capabilities approach, advocated by Amartya Sen (1999), suggests that instead of thinking about distribution in terms of the resources people are able to access, we should examine what their environmental context allows them to do or be. Capabilities encompass many of Rawls' social and natural goods, but also include the pursuit of "affiliation":

> being able to live with and toward others, to recognize and show concern for other human beings, to engage in various forms of social interaction; to be able to imagine the situation of another and to have compassion for that situation; to have the capability for both justice and friendship.
>
> (Nussbaum 2000: 79)

The idea of affiliation acknowledges the use value of urban space, which Lefebvre incorporates into his idea of city as "oeuvre," or a collective project in which all of its citizens participate. The tension between use value and exchange value fosters battles for urban land: "This city is itself 'oeuvre', a feature which contrasts with the irreversible tendency towards money and commerce, towards exchange and products. Indeed the oeuvre is use value and the product is exchange value" (Lefebvre 1996: 66). Residents have a right to the oeuvre, since it allows them to meet their social needs, which:

> include the need for security and opening, the need for certainty and adventure, that of organization of work and of play, the needs or the predictable and the unpredictable, of similarity and difference, of isolation and encounter, exchange and investments, of independence (even solitude) and communication, of immediate and long-term prospects.
>
> (Ibid.: 147)

As Fainstein (2010: 17) points out, the Rawlsian focus on equality among individuals sidesteps these issues of social affiliation and needs. Omitting the collectivity from the discussion means that certain types of goods—particularly those associated with social affiliation—are not considered important: "The starting point of individual liberty also avoids questions that bear on the character of collective goods—e.g. a high-quality built environment—if they are not necessary for the development of capabilities or remedying inequality."

Thus, it is perhaps not surprising tht some regionalist strategies have met with mixed success. If dispersal has not improved access to natural goods, such as health, and social goods, such as economic opportunity, then the move to the suburbs may actually hinder the development of capabilities. If the development of capabilities rests, in part, on meeting the need for social affiliation, then the disruption of social networks that occurs when the spatial distribution of the population changes, as in mixed-income neighborhoods, may likewise affect capabilities negatively. Strategies that purely promote physical access to jobs ignore the intricate social system through which people find jobs—let alone the workforce development system that, at its best, provides a valuable channel for information about the labor market (Chapple 2006).

Differing Needs

How do needs for primary goods differ among groups? From a Rawlsian perspective on how to create equality of opportunity, policymakers would first need to measure how residents of concentrated poverty neighborhoods are faring in terms of resources. This apparently assumes a homogeneous public with similar levels of needs (Young 2000). Yet, as noted by David Harvey in *Social Justice and the City* (1973), different groups have different elasticities in use of resources, so equality of opportunity depends on social context. For instance, if people lack "cultural motivation" to use parks, developing such facilities for them will not lead to a more just income distribution. Housing opportunity is another of Harvey's (1973: 85) examples: "Low-income groups, for example, often identify very closely with their housing environment and the psychological cost of moving is to them far greater than it is to the mobile upper middle class."[2]

Similarly, suppose that metropolitan areas were reorganized so that each individual had the same level of resources and opportunities, or at least a threshold level: social services, amenities, education and work opportunities are distributed equally across the region, in a utopian spatial allocation. This still would not create equal opportunity. As Martha Nussbaum (2000: 99) argues, utility differs: "giving resources to people does not always bring differently situated people up to the same level of capability to function." Coming from different backgrounds, some may lack the ability to use resources in order to function better. In fact, assuming resources benefit all equally "doesn't sufficiently respect the struggle of each and every individual for flourishing" (ibid.: 69).

Current urban and regional policy and planning does not always accommodate differing needs. Strategies for infill development have narrowly focused on large sites for high-density development. Redevelopment has tended to facilitate the location of entertainment and office jobs in the core, while ignoring other types of work. Housing choice vouchers will disproportionately benefit those with the mobility to assess housing opportunity throughout a region, as well as those without special housing needs—and will not necessarily meet the needs of those who are attached to their neighborhood and do not wish to move.

The Right to the City

Another approach to social justice is Henri Lefebvre's (1996) "right to the city," which encompasses the ideas of diversity, amenity, and visibility. Fostering diversity is key to justice because it helps us imagine alternative futures and life plans. The city makes possible encounters with people who are different, which, in turn, enriches experience. Thus, the just city "ought to provide spaces in which valuably different forms of human activity can flourish" (Nussbaum 2000: 60).

For the disadvantaged, being seen is just as important as seeing others. For Lefebvre, the right to the city is essentially the right to inhabit, or the right of individuals and groups to shape the conditions of their existence in space. With the right to inhabit, oppressed groups can stay visible in the public eye. Possessing this "space for representation" helps give groups legitimacy in their struggles (Mitchell 2003: 33).

As inner cities revitalize—and as public housing becomes mixed-income development—affluent newcomers squeeze out the disadvantaged. This threatens urban diversity and even the visibility of the least well-off. It also suggests another right: the right to enjoy "renewed centrality" (Lefebvre 1996: 179): "The right to the city ought to refer to more than mere inclusion—it needs to encompass access to an appealing city" (Fainstein 2010: 18).

Many regional sustainability plans, as well as the spatial solution offered by dispersal and mobility strategies, conflict directly with the right to the city. Regions from Shanghai to Copenhagen are reconfiguring the urban core to attract high-skilled workers. Displaced from downtown housing, the poor lose their centrality, visibility, and access to diversity. Commuting out to jobs in the suburbs, jobseekers lose their connections to the urban economy. And though this perhaps was not on Lefebvre's mind, industrial firms too have a "right to the city."

The Alternative

A large body of research documents the role of informal social supports in helping the poor cope with or even move out of poverty. Given the difficulty of entering the mainstream society and economy, many of the poor develop intricate survival systems based on social connections (Edin and Lein 1997; Kelly 1994). Because daily activity patterns for the poor occur mostly within a local area, social networks based in place may help the disadvantaged access "spur of the moment" job opportunities (Chapple 2001; Gilbert 1998; Hanson and Pratt 1995). These informal supports may provide the poor with "functional capabilities," or the freedom to achieve what they value. Nussbaum argues that depriving the poor of the ability to affiliate with others may be more harmful than reducing their utility or access to resources. The growing exclusion of the poor from the core, particularly of strong market regions, threatens to disrupt these social supports.

Writing about equity and diversity, Susan Fainstein (2010) makes the case for prioritizing equity. It comes down to whether we can accept that groups with shared identity may want to differentiate themselves by living in homogeneous neighborhoods. As Iris Marion Young (2000) argues, fairness comes from respecting group differences and institutions that allow their reproduction (including neighborhoods). Thus, to Fainstein (2010: 68), we need to embrace diversity at the metropolitan scale, but accept "relatively homogeneous neighborhoods with porous boundaries rather than proportionality in each precinct." This, then, means reconceptualizing policy and planning to provide more security to families in need across the region, regardless of where we think opportunity lies. Housing policy should continue to work to provide housing options across the region, but with the goal of integration at the scale of the district or place, rather than the neighborhood. Developing social seams is an opportunity to support integration goals without disrupting communities.

Adopting a capabilities approach and supporting the need for affiliation means a shift in the focus of regional sustainability planning from simply improving physical accessibility and increasing population and employment densities to supporting the existing residents and creating and maintaining institutional density. One general principle would be to ensure that all residents have the option to stay in their neighborhoods as it evolves and improves. Another is recognizing how local activity patterns (i.e., connection to a family support network, a diverse social network, and local workforce intermediaries) help shape life chances. As discussed in Chapters 3 and 4, this means a shift away from policies and plans that regulate diversity of uses and incomes at a local scale to those that accommodate it throughout the region. It would also need to be what Patrick Sharkey calls a *durable* policy: the experience with urban poverty policies from Model Cities has shown that these interventions are too short-lived or underfunded to be able to sustain their positive impact. In practice, durable policy for equitable development would likely need to follow two paths: one through the back door, and the other via the front.

Equitable Development via the Back—and Front—Door

As regions around the world conduct sustainability planning, many welcome equitable development through the back door. In many countries, a strong social safety net at the national level—often including education, health-care, social housing, and other social services—supports regional planning. In the United States, this means incorporating equity through federal and state programs and policies.

Some approaches are well known, such as civil rights enforcement or income supports such as the Earned Income Tax Credit. Others might be considered more of a stealth regionalism. For instance, the Affordable Care Act will support equitable development both by supporting the development of new community clinics and generating net new jobs of relatively high quality (Spetz et al. 2014). State and federal policies in support of the green economy, from energy efficiency to solar panel installation, tend to produce relatively high-paying jobs (Zabin et al. 2011). Increases in the minimum wage, whichever level of government implements them, will make it easier for low-wage workers to afford housing. Long-debated tax reforms such as the elimination of the mortgage interest tax deduction for second homes would help to level the unequal playing field for multifamily housing construction.

Still, sustainable equitable development will require some front door regionalism as well. Preserving the right to the city means ensuring that disadvantaged groups still have a place in the urban core as it undergoes the transformations of the twenty-first century. Sustainability planning shapes regions by allocating future growth through zoning, guiding public investment in infrastructure, and identifying mechanisms for design and finance. It thus offers the opportunity to transform equity from an afterthought in sustainable development, to its very foundation.

Notes

1. For a comprehensive review, see Fainstein (2010).
2. Also see Gans (1968).

References

Altshuler, Alan, William Morrill, Harold Wolman, and Faith Mitchell, editors. *Governance and Opportunity in Metropolitan America*. Washington, DC: National Academy Press, 1999.

Campbell, Heather. "Just Planning: The Art of Situated Ethical Judgment." *Journal of Planning Education and Research* 26, no. 1 (2006): 92–106.

Chapple, Karen. "Time to Work: Job Search Strategies and Commute Time for Women on Welfare in San Francisco." *Journal of Urban Affairs* 23, no. 2 (2001): 155–173.

Chapple, Karen. "Overcoming Mismatch: Beyond Dispersal, Mobility, and Development Strategies." *Journal of the American Planning Association* 72, no. 3 (2006): 322–336.

Dreier, Peter, John H. Mollenkopf, and Todd Swanstrom. *Place Matters: Metropolitics for the Twenty-First Century*. Lawrence, KS: University Press of Kansas, 2004.

Edin, Kathryn and Laura Lein. *Making Ends Meet: How Single Mothers Survive Welfare and Low-Wage Work*. New York: Russell Sage Foundation, 1997.

Fainstein, Susan. "Planning and the Just City." Paper presented at Searching for the Just City Conference, New York City, Columbia University, 2006.

Fainstein, Susan S. *The Just City*. Ithaca, NY: Cornell University Press, 2010.

Fried, Marc. "Grieving for a Lost Home, Psychological Costs of Relocation." In *Urban Renewal: The Record and the Controversy*, edited by J. Q. Wilson, 359–379. Cambridge, MA: MIT Press, 1966.

Fullilove, Mindy. *Root Shock: How Tearing Up City Neighborhoods Hurts America, and What We Can Do About It*. New York: One World/Ballantine Books, 2004.

Galster, George C. and Sean P. Killen "The Geography of Metropolitan Opportunity: A Reconnaissance and Conceptual Framework." *Housing Policy Debate* 6, no. 1 (1995): 7–43.

Gans, Herbert. "The Failure of Urban Renewal: A Critique and Some Proposals." In *People and Plans: Essays on Urban Problems and Solutions*, 260–277. New York: Basic Books, 1968.

Gilbert, Melissa. "Race, Space, and Power: The Survival Strategies of Working Poor Women." *Annals of the Association of American Geographers* 88, no. 4 (1998): 595–621.

Hacker, Jacob. *The Great Risk Shift: The Assault on American Jobs, Families, Health Care, and Retirement—and How You Can Fight Back*. New York: Oxford University Press, 2006.

Hall, Peter. *Cities of Tomorrow: An Intellectual History of Urban Planning and Design in the Twentieth Century*. 3rd Edition. Hoboken, NJ: Wiley-Blackwell, 2002.

Hanson, Susan and Geraldine Pratt. *Gender, Work, and Space*. London: Routledge, 1995.

Harvey, David. *Social Justice and the City*. Baltimore, MD: Johns Hopkins University Press, 1973.

Kelly, M. "Towanda's Triumph: Social and Cultural Capital in the Transition to Adulthood in the Urban Ghetto." *International Journal of Urban and Regional Research* 18, no. 1 (1994): 88–111.

Kneebone, Elizabeth and Alan Berube. *Confronting Suburban Poverty*. Washington, DC: Brookings Institution Press, 2013.

Lefebvre, Henry. *Writings on Cities*. Edited and translated by Eleonore Kofman and Elizabeth Lebas. Cambridge, MA: Blackwell, 1996.

Madanipour, Ali. "Sustainable Development, Urban Form, and Megacity Governance and Planning in Tehran." In *Megacities: Urban Form, Governance, and Sustainability*, edited by André Sorensen and Junichiro Okata, 67–91. Tokyo: Springer, 2011.

Mitchell, Don. *The Right to the City: Social Justice and the Fight for Public Space*. New York: Guilford Press, 2003.

Nussbaum, Martha C. *Women and Human Development: The Capabilities Approach*. New York: Cambridge University Press, 2000.

O'Connor, Alice. *Poverty Knowledge: Social Science, Social Policy, and the Poor in Twentieth-Century U.S. History*. Princeton, NJ: Princeton University Press, 2001.

Rawls, John. *A Theory of Justice*. Cambridge, MA: Belknap Press of Harvard University Press, 1971.

Schwartz, Barry. *The Paradox of Choice: Why More is Less*. New York: Harper Perennial, 2004.

Schwartz, Barry, Hazel R. Markus, and Alana C. Snibbe. "Is Freedom Just Another Word for Many Things to Buy?" *New York Times*, February 26, 2006.

Sen, Amartya. *Development as Freedom*. New York: Anchor, 1999.

Sharkey, Patrick. *Stuck in Place: Urban Neighborhoods and the End of Progress Toward Racial Equality*. Chicago, IL: University of Chicago Press, 2012.

Spetz, Joanne, Bianca Frogner, Laurel Lucia and Ken Jacobs Frogner. "The Impact of the Affordable Care Act on New Jobs." Unpublished paper, 2014.

Young, Iris M. *Inclusion and Democracy*. New York: Oxford University Press, 2000.

Zabin, Carol, Karen Chapple, Ellen Avis, Tory Griffith, Kate Stearns, Jane Peters, Nathaniel Albers et al. *California Workforce Education and Training Needs Assessment: For Energy Efficiency, Distributed Generation, and Demand Response*. Berkeley, CA: Institute for Research on Labor and Employment, University of California, Berkeley, 2011.

Appendix
Place-Based, Dispersal, and Mobility Approaches to Regional Equity

Place-Based Approaches

Neighborhood Grants

Community Development Block Grants (CDBG), which consolidated eight programs into one in 1974, provide discretionary funds for community and economic development to all states, as well as certain cities and urban counties based on a formula related to size, growth rate, share of poverty, and housing conditions (Kneebone and Berube 2013; Schwartz 2010). In the program, currently funded at $2.9 billion annually, 70 percent of expenditures must benefit those of up to 80 percent in area median income (with the remaining funds allowed to target blighted places or disaster relief). The program funds can be used for a variety of purposes including the acquisition and rehabilitation of property, social services, and economic development. HOME Investment Partnership is another block grant program that supports affordable housing needs for low- and moderate-income individuals (ibid.). It is distributed to cities and states based on a need-based formula. Since its inception in 1990, it has assisted more than 1.1 million renters and homeowners. Another form of grant-based approach is the array of foundation-funded, place-based revitalization campaigns, often referred to as comprehensive community initiatives.

Neighborhood Investment

The Community Reinvestment Act (CRA) has, since 1977, required depository institutions of a minimum size to meet the credit needs of the communities they serve, with penalties for failing to provide adequate service. Although shown to be effective at providing more home-purchase loans to lower-income and minority households (as well as preventing foreclosures), CRA has lost some of its influence because of a growing share of loans originating from institutions not subject to CRA (Schwartz 2010).

Nonprofits also play an important role in place-based approaches. Community development corporations (CDCs), community development financial intermediaries (CDFIs), and other community development intermediaries (such as the Local Initiatives Support Corporation, or LISC) comprise a "community development industry system" (Melendez and Servon 2007; Yin 1998). There are over 3,300 urban CDCs in the United States, 40 percent of which were launched after 1986. Though housing remains the predominant activity of CDCs, the majority also engage in other revitalization work such as commercial real estate development, commercial district revitalization, business assistance, social services, and job training.

CDFIs range from national banks and credit unions, to community development intermediaries, to small loan funds and venture capital providers, all with the mission of supplementing the conventional lending system with financial products and counseling targeted at low-income individuals and communities (Benjamin, Rubin, and Zielenbach 2004; CDFI Data Project 2003). This development finance industry, with almost 700 CDFIs, has doubled in size in the last decade due largely to the establishment of the CDFI Fund in 1994, which provides capital to CDFIs both directly and indirectly through investments from mainstream banks. The CDFIs support an array of financial services for both businesses and individuals, such as Individual Development Accounts (low-income savings accounts with matching funds), checking accounts, home loans, microloans, and business loans.

Enterprise zone programs, discussed in Chapter 7, provide tax credits for local hiring, equipment purchases, and R&D in order to develop new business and job concentrations in close proximity to existing urban neighborhoods. The New Markets Tax Credit helps finance commercial and retail development projects in disadvantaged areas.

Project-Based Approaches

HOPE VI (described in Chapter 5), authorized in 1992, provided funds to local housing authorities for the redevelopment of severely distressed public housing projects. HOPE VI projects typically involved displacement and relocation of public housing residents, and demolition to make way for newly constructed, mixed-income developments.

Most recently, under the Obama Administration, HUD has transformed HOPE VI into two comprehensive neighborhood-based efforts, the Choice Neighborhoods Initiative (CNI) and Promise Neighborhoods. These are small pilot programs and funds are awarded annually on a competitive basis. CNI recreates HOPE VI as a more comprehensive approach to redevelopment, involving the community in distressed public housing and surrounding neighborhoods to plan for safety, revitalization, schools, and services. Promise Neighborhoods, run through the Department of Education, bring a holistic approach to schools that addresses both educational programs and family and community supports.

Complementing federal and local programs are a number of foundation-funded comprehensive community initiatives, which build on the legacy of neighborhood improvement from the 1960s, from community development corporations that rebuild neighborhoods to social service providers addressing social and human capital needs (Kubisch 1996). In a reaction to these piecemeal community development efforts, these initiatives try to coordinate across organizations to build the capacity of local residents.

Dispersal Approaches

The Gautreaux consent decree—which was followed by others in at least 11 metropolitan areas—forced the Chicago Housing Authority to develop a "metropolitan-wide 'mobility program'" to partially compensate for its discriminatory practice of placing public housing in predominantly African-American or racially changing areas (Goetz 2003: 53). Over a 20-year period, over 7,100 families were relocated from virtually all-black urban areas to middle-income, overwhelmingly white areas in Chicago and its suburbs (Rubinowitz and Rosenbaum 2000).

Inspired by the success of Gautreaux and its tenant-based mobility structure, Congress authorized the Moving to Opportunity (MTO) demonstration program in 1992 in the cities of Baltimore, Boston, Chicago, Los Angeles, and New York City. Participants in an experimental group (which was paired with two control groups) moved from very high-poverty to low-poverty neighborhoods. MTO, then, was an early attempt to assess whether low-poverty areas translated into improved life chances for low-income households. These improvements would come, in part, from improved access to jobs, better schools for children, and the development of social capital, particularly in the form of social support and leverage provided by social ties and community institutions (Briggs 1998; Clampet-Lundquist 2007; Wexler 2001).

HOPE VI, described above as a place-based program, is also a dispersal program because it has involved significant relocation of residents of distressed public housing to different neighborhoods. It differs from Gautreaux and MTO in its larger scope, involving both demolition and construction, and much larger scale. The vast majority of relocated residents have not returned to the redeveloped public housing sites (Goetz 2013).

For new construction, the Low Income Housing Tax Credits (LIHTC), currently the most important source of federal funding for affordable housing, supports the development of rental housing via tax credits. From its establishment in 1986 to 2006, it had produced more than 1.6 million units, with 51 percent in cities, 35 percent in suburbs, and the remaining outside of metropolitan areas (Schwartz 2010). Although these developments are more likely to locate in low-income and minority neighborhoods, they are relatively less concentrated in such areas than traditional public housing development (ibid.).

Regional fair share housing strategies (described in Chapter 5) attempt to address inequities in the regional distribution of affordable housing, in order to shift more affordable housing provision to the outer suburbs (Bollens 2002; Listokin 1976). Typically, the approach relies on a formula for assigning affordable housing obligations to regional sub-areas, most frequently individual municipalities within a single metropolitan area.

Related to the fair share housing approach is inclusionary zoning (IZ) (discussed in Chapter 5), which mandates construction of affordable units, typically on-site within new housing developments. The country's 400 mandatory IZ programs have largely succeeded at serving low-income families and locating affordable homes in low-poverty areas (Hickey 2013; Schwartz et al. 2012).

Mobility Approaches

Beginning in 1999, the Federal Transit Administration began the Jobs Access and Reverse Commute program to develop either new or expanded transportation for low-income individuals to jobs and job-related services or reverse commute options to access suburban employment centers. Historically offering an average of $77 million in funding each year, grants were initially offered on a competitive basis, and then shifted to a formula basis in 2006. Most programs offer transit subsidies to individuals, rather than creating new transit services (Sanchez and Schweitzer 2008). Complementing this program are government and nonprofit programs that support car ownership for low-income groups. Over 150 nonprofit car ownership or loan programs for low-income groups have emerged around the country (Goldberg 2001; Lucas and Nicholson 2003).

References

Benjamin, Lehn, Julia S. Rubin, and Sean Zielenbach. "Community Development Financial Institutions: Current Issues and Future Prospects." *Journal of Urban Affairs* 26, no. 2 (2004): 177–195.

Bollens, Scott. "In Through the Back Door: Social Equity and Regional Governance." *Housing Policy Debate* 13, no. 4 (2003): 631–657.

Briggs, Xavier. "Brown Kids in White Suburbs: Housing Mobility and the Many Faces of Social Capital." *Housing Policy Debate* 9, no. 1 (1998): 177–221.

CDFI Data Project. "Community Development Financial Institutions: Providing Capital, Building Community, Creating Impact." 2003. Accessed January 20, 2004. www.cfed.org/enterprise_development/CDFIData.

Clampet-Lundquist, Susan. "No More 'Bois Ball: The Impact of Relocation from Public Housing on Adolescents." *Journal of Adolescent Research* 22, no. 3 (2007): 298–323.

Goetz, Edward. *Clearing the Way: Deconcentrating the Poor in Urban America.* Washington, DC: Urban Institute Press, 2003.

Goetz, Edward. *New Deal Ruins: Race, Economic Justice, and Public Housing Policy.* Ithaca, NY: Cornell University Press, 2013.

Goldberg, Heidi. *State and County Supported Car Ownership Programs can Help Low-Income Families Secure and Keep Jobs.* Washington, DC: Center on Budget and Policy Priorities, 2001.

Hickey, Robert. *After the Downturn: New Challenges and Opportunities for Inclusionary Housing.* Washington, DC: Center for Housing Policy, 2013.

Kneebone, Elizabeth and Alan Berube. *Confronting Suburban Poverty in America.* Washington, DC: Brookings Institution Press, 2013.

Kubisch, Anne. "Comprehensive Community Initiatives: Lessons in Neighborhood Transformation." 1996. Accessed June 2, 2013. www.nhi.org/online/issues/85/compcominit.html.

Listokin, David. *Fair Share Housing Allocation.* New Brunswick, NJ: Center for Urban Policy Research/Transaction Publishers, 1976.

Lucas, Marilyn and Charles F. Nicholson. "Subsidized Vehicle Acquisition and Earned Income in the Transition from Welfare to Work." *Transportation* 30 (2003): 483–501.

Melendez, Edwin and Lisa J. Servon. "Reassessing the Role of Housing in Community-Based Urban Development." *Housing Policy Debate* 18, no. 4 (2007): 751–783.

Rubinowitz, Leonard S. and James E. Rosenbaum. *Crossing the Class and Color Lines: From Public Housing to White Suburbia.* Chicago, IL: University of Chicago Press, 2000.

Sanchez, Thomas W. and Lisa Schweitzer. *Assessing Federal Employment Accessibility Policy: An Analysis of the JARC Program.* Washington, DC: Brookings Institution Press, 2008.

Schwartz, Alex F. *Housing Policy in the United States.* New York: Routledge, 2010.

Schwartz, Heather L., Liisa Ecola, Kristin J. Leuschner and Aaron Kofner. *Is Inclusionary Zoning Inclusionary? A Guide for Practitioners.* Santa Monica, CA: RAND Corporation, 2012.

Wexler, Harry J. "HOPE VI: Market Means/Public Ends—the Goals, Strategies, and Midterm Lessons of HUD's Urban Revitalization Demonstration Program." *Journal of Affordable Housing* 10, no. 3 (2001): 195–233.

Yin, Jordan S. "The Community Development Industry System: A Case Study of Politics and Institutions in Cleveland, 1967–1997," *Journal of Urban Affairs* 20, no. 2 (1998): 137–157.

Index

CPSIA information can be obtained
at www.ICGtesting.com
Printed in the USA
LVHW080252241118
598093LV00004B/16/P